# The
# Black Man
# and the
# American
# Dream

# The Black Man and the American Dream

*Negro Aspirations in America, 1900–1930*

*Edited with an Introduction by*
JUNE SOCHEN

CHICAGO: Quadrangle Books, 1971

*To My Mother and Father*

# CONTENTS

# The
# Black Man
# and the
# American
# Dream

# INTRODUCTION

BLACK AMERICAN thinkers and writers in the first thirty years of the twentieth century generally shared the values of white American society. They accepted the validity of the Declaration of Independence, the Constitution, and the democratic system; they believed in the importance of education, the right of individual development, and the role each person played toward his own improvement. The trouble was, according to the black man's criticism of white America, that these values were not equitably applied to black and white Americans. All black writers lamented the failure of white America to live up to its high-sounding ideals; they beseeched it to narrow the gap between ideal and reality for blacks. Still, these writers accepted the ideals, certainly those of freedom, equality, and liberty for all. Most of them also accepted the idea of economic advancement as a step toward achieving the "good life." The pursuit of happiness included a vision of political and economic opportunity and equality.

Thus did the American Dream motivate and inform much of black writing during the first third of this century. One could argue, in fact, that for the first time the dream was accepted by black Americans as a realizable goal for the twentieth century. Thirty-five years after slavery, blacks were told that mobility, opportunity, and rewards could, and would, characterize their lives in America. The dream, of course, had been used throughout American history to point out the tragic irony of slavery and the terrible denial to a portion of the population of those natural rights described in the Declaration of Independence. The Constitution, on the other hand, was often sneeringly referred to by abolitionists as an evil document because it sanctified slavery. Not until after emancipation, however, did the positive aspects of the American Dream become relevant for blacks. The generation of black Americans raised in freedom and nurtured on the American myth of success and individual opportunity came to maturity in the opening years of the twentieth century. And they used the rhetoric, methodology, and goals of the American Dream in their struggle for true equality.

Political, economic, educational, and social equality—none of these demands were outrageous, unreasonable, or radical. All were normally covered within the legitimate guarantees assured by the 14th Amendment, which was passed specifically to insure the new freedom of black Americans. When the articulate and able black leaders of the period demanded for all blacks the right to vote, the right to attend integrated schools, the right to join a union, and the right to live anywhere they wished, they were asking for delivery on the promises of the American Dream. If this land was a haven and refuge for hundreds of thousands of European immigrants at the turn of the century, then certainly, blacks argued, it ought to be a haven for its own citizens—many of whom were among the oldest Americans.

Most of the white audiences who heard these proposals thought them outrageous. A small core of white liberals did join hands with black leaders in organizations such as the National Association for the Advancement of Colored People and the Urban League, but most white people who read about the black struggle for equality either turned a deaf ear or assertively denied the validity of the claims.

Thus the period 1900–1930 is not one of significant accomplishment for black Americans. To be sure, this is a relative judgment from the vantage point of the 1970's. To W. E. B. DuBois, Booker T. Washington, Alain Locke, and Kelly Miller, just a few of the major black leaders of the time, the record was mixed. Examples of progress could be found along with recognized failures. Optimism, though, characterized the period. Note the following statement by DuBois, written in his monthly column in May 1921 for *The Crisis*, the organ of the NAACP:

> Far from being discouraged in the fight, we are daily more and more triumphant. Yesterday, 1650 Negro women voted in New Orleans. Never since 1876 have so many Negroes voted in the South as in the last election. Our fight for right has the enemy on the run. . . . Twenty-five years more of the intelligent fighting that the N.A.A.C.P. has led will make the black man in the United States free and equal.

True to their faith in the democratic process and the inevitability of progress, black American writers and leaders continuously demonstrated their belief in the eventual success of their struggle. This faith, I think, was inextricably tied to their belief in the validity of the American Dream as it applied to black Americans.

White liberal writers, who sympathized with the black struggle during these bleak years, used the same ideological framework as the black writers. They too urged enforcement of the 14th and 15th Amendments. They too argued for economic and educational opportunity for the black man. Both black and white writers held the reform Darwinist view of American society, that is, they believed in natural rights for all humans, and they considered the environment malleable and improvable. Contrary to the conservative Social Darwinist position, the reform Darwinists (as Richard Hofstadter has labeled them) considered social institutions dynamic and progressive. They felt that man played an active role, individually and collectively, in determining his own destiny. Man could, and they believed would, correct the wrongs around him once he knew what they were. If housing conditions were atrocious, they could and would be improved. If the school system was inadequate, it could be changed.

This same philosophy is in fact the foundation of all twentieth-century American reform efforts. Using the traditional American tools of reform, black and white writers urged the enforcement of constitutional provisions designed to protect black citizens. They attempted to publicize the evils of lynching and to propagandize for general support of the black man's quest. Inherent in the American scheme of things is the belief that ignorance is the chief evil to be overcome. Once the public is informed, they will rationally confront a problem and develop solutions to it. Ameliorative legislation will be followed by effective enforcement, thus solving the social ill. Thus reformers hoped to bring moral suasion to bear upon America to awaken her to her responsibility. Education, agitation, and legislative pressure were the key weapons in the reformer's armory.

The collection which follows, drawn from the periodical literature of the period 1900–1930, illustrates how black and a few white Americans expressed themselves on this most serious subject. The destiny of America—the conscience of America, as some writers called it— demanded a solution to the race problem. Through the writings of the period, one can easily determine that the intellectual framework of the writers was the American value system; one can also grasp the essential themes and concerns of those who dealt with the race issue.

Only during and immediately after World War I did the nation's magazines devote some attention to this problem. The drafting of black soldiers, the call to patriotism, the black migration to the North, the race riots, and the return of black soldiers to an unreconstructed America caused some writers to focus upon the larger theme. But only temporarily. The euphoria and general economic prosperity of the twenties made it a subject of small interest.* Just as the North had tired of Reconstruction, so did it tire of the modest early twentieth-century effort at Reconstruction. During the twenties, *The Crisis* and *Opportunity*, the major black magazines in America, continued the journalistic fight.

The magazines of the period offer a good barometer of the nation's attitudes and feelings. They also display the views of black and white thinkers who expressed themselves frequently during that period but have been forgotten by later generations. Some of the lesser-known black intellectuals, such as Eric Walrond, Eugene Gordon, and Abram Harris, for example, contributed interesting articles on the race problem. Taken together, all these articles, and especially those of black writers, put the black-white issue into an important historical perspective. All the major themes and "answers" to the race problem were articulated during the first third of this century. Because the nation chose to ignore the problem or not to discuss possible solutions, the dilemma is still with us. Thus the reader will find most of these articles surprisingly fresh and relevant: we failed to learn from history, so we are repeating it.

The documents in this volume—fiction and nonfiction—represent that fraction of writing on the race problem that dealt specifically with American values and goals. Most of the articles (and the total was not large) were concrete, pragmatic discussions of specific aspects of the life of the Negro American. For example, numerous articles discussed educational facilities for blacks and health conditions in the rural South. The popular magazines also liked to print articles on Negro music, the migration of blacks to the North, and labor problems. It could be argued, of course, that this overwhelming concern for specific aspects of the black problem implicitly acknowledged the American framework and recognized that adjustment had to be accomplished within the scheme of American values.

Articles from three black magazines of the period were used: The *Southern Workman* was the journal of Hampton Institute in Virginia. The first major black school established during Reconstruction, it typified the Booker T. Washington point of view, namely, that edu-

* In 1925, for example, at the height of the Harlem Renaissance, the *New York Times* had eleven articles on Pola Negri, the movie star, and only ten on Harlem (two of the ten being descriptions of shootings).

cation should be primarily vocational and industrial in order to develop economic independence for black Americans. Although mainly read in the South, its pages were filled with articles by prominent Northern blacks who spoke at Hampton. *The Crisis,* organ of the NAACP, was edited from its inception in 1910 until 1934 by W. E. B. DuBois. *Opportunity,* the journal of the National Urban League, was edited by Charles S. Johnson. These magazines focused on manageable aspects of the race problem, though they more often reflected, pleaded, or considered the larger conflict between American ideals and reality.

Two magazines of the period, on two separate occasions, devoted whole issues to the subject of race relations in America: the *Annals of the American Academy of Political and Social Science* for September 1913 was entitled "The Negro's Progress in Fifty Years"; its November 1928 issue was called "The American Negro." *Survey,* the journal of social workers, celebrated fifty years of emancipation in its February 1, 1913, issue; the March 1, 1925, issue, edited by Alain Locke, eventually became the basis for the book *The New Negro.* Both magazines included articles by leading black and white writers who treated, in minute sociological detail, the economic, political, religious, and social conditions of blacks. Black sociologists E. Franklin Frazier and Richard R. Wright, Jr., for example, contributed articles based upon their research on the black man's problems in the Northern cities.

The *Survey,* while emphasizing the economic and social problems of black America, also included discussions of black art, music, and literature. Thus the impression gleaned from the March 1925 issue, especially, is that real human beings, rather than mere statistics, were involved in the analyses. Except for these two journals, however, only sporadic, occasional articles may be found in the other popular journals of the period.

In many of the magazine articles written during the period 1900–1930, authors made repeated efforts to show the black man's progress since emancipation while gross inequities still remained. This was one of the paradoxes all writers faced; on the one hand they could cite concrete examples of black progress in America—the decrease in illiteracy, the improvement in health, and the accumulation of capital. On the other hand they had to report on continued poverty, deprivation, disfranchisement (especially in the South), and blatant discrimination experienced by blacks. The record was at best mixed. How could there be advances amid continued lynchings? Many reporters answered the question by optimistically concluding that the equal-protection laws, once they were enforced, would solve the race problem. Others thought positive change could not be expected without significant institutional guarantees. Individual accomplishment required society's cooperation in order to be real and meaningful. How extensive this social cooperation had to be (for example, was socialism a necessity?) was not fully explored during these years. Existing constitutional provisions seemed to most writers sufficient to deal with the issues. Although the NAACP campaigned for an anti-lynching law during the twenties, most of its legal activity centered on the enforcement of existing laws. The judicial system, then, was for many the answer to the problem; if the courts enforced the laws against residential and educational segregation, for example, major steps forward would be possible.

Education was the favorite solution advanced for the race problem: if black people received more and better education, they could better share in the abundance and mobility of America. This is, of course, a deeply held American view. Our schools have always been expected to fulfill great expectations, and black Americans shared them. Articles in the *Southern Workman*, for instance, frequently reminded their readers that more training and education would insure a better life.

The call for education and for judicial equality are also typical reform proposals. Just as Lincoln Steffens, the famous muckraker, believed that if people were educated to the principles of good government they would elect well-qualified officials, so Booker T. Washington and W. E. B. DuBois agreed that a proper education would free their people. As DuBois said on one occasion, "The very first step toward the settlement of the negro problem is the spread of intelligence. The first step toward wider intelligence is a free public-school system."[*]

American democratic values and the American dream of equal opportunity and individual advancement were iterated and reiterated by black writers from Washington to DuBois, and, in the more recent past, from James Weldon Johnson to Eldridge Cleaver. These black spokesmen have challenged America to realize its ideals, to insure tolerance, diversity, and individual rights for all Americans.

---

[*] See "The Training of Negroes for Social Power" in Part One following.

They have never tired of reminding white America of her heritage and her promise.

At times, black writers have dealt with this theme ironically rather than rhetorically. Primarily in their imaginative writings, they have chided the American dream amidst the lynchings, disfranchisement, and horrible prejudices experienced by black Americans. The fictional stories of black writers abound with examples of the seemingly unbridgeable gap between American goals and the reality of black America. Especially the work of the great black poets, such as Langston Hughes and Claude McKay, eloquently reminds America of her unfulfilled promises to a portion of her citizenry. It is in poetry that the sharp contrast between the beauty of America's ideals and the ugliness of her reality is most aptly expressed. A short poem, with its central theme of democracy or freedom, effectively captures the dilemma of black Americans. Short stories and novels written by blacks also deal with this subject. Jessie Redmon Fauset and Walter White, for example, both major black writers and leaders during the twenties, described in their fiction how black men and women with good educations and "natural" American ambitions failed because of their color. Time and again, their heroes found the color barrier impossible to overcome. Time and again they would carefully follow the American gospel of success, only to flounder because their skin was black.

Thus the imaginative writings of the period 1900–1930 also dealt extensively with the idea of the American Dream. Black writers were consumed with the terrible irony, and their fiction reflected this concern. But usually their stories ended on the hopeful note that white America would redeem itself, would become true to its own words and values. This was the enduring and persistent theme of most black writers. Just as the reportage of black writers invariably ended on a note of optimism, so did their fiction. The abiding commitment to progress within the American system informed all the writings of the period.

The black radical point of view does not receive much attention in the popular magazines. Monroe Trotter, A. Philip Randolph, and Chandler Owen, just a few of the black radicals of the period, wrote for their own respective magazines or papers and thus were not published in larger-circulation journals or in the white press. But one of the contentions of this introduction, and the theme that informs this interpretive collection, is that the American Dream, not rejection

of that dream, dominated the period. The radical magazines had a
tiny circulation and did not reach large numbers of black or white
readers. Since this collection concentrates upon popular magazines,
no selections from *The Messenger,* for example, have been included.
But there are selections representing the Marxist point of view as
discussed in the popular journals.

"We do not believe in revolution." So said W. E. B. DuBois in an
editorial in *The Crisis* in August 1921. DuBois and the NAACP, for
which he spoke, had 100,000 subscribers to *The Crisis*—subscribers
who shared his concern with achieving black equality through traditional American methods. Although the popularity of Marcus Garvey in the early 1920's demonstrated the fact that black leaders such
as DuBois did not speak to the masses of black people in Harlem,
the black middle and upper classes, as well as their white supporters,
did read *The Crisis* and *Opportunity.* Uneducated blacks, like their
white counterparts, did not read magazines; thus the audience
for these articles was a minority of black and white people—the
magazine-reading portion of both populations. Nonetheless, we know
that the articulate part of each constituency expresses and shapes
the views and feelings of its followers.

The repetition of the same themes, the appeals to the same principles, and the frequency with which the American Dream was mentioned confirmed the belief in its power. Black or white radicals who
advocated leaving America or working for a proletarian revolution
found few followers. Americans—and black Americans *were* Americans—believed in evolution, in progress within the system, and in
inevitable advancement. They believed, as suggested earlier, that
black Americans would eventually win economic success, and that
discrimination would gradually be replaced with tolerance and ultimately with brotherhood. The most realistic black thinkers of the
period would have settled for tolerance.

This collection is organized around four major themes: "The American Dream" demonstrates the predominant faith of black writers in
the validity of the dream. "The American Nightmare" provides illustrations of the agonies of lynching, discrimination, and disfranchisement that black Americans experienced every day of their lives. "The
Irony of the Dream" draws material largely from those black writers
and poets who so effectively expressed the paradox of American ideals
and reality. The final section, "Other Dreams," discusses those
few blacks who considered leaving America, those who wished to
create a separate state within the nation's boundaries, or those who

held a Marxist view of the race problem. Marcus Garvey represented the single most effective example of a black leader who rejected the value system and ideology of America. Articles on Garvey were by far the most numerous in the popular magazines. His colorful personality made good journalistic copy.

Garvey, a Jamaican, had not been raised on the rhetoric of natural rights, individual freedom, and an open society. He never believed, after arriving in America, that white Americans meant those beautiful words and concepts for black Americans. He had no quarrel with the ideas; he simply did not believe they pertained to blacks. Thus he advocated a "Back to Africa" plan. The scheme was not a new one, and Garvey never discussed it in practical terms; yet it was popular among those who were disillusioned with white America and who believed that its laws would never be applied equally to black Americans.

Garvey's black capitalistic schemes and black pride views were not original, nor was he the only black leader of the period who encouraged the development of black business or black pride. Among others, Booker T. Washington's National Negro Business League predated Garvey, and DuBois had long written articles favoring black ownership of business. The Harlem Renaissance, an outpouring of black art and culture, occurred in the twenties quite independent of Garvey. One of the major goals of the Harlem intellectuals was cultural pride. Langston Hughes said in one piece, reprinted in this collection, that black was beautiful. The *Southern Workman,* for example, also reminded its black readers frequently that knowledge of their past and admiration for their heritage was as important as learning a trade. Cultural autonomy was not considered incompatible with American ideals; it fit quite well. Preserving racial and cultural differences while practicing American virtues was considered a proper interpretation of Americanism. This is a crucial point, especially from the vantage point of the 1970's, when black power spokesmen argue that black pride means total black separatism. The advocates of black pride in the 1920's, both the Harlem intellectuals and the rural-oriented black writers for the *Southern Workman,* firmly believed that cultural autonomy was harmonious with political, economic, and educational integration into the white American scheme. They believed that biracial and bicultural harmony was not only feasible but desirable.

Viewing the subject from the perspective of 1970, it is important to note that from 1900 to 1930 the middle-class white American value system was labeled materialistic and therefore unworthy as a goal only by *desperate* black writers. When progress seemed impossible within the American system, some black writers left it and searched elsewhere for an ideology and an answer; the overwhelming majority of black writers remained hopeful. But the 1930's was a turning point. During and after the thirties, many black writers rejected the whole American framework of progress in race relations, that is, they denied the possibility of legal, educational, and social equality. They rejected the hope of economic independence and security as false, and despairingly and sometimes desperately repudiated the whole American value system. This could mean physically leaving America (as DuBois, the novelist Richard Wright, and James Baldwin eventually did) or becoming a Marxist, Maoist, or Africanist. It could express itself in a desire to elevate blacks to a level of mystical elitism, to portray the black as the chosen man and emphasize his uniqueness; or the rejection could take the form of identifying the black man with all the underprivileged classes of the world. This latter tactic minimizes black uniqueness and stresses the similarities between all oppressed peoples. (The view can also be perversely applied so that all oppressed peoples are "black," including the Chinese, the Vietnamese, and the Egyptians.) By universalizing the problem—abstracting the black American out of his context—the race issue is placed in the broader perspective of Marxian class struggle or the Third-World View.

Tactically, this position makes its adherents feel strong and powerful; after all, such a movement must elicit support from underprivileged millions. Further, it legitimizes a long historical struggle, of which the twentieth century is the culminating chapter. Clearly, the whole thrust of this ideology is radical and outside the mainstream of American thought—black and white. But it is also clearly a product of the frustration, hypocrisy, ineffectuality, and dehumanization that has characterized the black American's experience.

Black intellectual thought, supported by its few white helpers, has remained largely within the framework of the American Dream. This fact is amazing, given the modest gains. If the desperate radical voice becomes dominant in the last third of this century, it will be because the American system still refuses to respond to the legitimate demands of black Americans. The questions have not changed since 1900–1930. They were not heard or heeded then. Will they be now?

# PART ONE

# *The American Dream*

THIS FIRST SECTION, the largest in the book, presents magazine literature on the broad topic of the American Dream. The section is divided into sub-categories, each one depicting a component of the dream: politics, education, cultural equality, economics, and, finally, American values. Each of the black writers included here believed in the educability of white Americans and in the possibility of improving the black man's status in America. Certain writers, such as W. E. B. DuBois and Booker T. Washington, are represented by more than one selection because they wrote frequently for the popular magazines and their words were those most often quoted in the periodicals of the period.

In some selections the reader may glimpse something of the internal debates that occurred within the black intellectual community. Note, for example, the discussion between Langston Hughes, the poet, and George Schuyler, the journalist, on the question of whether there was such a thing as black culture.

POLITICS

*Archibald Grimké, a black member of a prominent South-
ern white abolitionist family, was a graduate of Harvard
Law School and a major spokesman for black rights in
the early twentieth century. He was a founder of the
NAACP and president of the Washington, D.C., branch.*

# Why Disfranchisement Is Bad

## By Archibald H. Grimké

IF THE DISFRANCHISEMENT of the negro by the South could settle permanently the negro question, I think that the action of that section
would find its justification in that achievement, according to the
jesuitical principle that the end justifies the means. But can disfranchisement of the negro settle the negro question? First: Can it do so
for the negro? Second: Can it do so for the South? Third: Can it do
so for the rest of the nation? I do not think that it can do so for the
negro, or for the South, or for the rest of the nation. And unless disfranchisement of the negro settles this question in its threefold aspect,
it will not settle it in such a way that it will long stay settled. If the
negro refuse to abide by such a settlement, the question will not be so
settled merely because the South has decided so to settle it. Neither
can the South of to-day settle the question by disfranchisement, if
disfranchisement of the negro be found in operation to injure the
South of to-morrow much more deeply than it does the negro. For
what is bad for the negro to-day will be found to be still worse for
the South to-morrow. The South must, therefore, awake some time to
this fact, unless she is indeed stricken with that hopeless madness by
which the gods intend to destroy her. But even if the South and the
negro agree so to settle the question, the question will not be permanently settled if the North, if the rest of the nation, refuses eventually to form a party to the compact. For the rest of the nation, quite
independently of the action of the South and the acquiescence of
the negro, will have something, something very decisive to say ultimately about the settlement of this question. The North has, in reality,
quite as much at stake in its settlement as either the negro or the

From *Atlantic Monthly*, XCIV (July 1904), 72–81.

South. Disfranchisement will not, therefore, prove a permanent settlement of the negro question if it be found in operation to affect injuriously Northern and national interests, or to work badly in the conduct of governmental affairs in respect to those interests.

I

Can disfranchisement settle the question for the negro? I do not think it can; I am sure that it will not, for the simple and sufficient reason that the negro will not consent to such a settlement;—a settlement which virtually decitizenizes him, and relegates him to a condition of practical servitude in the republic. He has tasted freedom, he has tasted manhood rights, he has tasted civil and political equality. He knows that his freedom, his American citizenship, his right to vote, have been written into the Constitution of the United States, and written there in three great amendments. He knows more: he knows that he himself has written his title to those rights with his blood in the history of the country in four wars, and he is of the firm belief that his title to them is a perfect one. . . .

So far as the negro is concerned, then, to disfranchise him will not settle the negro question. It will do anything else better than that. For it will make trouble, and no end of it. It will certainly make trouble if he rise in the human scale in spite of the wrong done him. Does any one think that he will ever cease to strive for the restoration of his rights as an American citizen, and all of his rights, if he rise in character, property, and intelligence? To think the contrary is to think an absurdity. But if he fall in the human scale in consequence of the wrong done him, he will surely drag the South down with him. For he and the South are bound the one to the other by a ligament as vital as that which bound together for good or bad, for life or death, the Siamese twins. The Enceladian struggles of the black Titan of the South beneath the huge mass of the white race's brutal oppressions, and of his own imbruted nature, will shake peace out of the land and prosperity out of the Southern states, and involve, finally, whites and blacks alike in common poverty, degradation, and failure in the economic world, in hopeless decline of all of the great social forces which make a people move upward and not downward, forward and not backward in civilization.

II

Disfranchisement of the negro is bad for the South. It is bad for her, in the first place, on account of the harmful effect produced by it on her black labor. It makes a large proportion of her laboring population restless and discontented with their civil and social condition, and it will keep them so. It makes it well-nigh impossible for this restless and discontented labor class to make the most and the best of themselves with the limited opportunities afforded them, with the social and political restrictions imposed by law upon them. It hinders employers of this labor from producing the largest and the best results with it, for the same cause. For to obtain by means of this labor the largest and best results, employers of it ought to do the things, ought to seek to have the state do the things, which will tend to reduce the natural friction between labor and capital to its lowest terms, to make labor contented and happy, surely not the things which will have the opposite effect on that labor. Otherwise, the energy which ought to go into production will be scattered, consumed, in contests with capital, in active or passive resistance to bad social and economic conditions, in effective or ineffective striving to improve those conditions. . . .

The grand source of wealth of any community is its labor. The warfare which nation wages against nation to-day is not military, but industrial. Competition among nations for markets for the sale of their surplus products is at bottom a struggle of the labor of different nations for industrial possession of those markets, for the industrial supremacy of the labor of one country over the labor of other countries. Industrialism, commercialism, not militarism, mark the character of our twentieth-century civilization. That country, therefore, which takes into this industrial rivalry and struggle the best trained, the most completely equipped, the most up-to-date labor, will win over those other countries which bring to the battle for world markets a body of crude, backward, and inefficient labor. Education, skill, quality, tell in production; tell at once, and tell in the long run. It is now well understood that the most intelligent labor is the most profitable labor. Ignorant labor is certainly no match in world markets for intelligent labor. It is no match in home markets either. Quality, intelligence, will prevail in such an industrial contest, whether in agriculture, manufactures, mining, or commerce. . . .

Thus it will be found that disfranchisement, which was intended to make the negro a serf, to degrade him as a man, to extinguish his ambition, to extinguish his intelligence, to fix for him in the state, in society, a place of permanent inferiority and subordination to the white race, has degraded the whole South industrially at the same time, and fixed for her likewise a place of permanent economic in-

feriority and subordination to the rest of the nation. The huge body
of her black ignorance, poverty, and degradation will attract to itself
by the social laws of gravitation all of the white ignorance, poverty,
and degradation of the entire section. . . .

III

It has been shown that disfranchisement of the negro is bad for
the negro and for the South. It remains to consider why it is bad for
the North, for the rest of the nation. But if it has been demonstrated
that disfranchisement is bad for the negro and for the South, it will
follow as a logical conclusion that it is bad for the rest of the nation.
For whatever injures a part injures the whole. The negro is a part
of the South, the South a part of the nation, in as real, as vital a sense
as feet and hands are parts of the human body. Hurt a hand, lame a
foot, and the whole body is hurt, lamed at the same time and for the
same cause. This is not sentiment. It is fact, it is common sense, it is
science. The old fable of the Members and the Belly is as true and
timely to-day as it was in ancient Roman days. Starve the belly and
the whole body is starved, suffers in consequence. Wither an arm,
shrivel a leg, dim an eye, and the whole body goes maimed and halt
and darkened.

Whatever, therefore, renders it impossible for the negro of the
South to make the most and the best of himself injures that section,
and this injury to the South hurts, in turn, the whole country. . . .

A superior laborer will produce better work and more of it than an
inferior one. How comes it that American labor, outside of the South,
holds to-day the front rank among the labor of the world, and has held
this foremost place for eighty years? Because it is the freest and most
intelligent labor in the world. For the freer and more intelligent the
labor, the more efficient as an industrial factor will be that labor.
The freest and most intelligent labor is the most productive, the most
profitable labor. To the superiority of American labor two things have
contributed more than any others: the free common school, and the
educative and stimulating function exercised on the minds of laboring men by the right to vote, by the part taken periodically by them
in government, in the choice of rulers, and in the consideration of
public questions. The wits of the children are developed, trained in
the public schools; the wits of the adults are educated, sharpened at
the polls. Labor thus developed mentally, and disciplined in these
two great schools of letters and practical civics, is doubly equipped,

doubly armed to defend well its own interests at home and abroad, and to defend those of the country also. It is alert, assertive, thoughtful, resourceful, independent, self-respecting,—capable of following and leading. It knows what it wants, what is good for it and what is not. It can take care of itself, can fight its own battle with organized capital at home, and with the rival labor of other countries in world markets. Herein lies the superiority of the labor of our American industrial democracy at the present time, with that one exception, Southern labor. . . .

The war for the Union decided the momentous conflict in favor of the democratic idea and its system of free labor. The Thirteenth Amendment destroyed slavery and the slave power; or such, at least, was its purpose. The Fourteenth Amendment provided forever against a revival of the old aristocratic idea of inequality of civil conditions between the races in the South—the real ground of difference between the sections—by declaring all persons born or naturalized in the United States to be citizens of the United States. There was not again to exist in the Southern states any system of labor to take the place of the old slave labor system except that of free labor, and there was not again to appear any corresponding political power in the South to take the place of the defunct slave power; or such, at least, was the plain purpose of the Fourteenth Amendment. But in order to make assurance doubly sure on this vital point, a supplementary provision was incorporated into the amendment, to reduce the representation in Congress of any state which shall deny to any portion of its voting population the right to vote, in the proportion which the number of such disfranchised citizens "shall bear to the whole number of citizens twenty-one years of age in such state."

The rest of the nation intended by these two great acts to destroy, root and branch, the old constitutional provision which entitled the South to count five slaves as three freemen in the apportionment of representatives among the states. It was determined to rid the country for all time of any future trouble from that cause. The Reconstruction measures attempted to introduce into the old slave states the democratic idea, and a labor system corresponding to that idea. But in the event of failure in these regards, and the ultimate revival on the part of those states of the aristocratic idea, and a labor system corresponding to that idea, it was carefully provided that such revival of the old aristocratic idea and labor system should be accompanied by an equivalent loss of political power on the part of those states. They were no longer to eat their cake, metaphorically speaking, and keep it, too. For this eating and keeping something at one and the same time means that the something kept belongs to some one else than the eater. The political power which the South manages to retain in spite of her disfranchisement of the negro does not, therefore, belong to her. If she deprives the negro of the right to vote without being deprived in turn of a proportionate share of her representation in Congress, she has possessed herself wrongfully of a power in national politics, in national legislation, which rightfully belongs to the negro. And this power she may and does exercise against the negro and the North at the same time. It will be seen by the North some day, as it is seen to-day by the negro, that while her old rival has lost on paper the old three-fifths slave representation under the Constitution to which she was entitled before the war, she has not practically suffered any loss at all in this respect, but the contrary. She has actually gained since the war the other two fifths in the apportionment of representatives among the states. For five of her disfranchised colored citizens count to-day the same as five Northern voters, instead of the proportion prevailing in ante-bellum times, when it took five slaves to equal three freemen in Federal numbers.

Following the adoption of the Fourteenth Amendment the North seemed still uneasy on this head. For very early coming events in the South were casting shadows before them to the manifest disturbance of the Northern mind. Heeding these shadows of ill omen along the Southern horizon, the North decided to clear the national sky of every shadowy possibility of a return of conditions which existed before the war, and which vexed her sorely during those bitter years. Apprehensive, then, lest the Fourteenth Amendment had not made a repetition of this history impossible, the nation adopted the Fifteenth Amendment, which ordains that "the right of citizens of the United States to vote shall not be denied or abridged by the United States or by any state on account of race, color, or previous condition of servitude." Each of those three great steps was taken by the North to rid the country of the Southern aristocratic idea, and of its corresponding labor system; to plough into Southern soil the democratic idea and its corresponding system of free labor; to purge the Constitution of its hateful three-fifths slave representation principle; to redress, in short, the old balance of political power between the sections in order to secure forever the domination of our Northern industrial democracy in national affairs.

Then ensued naturally enough in the wake of a period of great emotions a period of strong reaction at the North. That section grew weary of the everlasting negro question, and began to yearn for peace, for a cessation of strife between the sections; began to yearn for change, for other sensations, for other interests of a more material kind,—for dollars and dividends, for railroads and mines and factories, for buying and selling, for the thousand and one things which make up the busy life, the activity of a great and enterprising people. The spirit of modern commercialism descended like a consuming flame on the new generation which followed the war. Modern industrialism sucked like a huge maelstrom the whole multifarious and multitudinous life and forces of the nation into itself, with that one exception, the South.

The democratic idea of government has been put to rout in every Southern state by the old aristocratic idea founded in race prejudice and race distinctions. A labor system is fast growing up about this idea,—a labor system as much opposed to the labor system of the rest of the nation, as was the old slave system to the free labor of the North. There can be no lasting peace between them now, any more than such peace was possible between them in the period before the war. The political and industrial interests of the sections are not the same, and cannot be made the same so long as differences so fundamental in respect to government and labor exist between them. The conflict of the two contrary ideas of government, of the two contrary labor systems, for survivorship in the Union, may be postponed as it is to-day, but it cannot be extinguished except by the extinction of one or the other of the old rivals. For they are doomed, in one form or another, by economic and social laws, to ceaseless rivalry and strife.

In this strife the disfranchisement of the negro by the South is a distinct victory for the Southern idea, for the Southern rival, over the Northern idea, the Northern rival. The Southern idea has taken on new life, is re-sowing itself, striking powerful roots into Southern soil. And while it is steadily strengthening its ascendency over those states, its pollen dust is slowly spreading in many devious ways, blown by winds of destiny beyond the limits of those states, attacking with subtle, far-reaching, and deep-reaching influences the democratic idea of the rest of the nation, giving aid and form to all those feelings, thoughts, purposes, hidden or open, but active, in the republic, hostile to popular government, to the democratic principle of equality and universal suffrage. The South has thrown down its gage of battle for the aristocratic idea, for the labor system which grows out of that idea. This gage of battle is the disfranchisement of the negro because he is a negro, and the consequent degradation of him as a laborer. Will the North accept the challenge of its old rival, will it pick up the gage of battle thus thrown down? I think that it will. I am sure that it will. When? I confess frankly I do not know. But of this I have no doubt, that when this time comes, as come it must, the negro will mark again, as he did formerly, the dead line between the combatants,—between the aristocratic idea of the South and the democratic idea of the rest of the nation; between the labor system of the South and the labor system of the rest of the nation.

# The American Negro and the World War

## By Robert R. Moton

THERE HAVE BEEN so many marvelous and unexpected changes in
the mental attitude of stronger groups toward weaker ones, and so
many efforts to bring about universal democracy, that the Negro
himself has experienced much more of a genuinely friendly attitude
toward himself from the white race. He has also found so many more
doors open to him than hitherto, until he sometimes wonders what it
all means. Many sincere people had, just prior to, as well as at the
beginning of the war, wondered whether the Negro, because of the
many limitations which, as a race, he experienced in this country
and the protests which he frequently uttered, would allow himself
to become identified with the disloyal elements of this country and
fall an easy prey to German propagandists. Others wondered whether
Negro leaders would unconsciously or willfully encourage their
people to assume an indifferent if not wholly hostile attitude toward
the country. But educated and patriotic Negroes knew that these
anxious qualms were due rather to lack of knowledge and understanding of Negroes. As a matter of fact, without advice or counsel
from any organized body, official or otherwise, the educated Negroes,
professional and business men and educators generally, showed themselves as loyal and patriotic as any other Americans, and not only
counseled their people to be loyal, but urged them to avoid loose
expressions even in jest which might lead others to misunderstand.
Not only so, but they urged their people to raise food, to buy Liberty
Bonds, to respond to every other demand of the Government, and to

From *World's Work*, XXXVI (May 1918), 74–77.

serve along any lines that would help in the struggle that was being waged for humanity. Negroes, as other citizens, responded with enthusiasm that is now proverbial. One Negro fraternal organization, the Mosaic Templars of Arkansas, purchased $80,000 worth of Liberty Bonds, and throughout the South more food stuffs were raised by Negroes than ever before in their history. In the appeal from the Food Administration for conservation or saving of these food products for man and beast there was a response such as has never before been witnessed. It is reported by families who employ Negro domestic servants that they have never known their cooks to be more thoughtful and economical than at present. Chancellor D. C. Barrow of the University of Georgia reported that the Negro cook who had been in his family for a great many years, and who was inclined at first to take the matter of saving as a joke, had come to the point where she was preparing and serving the family dainty, appetizing, nutritious meals from the leftovers and took great delight in so doing. This is the opinion of scores of other people with whom I have talked regarding this matter. Negroes in their own homes, from the lowliest cabin to the best Negro residence, are vying with their white neighbors and their country in helping our government in this struggle, by saving food, and practising every economy.

### PERCENTAGE OF NEGRO VOLUNTEERS

It is notorious that when President Wilson asked for 70,000 volunteers, in many cities the Negro volunteers were out of proportion to their percentage of the population. Investigation in three cities has shown that these Negro volunteers were not doing so in a thoughtless, adventurous way, for many of them had jobs and reasonably comfortable homes, but they felt it their patriotic duty to offer their services to their country. In several cities where Negroes volunteered for the Navy, they were frankly and abruptly told that Negroes were only wanted for the mess departments. Many of these same men went from the navy recruiting station to the army and volunteered their services where they could be assigned to direct combative service. When the War Department, as a result of the earnest and persistent efforts on the part of colored people and their white friends, opened a camp for the training of Negro officers at Des Moines, Iowa, and asked for 1,200 Negroes to offer their services for training, notwithstanding the fact that it was less than 30 days, the required number reported for three months' training. Out of the number that took the training, 625 received commissions. Some people have ventured the suggestions that this present crisis is an opportune time for the Negro to demand "his rights," but subsequent developments have shown that the Negro, while clearly conscious of what he considers his rights, has been most earnest and persistent in his efforts to be granted the chance to do his duty by his country. The leaders have felt that that was sufficient for the present. Just now the important thing is the opportunity to serve in the great struggle for democracy.

### A NEGRO DIVISION

Major Thomas B. Spencer, who is on the staff of Gen. C. C. Ballou, of the 92nd Division, a division to be composed of Negroes, has been making a tour of Negro schools and colleges of the country with a view to selecting four or five hundred men for a particular branch in this division. At every school visited he has been asking for men who were below the draft age. He has received a most hearty response in volunteers from practically every school to which he has gone. At Tuskegee Institute thirty of the upper class men with whom he talked offered their services and left within 48 hours for Chillicothe, Ohio, where they are now being trained. About one hundred thousand Negro soldiers are under arms at the present time, as follows:

These troops are divided among many states and many regiments. They are in the infantry, the cavalry, and in considerable numbers in the National Guard, not only in Southern States but also in Northern and Western States. In many instances their officers are men of their own race, but white officers assigned to Negro regiments are almost invariably pleased with their men, and convinced that they are excellent material of which to make soldiers. The Negro is ordinarily proud of his uniform, falls readily into the discipline so necessary to military proficiency, and when occasion demands, he is faithful to his trust even against overwhelming odds. He is of the stuff from which good soldiers are made, and properly officered he becomes a soldier in the best meaning of the word. About 75,000 Negro men were called in the first draft, making as stated, a total of about one hundred thousand men. This, however, is not the largest number of Negro soldiers who have been under arms, for in the Civil War, 178,000 black men bore arms on the Union side.

Including those who were commissioned at the officers' training camp at Ft. Des Moines, those who were already officers in the four regiments and companies, there are now about one thousand Negro officers in the United States Army.

## THE ATTITUDE OF THE NEGRO SOLDIER

But all of the foregoing is wholly physical. One naturally asks what is the inner feeling of these men? How do they feel about the whole thing? I have talked with many of the rank and file of Negro draftees and volunteers as well as of state guards. I talked to one group of a half dozen Negro soldiers in Atlanta, who were at Camp Gordon. I put the question something like this:

"I suppose you feel proud to wear the uniform of your country?"

"Yes," said one.

"Do you like army life?"

"Not very well. We have not been fitted out yet with all of our equipment. I reckon we'll like it better when we git *more* used to it."

"Would you rather be home?"

"In some ways, yes. We would like to be home with the old folks and with our friends, but I don't b'lieve we colored folks will ever git a chance again like this to serve our country, so for our own race and our country, we feel it's our duty to go."

I talked with men also at Camp Meade, in Petersburg, Virginia, and from the two camps at Newport News—Stuart and Hill. These gave similar answers, the language sometimes crude, but all expressing the same loyal spirit. A colored man who was made a captain at Des Moines leaves an aged mother to care for four children, his wife having died a few years ago. "I could probably resign in view of home conditions but my country is first. I have made ample provisions by insurance, etc., for my mother and children so far as I am able. I feel my country needs me, and I must help my government in the training of these untrained colored soldiers as well as leading them in battle for the protection of our own flag," this man told me. I got a similar expression from a very prominent Negro lawyer and physician, now an officer in the Ohio National Guard. Thousands of black mothers and wives and sisters, to say nothing of fathers, have wept as these men have left home, and very few, if any, have raised a voice in protest on account of the past unfairness which the Negro has had to undergo.

## MR. GOMPERS' OPINION

Mr. Samuel Gompers, of the American Federation of Labor, expresses what in my opinion is not only the Negro's sentiment throughout the country but what is becoming the true American sentiment, when he says:

"What will come out of the war for labor? In a word, emancipation from every vestige of wrong and injustice. Out of this war the men of labor of the democracies of the world will come, standing upright; no longer like the men with the hoe. There is a new concept among mankind—the question 'Am I my brother's keeper?' this war and the democracies of the world are going to answer in the affirmative. If I have read history right there has never been any great struggle in the history of the world that has not had its baptism in blood. And the great cause of human liberty and justice is being baptized in human blood; and the spirit of freedom, of human justice, of human brotherhood, will triumph here, as in Europe. I ask you to believe in the loyalty of the great mass of the people who toil."

And Secretary Daniels, a Southerner, expresses the same democratic idea with equal force, when he says:

"We have done more for democracy in six months of war than in six years of peace. Our soldiers who come back from France aren't going to be anything but men. For in this war we are establishing a new spirit of universal equality and brotherhood. Too long has America been enslaved, too long has caste been enthroned. Kings will be relics, thrones will be in museums, here and abroad."

No finer tribute has been paid the Negro soldier than by Colonel James A. Moss, who recently said:

"Understanding the Negro as I do, and knowing his responsibilities as a soldier, I consider myself fortunate in having been assigned to the command of a colored regiment. Of my twenty-three years' experience as an officer, I have spent eighteen with colored troops, having commanded Negro troops in the Cuban campaign, and in the Philippine campaign, so that what I say about the Negro soldier—my faith, my confidence in him—is based on long experience with him in garrison and in the field; in peace and in war. I do not hesitate to make the assertion that if properly trained and instructed, the Negro will make as good a soldier as the world has ever seen. The proper training and instruction of the Negro soldier is a simple problem—it merely consists in treating him like a man, in a fair and square way, and in developing the valuable military assets he naturally possesses in the form of a happy disposition, pride in the uniform, tractability, and faithfulness. Any one who says that the Negro will not fight, does not, of course, know what he is talking about.

"The first fight I was ever in, the battle of El Caney, Cuba, July 1,

1898, I had Negroes killed and wounded all around me, 20 per cent of my company having been killed and wounded in about ten minutes' time, and the behavior of the men was splendid. At no time during that, and in subsequent fights, did my men hesitate at the command to advance or falter at the order to charge. I expect my colored regiment to be fully as well drilled, as well instructed, as well behaved, and as good fighters, as any other regiment in the National Army. Lest some might think that what I have to say about the Negro soldier is only the fulsome words of a "Yankee" Negro-phile, let me say that I am a native Louisianian who did not leave the confines of the State until I went to West Point at the age of eighteen."

## THE POINT OF VIEW OF PUBLIC MEN

We have had no finer interpretation of the fundamentals of democracy than from our own President Wilson, and the appointment of Mr. Emmett J. Scott, Secretary of Tuskegee Institute, as Special Assistant to the Secretary of War, is evidence of a growing faith in the Negro race and in its capacity for citizenship. Secretary Baker, in his telegram to the Chicago Colored Branch of the National Security League, said of democracy:

"After all, what is this thing we call 'democracy' and about which we hear so much nowadays? Surely it is no catch phrase or abstraction. It is demonstrating too much vitality for that. It is no social distinction or privilege of the few, for were it that, it could not win the hearts of peoples and make them willing to die for its establishment. But it is, it seems to me, a hope as wide as the human race, involving men everywhere—a hope which permits each of us to look forward to a time when not only we, but others, will have respective rights, founded in the generosity of Nature, and protected by a system of justice which will adjust its apparent conflicts. Under such a hope nations will do justice to nations, and men to men."

## NEGRO TROOPS IN THE FRENCH ARMY

When one talks face to face with such a man as Colonel E. M. House as well as other men, newspaper editors, Southern and Northern, as well as certain French officials, as has been my honor and pleasure to do during the past few months; when one remembers that France called to her aid her black troops from Senegal as well as her thousands of black Arabian troops, and when we remember how France has treated these men, not as black men, but as soldiers and patriots who gladly placed their lives at the service of their country, permitting them to have equal share in the blessings and privileges of French democracy in proportion as they have measured up to democracy's requirements, the Negroes of America feel that the world is going to be made safe for democracy. When through the discipline which it is now undergoing, it is stripped of arrogance, selfishness, and greed, and when those who arrogate to themselves the making and execution of the laws, feel, as they ultimately must, that it is their patriotic duty and sacred obligation to see that the humblest citizen is given every privilege to live and to serve that is granted every other citizen within the limits of the law, then we shall have a real democracy in America. We cannot believe these sincere exponents of world democracy mean that the Negroes, 12 million now perhaps in this country, should not be given an equal chance to live, to work, to secure an education, and to ride on public conveyances, without embarrassment, and under conditions equal in comfort and safety to that enjoyed by any citizen.

## EQUALITY OF OPPORTUNITY

War is teaching us that we are inseparably linked together here in America. Races, creeds, colors, and classes all have their interests interrelated and interdependent. The test of our greatness as a nation is not in the accumulation of wealth, nor in the development of culture merely. The great test is for the fortunate to reach down and help the less highly favored, the poor, the humble—yes, even the black. My race asks no special favors and deserves no special favors. It simply asks an equal chance on equal terms with other Americans, and nothing in the Negro's past record indicates other than that he will give a strict account of his stewardship. Give the Negro race responsibility, and in proportion as he has these race responsibilities placed upon him, in like proportion will his experience broaden and his service in all lines reach a higher level of satisfaction. The social problems of America will never be solved by mobbing or segregating black men in the North, nor by burning or lynching in the South. Injustice and unfairness will never do it. The great Nazarene said: "Inasmuch as ye did it unto one of the least of these ye have done it unto me."

*The two following articles, by Robert Moton and by Kate Herring, director of publicity of the North Carolina War Savings Committee, effectively demonstrate the propaganda effort undertaken during the First World War to rally black support for the war and to convince white America that black people supported the war effort.*

# Fifty Thousand and Fifty Million

### By Robert R. Moton

"I'm sometimes up,
I'm sometimes down,
Oh, yes, Lord.
I'm sometimes almost level with the ground.
Oh, yes, Lord."

THESE ARE SOME LINES from a famous Negro folk song which we sometimes sing when in a somewhat despondent mood. These lines frequently express, even now, the emotions of my race, and, I suspect, often of some white people too.

I attended a very significant gathering of something like a thousand men, under the auspices of the Fifth Avenue Association, at the Waldorf Astoria, in New York City. . . . The gathering was a diplomatic luncheon. The object was to sell twenty-two million dollars' worth of Liberty Bonds. The meeting was presided over by a master of business as well as a master of men, and one who represents the highest ideals of American citizenship, Mr. Charles M. Schwab, whom President Wilson, with his usual rare foresight, placed at the head of the United States Shipping Board. In a simple, direct, brief, yet forceful address, Mr. Schwab stated the object of the meeting; told of the work the Shipping Board had done, described how American labor as well as capital had combined in ship-building to the extent that the submarine had been practically put out of business, speaking in a way to bring that audience of dignified bankers, merchants, etc., to its feet with such cheers and enthusiasm as one seldom

Both articles from the *Outlook*, CXX (November 1918), 451–453.

witnesses except perhaps at a college football game. It was an *orderly disorderly* crowd. Mr. Schwab said, among other things: "We have entered upon a social war, in which the aristocracy of the future will be men who have done something for humanity and for their nations. There will be no rich or poor classes. The rich men are learning this—and I am a rich man, I'm told. But there has never been a time in my life that I had the sense of possession or that my riches gave me any happiness. It is the doing of something useful that has made me happy." In about an hour that audience subscribed fifty-two million dollars in Liberty Bonds, and then the meeting adjourned to permit those present to attend the launching of two ships.

I left the magnificence of the hotel and the enthusiasm of the party, feeling proud of my country and proud of my citizenship therein. That was one of the times when, in the words of the song, I felt that I was "up."

As I walked down Thirty-fourth Street towards Broadway and Sixth Avenue, unconscious of the noonday crowd which was surging past me, I remembered that I was to participate in another Liberty Loan meeting the next day, among my humble, far-from-wealthy, and yet reasonably comfortable, but nevertheless patriotic people. I suspected that at the Liberty Loan meeting in Harlem there would be present perhaps three or four thousand of my own race, and I wondered if in two hours four thousand of my people in New York could raise ten thousand dollars. I hoped they would raise fifty-two thousand—a thousand for each million raised by the leading business men and the real captains of American industry at the Waldorf. I felt reasonably sure that they could not raise $52,000 in one meeting. This was one of the times when I was "down" in my spirits and "almost level with the ground."

According to arrangements made by an excellent committee composed of both white and colored people, a great audience of black people, with perhaps a hundred white people, assembled the next evening at the Palace Casino in Harlem. A parade of the Fifteenth Regiment of the New York State Guard, under Colonel William Jay Schieffelin, preceded the meeting.

I do not know how many people were present; no one knows—some said three thousand, others said five thousand; this we are sure of, the hall was filled to its capacity. That was also an *orderly disorderly* crowd. The presiding officer, Colonel Schieffelin, was fittingly introduced by Mr. John E. Nail, a successful Negro real estate dealer in Harlem, who in turn, in a short but effective address, outlined the object of the meeting. There were several other very brief and telling addresses, by Mr. James W. Johnson, contributing editor of the New York "Age"; by Mr. J. F. Leech, of the New York Liberty Loan Committee; and by Captain Marcel Knecht, who served two years with the French army, after which he came over with the French High Commission. The Principal of Tuskegee Institute also spoke.

In a comparatively short while, amid as much enthusiasm and patriotism per individual and as much of genuine American spirit, expressed perhaps differently, and with as much disorderly order as I had witnessed a few hours before at the Waldorf, sixty thousand dollars in Liberty Bonds had been subscribed for by that audience. Then I was neither "up" nor "down."

I asked myself, "What is sixty thousand dollars against fifty million?" But then when I looked over the audience I shared the irresistible enthusiasm of the true Americanism which manifested itself by that throng of people. And when I thought of the love and devotion of that audience and the millions whom they represent, and as I remembered how the mention of the flag and loyalty, and President Wilson, and our boys in France, white and black, and General Foch and General Pershing, brought that mass of humanity to its feet; and when I thought of the yearnings and longings and strivings of that audience for right and justice; and the efforts they and their brethren North and South are making in schools, on the farms, in shops, in factories, in domestic service; and of the increasing sympathy and co-operation they are receiving from their white friends of both sections to fit them for democracy; and as a black man, yearning and struggling with them for all that is true, for all that is best and noblest in American civilization, and knowing how sincere they were in their desire for the real freedom of all humanity and the ultimate triumph of right, my pride in my race was again deepened.

That was one of the moments when I was *"up"—"away up"*—because I knew that the audience, composed of the rank and file of the laboring people of my race, out of their devotion and patriotism had been as responsive as the million-dollar audience. I realized fully that sixty thousand dollars from that audience meant as much in devotion and in loyalty to the Old Flag as the fifty-two millions taken at the Waldorf represented. The magnificent gathering at the Waldorf of some of America's greatest captains of industry and finance, out of their abundance and with true American spirit, did their best; the significant gathering at the Palace Casino, not of captains of industry or masters of finance, but largely of laborers and representatives of a cramped and as yet more or less poverty-stricken people, did their best, and I knew that both groups, one white, one black, were yearning for the triumph of human rights and the crushing forever of autocracy and all of the representatives of inhumanity wherever found.

And then when I thought of how our Tuskegee teachers, out of their all too meager salaries, had subscribed twelve thousand dollars to the Fourth Liberty Loan, and how a few of us from Tuskegee went out on a Sunday afternoon during the drive to several of the gatherings and church services of the colored farmers in our own county here in Alabama, and how readily these humble people in true American fashion had subscribed for seven thousand dollars' worth of bonds, their spirit, while not exactly of almsgiving, reminded me of the sentiment in that beautiful passage of Lowell's,

> "Not what we give, but what we share,
> For the giver without the gift is bare;
> Who gives himself with his alms feeds three,
> Himself, his hungering neighbor, and Me."

I could not but feel that my people by their contribution, their loyalty, and their spirit along all lines, realized fully that they are heirs of America, and that as such they must be sharers of her struggles as well as partakers of her glory.

The fine spirit of Northern and Southern people, of white and colored people, infused me with new life, gave birth to new hope for my country's ultimate triumph and glory; and I was able to look into the future and behold the great opportunities of America, united on essentials of justice and human brotherhood, and I was still exceedingly glad to be a NEGRO AMERICAN.

# How the Southern Negro Is Supporting the Government

*By Kate M. Herring*

WHAT TO DO with the Negro in the War Savings Campaign was one of the most puzzling questions that confronted the National Committee. The proposition to apportion to each State its allotment of War Savings Certificates on the basis of twenty dollars per capita was earnestly objected to by representatives from the South. They claimed that this method of determining the quotas was inequitable to the South for the reason that a large part of its population consists of Negroes, and that they cannot buy an average of twenty dollars per capita of War Savings Certificates. They urged the Committee to put the apportionment upon some other basis than population. But the Committee was obdurate and held the South to the same basis of apportionment as other sections.

When the National War Savings Committee saw fit not to make the Negro an issue or an exception in the War Savings Campaign, but to consider him an American citizen with responsibilities the same as other citizens, all the States of the South, except South Carolina, proceeded with their campaigns, altogether ignoring race. South Carolina, however, made a reapportionment of her quota, assigning to the Negroes only two dollars per capita and to the white people enough over twenty dollars to make up the balance. North Carolina made no distinction between the races, expecting Negroes to invest twenty dollars per capita in War Savings Certificates the same as white people.

One of the first things to be attempted by the North Carolina War Savings Committee was to plan for the colored people. The State Director asked each of his county chairmen to name the most representative and influential Negro in his county to be called to a conference to make plans for promoting the War Savings Campaign among the Negroes. As a result of this conference the State was divided into ten districts, in each of which a leading Negro was appointed supervisor of the War Savings activities. In addition to this, separate War Savings headquarters for the colored people, with a capable colored man as executive secretary, were established. This office has been in close touch with and operated under the supervision of State headquarters for the white people.

In North Carolina very much the same educational work has been done for the Negroes as for the whites. The colored War Savings Committee considered that the greatest need of the colored people was to be informed both as to what War Savings Securities were and what they as patriotic citizens should do about them. One of the first efforts of the Committee to educate their people in thrift as well as patriotism was to issue the following leaflet:

## TO THE COLORED PEOPLE OF NORTH CAROLINA—
### GREETING

Our interests are collective, but they are also racial and individual. They are indissolubly wrapped up in the issues of the war. If the United States and her allies win, it will be, in an important sense, our victory, and will herald the dawn of a new day. If the enemy win, it will be, in a vital sense, our loss, and will betoken the approach of another long night of gloom.

You must see this matter from the point of view that your individual, personal attitude and activity MUST and WILL help to win this war, or lose it. YOU CANNOT BE NEUTRAL! You cannot say as Pilate: "I wash my hands of this matter." To assume an attitude of indifference or even of passive sympathy is to give comfort and help to the enemy. "HE THAT IS NOT FOR US IS AGAINST US!"

#### HOW YOU CAN HELP

1. Conserve speech. Be careful to utter no word calculated to beget mischief.
2. Conserve food. Waste no flour, sugar, meat, or other staples.
3. Conserve fuel. Burn no more wood, coal, gas, or oil than comfort and safety require.
4. Conserve time and energy. Find some useful, gainful employment. Do some constructive work putting in full time.
5. Conserve money. Save every penny of your money and buy Thrift and War Savings Stamps. By so doing you will develop self-reliance, independent manhood and womanhood, and become a creditor to the Government. You will fire a deadly missile at the enemy.

Your Thrift and War Savings Stamps are the best investment in the world. They are mortgages on the United States of America. They are tangible evidence of your loyalty. They insure the success of our Army.

Our fathers left us a proud heritage of faithfulness, patriotism, and valor, but for the first time in our history we are called upon to help furnish the sinews of war. Shall we be less faithful, patriotic, and valorous? A thousand times, No!

Patriotic meetings of colored people have been held in their schools, churches, and community centers, at which War Savings speeches were made by both white and colored field workers. War Savings Societies have been organized in their day schools, Sunday schools, churches, lodges, and working places the same as among white people. In fact, the first War Savings Society organized in the State was among colored people. This was the Warren Place War Savings Society, at Pendleton, Northampton County, and was composed of the tenants of the Warren plantation. The President and moving spirit of this organization is W. J. Lassiter, a Negro tenant, who subscribed $200 to the War Savings Campaign and who has already bought that amount.

Few white citizens of the State have given more liberally of their time and money than a score or more of loyal colored citizens. Negro educators, ministers, and business men of ability have labored unceasingly and without remuneration to arouse their people to a full sense of their full duty toward the Government's requests and to their responsibilities as American citizens. Prominent among those who have labored most faithfully to carry the gospel of thrift and patriotism to the people of their race, even in the remote corners of the State, are: Dr. R. B. McCrary, a leading business man of his race and Chairman of the Colored War Savings Committee; S. G. Atkins, Principal of the Slater Normal School, Winston-Salem, and Executive Secretary of the Colored War Savings Committee; C. S. Brown, Principal of the Watters Normal School, Winton; T. S. Inborden, Principal of the Bricks School, Enfield; Bishop G. W. Clinton, A. M. E. Church, Charlotte; H. L. McCrory, W. H. Coler, Colonel James H. Young, John Merrick, E. G. Storey, S. H. Vick, and C. M. Epps—men of prominence and ability.

Colored people have considered and accepted the calls that have come to them in the War Savings Campaign as privileges of service and as a direct summons from the Government. The quick and wholehearted response made by the Negroes of Greene County in the pledge drive of June 23–28 illustrates this fact.

Early one morning in June Ambrose Best was notified that he had been appointed chairman of an adjoining township to raise the War Savings quota of the colored people of the township in pledges. On receiving his summons he left his mule and plow in the field in the hands of his young son, and went afoot over into the township assigned to him. Before sunset he had visited every colored person's home and actually had secured an over-subscription of his allotment.

Jesse Williams was another colored township chairman of Greene County who on June 28 was not found deserting his post. He arranged for a schoolhouse meeting Friday night, and kept his audience until three o'clock in the morning signing War Savings pledges. As a result of his energy and enthusiasm he raised his War Savings quota in pledges three times over.

As a result of all these activities of the colored people in the War Savings Campaign, the records show that they have bought and have pledged to buy War Savings Stamps far more extensively in comparison with their ability than the white people.

From inquiries made of War Savings directors of other Southern States, it appears that their experience with the Negro has been not unlike North Carolina's. Florida reports that the ten counties in that State making the best showing in the War Savings pledge drive in June had from forty to fifty per cent colored population, and that the ten counties making the poorest showing had from thirty to forty per cent colored population. Mississippi reported that the Negroes of that State have given a support to the campaign that in proportion to their means equaled or surpassed that of the white people. Unofficial reports from other Southern States show that the record of the Negro, in the loyal support he has given the War Savings Campaign, has been extremely gratifying. Apparently the misgiving in the beginning lest the Negro would handicap the directors of the Southern States in raising their quotas on a basis of population was unfounded. On the contrary, it would seem that the loyal support of the Negro has more than made up for his poverty.

In justice to the Negro as well as to enthusiastic War Savings workers, particularly pledge canvassers, it can be and should be said that the spirit to coerce the Negro into buying and subscribing for War Savings Stamps has not existed, not even in individual cases, in North Carolina. No threats, scares, or other means of intimidation have been used to make him pledge or buy either in keeping with or beyond his ability. On the other hand, wherever the Negro has been informed as to his duty as a patriotic American citizen, regardless of other calls, he has responded most liberally and cheerfully. It has been a noticeable fact that he responded most readily to the patriotic appeal. The plea that Uncle Sam needed him to uphold his hands while he delivered the blow that would crush the Hun was argument enough for him. The plea that War Savings Stamps are a good investment, that they bear four per cent compound interest and are non-taxable, meant not half so much to the average Negro as the fact that Uncle Sam and the boys at the front needed him and his money to drive back the Germans across the Rhine and to make the world safe for women and children.

But the real explanation of the Negro's co-operation and success in the War Savings Campaign in North Carolina lies in the fact that he has been recognized as an American citizen and given responsibilities the same as white men. Moreover, he has been made to realize the opportunities that have come to him through this call of the Government, and, like the colored soldier at the front, he has responded in a spirit of service and sacrifice that marks him a worthy patriot.

# The Republicans and the Black Voter

## By W. E. B. DuBois

IF WE TAKE as our basis the election of 1916 and assume that women will vote, it would seem probable that the balance of power which will determine the way in which the electoral votes of eight pivotal States will be cast will depend roughly upon the following number of voters: Illinois, 100,000; Indiana, 10,000; Kentucky, 60,000; Maryland, 40,000; Michigan, 90,000; New Jersey, 120,000; New York, 220,000; Ohio, 180,000. The electoral votes of Connecticut, Delaware, Iowa, Kansas, Massachusetts, Minnesota, Missouri, Pennsylvania, and West Virginia may depend on an equally narrow marginal group, and the decision in these seventeen States will determine the election. Recently there has been a large migration of adult Negroes from the South. It seems probable, then, that in the next election the number of Negroes eligible to vote will be: Illinois, 125,000; Michigan, 25,000; Indiana, 45,000; Kentucky, 150,000; Maryland, 150,000; New Jersey, 75,000; New York, 125,000; Ohio, 100,000. If this estimate should prove true then in the first mentioned four States, the Negro voter easily holds the balance of power. In four others he might hold the balance in a fairly close election. Moreover, he holds large power and in many Congressional districts decisive power in the other nine States mentioned. He could then, if he voted intelligently and with an eye single to his greatest political advantage, decide the election of 1920.

He could not only decide who would be President but more important, he could greatly influence the complexion of Congress. The

From *Nation*, CX (June 5, 1920), 757–758.

present Senate has forty-seven Democrats and forty-nine Republicans, so that without the indicted Senator from Michigan the Republicans lead by one. Nine senators are to be elected from Iowa, Kansas, Ohio, Kentucky, Illinois, Maryland, Missouri, Indiana, and New York. The Negro vote might easily decide which party should control the Senate. The House Republican majority is forty-one, and Negroes by voting carefully in the forty-one Districts might easily cut down if not destroy it.

The reader will immediately say: This is all very well and would call for careful attention if the Negro voter were intelligent, experienced, and determined. But he has a large percentage of illiteracy; he has had no political experience; and hitherto he has voted with his heart and not his head. We may, therefore, be sure that the Republicans are not losing much sleep over the Negro vote. They are saying that Wilson has made it impossible for any Negro to vote Democratic, and therefore there is nothing else for him to do but vote Republican. This calculation may be sound, but there are other considerations. First, the Negroes as a mass have done more thinking in the last four years than ever before. Second, they have long-standing grievances against the Republican Party, and it cannot therefore count on the absolute necessity of a black man voting Republican.

Americans must not forget the deep distrust and resentment left among the Negro population by the later Taft and Roosevelt policies. When they turned over the patronage of the South to its whites they did not prevent Republicanism in the South from continuing to be mainly a matter of patronage, and thus they joined the South in disfranchising the best of the Negroes in the counsels of the party. It was then that a small group of Negroes conceived the idea that there might be a chance to interest farseeing Democrats. They believed Mr. Wilson to be a new type of politician. They thought that he must see that present political conditions in the South could not be permanent and they inquired if it might not be possible to make a tentative alliance between the forward-thinking northern Democrats and intelligent Negroes, with the idea of dividing the northern Negro vote and gradually bringing a real government of the people in the South. The first overtures toward this end brought instant response. In a letter to Alexander Walters, a colored bishop, written just before the election of 1912, Mr. Wilson expressed his "earnest wish to see justice done them [the colored people] in every matter; and not mere grudging justice, but justice executed with liberality and cordial good feeling."

This induced a considerable number of Negroes to vote the Democratic ticket in 1912 and those that were not persuaded by Wilson's words were helped by the extraordinary attitude of the Progressive Party under Mr. Roosevelt, which despite its vast enthusiasm of song and tears absolutely refused even to consider a plank which said, "The Progressive party recognizes that distinctions of race or class in political life have no place in a democracy." Wilson's election followed, and the Republican split made it difficult to determine just what the Negro vote meant. Needless to say, in 1916 it went solidly for Hughes.

Coming now to 1920 we have first to note that these experiences have not improved the temper of the Negro voter. In the first place, intelligence, not only as measured by formal schooling but as measured by wider social experience, is spreading fast in the Negro race and was quickened by the Great War. Black men are determined as never before not simply to vote but to make their votes tell. Intelligent leaders do not yet represent or control the majority of Negro voters, but this type of leadership is more widely effective today than ever before.

The calculations of the Republicans may first go awry in assuming that Negroes will not vote for Democrats. So far as the national Democratic ticket is concerned, this is of course perfectly true. No black man could vote for the "Solid South" and no Democratic candidate dare repudiate the support of this rotten borough system. But the Democratic organizations in certain northern States, and particularly in northern cities, have been giving a great deal of solicitous attention to Negroes. In New York City, for instance, there is a strong and intelligent Negro Democratic organization. The Negroes can get more consideration from the Democratic Congressman in the one black Harlem district than from any of their Republican Congressmen. They have consequently been voting more and more independently in Harlem in local elections and have their own representatives on the Board of Aldermen, in the Legislature, and in various branches of the civil service. In other cities and States the Democrats have made similar inroads.

It is quite possible, then, for Democratic Congressmen, legislators, and governors to attract a considerable number of Negro votes and it is noticeable in this election that Negroes recognize that they are not nearly so much interested in the President of the United States as they are in their local aldermen and members of their State legislatures and particularly their Congressmen.

Again the radicals have begun to see light with regard to Negroes. They realize that they must do more than flourish and beckon to get Negro support. The Committee of Forty-Eight has demanded: "equal economic, political and legal rights for all, irrespective of sex or color." The Socialist Party has put this plank in its platform: "Congress should enforce the provisions of the Fourteenth Amendment with reference to the Negroes, and effective Federal legislation should be enacted to secure to the Negroes full civil, political, industrial educational rights." The Labor Party has not been as explicit but it is making distinct overtures. Without doubt there will be a large Negro radical vote.

On the other hand, the Republicans are following placidly the old path. In the South they are encouraging the "Lily Whites" to "contest" the Negro delegates. Tennessee is typical. In that state a strong, intelligently led colored Republican movement has gained much headway, yet when their convention met, white men, both Republicans and Democrats, held a rival convention and will send rival delegates to the national convention. At the convention the Republican Party will be obsessed by the idea of building up a white Republican Party in the South. The "Lily Whites" will gain most of the "contests." The only appeal that the Republicans are now making to the colored vote is the old appeal of bald money bribery. *The Crisis* says:

> Every four years the disgrace of the buying up of certain delegates for the Republican convention is repeated in the Southern South. In South Carolina, Georgia, Florida, Alabama, Mississippi, Louisiana, and Texas, there are a few professional grafters, black and white, who assume to represent the "Republican Party." They are for sale to the highest bidder. Republican candidates begin their campaign by sending men into the South to buy the support of these men, and the whole Negro race is blamed for this recurring disgrace. But whose is the fault? The fault lies at the doors of the National Republican Party. Not only are the party and its candidates willing and eager to buy up this support, but they have repeatedly refused support or countenance to the better class of colored leaders who seek to oust these thieves.

What do Negroes expect to gain by political action? How far are they to be satisfied by platform dissertations on the Rights of Man?

Do they expect to be legislated into complete modern freedom or have they thought out a clear straight political path leading to their ideals? Four years ago I could have answered these questions only by stating my own personal opinions. Today I can do more. The National Association for the Advancement of Colored People sent to seventeen presidential candidates and near candidates the following questionnaire:

    1. Will you favor the enactment of laws making lynching a federal offense?

    2. What is your attitude toward the disfranchisement of Americans of Negro descent: (a) will you advocate that Congress enforce the 14th Amendment and reduce the representation of States which disfranchise their citizens, or (b) will you advocate the appointment of United States Commissioners to enforce the 15th Amendment ?

    3. Will you endeavor to bring about the abolition of "Jim Crow" cars in interstate traffic?

    4. Will you withdraw armed or other interference with the independence of Haiti?

    5. Will you urge national aid to elementary education, without discrimination against Negro children?

    6. Will you pledge the apportionment of Negro soldiers and Negro officers in the armed forces of the United States in proportion to their numbers in the population?

    7. Will you abolish racial segregation in the Civil Service of the United States?

Fifteen of those questioned preserved a discreet silence. Two replied but avoided committing themselves. Very well. The same or a similar questionnaire will go to every candidate for Congress. Some of these will refuse to answer while others like Dyer of Missouri and Madden of Illinois will hasten to answer favorably and in detail because a majority of their constituents are black and because, within the next four years, these men will be succeeded in Congress by black men. Other Negro Congressmen loom in the far horizon in New York and Pennsylvania. The dilly-dallying of the Republicans has already beaten the Harlem district of New York into the most independent voting district in the city. Party labels mean nothing there: A hundred thousand Negroes simply ask the candidates: Where do you stand on OUR problem?

This is symptomatic. The Republicans may ignore the Negro or pat him graciously on the back as in the past. The Democrats may continue to depend on oligarchy and mob rule in the South. Neither attitude will disturb the new Negro voter, for he expects it. He is simply going to seek to keep the Negro hater and the straddler out of Congress and the legislatures, and wherever possible he will support the candidate that stands for his Seven Points.

## Is Al Smith Afraid of the South?

*By W. E. B. DuBois*

ALFRED SMITH is not the first American politician for whom the Negroes of the United States have proved a most embarrassing stumbling block. But seldom have the implications of this situation been so clear to all Americans who are willing to think.

Mr. Smith is posing as liberal. His attitude toward super-power, toward non-partisan appointments to office, and toward prohibition give him some color of right to this definition. Toward the greater and ever more pressing problems of the distribution of income and ownership of property, he is making a tentative approach by noting the economic distress of the American farmer. But all this does not prove his case, and does not make his appeal to American liberals by any means clear; for he has also made desperate effort to reassure entrenched American capital that he cannot be counted as its enemy; that he will be considerate of corporations like General Motors; and that he will take care of the interests entrenched behind the tariff. All this would make liberal support of Mr. Smith debatable. But there is another matter where there can be no debate.

Mr. Smith is silent about the Negro. Why? Certainly it is not because he has no need of the Negro vote. Migration from South to North, and from country to city, has increased the effective vote which Negroes cast very appreciably over 1916, and considerably over 1920 and 1924. We must, of course, depend upon estimates instead of actual figures, but in States where the real battles of this campaign are apparently being fought, there is a large Negro vote: in New York, 150,000; in New Jersey, 75,000; in Ohio, 125,000; in Indiana, 70,000; in Illinois, 175,000; in West Virginia, 50,000; in Kentucky, 125,000; in Tennessee, 225,000; in North Carolina, 25,000; in California, 40,000. Even Massachusetts has 21,000 Negro voters, and Connecticut, 15,000. There are probably 60,000 Negro voters in

Michigan and 125,000 in Missouri. Kansas has 35,000, Delaware, 15,000, and Maryland, 140,000. Of course, in the Southern hinterland, there is little chance that any appreciable Negro vote will be cast or counted. And yet in Virginia, South Carolina, Georgia, Florida, Texas, and Oklahoma the Negro vote of 100,000 might conceivably be of importance if any real rift were made in the governing oligarchy.

This is an asset that no astute politician—and no one has accused Mr. Smith of not being astute—would ordinarily neglect. Moreover, the Negroes are incensed against the Republican Party and against Mr. Hoover as never before. Some defection from the ranks of Negro Republicans was felt as early as 1912, and Woodrow Wilson went out of his way to encourage it. He openly promised Negroes "Justice and not mere grudging justice." Led by the late Bishop Alexander Walters, a Negro bureau was established at Democratic headquarters and a considerable Negro vote was cast for Woodrow Wilson. But the Wilson administration disappointed Negroes even more than it disappointed other people. Wilson refused to appoint the fact finding commission which he had promised to Oswald Garrison Villard; he refused to recognize the Negro in any important appointments; his whole Negro program succumbed to the Southern oligarchy, except during the war scare. By 1916 the revolt was well over and Negroes went back and voted with docility for Mr. Hughes.

In 1920, Cox made no appeal to the colored vote and it went almost solidly for Harding. In 1924, however, a revolt began again. Davis was a favorite among West Virginia Negroes, and led by William H. Lewis, the Boston lawyer, many colored voters bolted Coolidge. But all the revolt was as nothing to that which was brewing among Negroes in 1928. If Al Smith would raise a finger to assure American Negroes that, while he was not necessarily a warm friend, at least he could not be classed as an enemy, he would receive more Negro votes than any Democrat has ever received. For the first time in the history of colored Republican politics, leading colored politicians, like R. R. Church of Tennessee, refused to sit upon the colored Advisory Committee; the head of the Negro Elks openly pledged his organization against Hoover, and there was every sign that the defection thus begun was going to reach large proportions.

Nor were the reasons for this far to see. If leading Negroes repudiated Coolidge in 1924, they were even more estranged in 1928. Moreover, Hoover's silence on them and their problems has been nearly as great as Smith's. He has not said a single public word

against lynching, disfranchisement or for Negro education and uplift. When it was brought to his attention that the Red Cross was
discriminating outrageously against Negroes suffering from the Mississippi flood, Hoover at first denied it vehemently; afterward he
named a Negro committee of his friends, headed by R. R. Moton of
Tuskegee, and when this committee confirmed the evidences of discrimination he refused to let the committee publish its findings.

In addition to this, Hoover has joined openly with the "Lily Whites"
of the South,—that is, with those active Southern politicians who
propose, not simply to keep the Southern Negro disfranchised, but
to prevent the organization of any effective minority party in which
the Negro has representation. Hoover knows perfectly well that the
disfranchisement of the better class Negroes in the South delivers
them into the hands of venal politicians, black and white. Hoover,
Coolidge, Hughes, Harding, and all Republican candidates receive
gladly the political support of these men in the national conventions.
After the convention, Mr. Hoover proceeds to recognize only the
white politicians who have supported him. It was very easy to find
evidence for accusing Southern Negro politicians of traffic in public
office. But the same accusations have been made and proven against
white politicians. There is no reason to think that the accusations
were any more true in the case of the colored Perry Howard than in
the case of the white Bascom Slemp, once Secretary to President
Coolidge. But under Hoover's political organization, Howard was
kicked out and prosecuted, while Slemp was put in charge of his
Southern campaign! Every Negro political leader in the South regardless of his standing—and there are some who are honest and
brave—has been unceremoniously ousted by Hoover and his
lieutenants.

Here, then, was a chance and an unusual chance for Al Smith,
and not simply a chance for political maneuvering. It was a chance
to attack in its stronghold the central danger of American democracy;
the thing that makes it impossible for the American people today to
vote logically or coherently on any subject whatsoever; and that
incubus is the bloc of 114 to 139 electoral votes which are out of
politics in the sense that no political discussion, no appeal to intelligence or justice, has any influence on them. This was the time for
a really great statement. The Governor of New York might have
stepped into the arena and said: "I believe in democracy. I believe
that no one is good enough to cast a vote for his neighbor. I be-

lieve that poverty and misfortune, even if coupled with slavery and color, are in themselves no reason for caste and disfranchisement. If in spite of misfortune, poverty, and handicap a man meets the qualifications laid down for voting, he ought to vote and to be protected in his vote. He and his ought not to be interfered with by lawlessness and lynching. Education and encouragement ought freely to be offered, and every opportunity for development placed before such people."

Is there any reason why any American citizen, Democrat, Republican, or Socialist, should not subscribe to such a creed and publicly announce it? If there is, then American democracy is already a failure. If there is not, then Alfred Smith ought to have made such a statement. Moreover, I violate no confidence in saying that he was asked and urged to do it and that he refused.

A number of enthusiastic colored folk and friends of colored people put before the advisers of Governor Smith several possible statements which he might make to show that at least he was not an enemy of the American Negro. He refused to say a single word. He refused to let even indirectly anything go out from his headquarters which should seem to represent him as friendly to black men. Negro Democratic headquarters were indeed established but they were not allowed to have offices in the regular Democratic headquarters but were given a small "Jim Crow" annex where they exist without real authority, without explicit recognition, and without the slightest initiative.

On the other hand, explicit and repeated anti-Negro propaganda is being sent out by Democratic headquarters. When the Klan accused Governor Smith of having as his private stenographer "a Negro wench," Democratic headquarters at Washington on September 8 sent out the following release:

> Governor Smith does not have, and never has had, a Negro stenographer, and in the employment of Negroes by the State of New York under his administration this has been done only to fill such jobs as are given in the South, to wit: porters, janitors, charwomen, etc.

The interesting thing about this statement is that it is perfectly true. In all Governor Smith's long career, he had sedulously avoided recognizing Negroes in any way. He has twice vetoed bills which would have given a colored magistrate to Harlem. He has never given a Negro any major appointment. He has seldom been willing to receive a Negro delegation and it is doubtful if he has met personally in all his career a half-dozen of the 250,000 Negroes of his State.

At one time the leaders of his party in New York City recommended that the late Colonel Charles Young be made head of the new Negro regiment authorized under the direction of the Democratic Governor Sulzer. This regiment had not been organized because of the question of colored officers. The State National Guard was determined that there should be no colored officers, and gave as an excuse that none was qualified. But Charles Young, then a Major in the regular army and a West Point graduate, was a man not only of stainless personal character, but of well-known military ability. The army would have been perfectly willing to lend him to the National Guard. Governor Smith was asked to appoint him. He peremptorily refused and placed a white man at the head of the colored 15th Regiment.

Now why should a man otherwise in many respects liberal and likable, who has himself come up from the common people, show himself so illiberal and petty toward the Negro? It is because Smith has been afraid of the South, and is so today. He probably first ignored the Negro because, with East Side ignorance, he knew nothing about him, and shared the East Side's economic dislike of Negro labor competition: a dislike which was back of the Irish anti-Negro riots before and during the war, in Philadelphia and New York. As Smith began to develop in political power and ambition, he recognized that if he wanted to carry the South he must be orthodox on the Negro according to Southern traditions. He has been so, and, in the future, according to Congressman Hill of Alabama, "Governor Smith says he will let us handle the Negro problem as we see fit. What more could we ask?" Then, again, his liquor program and his religion have stirred up enough trouble and revolt south of the Mason and Dixon line. Smith is determined, therefore, not to say a single word that will enable his enemies and the Ku Klux Klan to fasten the title "Nigger-lover" upon him.

This is unfortunate for the Negro. But it is far more unfortunate for the American people. It means that no attempt to liberalize either the Republican or the Democratic Party, or to start a new third-party movement, can succeed as long as the present disfranchisement of the Negro supports a Solid South. Few Americans yet realize this. Many simple souls have a distinct hope that the Democratic Party may yet figure as a liberal party. They have an additional hope that it will never be necessary in the future, as it has not seemed necessary to these liberals in the past, to take any stand or attitude with regard to the so-called Negro problem. They propose to go on, ignoring the fact that the eleven Southern States, with an increase of population of more than 200 per cent since 1870, and with a theoretical doubling of the electorate by woman suffrage, did not, between the election of 1872 and that of 1924, increase its voting population more than 131 per cent, and that in five States of the Southern South the voting population has actually decreased in fifty years. In other words, a rotten borough system has been built up in the South which has disfranchised 5,000,000 voters and put the political power of a third of the nation in the hands of fewer than a million voters!

The political power of this rump electorate is astonishing. They send forty-five congressmen to Washington, while a million voters on the Pacific Coast send but twelve! They keep their Congressmen in office for long periods, thus enabling the South to monopolize a large number of the chief committee appointments. What chance is there that this political power will become radical or even liberal? Not the slightest. Now and then we may get some wild talk from Tillman or Jeff Davis or Caraway. You may get gestures from Carter Glass and taunts from Pat Harrison and solemn rhodomontades from Swanson of Virginia. But when it comes to votes, in every case the Solid South will be found to be the tail of the conservative reactionary North, and not a single reform movement, no punishment of swindlers, no real investigation of political evils, can depend upon Southern support. The Solid South cannot be liberal. It is built upon the disfranchisement, not only of 2,000,000 Negroes, but of many more than 2,000,000 whites. It is built on widespread ignorance and intolerance; crime and lynching; peonage and slavery. Its business is to choke off all discussion among liberal whites in the South; to stop all political independence, social freedom, or religious liberalism. For any sane liberal in the United States to think that this body of death is going to be permeated by liberal opinions is clear evidence of incipient softening of the brain.

If now the Southern Democratic bloc cannot become liberal, what chance is there that the Northern Democrats will become liberal? None at all. In Northern States they may temporarily follow liberal principles. But nationally they must do as Smith has done: make peace with plutocracy and repudiate the simplest principles of democracy.

There are a number of hopeful souls who continue to believe that the very ineptitude of the two old parties is going to lead, one of these days, to a triumphant third party. These dreamers insist that this already would have happened if third party advocates could only "agree." This is nonsense. When and where have liberal reformers ever agreed in advance on main matters of reform? Certainly not at the birth of the Republican Party in the United States or at the birth of the Liberal or Labour Party in England. Widely divergent liberal panaceas are slowly pounded into shape at successive elections as certain of them gain popular support. By a slow process of selection and elimination, the program of a third party is clarified and solidified, and slowly one of the old parties dies. This program is impossible in the United States because the one political party, the Democrats, which is nearest moribund in its ideas, cannot die; it uses the political power of disfranchised Negroes and disfranchised whites to keep itself so large a minority party that any diversion of liberals from the Republican Party simply throws this more reactionary party into power. That was the clear case in the celebrated election of 1912. It was the largest influence in the election of Coolidge, when at the last moment voters became convinced that a vote for La Follette was practically a vote for the Democrats.

The same situation is before us today. Liberals may, if they will, vote for Al Smith. But a vote for Al Smith is a vote for the Bourbon South, and that reactionary bloc will not let Smith take a single really liberal step. They will stand with the Republicans for super-power, for high protection, for disfranchisement, and for war made by an army and navy which they overwhelmingly dominate. On the other hand, if the liberals turn and vote for Norman Thomas they throw their votes away just as surely as when they voted for Robert La Follette. Under the present distribution of electoral votes Norman Thomas has no chance of carrying a single State even if he should receive 6,000,000 popular votes. All of which shows that the problem of Negro disfranchisement is not a problem of the Negroes; it is a problem of democratic government in the United States.

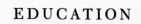

EDUCATION

*The* Outlook *was a rather traditional popular magazine during the early years of the century. The following editorial effectively captures the dominant views of white Americans on education for blacks.*

# Shall the Negro Be Educated?

WE ARE SORRY to see the proposition seriously made in some of the Southern States to divide the school fund so as to give all the taxes derived from the whites to the education of white children, and only the taxes derived from colored people to the education of colored children. We are glad to see this proposition condemned, as it ought to be, by the best citizens in the South, without regard to party, and generally regarded by them as an appeal by politicians to the prejudices of the lower classes, not as a practical proposition to be seriously entertained. No doubt there is something in the proposition which may seem, on a mere casual and careless consideration, to have in it an element of fairness. We have occasionally heard the same proposition in a different form in the North. It has been sometimes seriously proposed to relieve all Roman Catholics from the school tax, and leave them to educate their own children in their own Church. It has been sometimes seriously questioned why the rich man with one or two children whom he sends to a private school should be taxed to pay for the education of the poor man's half a dozen children in a public school. Why should not Protestants educate themselves, and leave Roman Catholics to provide their own education? Why should not the rich educate their children, and leave the poor to educate theirs? Why should not a feudal aristocracy educate their children at Eton and Rugby and Winchester, and leave the workingmen and the laborers to provide for their children such education as they desire? Why should not the whites educate themselves, and leave the colored people to provide for their own education? These questions are simply different forms of the same question—namely, Why should not the strong and rich and cultivated take care of themselves, and leave the poor and unprosperous and ignorant to take care of themselves?

From *The Outlook,* LXVIII (May 4, 1901), 13–15.

In a Christian country, in this year of grace 1901, it ought not to be possible to ask this question; but since it is asked, let us try to answer it. Those who ask it ought not to suffer any illusion. It is really the question, Why should any intelligent community object to have attached to it and forming a part of it a mass of ignorant and immoral persons, living perhaps in a state of dull content with their animal conditions, perhaps in a state of chronic envy of their more prosperous neighbors? Surely history has given in more than one tragedy an answer to that question. It was the ignorant plebs who destroyed Rome. It was the uneducated mob whose irruption inflicted on France the excesses of the Revolution. It is the unschooled peasantry of Ireland which keeps in hopeless poverty an island rich in agricultural and commercial possibilites. It is the ignorant population in our great cities which every now and then inflicts upon them an ugly, dangerous, and costly mob. These seven millions of colored persons are going to remain in the South. To deport them is physically impossible. To absorb them by intermarriage with the Anglo-Saxon race is not thought of as possible by any one whose judgment is determined by facts, not by *a priori* theories. They are not dying off, and will not thus disappear from the American continent. They cannot be reduced into a condition of slavery, and no one wishes so to reduce them.

What remains? But one alternative: to give them the best education they are capable of receiving, or to leave them to increasing degeneration and decay, a burden and a peril alike to themselves and to their neighbors. The answer to the question, Why not leave the colored people to grow up without education? is well put in a sentence by Dr. J. L. M. Curry: "We must elevate this race or it will drag us down." The colored people educated and made a component part of the industrial and political organization of the South, contented and prosperous, self-respecting because worthy of respect, will add to the wealth, the prosperity, the happiness of the South. Left uneducated to drop in successive generations into ever lower stages of barbarism, they will be a burden bound upon the back of the South, if not a millstone bound about its neck.

For the South now to abandon the colored people to themselves would be not only a public calamity, it would be a public dishonor. It is estimated that since the close of the Civil War the South has expended in taxes for the education of the emancipated slaves something like $120,000,000. This is a splendid record. We recall nothing analogous to it in all history. Fifty years ago there was not a public-school system in any Southern State, and in most of the Southern States it was a criminal offense to teach the slaves. Slavery was abolished, not with the consent of the South, but against her vigorous protests and her heroic resistance. Yet no sooner is emancipation an accomplished fact than she begins in her poverty to see what can be done to educate the emancipated slaves for freedom. In every Southern State there is now a public-school system; and in every State the public provision for the one race is substantially equal to that made for the other. For the South to throw away in its growing prosperity this honorable distinction achieved in its desolation and poverty is not to be thought of; we have faith to believe that the suggestion will be thought of only to be indignantly repudiated. This work of education has been carried on under great difficulties. The money had to be raised, the school-houses built, the teachers to be educated, a curriculum adapted to the conditions of the race to be chosen, a system to be organized. Of course there have been mistakes. The education has been too exclusively literary, and should be developed along the lines of manual and industrial training; it has been too exclusively intellectual, and should be developed along the lines of moral training. But the fact that mistakes have been made is a reason for correcting the mistakes, not for abandoning the endeavor. Italy and France have established schools for their peasant children; Ireland has abandoned her hedgerow schools and is maintaining recognized parochial schools for her poorest population; England, by her Board Schools, is educating the children of the citizen and the laborer; America is planting the common school in Cuba, Porto Rico, and the Philippines. Those in the South who propose to abandon the attempt to educate the colored people, whom the South has thus far with such self-sacrifice endeavored to educate, propose to transfer the Southern States from the front to the rear of the column of free States, to revert in the twentieth century to the conception of education which the civilized world was already beginning to abandon by the close of the eighteenth.

It is true that if any Southern State were to abandon its attempt to educate her colored population the education would not be wholly abandoned. She would by that very act make her territory missionary ground; the efforts of missionary and charitable organizations in the North would be redoubled; public charity would take up the work laid down by the State; and Northern schools, supported by Northern contributions and officered by Northern teachers, would be multiplied. Of course this work would be undertaken under great disadvantages. It would be difficult to raise adequate funds. The Northern teachers would not and could not understand either the nature of the negro or the demands of the community as well as the Southerner understands them. The schools would be charity schools, not public schools; and the difference between the two is real and vital. The fact that Northern charity had to be appealed to for the continuance of a work which the South had once carried on, and then abandoned in discouragement because it presented obstacles, would be galling to Southern pride, as it ought to be. But, worse than all, the colored people, publicly and officially notified, by an action which would speak much more loudly than words, that the Southerner was no longer his friend and did not care whether he obtained an education or remained in ignorance, would accept the separation which such an act would inevitably involve. Indifference is harder to bear than enmity; and whether the abandonment of the public-school system for the colored people was based on the affirmation that they are incapable of receiving an education, or on the affirmation that the Southerner does not care whether they are educated or not, the effect would be to increase that separation of the races in the South which all philanthropists and statesmen have justly regarded as disastrous alike to the white and to the colored people.

We do not anticipate the division of the school funds in any Southern State. But the way to insure the defeat of this proposition is to protest against it wherever and whenever it makes its appearance, and to compel its advocates to present some other argument in favor of it than an appeal to the prejudices or the pockets of the taxpayers. We believe that The Outlook in this matter reflects the almost unanimous sentiment of the best people in the South; our only fear is that, in their contempt for so undemocratic a proposition, they may allow it in some sections to gather a headway which it never could secure if it were met in the very outset with a challenge to debate from Southern men.

*The Rev. Reverdy C. Ransom was a leading Social Gospel minister who worked in black settlement houses in New York and Chicago during the first years of the century. From 1912 to 1924 he edited the A.M.E. Church Review. The following address was delivered to a union meeting of preachers, teachers, and farmers at Hampton Institute in June 1921.*

# Educational Problems

## By Reverdy C. Ransom

ALONG THE LINE of education we have in this country two great big outstanding problems. One of them bulks large in the North and the other bulks large in the South. In the North it is the problem of the children of the immigrants:—to absorb them and to assimilate them through free public schools into American citizenship, so that, as they come by the thousands and tens of thousands from Southern Italy and Central Europe and Russia and elsewhere, as they come into great centers like Chicago, Pittsburgh, Philadelphia, and New York, the problem of the teacher, the problem of the public schools, among others, is to assimilate that particular group so that it may become Americanized.

In the South the great problem is—or should be, rather—the problem of assimilating and training the great bulk of those millions of Americans of African descent who have only had a little over fifty years in this country. The problem is difficult as far as this element is concerned, and both the teacher and the preacher must meet it.

According to the latest report issued by the United States Bureau of Education, fifteen Southern States, among them Delaware, Maryland, and Kentucky, expended annually for the education of white children $36,649,827. In the same period they spent for the education of colored children $5,860,876. On a per capita basis this means that $10.30 is expended for the education of each white child in the South per annum. To be more specific, the State of Virginia spends

From *Southern Workman*, L (September 1921), 417–420.

annually $9.64 for the education of each white child. It expends $2.74 for each colored child. North Carolina spends $5.27 for each white child, $2.02 for each colored child; Georgia, $9.58 for the white child, and $1.76 for the colored child; and Louisiana, $13.73 for the white and $1.31 for the colored child.

This means a great many things to you teachers and it means a great many things to our American citizenship in those States and throughout the Nation, from the angle of the colored people, and it should from the angle of the white also. We do not need any jim-crow cars or any other segregation, any oppression or repression to "keep the Negro in his place." All we need to do is to spend $10 on a white boy and $1.31 on a black boy. That is enough without all this other stuff. It seems to me that these other abominations are works of supererogation.

Those are plain, cold facts published by the Government of the United States. Now what is your problem? You are trying to bridge the chasm between the $10 child and the $1.31 child. That is the meaning of Hampton and of Fisk University and of the schools on the hills around Atlanta, Ga. It is the meaning of the schools supported by the denominations and those other schools that have sprung up and I hope will continue to spring up through all the Southland. It is to bridge the gulf in order that all may be more equally endowed. That is the great thing that confronts us, not only colored people, but all Americans.

It is not simply a question of color and race; it is a question that affects our common country and our citizenship. These young women before me are a part of this problem: to bring the one-dollar boy and the one-dollar girl up to the standard so that they will be able to meet, on equal terms, the ten- and twelve-dollar boy and girl in the battle of life. When the Germans came with poison gas the Allies had to invent poison gas to meet poison gas. In other words they could not contend except on equal terms with equal instruments with the men who were confronting them.

So in our American democracy. In New York City we say that the children of the immigrants must be taken through the public schools and equipped so that they shall be able to go out into this great country and be absorbed in this life and meet the children of other Americans; that they shall become Americans on equal terms. So the children of Americans of African descent must be so trained that when the black boy and girl of to-day, fifteen or twenty years hence, go out into the battle of life, they shall be equipped and trained intellectually, so that, in the struggle for the prizes of life, they will not have to fight with unequal weapons.

Our America cannot go forward—and you might just as well face it—on the idea that any class of people in our common land can be handicapped by such circumstances as will by force cause them to take a secondary place in our civilization.

There are two things I want to speak of briefly to the teachers here. I look at some of the textbooks. It seems to me that the colored teacher everywhere should equip herself so as to supplement the teaching of history. I think that each teacher should specialize in the teaching of Negro history. If you do not do it how do you expect the generation that is coming up to hold up its head in the United States, when they read a so-called history of the United States with not a single line in it about the Negro. Your children should be taught the fact that the first ship ever built in the United States sailed from the United States to Newfoundland and was built by Paul Coffey and his brother—two Negroes. Of course you know the story of Crispus Attucks, but keep on telling it. Boston, Massachusetts, put it in bronze on the Common. Tell it!

Just a few weeks ago President Harding came over from Washington to assist us in dedicating a statue to Simon Bolivar, but there was not one line about us. What are the facts? Simon Bolivar had failed in his campaigns and battles to win the Independence of South America and in his discouragement and failure he put into the harbor of Port au Prince, and it was the president of that Negro republic who gave him money and ships to enable him to go back and win independence.

How is the colored child to get its inspiration? How is it to have its pride in achievement, when others are reading about their fathers as heroes and there is not one word about the great deeds of Negroes?

Not only in war but in the realm of invention as well the Negro has a place. I published not long ago some information furnished me by the United States Shoe Machinery Company. All the lasting of shoes in all the shoe factories of America had been done by hand until a colored man invented a machine to do the lasting. It was some years before they got it to operate, but to-day it is used, not only in all the factories of America, but in England and Europe as well. That machine is called "The Nigger." It is a mighty good "nigger." It cheapened the price of shoes. Every person who walks in shoe leather is able to do it more cheaply and perhaps more comfortably because a man of your race invented the machine that enables them to do it.

I simply say this much in order to emphasize the fact that the teacher must get busy, if she has not already done so, and supplement the histories by teaching also Negro history.

There is one other thing. Somebody must look out for the exceptional boy and the exceptional girl. The preacher must do it and the teacher must do it. I take great satisfaction in saying that more than once I have done that thing. I am a native of Ohio. When Paul Dunbar published his first little volume of poems called "Open Eyes," he got it to the printer but he could not get it out. I said, "Paul, go tell the printer to let you have a hundred copies and we will pay for them to-morrow." He got them and brought them down to the church and when the people saw them, they bought them. Later, when Dr. Howells said Dunbar was a poet, that settled it!

I think we should be on the lookout for these exceptional boys and girls and encourage them. That is one of the great needs of the hour. Perhaps in almost every community there is one such boy or girl. It may be a girl who has some special skill with the needle. Push her forward! Or it may be a boy with mechanical ability. Or it may be a writer or an artist. If you find exceptional ability, get behind it. I would get behind a white child just as quickly. He is among the favored ones, but he often has to fight against obstacles. We should be on the lookout for exceptional ability, if not for genius.

*Eugene Kinckle Jones was Executive Secretary of the National Urban League in the 1920's. The following article was a commencement address at Hampton Institute, May 29, 1928.*

# Negro Youth Goes Out into Life

## By Eugene Kinckle Jones

THE NEGRO youth of today is passing through the door leading to a full life in America. He wants to know what his experiences will be; what preparation is necessary; what obstacles he will meet; what opportunities are his; what assistance he may call on in need. What should be his preparation? This is the age of preparedness. Athletes train for years for a great event. Soldiers train for years for one great battle. Physicians train for a lifetime to save a man through one grave operation. Engineers perform innumerable difficult engineering feats to gain undying fame through the construction of one great bridge, tunnel, or dam.

Whatever may be the future life of an individual he is entitled to the fundamentals of education. Modern society owes to every human being the chance for this primary education. There is no State in our Union which is too poor to establish and enforce compulsory education laws. These laws should apply alike to black and white up to the age of fourteen, yea, better, to the age of sixteen. America needs people of understanding and intelligence, and universal, compulsory education laws properly enforced will insure this result. If all Negro youths at fourteen years of age were possessed of primary education, it would be a very easy task to follow up this training with secondary training designed according to the individual's talent and bent. We have about reached the point in our development as a race in America at which Negroes can enter almost every occupation. In fact, Negroes are entering from time to time into lines of work hitherto closed almost completely to them, and as one enters his record commends itself to the point that those in control of such occupations definitely

From *Southern Workman*, LVII (August 1928), 297–302.

and consciously at times ask for other Negroes when vacancies occur. Our schools need psychologists, vocational counsellors who can advise our youth and their parents on the peculiar mental traits and characteristics of school children and counsel with them on the training they should seek for their life's work. They should study the changes in employment and in the preparation needed to meet changing needs in industry and in commerce and in professions. The course of study in our schools and colleges should be altered, revised, or overhauled to prepare the student for his place in the world as it is today. The curricula and training methods in our schools should not be considered just formulae to provide mental gymnastics for teachers who are satisfied with time-worn pedagogical methods and for students who consider their diplomas a magic wand capable of producing lucrative jobs when waved in the sight of employers. Diplomas dated May 29, 1928, should simply mean that the holder thereof has the sheepskin evidence that he has been fully informed of the world we live in and is fitted to begin his labors in a field in preparation to enter which special training has been received.

Personally, I think every boy and girl should be taught to be useful with his hands regardless of the position in life one holds. Incidentally, he should know how to clean a house, cook a meal, sew on buttons, and to make other minor clothing repairs. It means much to the spirit of independence and self-reliance which the young should have instilled to be sufficiently self-contained to pass through emergencies, when one sometimes must depend entirely upon himself. This parents can achieve but I think it is so important to society that self-reliant men and women make up society, that the obligation to effect this result is the function of public instruction.

Obstacles to be met by the Negro youth today are too numerous to present in full but it would be well to mention a few: First, there is the prejudice of race which he should be brought to face. This prejudice can be met effectively only by a subjective approach. Within each man's spirit is the most potent weapon against it. Men are often prejudiced because of traditions which they did not make and are not inclined to ignore. One's demeanor can overcome some of the effects, however. Then there is the competition for getting and for holding jobs. This, no man can escape. This competition is not only with members of the white group but also with members of the Negro race. Low wages and occasional unemployment are inevitable in the careers of most men. Thrift is necessary, in preparation for periods of unemployment and other emergencies.

Another obstacle is the intolerance of employers in the matter of the manhood rights of the employed. Have the interest of your fellow-workers at heart and be prepared to unite the strength of your support to that of other workingmen and women in the effort to bring lasting and merited reforms in the field of labor. Organization of men who work has raised the standard of wages and of self-respect among working men. Be prepared to do your bit to help dignify all labor and to raise the standards of living and working among the masses of the people.

The temptation of the "easy life" is a great deterrent to progress. The law of inertia is a two-sided law. "A body at rest, remains at rest, and a body in motion remains in motion, unless acted upon by some external force." You can enter any community and see how the people move and hear how they talk and at once know whether they are an alive, wide-awake group of people or whether they are indolent, slothful, and lacking in ambition. "Keep on your toes for the word 'go'!" is figuratively what your principal will say to you as you leave here today to run the race of life.

The greatest enemy of the human family is "General Apathy." He controls much of our life and must be removed to assure progress.

The last obstacle which I shall mention is one which I think needs special emphasis. It is a feeling akin to inferiority which many Negroes possess. There is no such thing as racial inferiority. There is as much difference between individual members of the white race and between individual members of the Negro race as between any member of the white race and any member of the Negro race. The difference in the standards of any two races is due to the difference in the training, the outlook, the confidence, and the number of the leaders of each race.

I should think that the first requisite in the development of leadership in the Negro, possibly even more important than his general training, is self-confidence and belief in his own racial capacity. Practically every dependable anthropologist, sociologist, and psychologist today admits that there has never been produced anywhere or at any time any reliable evidence of difference in racial capacity. Whatever difference one may observe in groups can be traced to historical forces and cannot be ascribed to inherent racial characteristics.

There is no need for any Negro youth to hesitate to engage in any profession or undertaking in the mistaken belief that there is a racial inhibition to his entree and success. In agriculture and mechanics, engineering, in the field of teaching and the social sciences, in music, law, fine arts, in dramatics, and in business, Negroes are finding opportunities to apply their talents.

There never was a time in the life of the Negro in which there was greater demand for men and women of the very best possible training, and well informed, ambitious young men are seeking graduate training and the most advanced degrees to enter the professions. To meet the exacting demands by the public today on persons engaged in these professions, the Negro must be prepared to deliver high class, dependable, thorough, and efficient technical service. He has proved his capacity as a race for producing such minds and no Negro who wants to meet with success today in any of these chosen fields should stop short of such training as is afforded by the best colleges and technical schools designed for such preparation.

In service to the Negro race opportunities are increasing, and in services where the racial element does not enter there are many chances being offered and accepted by members of the race. I cite a few of the unusual instances of splendid accomplishments of Negroes where the general respect for their race is elevated thereby: physicists in a large industrial plant in Jersey City; metallurgists in a Canton, Ohio, watch factory and in a hardware manufacturing concern in Cleveland; a woman chemist and a man assistant in a hardware company in Cleveland; an engineer in Des Moines, Iowa, who has built many bridges in Southern Iowa and designed and constructed the heating plant of his Alma Mater—the University of Iowa —and is bidding for large sewer and asphalt-laying contracts in large cities of the Middle West; physicians on the staffs of the Bellevue and its allied hospitals, and an associate surgeon on the staff of the Broad Street Hospital, New York, and on the staff of a hospital in Altoona, Pa.; a building contractor in Philadelphia who has just completed all of the concrete work in a two and a half million dollar unit of a seven million dollar apartment hotel,—all of the frame work of which being concrete; a contractor for the building of all of the molds for the pouring of the concrete for the foundations to the $12,000,000 Columbia-Presbyterian Hospital in New York City; an architect in Los Angeles who has recently completed important office buildings, a hotel, and a Y. M. C. A.; the western manager of a large steel concern—the western headquarters being in Chicago; case reader of the Minneapolis Associated Charities—one of the most important positions held in this large social service organization; medical men and dentists in many cities of the North and Middle West whose percentage of white practice ranges from 20 per cent to 95 per cent; Negro certified accountants with large clientele in New York and West Virginia; Negro musicians who are singers in white church choirs and organists in important churches and other institutions of the white group; actors and other performers in Broadway shows, many of them in leading parts; an assistant professor of biology in the University of Chicago; a biologist at Marine Biological Laboratory, Wood's Hole, Mass.; poets, authors, literary men acknowledged as ranking among the best America is now producing—in fact, one of the books of poetry composed by a Negro is ranked with the best sellers; and experts in the social research field. These are records which could be multiplied to encourage the Negro youth as he enters the life of the nation! In New York City, 316 of the 321 occupations listed in the 1920 Census included some Negroes, and 175 of them included more than 50 Negroes each.

In meditating over the difficulties and the proscriptions under which Negroes are forced to live and work, bring into conscious thought the greatly increased opportunities that are the Negro's today compared with a few years back. Take on new life. Increase your confidence in your race. Pass on out into life with a fresh determination to make your contribution to America, and thus help her to get rid of her prejudice and to become the great democracy which she should be as an example to the rest of the world!

*John Hope was president of Morehouse College in At-*
*lanta and a leading black educator of the period. The*
*following speech was originally given at a Washington*
*Interracial Conference.*

# Educational Achievements and Needs

*By John Hope*

I REMEMBER when I was a boy thirteen years of age I had to leave
the public schools at the end of my 8th grade preparation—or, rather,
preparation in the 8th grade—and work for five years before having
another chance at going to school.

When I got back to school, it seemed to me that I had lost five
years. In fact, it seemed that way to me for a long time. It is only in
recent years that I have come to think that possibly that five years
when I was not going to a formal school was about as educative as
any five years of my life. I had to work for a living and I had to get to
work on time. I had to give satisfaction to the people for whom I
worked. I came in contact with a great many people and I had to
make friends. Incidentally, I met some people who were not friends
and I had to adjust myself to them. I had to think of what I would do
with the little money I made, and I learned how to buy a suit of
clothes on the instalment plan and pay for it—which I think is quite
an achievement. Taking it all in all, I had a really good schooling for
five years.

I have been thinking of the possibility of that sort of thing having
obtained with the Negro people. Here we have had in the United
States sixty-five years of formal school work where we go to school
at nine o'clock in the morning and carry our books under our arms
and recite in classes. We have had this about sixty-five years. Out
of 300 years in this country, it certainly cannot be that all our educational achievement is in these past sixty-five years.

I think of some of the remarkable things we had to do. We came
into a new climate. We came into a new civilization, with a new

From *Southern Workman*, LVIII (April 1929), 147–154.

people, with a new language. We learned the language so well that at the end of a long period of enforced slavery, we had acquired the language. We learned it so well that some of us wrote poetry. I might not say we wrote it—we composed it, and it has come through some generations as a sort of folk lore handed down. And we composed the music for it. I think this a great achievement.

Whether we forgot our religion or not, I do not know; but we took on another religion, and somehow we got the principles of it so that they became vital in our life and enabled us to go through great trials without doing much violence to ourselves or to anybody else.

The customs were entirely new to us. We learned those. Even to a certain extent we learned the laws and got into the spirit of the country. We learned new trades and learned them well, becoming so skilled in those trades that some Negroes became managers and foremen and business men to such a degree that they could actually do what was called in slavery, "hiring their time." A number of Negro slaves were of sufficient value to pay their masters a certain charge for their time and yet clear money besides. I call that a good industrial achievement.

Then we learned some of the social responsibilities, necessarily so. We developed a family life—a monogamous family life. Family life was so precarious under the conditions of slavery that no Negro man could look in his new-born baby's face and have any degree of certainty that he could rear him to manhood. We nevertheless had a fine idea about the monogamous family, so that when we came out of slavery we developed a good family life.

But family life was so precarious that many times a man or woman would have to step in, and in odd moments give assistance to an orphaned child or to a widowed wife. I sometimes think that the ease with which young educated colored men and women take so quickly and efficiently to social service is a sort of "hang over" from ante-bellum days.

They used to laugh a great deal in the South about Negroes "sitting up with the sick and burying the dead"; but I think it is a fine tribute to colored people. It is a very fine thing that we learned, and I hope that no amount of scientific methods of looking after the sick and burying the dead will deprive Negroes of the generous, unselfish feeling towards one another that up to this time has been exemplified in our relations with one another.

Then there came Emancipation. By that time Negroes had de-

veloped to such a degree that they had really a sort of social stratification. In fact, there are relics yet in some places in the South of
the old ante-bellum social stratification of Negroes. I do not know
how that would be working out today if it were not that there came,
right along with emancipation, the founding and operation of mission
schools and colleges. They made a tremendous change in Negro life,
in the long run basing the stratification on something different. All
classes of Negroes, rich and poor, advantaged and disadvantaged,
were brought very early into these home mission schools and, by the
sheer process of education and daily association, there developed
among colored people a new ideal of society based upon education.

And so we have today among Negroes, whether we realize it or
not and whether we want it or not, a democracy, or an aristocracy,
a social group that is more or less to be explained by its degree of
education; and Negroes that are not educated adhere in some respects
to the ideals of this group, if they wish to come into it.

There was something else that this home mission college did. It
taught something quite new. I would not say "quite new," but perhaps as a pedagogic principle, it was new; that is, so far as teaching
it to the whole crowd, to the rank and file, it was new. Up until that
time people had been educated for their own advantage, for power.
Now there came along a finely educated group of people who taught
a different principle. They said, "You must be educated in order that
you may help somebody else."

And so there is bound up in the mind and life of the average educated Negro even until this time, with all of the temptations for him
to become otherwise,—there is bound up in his life even yet that
feeling that he must do something, that he must accomplish something for somebody else.

When I think about education and its achievement in the last
sixty-five years, I think of some of the shocks that have come to Negroes in that length of time. I was stating last summer to a group of
teachers that when a small boy, I heard somebody say "The bank
is broke." That meant that the very first challenge to Negroes, after
they had come out of slavery, to cultivate thrift had been a failure.
They had put their small earnings into the bank and the bank had
"gone broke." The first thrift experience of their free days was one of
discouragement. And I should say that it must have taken many,
many years for the average of those people to think of putting money
in any more banks. They had had great faith in that bank. It was

called the Freedmen's Bank; and that word had a significance with Negroes at that time. That experience was a distinct shock.

Then we went into politics and thought that was going to work out all right, but by and by it didn't work out all right. The change came rather suddenly, so suddenly that I can at this moment remember two or three instances that make that epoch stand out quite prominently in my mind.

Then they said, "We will do away with politics. Don't flock to the cities. Buy farms." And we did that. But we did not have as much protection in the country as we ought to have had. We do not have it even now. Besides that, the boll weevil came along and did its worst for us. Poor protection, poor chance to make a living, poor public-school advantages in the country for children.

Well, we grew restless. Then the war came on, and one or two million of us picked up and moved hundreds and hundreds of miles into an entirely new locality, into an entirely new situation, and we experienced the shock of changing  from a rural people in a warm climate to an urban people in a cold climate. But in the midst of all of these shocks, we have managed to carry on a rather steady development, so that, by and large, without stopping to go into our various difficulties, it might be said that for a people who have developed from four million to twelve million in sixty years and felt these shocks that I have mentioned, in addition to others, and trekked from place to place, our achievements have been fairly remarkable.

It is hardly necessary for me to speak of the needs. We do need better public schools. It is my impression that the colored children in my native city in Georgia are being relatively more poorly educated today in the public schools than I myself was,—and I left the public schools in 1881.

In my boyhood Negroes were taught about as well in the public schools as white people were, but the white schools have gone forward so rapidly in recent years that I should say that the Negro boy in my town is receiving a relatively poorer education at the expense of the county than we received when I was a boy. I hope that will be changed. I think much of crime itself, to say nothing of public health, could be changed for the better if we had better schools. I live, for instance, in a city which has tried in recent years to improve its public schools for Negroes yet there are instances there today of what is called the triple session, and a very large number of colored children go into what is called the double session.

As a matter of education, one of our greatest needs is better medical schools for colored people in the United States. At least there are only two that are highly accredited. One of those is right on the edge of Southern Negro population, in Washington. The other is in Nashville. Yet you have Negroes by hundreds of thousands away back to the Texas-Mexico line. There is no particular plan for anything like organized public health with courses for Negro doctors and Negro nurses. When I think of pretty nearly fifty Negro physicians in my own city having practically no clinical opportunity at all, it is amazing that my doctor has kept me alive for all these years!

I was talking with a white physician in Atlanta less than a week ago and I was glad to find him of the same mind. I am hoping to see in my city Negro doctors practising at least in the Negro ward of the public hospital. I am hoping to see nurses properly trained. I am hoping to see Negro physicians and Negro nurses with a sufficiently broad academic background before they enter the field of medicine and nursing—with a sufficient background to have some conception of public health so that they will go into it with intelligence as well as zeal.

There is another thing that I would like to speak of, but I rather dread to because I was embarrassed in mentioning it a few weeks ago. I went with a friend of mine to see if we could get financial assistance for a country life project, and the gentleman that we talked to told me that I betrayed my age to talk about country life; that we were now living in an urban epoch! So I rather hesitate to say that one of the great needs today, to my mind, is to make life in the country places livable, attractive, and inspiring to Negroes so that they may live there and develop, and from that point of vantage render a service to society that I am afraid we will not be able to render if too many more of us crowd into the cities.

Then, as to whether we have any particular religious belief or not, I think I might mention that there is a need in connection with the church. A friend of mine said today that his beliefs had narrowed down to the place where his confession of faith was the National Association for the Advancement of Colored People! Even assuming that your beliefs are like that, I should say that the church is by no means out of date; and the Negro church, with all that it may be or may not be, and with all of the criticisms of an adverse sort that are hurled at it, is the great center of Negro life, and it is going to remain that way for a long time. So it would be greatly to the advantage of

Negroes and other people also in this country if we should make the church the most intelligent and the cleanest and most spiritual center that it could be made. I believe that we ought to have more of our men and our women turning towards the ministry or other sorts of work in churches. It is now, and it is going to be for some time, the rallying ground in Negro life.

Then I would like to speak about the college. I do not know whether to call it the Negro college or the college for Negroes. I mean the college where only Negroes attend.

I sometimes wonder whether we are getting as much as we ought out of the Negro college for Negro society and Negro life. It may be that we are over sensitive about our colleges, that we are afraid that we might be doing something that other colleges are not doing and that we might not appear so intelligent and educated and well-behaved as the colleges for white people. Assume and grant the limitations there may be for an institution of learning that is designated by charter and law to be for only one race—assume that, if you will, and let me raise the question: May we not take our college and make it into something that will be very definitely to the advantage of the people that are in it?

One thing that we ought to consider in the Negro college is some sort of technique for the minority, that minority being Negroes; not only a minority as to numbers, but a group still further embarrassed by poverty and by disease, by ignorance, and by prejudice and discrimination. Is it not possible for teachers and students to sit down and think together and plan out some method whereby Negroes may more nearly get their dues so that Negroes may more perfectly function in society than they are today functioning?

I raise that question, whether it might not be possible for the Negro college to do something very definite in the line of developing a technique for minorities. It might be that in making that study we should discover something that would be of great advantage to some other minorities that are not Negroes.

We talk a good deal about racial relations, interracial relations. We have an organization represented in this conference, a Commission on Interracial Relations. White people and colored people belong to that organization and we have meetings and a good time for all present; but I am wondering whether in these organizations where white and colored people come together to see about better interests of Negroes—for that is what most of those organizations are for—

it is not too much a one-sided thing. It may be that we have got to think a little deeper and think about the best interests of both races. Is it not possible for us in our schools to consider questions like that? What may be a method in our relations with each other whereby the best things may occur and result?

A few years ago we had a great Negro insurance company. I am so short a time from that catastrophe that I hesitate to speak of it. The unfortunate happening to that insurance company was one of the awful shocks to Negro society. As we look back at it and think of business as it is run today, we see that that company failed for lack of a very small amount of money in a city of powerful banking institutions, with a population of over 200,000. For lack of a little timely help, that organization was allowed to fall into the hands of money lenders who might almost be regarded from their methods as buccaneers; and all the while there stood by a group of perfectly nice people, fine business men, a chamber of commerce, and the like, and there was an interracial commission functioning. But they stood by and watched and waited for months and months. It seemed impossible for the Negroes to make a step to the white people or the white people to make a step to the Negroes that would result in the great organization's being righted and allowed to function.

I should say that with twelve millions of people in the midst of a hundred and eighteen millions, it is virtually out of the question to talk about solidarity in some things; you may have isolation; in some things you may be as separate as the fingers. But when it comes to business, business is so intricate today, so high-powered, so complex, that it is impossible practically for Negroes to think of functioning in any large way in business unless they have some sort of understanding, cooperation, and friendship with white people.

A certain number of young people talk about the "Uncle Tom" and the "hat-in-hand" Negro, but it must be said that Uncle Tom and the old hat-in-hand fellow, as far as he went, had some sort of understanding. It is quite possible, and I regard it as obligatory upon us, that educated Negroes learn how, in a manly and womanly way, to join in with the other forces of society and make it go; and I believe that that is a thing we need to have taught properly and intelligently in our institutions of learning.

Then take the Negroes among themselves. Some college people and I were recently discussing the labor situation. The labor situation among Negroes is very embarrassing if we only know it. Some new places are opening to us, but some places are closing, and it is by no means certain that the Negro is going to have anything like a sure thing in the industrial and business world. One of these men referred to a certain city where the porters at the station are organized into a club. He said he heard that entrance into that club called for a college education, and he laughed about it. Well, I didn't want to be ugly about it, but I said, "I don't think that is funny. If a certain number of Negroes have to be porters, they can enjoy life better if they are college graduates." Why is it that we need to think about any occupation calling for ignorance? That is a great mistake. If Negroes do not look out, that sort of thing in Negro society will bring snobbery that would do credit to the Nordics.

I should not be surprised if a large number of colored men and women in college today would find themselves in what are regarded as the humbler pursuits of society. But by no means would I tell Negroes to stop going to college.

There is another side of that which should be emphasized. If the Negro working man is to be received as an equal among the working classes and to get a guarantee of continued work in this generation and for several generations to come as things are in this country, the educated Negro has got to make common cause with the Negro in the humbler pursuits; and a certain number of Negroes of college training and college preparation may, in a perfectly missionary fashion, have to choose one of those jobs in order that they might get among people to lift them up.

# CULTURAL EQUALITY

*W. E. B. DuBois wrote frequently for popular journals as
well as his regular monthly column in* The Crisis. *His
enduring theme in much of this writing was the great
progress black Americans had made despite the terrible
hardships they faced.*

# Social Effects of Emancipation

## By W. E. B. DuBois

IN ENDEAVORING to sum up the results of emancipating the Negro
slaves in the United States fifty years ago, it will be natural to note the
material and educational advances the colored people have made;
the evidences of group consciousness among them; their present legal
and political status and the outlook for social reform.

In 1863 there were about 5,000,000 persons of Negro descent in the
United States. Of these 4,000,000 and more were just being released
from slavery. These slaves could be bought and sold, could move from
place to place only with permission, were forbidden to learn to read
or write, legally could never hold property or marry. Ninety per cent
were totally illiterate and only one adult in six was a nominal Christian. Until 1863 the total slave population had been steadily increasing, and the South was passing laws to enslave free Negroes. The
three-quarters of a million free Negroes had been equally divided between the North and the South. Those in the South were a wretched,
broken-spirited lot for the most part and slaves in all but name. Here
and there in cities there were a few among them who were prosperous
mechanics and property holders to a small extent.

The 250,000 Negroes of the North were the leaven and had been
making for nearly a century a struggle for survival. They aided in the
anti-slavery movement, had a few newspapers, and had produced
leaders like Frederick Douglass and Harriet Tubman. They had
planned and carried through a systematic migration to Canada where
several prosperous settlements sprang up. They started schools in a
number of cities and founded the catering business in Philadelphia.

From the *Survey*, XXIX (February 1, 1913), 570–573.

They had held several general conventions appealing for justice. For the most part these appeals fell on deaf ears, although Garrison, Sumner, Phillips, Harriet Beecher Stowe, and John Brown had come to their aid.

Nevertheless, up to the time of the opening of the war, the Negroes in the North were forced to live in the worst slums and alleys, were either excluded entirely from the public schools or furnished cheap and poor substitutes, and in 300 years only twenty colored men had received a college education. Except in parts of New England and partially in New York, the Negro was disfranchised and largely without civil rights. Indeed, the Fugitive Slave Law of 1850 made personal freedom difficult, and in 1857 the Supreme Court had declared that Negroes were not citizens, and that they had always been considered as having "no rights which the white man was bound to respect."

Then came the war, which was not started with the idea of liberating the slaves, but which soon showed the North that freedom for the Negro was not only a logical conclusion of the war, but the only possible physical conclusion. Two hundred thousand black men were drafted in the army and the whole slave support to the Confederacy was threatened with withdrawal. Insurrection was in the air and the emancipation of the slaves was needed to save the Union. Such, then, was the situation in 1863.

Fifty years later, in 1913, there are in the United States 10,250,000 persons of Negro descent, an increase of 105 per cent. Legal slavery has been abolished, leaving, however, vestiges in debt peonage and the convict lease system. The freedmen and their sons have

"Earned a living as free men; shared the responsibilities of government; developed the internal organization of their race, and aspired to spiritual self-expression."

### ECONOMIC PROGRESS

The Negro was freed as a penniless, landless, naked, ignorant laborer. Very few Negroes owned property in the South; a larger number owned property in the North; but 90 per cent of the race in the South were field hands, servants of the lowest class. Today 50 per cent are farm laborers and servants, and over one-half of these are working as efficient modern workmen under wage contract. Above these, to use the figures of 1900, there are 750,000 farmers, 70,000 teamsters, 55,000 railway hands, 36,000 miners, 15,000 sawmill employees, 28,000 porters, 21,000 teachers, 21,000 carpenters,

20,000 barbers, 20,000 nurses, 15,000 clergymen, 14,000 masons, 13,000 dressmakers and seamstresses, 10,000 engineers and firemen, 2,500 physicians, and, above all, 200,000 mistresses of independent homes, and 2,000,000 children in school.

Fifty years ago the overwhelming mass of these people were not only penniless, but were themselves assessed as real estate. By 1875 the Negroes probably had gotten hold of something between 2,000,-000 and 4,000,000 acres of land through their bounties as soldiers and the low price of land on account of the war. By 1910 this had increased to about 18,000,000 acres.

In 1890 Negroes owned 120,738 farms; in 1900 they owned 187,799; in 1910 they owned about 220,000. Thus, over 25 per cent of the Negro farmers owned their own farms, and the increase of farm owners between 1890 and 1910 has been over 83 per cent. The value of land and buildings owned by Negroes in the South was in 1910 $272,-992,238. This is an increase of nearly 90 per cent in a single decade. This does not include land owned by Negro farmers but rented out. On a basis of the value of farm property in 1900, a committee of the American Economic Association estimated the value of Negro wealth in the United States at $300,000,000. On the same basis we can estimate the total Negro wealth today at $570,000,000.

### THE NEGRO AND ORGANIZATION

Today the Negro is a recognized part of the American government; he holds 9,000 offices in the executive service of the nation, besides furnishing four regiments in the army and a large number of sailors. In the state and municipal civil service he holds at least 10,000 other offices, and he furnishes 500,000 of the votes which rule the Union.

In these same years the Negro has relearned the lost art of organization. Slavery was the absolute denial of initiative and responsibility. Today Negroes have 35,000 church edifices, worth $56,000,000, and controlling nearly 4,000,000 members. They raise themselves $7,500,000 a year for these churches.

There are 200 private schools and colleges managed and almost entirely supported by Negroes, and other public and private Negro schools have received in forty years $45,000,000 of Negro money in taxes and donations. Five millions a year are raised by Negro secret and beneficial societies, which hold at least $6,000,000 in real estate.

Above and beyond this material growth has gone the spiritual uplift of a great human race. From contempt and amusement they have passed to the pity and perplexity of their neighbors, while within their own souls they have arisen from apathy and timid complaint to open protest and more and more manly self-assertion. Where nine-tenths of them could not read or write in 1859, today two-thirds can; they have 200 papers and periodicals, and their voice and expression are compelling attention.

Already the poems of Dunbar and Braithwaite, the essays of Miller and Grimké, the music of Rosamond Johnson and the painting of Tanner are the property of the nation and the world. Instead of being led and defended by others, as in the past, they are gaining their own leaders, their own voices, their own ideals. Self-realization is thus coming slowly but surely to another of the world's great races, and Negroes are today girding themselves to fight in the van of progress, not simply for their own rights as men, but for the ideals of the greater world in which they live—the emancipation of women, universal peace, democratic government, the socialization of wealth, and human brotherhood.

This, then, is the transformation of the Negro in America in fifty years; from slavery to freedom, from 5,000,000 to 10,250,000, from denial of citizenship to enfranchisement, from being owned chattels to ownership of $570,000,000 in property, from unorganized irresponsibility to organized group life, from being spoken for to speaking, from contemptuous forgetfulness on the part of their neighbors to uneasy fear and dawning respect, and from inarticulate complaint to self-expression and dawning consciousness of manhood.

### LEGAL DISABILITIES

Notwithstanding this creditable showing the present situation has dark and threatening aspects. First, we have in the United States the distinct growth of a caste system. It has been adjudged in many states a misdemeanor to call a white man a Negro; it has been adjudged in many states that a person having the slightest degree of Negro blood is a "Negro"; intermarriage of Negroes and whites is prohibited in twenty-six states even if the persons are living as man and wife; travel is interfered with by separating whites and Negroes in the South and it has been decided that Negroes do not have to be given absolutely "equal" accommodations; colored and white people are separated in the South on street cars, in waiting rooms, on many elevators, on steamboats, etc. In practice Negroes are liable to discrimination in hotels, restaurants, saloons, soda fountains, theaters, cemeteries, insane asylums and in the militia. This is forbidden by many northern states, but the law is difficult to enforce. Church organizations either refuse Negro members entirely, as in the case of most white churches of the South, or put them in an allied organization or in separate congregations. Separate school systems are compulsory in the South and allowed in a few northern cities, as Indianapolis.

In the courts, Negroes are not legally discriminated against, but an extra-legal system has arisen in the South, to a less extent in the border states and to some extent in the North, which tries and punishes the Negro criminal on an entirely different basis from the white criminal. The result is that the number of long-term Negro convicts is extraordinary. In the South it is unusual to send a white man to the penitentiary or to capital punishment, or to punish a white woman under any circumstances. The penitentiaries, therefore, are filled with Negroes, and are among the worst penal institutions in the world. They are, most of them, run for profit under the convict lease system. There are very few reformatories for colored children, and their conviction, therefore, means the manufacture of confirmed criminals. There is a widespread tendency, which shows no decided reduction, to murder by mob violence Negroes accused of crime. Since 1885, 2,584 such murders have taken place. Only 25 per cent of those lynched have been even accused of crimes against women, and in most of these accusations the offense alleged was not criminal.

Since 1890 five and a half million Negroes, over half of whom can read and write and who own fully $300,000,000 worth of property, have been practically deprived of all voice in their own government. The restrictions by which this has been accomplished are eight in number: 1. Illiteracy: the voter must be able to read and write. 2. Property: the voter must own a certain amount of property. 3. Poll tax: the voter must have paid his poll tax for the present year or for a series of years. 4. Employment: the voter must have regular employment. 5. Army service: soldiers in the Civil War and certain other wars, or their descendants, may vote. 6. Reputation: persons of good reputation who understand the duties of a citizen may vote. 7. "Grandfather" clause: persons who could vote before the freedmen were enfranchised or descendants of such persons may vote. 8. Understanding clause: persons may vote who understand some selected clause of the constitution and can explain it to the satisfaction of the registration officials.

If these laws were impartially administered the result would be bad enough; but they are deliberately, openly and avowedly administered so as to admit any white man, however ignorant, to the polls and to exclude any colored man however intelligent.

To illustrate the immediate effect of these disfranchising laws, the following statistical tables are given:

LOUISIANA

|  |  | White | Negro |
|---|---|---|---|
| 1900 | Population | 729,612 | 650,804 |
| 1900 | Males 21 years or over | 178,595 | 147,348 |
|  | Literate | 146,219 | 57,086 |
|  | Illiterate | 32,376 | 90,262 |
| 1908 | Registered voters | 152,135 | 1,743 |

LOWNDES COUNTY, ALABAMA

|  |  | White | Negro |
|---|---|---|---|
| 1900 | Males 21 years or over | 1,138 | 6,455 |
|  | Illiterate | 81 | 4,667 |
|  | Literate | 1,057 | 1,788 |
| 1902 | Registered voters | 1,097 | 39 |
| 1906 | "          " | 1,142 | 52 |

Under a strict educational qualification the literate Negroes of Lowndes county could outvote all the whites, literate and illiterate, yet only fifty-two are given the franchise!

### SOCIAL REFORM AND EDUCATIONAL OPPORTUNITIES

The result of all this has been to retard public education and social reform among colored people except that which can be carried on in private institutions or by voluntary taxation.

In the North they share somewhat in the general results of social reform work. There is, however, in this field a great deal of discrimination. Social settlements often exclude them—the "Lincoln" settlement, for instance, in Boston; fresh air funds sometimes make no provision for them; day nurseries discriminate; and even where they are not actually discriminated against, they are not made to feel welcome. On the other hand, they have their full share, heaped up and running over, of all the disabilities due to city congestion and municipal misrule. So too they are common sufferers with the rest of the South, in the general backwardness of the southern states in education, in public health regulation, in inadequate provision for the insane, the feebleminded, and the delinquent. They are sufferers without the power to vote for change.

The colored people through their women's clubs are bearing almost the whole burden of their own internal social reform. They have one hundred old folks' homes and orphanages, about 40 hospitals (some of which have partial public support), at least 500 private cemeteries, and a large number of charitable organizations of various kinds.

Not only has the general enrollment and attendance of Negro children in the rural schools of the lower South and to a large extent of the city schools been at a standstill in the last ten years and in many cases actually decreased but many of the school authorities have shown by their acts and in a few cases expressed declaration that it was their policy to eliminate the Negro schools as far as possible.

There is a distinct endeavor to curtail the facilities of education which the Negroes already possess. This can be seen in the persistent campaigns carried on in the North and directed toward the North which say, in effect, that the Negroes' education as carried on by northern philanthropists has been a mistake, that it is an interference with the local conditions in the South, and that the stream of benevolence ought to be stopped. There is no doubt but that this argument has had tremendous influence upon the benevolent public.

Again, there has been a continual effort to curtail Negro education by reducing the number of grades in the Negro public schools. Macon and Augusta, Ga., and New Orleans, La., are typical in this connection. The lack of public high schools for Negroes is one of the greatest drawbacks of the southern school system.

At the same time the Negroes are helping to pay for the education of the whites, in the sense that public monies which Negroes pay in indirect taxation or which are endowments from past generations are diverted entirely to white schools. . . .

On the whole, then, it may be said that the efforts of the Negroes since emancipation have been very promising and beyond what could be reasonably expected; that, on the other hand, the caste system which attempts to exclude Negroes from the benefit of the general social and political organization of a great modern state is strong and growing both North and South, and is not only a hindrance to Negro-Americans but a serious menace to American democracy.

*Dr. Brown, of Washington, D.C., was a graduate of Hampton Institute in the Class of 1887. Ten years later she received the B.S. degree from Cornell University and in 1904 an M.D. from Howard University. She was active in social work and was the organizer in 1908 of the College Alumnae Club, composed of colored women graduates of Class A colleges throughout the United States.*

---

# Fundamentals of Race Progress

### By Sara W. Brown, M.D.

THE FUNDAMENTAL basis of the progress of a race is self-respect, growing out of a sense of personal dignity, or moral worth, of belief in one's self, of an appreciation of one's inherent ability. Being different from others is not an evidence of inferiority. It could mean just the opposite. As to racial inferiority many ethnologists and anthropologists teach that there is no such thing as a superior race or an inferior. Neither superiority nor inferiority can be proved. We are in need of some definite propaganda to counteract in public opinion the effect of heedless, hostile, prejudiced writers, and to support friends, both within our group and outside of it. How many of us appreciate what it means to have Professor Kerlin, lately of the Virginia Military Institute, explore so diligently into the records of our Negro newspapers, and into our music and poetry in a holy desire to interpret us favorably to those who mingle with us daily and to whom we are utter strangers? He even reveals us to ourselves. His recent contribution, "Contemporary Poetry of the Negro," should be the personal possession of every man, woman, and child.

It becomes a paramount duty to inculcate race pride as a stimulus to action and as a definite offset to our past training. With every subject people the aim of the master is to make the subjugated ones believe that they are inferior and weak, and at the same time give them just enough praise and appreciation to play upon their ego instinct so as to keep them contented and satisfied to remain in their place.

From *Southern Workman*, L (December 1921), 538–544.

The fact of slavery should not cause a feeling of inferiority or of humiliation. The shame is not the Negro's. The day must now be at hand when a man will never again allude with pride to the number of slaves held by his family. The memory of it will be hateful to him. Our slavery is not sufficiently remote in the history of this country for us to consider it dispassionately, but the universality of slavery is a well-known fact. The part it has played in the evolution of society is an interesting study.

Our African ancestry is not to be despised. On the contrary, from interviews with missionaries, with native men and women, through study of recent archeological discoveries and of scientific treatises, one finds much to awaken and stimulate race pride. I was constrained to get at the truth as fully as I could lately when meeting groups of colored girls and women, because there was such ready response to the little information I had in regard to the worth-while character- istics, intellectual, moral, and physical that were the African's own. The accounts of the Yoruba country, the history of the people, their industries, the government and customs, are very gratifying. A large number of American Negroes are accredited to the Yoruba country. These people, the Matabele, the Hottentots, and numerous others are credited with having a very high standard of sex-morality—adultery and bastardy being almost unknown before the natives were contam- inated by outsiders. We have long known that Africans gathered their girls and boys at the age of adolescence into separate groups in the bush schools for secret instruction pertaining to individual and racial health. Professor Aggrey, of Livingstone College, N. C., a native Afri- can who was a member of the African Educational Commission under the Phelps-Stokes Fund, gave me when I was at Livingstone College last year some most illuminating information in regard to the mys- teries of the bush schools. He took great pride in pointing out how in sex-education his people had been in advance of some modern nations for a thousand years. I was made to feel that eugenics had originated with them. A scientist lately returned from Africa states that if safety of life and of property are a measure of civilization, then Africa and China are ahead of New York City.

With due consideration to self-respect, to tradition, and to racial inheritance, a chief factor in our power to achieve is personal health. We are helpless without this asset. The revelation of the physical in- efficiency of the young men of the United States during the period of the draft shocked the Nation and aroused the determination to improve the standards of health among its youth. We do not have the exact figures to guide us in the case of women as with men, but we can assume that the physical status of women is no better. Think of Massachusetts with 48 per cent of its young manhood, from 19 to 30, below the physical standard and other States as low or lower. The problem of health is the most urgent before us to-day, and the activities of the Y. M. C. A., the Y. W. C. A., the U. S. Public Health Service, and State Boards of Health demand our constant cooperation.

Mr. Lothrop Stoddard states that the black man's outstanding quality is superabundant vitality. That is an invaluable gift out of which the greatest blessings to man may come. But, as with all great forces, it must be rightly understood, conserved, and subdued to intelligent and desirable ends. Possibly this abounding vitality is the secret of our joyous nature, our kindly disposition, our patience and endurance under all manner of affliction and persecution. The preservation and right use of this fundamental quality concern us very, very seriously if we are to continue to survive and achieve the highest development. Mortality statistics from the United States Census and from State Boards of Health unfortunately do not corroborate Mr. Stoddard's belief. Civilization has brought in its train evils which are not conducive to our best health. In the data compiled recently for Negro Health Week, it is estimated that 450,000 colored people in the South are seriously sick all the time; that 50 per cent of every 100 cases of annual sickness can be prevented; that the annual loss of earnings from sickness and death is $300,000,000; that $150,000,000 in earnings can be saved annually by hygiene and sanitation. The death rate in 1910 per 1000 for 81 cities was 14.8 for whites to 25.9 for colored; for the whole registration area (which is only one-third of the United States) white 13.5, colored 20.5—significant and discouraging figures, but not hopeless, as each succeeding year since 1910 shows a steady reduction.

The Director of the United States Census states that substantial improvement in mortality may be designated as a social obligation resting upon the Negro population, although responsibility for the excessive mortality in this class undoubtedly rests in some degree upon the community as a whole. The combined efforts of Tuskegee Institute, the United States Public Health Service, the Young Women's Christian Association, and other organizations in the recent health crusade indicate an initial response to the suggestions of the Director of the Census.

Upon woman rests the special, sacred obligation of protection to maternity, infancy, and childhood. The Virginia Health Bulletin in its report of the Bureau of Vital Statistics, Dec. 1920, contains this statement: "The death rate of infants under one year of age is now considered as one of the surest indications of the degree of civilization of a state or country." The Children's Bureau Report, 1919, informs us that over 200,000 babies less than a year old die annually in the United States, which places our country seventh from the head in the list of countries judged by the favorable character of their infant mortality rates. More than 16,000 mothers of all classes die yearly from the causes incident to child bearing, and ill health is suffered by a vast number of others from the same causes. These deaths and disabilities are now known to be needless in large measure. The best available figures for maternal mortality show that the United States is fourteenth down the list of civilized countries.

Women are going to attack with tremendous energy these problems that strike at the root of the Nation. They will assemble all the forces within their reach—individual and organized. They will bring State and Federal government to the rescue of motherhood, infancy, and childhood. Note the resolutions and programs of influential women's organizations and of women leaders. The League of Women Voters, the National Woman's Party, the National Federation of Colored Women's Clubs, and many others,—all of one accord are in favor of legislation for the public protection of maternity and infancy; for universal elementary education; for the prompt and immediate abolition of illiteracy, and of child labor. Individuals should be educated to demand, and communities to supply, public-health nurses, prenatal centers, dental and venereal clinics, maternity hospitals and wards.

Next to health I would place education. The illiterate Negroes in 1920 were 1,842,161 in number and represented 22.9 per cent of the total Negro population 10 years of age and over, as compared with 30.4 per cent in 1910, 44.5 in 1900, and 57.1 in 1890. The percentage of Negro illiterates decreased in the District of Columbia and in every State except four—Vermont, Rhode Island, Wyoming, and Oregon. The largest proportional increase, from 3.4 in 1910 to 4.7 in 1920, appears in Oregon. The largest proportional decrease is that for New Mexico; in which State the percentage of illiterates declined from 14.2 in 1910 to 4.3 in 1920, or more than two-thirds. The explanation of this pronounced decrease is found in the fact that a large increase took place in the total Negro population of New Mexico, due in part to the presence of Negro troops in the State in 1920, and that there were few illiterates among the newcomers.

As the returns from the Census of 1920 for school attendance by color will not be available for some months, it will be impossible at this time to correct the 1910 figures, which showed that only 47.3 per cent of the colored children in the United States between six and twenty years of age were in school. In the South 46.4 per cent of the Negro and 62 per cent of the white school population were enrolled. In the North and West the Negroes in school ranked closer to other racial groups.

Statistics on school education may be very misleading unless interpreted with an understanding of such disparities as the varying length of the term covered by the school year, the varying grade of teachers employed, the varying character of the curriculum. A school year of forty weeks is more productive of results than one of ten or twelve weeks; a graduate of a high-grade normal school is a better teacher than a graduate of a local grammar or high school; a system of graded schools is of far greater educational value to a community than the ordinary ungraded school of remote country districts.

These figures and facts from the United States government reports are convincing testimony as to the educational status of our people. The realization of the import of these facts has already set machinery in motion for improvement. Since these figures were obtained all of us know of the genuine awakening of activities throughout the Southland to give better educational opportunities to all the children. But those of us who have seen dilapidated, insanitary school buildings thronged with numbers far beyond the capacity of the structure or of the teaching force, realize that equal opportunity is not yet given our children, and that there is a vast amount yet to be done to make anything like adequate provision for the need.

The need for teachers is pressing. The necessity of education for all classes of children in the South is clearly indicated by the above figures, and the proper race relationship between the two large groups in those States must depend primarily on the spread of the right kind of education. A colored bishop from Mississippi made the statement to me last year in North Carolina that for the sake of racial peace and happiness, it would pay the colored people to take the money out of their own pockets and use it in the education of the ignorant whites. Rather a unique proposition! He was not far wrong as to the need in the case.

In the matter of occupations of colored men and women we will present several having the smallest numbers and several having the largest numbers, as given by the Census of 1910.

| | | | |
|---|---|---|---|
| Sculptors | 10 | Clergymen | 17,996 |
| Inventors | 19 | Janitors and sextons | 22,419 |
| Journalists | 24 | Carpenters | 22,464 |
| Librarians | 30 | Teachers | 29,722 |
| Architects | 59 | Laundry workers | 368,128 |
| Editors | 146 | Domestic and personal | |
| Bankers and brokers | 241 | service | 1,074,543 |
| Dentists | 478 | In agriculture | 2,893,375 |

These facts indicate the nature of the education needed by the Negro. Serious consideration should certainly be given to those occupations in which we find our greatest numbers employed. For instance, agricultural education, aside from its cultural value, offers great economic opportunities in a field already open to us. Life in rural communities, of course, must be enriched by provision for education, physical and intellectual, and by suitable amusements and recreation. The art and science of home making should be taught to fit us to continue in the field of industry already at our command, and to enable us by superior work to demand a more adequate wage; or better still, to prepare our young women for their own homes, where the husband and father must earn enough to make it possible for the wife and mother to devote her energy and ability to the nurture and training of her children. The moral crisis demands this. In the words of President Harding, "We want an America of homes, illumined with hope and happiness, where mothers, freed from the necessity of long hours of toil beyond their own doors, may preside as befits the hearthstone of American citizenship."

Judged by standards in the white population it would appear that each of the professions, with the single exception of the clergymen, is undermanned among the Negroes.

| | AMONG NEGROES | AMONG WHITES |
|---|---|---|
| Population per dentist | 20,560 | 2070 |
| " " physician | 3,194 | 553 |
| " " college president or professor | 40,611 | 5301 |
| " " lawyer, judge, or justice | 12,315 | 718 |
| " " school teacher | 334 | 145 |
| " " minister | 562 | 815 |

Surely we must be impressed by the fact that there is no over-
crowding in the ranks calling for higher education and superior intelligence. We must diligently seek out the able and gifted and
inspire them with zeal for achievement in those activities which
require years of continued application and devotion. The development of this type is a real need of the hour. And the encouragement
by all classes of such individuals to accomplish their life work in the
South is an urgent necessity.

Colored women are not going to be indifferent to the new citizenship which has been conferred on all women. The following significant statement is taken from a Memorial presented to Miss Alice
Paul of the National Woman's Party by a deputation of colored
women: "The world has moved forward in these seventy years, and
the colored women of this country have been moving with it. They
know the value of the ballot if honestly used to right the wrongs of
any class. Five million women in the United States cannot be denied their rights without all the women of the United States feeling
the effect of the denial. No women are free until all are free." The
woman's cause is one.

Our attitude is well expressed by the woman orator who said,
"All women want to use their new political power in such a way as
to help humanity. There are all the human problems of poverty,
crime, the social evil, sickness, old age. The nineteenth century has
stood for the awakening of the social conscience. Thoughtful people
cannot be happy so long as there is a submerged tenth. Legislation
and education are at present the chief means of securing progress."
It is only by trying to understand others that we can get our own
hearts understood. There must be mutual sympathy, understanding,
and co-operation between the two great groups in our country. Antagonism, prejudice, hatred, persecution, must be abandoned so that
the era of good will can enter and abide. "Service," the one word
which epitomizes all that Hampton means to its graduates, which
includes all our obligations to alma mater, to our neighbors, and to
our country, in the language of our President, "is the supreme commitment of life."

*Carter G. Woodson, a leading black historian, helped to form the Association for the Study of Negro Life and History and, in 1916, the* Journal of Negro History *which was published under the Association's auspices. Mr. Woodson was editor of the journal for many years.*

# Some Things Negroes Need To Do

## By Carter G. Woodson

THERE ARE certain things the Negroes in this country must do if they hope to enjoy the blessings of real democracy, if it ever comes.

In the first place, we need to attain economic independence. You may talk about rights and all that sort of thing. The people who own this country will rule this country. They always have done so and they always will. The people who control the coal and iron, the banks, the stock markets, and all that sort of thing, those are the people who will dictate exactly what shall be done for every group in this land. More than that, liberty is to come to the Negro, not as a bequest, but as a conquest. When I speak of it as a conquest, I mean that the Negro must contribute something to the good of his race, something to the good of his country, and something to the honor and glory of God. Economic independence is the first step in that direction.

I was in Washington the other day and a man told me that the colored people were about to have a new bank there—"and they have two already," he said. I answered, "They should have had ten banks forty years ago." Two banks among a hundred thousand Negroes! We must learn to take these things more seriously.

I was speaking to a gentleman the other day about the organization of an insurance company, and he was telling of the wonderful things we have done in the way of insurance. After he had summarized the receipts of the various companies now organized among Negroes it was just a little modicum, so to speak, compared with the great achievements in insurance on the part of members of the white race. Here we are, rejoicing over these little things, and we have hardly begun to make a beginning.

From *Southern Workman*, LI (January 1922), 33–36.

Then we must have educational independence. If the Negro is not going to become an educational factor among his own people, then education is not the leverage to lift him, in the sense it has lifted other people; for a man is educated when he can do without a teacher, when he can and will develop and grow without the stimulus of instruction. So must it be with a race. If we are not going to reach that point some day in our lives when we shall be able to go out and establish schools and become persons well rounded in philosophy and science and history and what-not, and be able to help one another; if we are not going to prepare ourselves here, three generations from slavery, to do that work for ourselves, then we cannot say that education has done for our group what it has done for others.

Then the Negro needs to develop a press. Some of us never read a Negro newspaper—and some are not worth reading. A few, however, tell the story of the Negro in a cool, calm way. They tell of the strivings of the Negro in such a way as to be an inspiration to youth. Every Negro ought to read the publications of his own race.

I was impressed in California to find that, although there are only ten thousand Japanese in San Francisco, they have two daily papers —only ten thousand, but they have two daily papers of eight pages each. We have over ten million in the United States and we have not yet developed a real daily newspaper. We should not complain if the white papers do not tell our own story. We complain because they publish our crimes and tell of the evils that we do but do not say anything of our achievements in those lines that tend to stamp us as people of the world. We must learn to tell the story ourselves. It is our duty to develop a press.

We should also develop a literature. Negroes should read some things written by their own people that they may be inspired thereby. You will never be a George Washington or a Thomas Jefferson—you will never be a white man—but you will be a Negro, and we must realize that there are certain things in the Negro race worth developing. Those things may be worth as much to the world as the things of the white race when they are properly developed. We must cease trying to straighten our hair and bleach our faces, and be Negroes— and be good ones.

In this literature you will get the inspiration you need to be like Frederick Douglass, Booker Washington, S. Coleridge-Taylor, or Paul Laurence Dunbar. If you can contribute to the world what those men have you will have no reason to regret that you cannot be a

George Washington or a Thomas Jefferson, because you will still be identified with some of the greatest men who have ever appeared in the history of the world.

The Negro must learn to preserve his own records. He must learn the value of tradition. I was speaking to a teacher the other day. I wanted to get some information as to his people. I asked him who his grandfather was. "I am not sure," he said, "what my grandfather's name was." It may be that some of you do not know your grandfathers. You have not thought they were worth while. Although they perhaps could not read and write, they contributed much to the making of the race. They made it possible for you to be where you are to-day. They bore the burden and heat of the day. Some of them achieved a great deal more than some of us could have achieved.

If you should go to Cincinnati and speak with some of the old citizens—those who lived there before the Civil War—they would tell you that the Negroes of Cincinnati achieved more prior to the Civil War than they have since. There was a man who had patented a cord-bed which became popular throughout the United States, just as the spring-bed is popular to-day. In the exploitation of that patent he built up a large business and employed scores of white men and Negroes. He was worth thousands of dollars.

There was a Negro who went from this State—a Negro from Richmond, Va., who had worked in a blacksmith shop. His master permitted him to sell the slack of the coal. He accumulated a large sum of money, about $15,000, and he went to his master and purchased himself. He then went North and settled finally in Cincinnati. He knew the coal business and entered that business there. The people thought they would run him out of business and they said, "We coal dealers will get together and lower the price of coal to such an extent that he will be ruined." This Negro was wise. He sent mulattoes around to fill all his orders at the white coal yard, so that his supply would be kept on hand. The white coal dealers exhausted their supply and there came a great freezing. No coal could get through up the river and the railroads had not been constructed. This Negro had all his coal on hand. Nobody else could get any, and he sold out at a handsome profit. He then had so much money to enlarge his business that they never thought of combining against him again. That was in 1869. That Negro was worth something like $60,000. There isn't a Negro in Cincinnati to-day worth $60,000.

We have a wonderful history behind us. We of the *Journal of*

*Negro History* shall have going the rounds soon a lecture on the ante-bellum period, setting forth the stories of Negroes who did so much to inspire us. It reads like the history of people in an heroic age. We expect to send out from time to time books written for the express purpose of showing you that you have a history, a record, behind you. If you are unable to demonstrate to the world that you have this record, the world will say to you, "You are not worthy to enjoy the blessings of democracy or anything else." They will say to you, "Who are you, anyway? Your ancestors have never controlled empires or kingdoms and most of your race have contributed little or nothing to science and philosophy and mathematics." So far as you know, they have not; but if you will read the history of Africa, the history of your ancestors—people of whom you should feel proud —you will realize that they have a history that is worth while. They have traditions that have value of which you can boast and upon which you can base a claim for a right to a share in the blessings of democracy.

Let us, then, study this history, and study it with the understanding that we are not, after all, an inferior people, but simply a people who have been set back, a people whose progress has been impeded. We are going back to that beautiful history and it is going to inspire us to greater achievements. It is not going to be long before we can so sing the story to the outside world as to convince it of the value of our history and our traditions, and then we are going to be recognized as men.

*The following article, written by a black schoolteacher, describes in a forthright manner the great need for teaching black pride to black children.*

# Negro Literature for Negro Pupils

## By Alice Dunbar-Nelson

THE ANCIENT GREEKS, wishing to impress upon their children the greatness of Hellas, made the schoolboys memorize Homer, particularly those passages dealing with wars and conquests. The Romans saturated their youth with Roman literature, history, and law. The Hebrew children of all ages are versed, grounded, and crammed with the Mosaic and Rabbinical law. The Chinese child learns volumes of Confucius. The French child recites La Fontaine, even before he can read. Spain drives home the epic of the Cid to the youth of her land —and so on, through all history, ancient and modern; each land, each nation, impresses most painstakingly upon the rising generation the fact that it possesses a history and a literature, and that it must live up to the traditions of its history, and make that literature a part of its life.

The reason for this is obvious. If a people are to be proud and self-respecting they must believe in themselves. Destroy a man's belief in his own powers, and you destroy his usefulness—render him a worthless object, helpless and hopeless. Tell a people over and over again that they have done nothing, can do nothing, set a limitation for their achievement; impress upon them that all they have or can hope to have is the product of the minds of other peoples; force them to believe that they are pensioners on the mental bounty of another race,—and they will lose what little faith they may have had in themselves, and become stultified non-producers. Any parent or teacher knows how disastrous is the result of telling a child how splendidly some other child has done, and asking why he does not go and do likewise. The one so adjured usually does the exact opposite, in a bitterness of resentment and gloom, it being one of the vagaries of human nature to act contrariwise.

From *Southern Workman*, LI (February 1922), 59–63.

97

All this is by way of reminding ourselves that for two generations we have given brown and black children a blonde ideal of beauty to worship, a milk-white literature to assimilate, and a pearly Paradise to anticipate, in which their dark faces would be hopelessly out of place. That there has not been a complete and absolute stultification of the efforts of the race toward self-expression is due only to the fact that we are a people of peculiar resiliency and combativeness. The effect of this kind of teaching is shown in the facts that the beautiful brown dolls, which resemble their tiny play-mothers, still have some difficulty in making their way into the homes of our people; that some older religionists still fondly hope that at death, and before St. Peter admits them into Paradise, they will be washed physically white; that Negro business enterprises are still regarded with a doubtful eye; and that Negro literature is frequently mentioned in whispers as a dubious quantity.

There is a manifest remedy for this condition, a remedy which the teachers of the race are applying gradually, wherever the need has been brought to their attention. We must begin everywhere to instill race pride into our pupils; not by dull statistics, nor yet by tedious iterations that we are a great people, and "if you do not believe it, look at this table of figures, or at the life of so-and-so." Idle boasting of past achievements always leaves a suspicion in the mind of the listener that the braggart is not sure of his ground and is bolstering up his opinion of himself. But we will give the children the poems and stories and folk lore and songs of their own people. We do not teach literature; we are taught by literature. The subtlest, most delicate, and lasting impressions of childhood are those gained by the chance poem, the eagerly absorbed fable, the lesson in the reader, the story told in the Sunday-school lesson. The fairy prince and the delectable princess have their charm, as opening up a vista into an enchanted land, but the poem that touches closely the heart of a child, and belongs to it because of its very nearness to his own life, is the bit of literature that lifts him above the dull brown earth and makes him akin to all that is truly great in the universe.

Three pictures project themselves upon the screen of memory, deeply suggestive of the futility of some of our efforts to reach child-life. One is that of a plaintive child, to whom the world of books was the real world, hugging to her thin little breast a big book of poetry, and passionately praying, "Oh, please, dear Lord, let me grow up and write things, because none of us have ever written anything, and we ought to, dear Lord, because its *awful* that we don't write stories or things." Now this was a Southern child in a Southern city in a school taught by colored teachers, and her eager little soul was convulsed with shame that her own people had never accomplished anything in the realm of the books she loved.

The second picture shows a young girl teaching in a Southern city before it was supplied with modern sewerage, when to dig even eighteen inches in the ground brought one to water. The Second-Reader lesson cheerfully told of the joys of storing red apples in the cellar to eat when the snow was on the ground. To explain snow to these children in a semi-tropical clime was a feat requiring Herculean efforts, and the modicum of impression made was tempered by open skepticism on the faces of the boys. But when the cellar problem was attacked all faith in the teacher's omniscience was blown to the four winds. What, a room under-ground? Why, everyone knew that you couldn't even dig a grave without its filling with water, much less have a whole room underground! Prudence and decorum went to the winds, and the little teacher mopped her agitated forehead and prayed for Second Readers with Southern stories in them.

Third: a splendidly equipped school in a sea-side town. The windows of all the rooms on one side of the building overlooked the Atlantic Ocean, and every pane of glass framed a perfect vignette of cloud and wave and white-winged fishing smack, driving before the wind, or lying at anchor with graceful spars silhouetted against a myriad-hued sky. Yet every child in the art classes was busily painting apple orchards in full bloom, it being spring, and time for the apple orchards of New England and inland places to flower into whiteness and pinkness. There are no apple trees anywhere near this sandy strip of white coast that is pounded by the great waves, and spring for that section means the shy wild flowers that bloom in heaped sand dunes, or brilliant marshmallows flushing amidst swaying reeds. It means little saucy-frocked fishing smacks running through white-capped ultramarine waves. Yet in all that school not a child had been told to look out of the window and see the beauties of his own environment. They were copying the reputed beauties of a land miles inland.

These three pictures stand out in my mind because it seems to me that they symbolize the kind of teaching that we do so much of in our schools—the colored child, hungry for information, and yet ignorant of the history and achievements of its own race; pupils forced to insult their budding intelligence with an unnecessary situation; youthful artists turning their backs on the beauties about them and copying the counterfeit landscapes which they have never seen. It is high time that we throw off the shackles which convention binds around our educational methods and "let down our buckets where we are."

Every teacher in a colored school is a missionary. More than the mere instilling of so much knowledge in the heads of the pupils must he or she teach many other things, character through pride of race being one of the greatest. For the youth who is proud of his race and will endeavor to live up to its traditions, and will hesitate to do mean things lest they sully the escutcheon. As we have said before, the sentiment of pride and honor fostered in the Negro youth will fire his ambition, his desire to accomplish, even as others of his race have done before him. It is only the exceptional case, the overmastering genius who is thrilled with the desire to conquer because no other has done so. The ordinary one—and there are so many more of him than there are of any other kind—needs encouragement from the deeds of others.

But statistics mean nothing to children; they are colorless things, savoring too much of tables in arithmetic to be deeply intriguing. The child mind must have concrete examples, for it is essentially poetic and deals in images. It is not enough to say that black men fought in the Revolutionary War to the extent of so many in so many regiments. But there are a number of well-told, crisply narrated stories of Crispus Attucks, and even some narrative poems celebrate the first blood shed in the Revolutionary War. It is not enough to say that black slaves, from Massachusetts to Maryland, stood by the Nation when red-coated Tories overran the land. Dunbar's spirited ballad of "Black Samson of Brandywine" will fix the idea in the youthful mind, even as "Paul Revere's Ride" has fixed the date of the battle of Concord and Lexington in the minds of generations of young Americans, white and black, from Maine to California.

It is well for Negro children to know that the delightful fables of Æsop are the satires of a black slave, and that the author of the incomparable "Three Musketeers," which rejoices the swashbuckling instincts of the adolescent, was of Negro descent. There are exquisite little nature lyrics, particularly snow scenes, by Pushkin (obtainable in translation) as perfect in their picturization, in a way, as those of Bryant, or that of Lowell's "First Snowfall"; and it would make the young chests swell with pride to know that these are the work of one of the greatest of Russian poets—an acknowledged Negro.

Apart from these exotic instances, the children might well be taught the folk tales of the race, as rich in content and moral lesson as can be found in any folk tales, from Æsop and Reynard the Fox to Uncle Remus. There is a mine of suggestion in Alphonso Stafford's "African Folk Stories." That classic, "The Seedling," by Dunbar, has delighted the little folks of a generation, with its botanical lesson encouched in delicate verse, and the inevitable moral admonition, which all children secretly love, at the end.

By the side of Maggie Tulliver we may place Zora, of "The Quest of the Silver Fleece (DuBois)"; against Spartacus and his address to the gladiators, is Dessalines and his defiant reminiscences; thrilling rescue stories might be matched by the rescue of the lad in Durham's "Diane"; or by the round-up scene from "The Love of Landry" (Dunbar), to give the proper Western flavor to the boy or girl in love with the Bill Hart type. In company with "The Charge of the Light Brigade" is the "Second Louisiana," and the "Finish of Patsy Barnes" (Dunbar), for those who love the small boy who overcomes obstacles for the sake of the mother ill at home. Thanksgiving is commemorated by Braithwaite as delightfully as ever Stevenson "gave thanks for many things" not to mention "Christmas," by Dunbar, or similar poems by those others who have followed in his tread.

And the winged words of Booker Washington and Frederick Douglass! The biographies of those who have accomplished great things in the face of heavy odds! Romances of lives as thrilling as the romances which have grown up around Lincoln and Daniel Boone! The girl, Phyllis, and the lad, Paul! How much finer for the Negro boy and girl to know of these lives, and of the work they did; to read the burning, living words that are the work of their own blood and kin; to feel that the lowly ones of the cabins in the country, or the tenements and alleys in the city, may yet give to the world some gift, albeit small, that will inspire and ennoble countless dark-faced children struggling up towards the light.

Assuredly we will teach our boys and girls, not only their own history and literature, but works by their own authors. We will, ourselves, first achieve a sense of pride in our own productions, with a fine sense of literary values which will not allow us to confuse trivialities and trash with literature. We will learn to judge a thing as good, because of its intrinsic value and not because it is a Negro's!

We will be as quick to throw away valueless stuff written by a black man or woman, as if it were written by a white man or woman. In other words we will recognize but one absolute standard, and we will preserve for our children all that approximates that standard, and teach them to reverence the good that is in their own because it is good.

And by so doing, we shall impress most deeply upon the young people of our race, by our own literature, that most valuable of all lessons:—

> Be proud, my race, in mind and soul:
> Thy name is writ on glory's scroll
>      In characters of fire;
> High, midst the clouds of Fame's bright sky,
> Thy banner's blazoned folds now fly,
>      And Truth shall lift them higher.

*The following article by Alain Locke was part of the issue
of* Survey *magazine that was devoted entirely to black
Americans and eventually became the book* The New
Negro, *edited by Locke.*

---

# Enter the New Negro

### By Alain Locke

IN THE LAST DECADE something beyond the watch and guard of statistics has happened in the life of the American Negro and the three
norns who have traditionally presided over the Negro problem have
a changeling in their laps. The Sociologist, The Philanthropist, the
Race-leader are not unaware of the New Negro, but they are at a loss
to account for him. He simply cannot be swathed in their formulae.
For the younger generation is vibrant with a new psychology; the
new spirit is awake in the masses, and under the very eyes of the
professional observers is transforming what has been a perennial
problem into the progressive phases of contemporary Negro life.

Could such a metamorphosis have taken place as suddenly as it has
appeared to? The answer is no; not because the New Negro is not
here, but because the Old Negro had long become more of a myth
than a man. The Old Negro, we must remember, was a creature of
moral debate and historical controversy. His has been a stock figure
perpetuated as an historical fiction partly in innocent sentimentalism,
partly in deliberate reactionism. The Negro himself has contributed
his share to this through a sort of protective social mimicry forced
upon him by the adverse circumstances of dependence. So for generations in the mind of America, the Negro has been more of a
formula than a human being—a something to be argued about,
condemned or defended, to be "kept down," or "in his place," or
"helped up," to be worried with or worried over, harassed or patronized, a social bogey or a social burden. The thinking Negro even has
been induced to share this same general attitude, to focus his attention on controversial issues, to see himself in the distorted perspective

From *Survey*, LIII (March 1, 1925), 631–634.

of a social problem. His shadow, so to speak, has been more real to him than his personality. Through having had to appeal from the unjust stereotypes of his oppressors and traducers to those of his liberators, friends and benefactors he has subscribed to the traditional positions from which his case has been viewed. Little true social or self-understanding has or could come from such a situation.

But while the minds of most of us, black and white, have thus burrowed in the trenches of the Civil War and Reconstruction, the actual march of development has simply flanked these positions, necessitating a sudden reorientation of view. We have not been watching in the right direction; get North and South on a sectional axis, we have not noticed the East till the sun has us blinking.

Recall how suddenly the Negro spirituals revealed themselves; suppressed for generations under the stereotypes of Wesleyan hymn harmony, secretive, half-ashamed, until the courage of being natural brought them out—and behold, there was folk-music. Similarly the mind of the Negro seems suddenly to have slipped from under the tyranny of social intimidation and to be shaking off the psychology of imitation and implied inferiority. By shedding the old chrysalis of the Negro problem we are achieving something like a spiritual emancipation. Until recently, lacking self-understanding, we have been almost as much of a problem to ourselves as we still are to others. But the decade that found us with a problem has left us with only a task. The multitude perhaps feels as yet only a strange relief and a new vague urge, but the thinking few know that in the reaction the vital inner grip of prejudice has been broken.

With this renewed self-respect and self-dependence, the life of the Negro community is bound to enter a new dynamic phase, the buoyancy from within compensating for whatever pressure there may be of conditions from without. The migrant masses, shifting from countryside to city, hurdle several generations of experience at a leap, but more important, the same thing happens spiritually in the life-attitudes and self-expression of the Young Negro, in his poetry, his art, his education and his new outlook, with the additional advantage, of course, of the poise and greater certainty of knowing what it is all about. From this comes the promise and warrant of a new leadership. As one of them has discerningly put it:

We have tomorrow      Yesterday, a night-gone thing
Bright before us       A sun-down name.
Like a flame.

And dawn today
Broad arch above the road we came.
We march!

This is what, even more than any "most creditable record of fifty years of freedom," requires that the Negro of today be seen through other than the dusty spectacles of past controversy. The day of "aunties," "uncles" and "mammies" is equally gone. Uncle Tom and Sambo have passed on, and even the "Colonel" and "George" play barnstorm roles from which they escape with relief when the public spotlight is off. The popular melodrama has about played itself out, and it is time to scrap the fictions, garret the bogeys and settle down to a realistic facing of facts.

First we must observe some of the changes which since the traditional lines of opinion were drawn have rendered these quite obsolete. A main change has been, of course, that shifting of the Negro population which has made the Negro problem no longer exclusively or even predominantly Southern. Why should our minds remain sectionalized, when the problem itself no longer is? Then the trend of migration has not only been toward the North and the Central Midwest, but city-ward and to the great centers of industry—the problems of adjustment are new, practical, local and not peculiarly racial. Rather they are an integral part of the large industrial and social problems of our present-day democracy. And finally, with the Negro rapidly in process of class differentiation, if it ever was warrantable to regard and treat the Negro en masse it is becoming with every day less possible, more unjust and more ridiculous.

The Negro too, for his part, has idols of the tribe to smash. If on the one hand the white man has erred in making the Negro appear to be that which would excuse or extenuate his treatment of him, the Negro, in turn, has too often unnecessarily excused himself because of the way he has been treated. The intelligent Negro of today is resolved not to make discrimination an extenuation for his shortcomings in performance, individual or collective; he is trying to hold himself at par, neither inflated by sentimental allowances nor depreciated by current social discounts. For this he must know himself and be known for precisely what he is, and for that reason he welcomes the new scientific rather than the old sentimental interest. Sentimental interest in the Negro has ebbed. We used to lament this as the falling off of our friends; now we rejoice and pray to be delivered both from self-pity and condescension. The mind of each racial

group has had a bitter weaning, apathy or hatred on one side match-
ing disillusionment or resentment on the other; but they face each
other today with the possibility at least of entirely new mutual
attitudes.

It does not follow that if the Negro were better known, he would
be better liked or better treated. But mutual understanding is basic
for any subsequent cooperation and adjustment. The effort toward
this will at least have the effect of remedying in large part what has
been the most unsatisfactory feature of our present stage of race relationships in America, namely the fact that the more intelligent and
representative elements of the two race groups have at so many points
got quite out of vital touch with one another.

The fiction is that the life of the races is separate, and increasingly
so. The fact is that they have touched too closely at the unfavorable
and too lightly at the favorable levels.

While inter-racial councils have sprung up in the South, drawing
on forward elements of both races, in the Northern cities manual
laborers may brush elbows in their everyday work, but the community and business leaders have experienced no such interplay or far
too little of it. These segments must achieve contact or the race situation in America becomes desperate. Fortunately this is happening.
There is a growing realization that in social effort the cooperative
basis must supplant long-distance philanthropy, and that the only
safeguard for mass relations in the future must be provided in the
carefully maintained contacts of the enlightened minorities of both
race groups. In the intellectual realm a renewed and keen curiosity is
replacing the recent apathy; the Negro is being carefully studied, not
just talked about and discussed. In art and letters, instead of being
wholly caricatured, he is being seriously portrayed and painted.

To all of this the New Negro is keenly responsive as an augury of
a new democracy in American culture. He is contributing his share
to the new social understanding. But the desire to be understood
would never in itself have been sufficient to have opened so completely the protectively closed portals of the thinking Negro's mind.
There is still too much possibility of being snubbed or patronized for
that. It was rather the necessity for fuller, truer self-expression, the
realization of the unwisdom of allowing social discrimination to seg-
regate him mentally, and a counter-attitude to cramp and fetter his
own living—and so the "spite-wall" that the intellectuals built over
the "color-line" has happily been taken down. Much of this reopen-

ing of intellectual contacts has centered in New York and has been richly fruitful not merely in the enlarging of personal experience but in the definite enrichment of American art and letters and in the clarifying of our common vision of the social tasks ahead.

The particular significance in the reestablishment of contact between the more advanced and representative classes is that it promises to offset some of the unfavorable reaction of the past, or at least to re-surface race contacts somewhat for the future. Subtly the conditions that are moulding a New Negro are moulding a new American attitude.

However, this new phase of things is delicate; it will call for less charity but more justice; less help, but infinitely closer understanding. This is indeed a critical stage of race relationships because of the likelihood, if the new temper is not understood, of engendering sharp group antagonism and a second crop of more calculated prejudice. In some quarters, it has already done so. Having weaned the Negro, public opinion cannot continue to paternalize. The Negro today is inevitably moving forward under the control largely of his own objectives. What are these objectives? Those of his outer life are happily already well and finally formulated, for they are none other than the ideals of American institutions and democracy. Those of his inner life are now in process of formation, for the new psychology at present is more of a consensus of feeling than of opinion, of attitude rather than of program. Still some points seem to have crystallized.

Up to the present one may adequately describe the Negro's "inner objectives" as an attempt to repair a damaged group psychology and reshape a warped social perspective. Their realization has required a new mentality for the American Negro. And as it matures we begin to see its effects; at first, negative, iconoclastic, and then positive and constructive. In this new group psychology we note the lapse of sentimental appeal, then the development of a more positive self-respect and self-reliance; the repudiation of social dependence, and then the gradual recovery from hyper-sensitiveness and "touchy" nerves, the repudiation of the double standard of judgment with its special philanthropic allowances and then the sturdier desire to objective and scientific appraisal; and finally the rise from social disillusionment to race pride, from the sense of social debt to the responsibilities of social contribution, and of setting the necessary working and commonsense acceptance of restricted conditions, the belief in ultimate esteem and recognition. Therefore the Negro today wishes to be known for what he is, even in his faults and shortcom-ings, and scorns a craven and precarious survival at the price of seeming to be what he is not. He resents being spoken for as a social ward or minor, even by his own, and to being regarded a chronic patient for the sociological clinic, the sick man of American Democ-racy. For the same reasons, he himself is through with those social nostrums and panaceas, the so-called "solutions" of his "problem," with which he and the country have been so liberally dosed in the past. Religion, freedom, education, money—in turn, he has ardently hoped for and peculiarly trusted these things; he still believes in them, but not in blind trust that they all will solve his life-problem.

Each generation, however, will have its creed, and that of the present is the belief in the efficacy of collective effort in race coopera-tion. This deep feeling of race is at present the mainspring of Negro life. It seems to be the outcome of the reaction to proscription and prejudice; an attempt, fairly successful on the whole, to convert a defensive into an offensive position, a handicap into an incentive. It is radical in tone, but not in purpose and only the most stupid forms of opposition, misunderstanding or persecution could make it other-wise. Of course, the thinking Negro has shifted a little toward the left with the world-trend, and there is an increasing group who affili-ate with radical and liberal movements. But fundamentally for the present the Negro is radical on race matters, conservative on others, in other words, a "forced radical," a social protestant rather than a genuine radical. Yet under further pressure and injustice iconoclastic thought and motives will inevitably increase. Harlem's quixotic radicalisms call for their ounce of democracy today lest tomorrow they be beyond cure.

The Negro mind reaches out as yet to nothing but American wants, American ideas. But this forced attempt to build his Americanism on race values is a unique social experiment, and its ultimate success is impossible except through the fullest sharing of American culture and institutions. There should be no delusion about this. American nerves in sections unstrung with race hysteria are often fed the opiate that the trend of Negro advance is wholly separatist, and that the effect of its operation will be to encyst the Negro as a benign foreign body in the body politic. This cannot be—even if it were desirable. The racialism of the Negro has no limitation or reservation with re-spect to American life; it is only a constructive effort to build the ob-structions in the stream of his progress into an efficient dam of social

energy and power. Democracy itself is obstructed and stagnated to
the extent that any of its channels are closed. Indeed they cannot be
selectively closed. So the choice is not between one way for the Negro
and another way for the rest, but between American institutions
frustrated on the one hand and American ideals progressively fulfilled
and realized on the other.

There is, of course, a warrantably comfortable feeling in being on
the right side of the country's professed ideals. We realize that we
cannot be undone without America's undoing. It is within the gamut
of this attitude that the thinking Negro faces America, but the varia-
tions of mood in connection with it are if anything more significant
than the attitude itself. Sometimes we have it taken with the defiant
ironic challenge of McKay:

> Mine is the future grinding down today
> Like a great landslip moving to the sea,
> Bearing its freight of debris far away
> Where the green hungry waters restlessly
> Heave mammoth pyramids and break and roar
> Their eerie challenge to the crumbling shore.

Sometimes, perhaps more frequently as yet, in the fervent and almost
filial appeal and counsel of Weldon Johnson's:

> O Southland, dear Southland!
> Then why do you still cling
> To an idle age and a musty page,
> To a dead and useless thing.

But between defiance and appeal, midway almost between cynicism
and hope, the prevailing mind stands in the mood of the same author's
To America, an attitude of sober query and stoical challenge:

> How would you have us, as we are?
> Or sinking 'neath the load we bear,
> Our eyes fixed forward on a star,
> Or gazing empty at despair?
>
> Rising or falling? Men or things?
> With dragging pace or footsteps fleet?
> Strong, willing sinews in your wings,
> Or tightening chains about your feet?

More and more, however, an intelligent realization of the great
discrepancy between the American social creed and the American
social practice forces upon the Negro the taking of the moral advan-

tage that is his. Only the steadying and sobering effect of a truly
characteristic gentleness of spirit prevents the rapid rise of a definite
cynicism and counter-hate and a defiant superiority feeling. Human
as this reaction would be, the majority still deprecate its advent, and
would gladly see it forestalled by the speedy amelioration of its
causes. We wish our race pride to be a healthier, more positive
achievement than a feeling based upon a realization of the shortcomings of others. But all paths toward the attainment of a sound
social attitude have been difficult; only a relatively few enlightened
minds have been able as the phrase puts it "to rise above" prejudice.
The ordinary man has had until recently only a hard choice between
the alternatives of supine and humiliating submission and stimulating
but hurtful counter-prejudice. Fortunately from some inner, desperate resourcefulness has recently sprung up the simple expedient
of fighting prejudice by mental passive resistance, in other words by
trying to ignore it. For the few, this manna may perhaps be effective,
but the masses cannot thrive on it.

Fortunately there are constructive channels opening out into which
the balked social feelings of the American Negro can flow freely.
Without them there would be much more pressure and danger
than there is. These compensating interests are racial but in a new
and enlarged way. One is the consciousness of acting as the advance-
guard of the African peoples in their contact with Twentieth Century
civilization; the other, the sense of a mission of rehabilitating the
race in world esteem from that loss of prestige for which the fate and
conditions of slavery have so largely been responsible. Harlem, as we
shall see, is the center of both these movements; she is the home of
the Negro's "Zionism." The pulse of the Negro world has begun to
beat in Harlem. A Negro newspaper carrying news material in
English, French and Spanish, gathered from all quarters of America,
the West Indies and Africa, has maintained itself in Harlem for over
five years. Two important magazines, both edited from New York,
maintain their news and circulation consistently on a cosmopolitan
scale. Under American auspices and backing, three pan-African
congresses have been held abroad for the discussion of common interests, colonial questions and the future cooperative development
of Africa. In terms of the race question as a world problem, the Negro
mind has leapt, so to speak, upon the parapets of prejudice and extended its cramped horizons. In so doing it has linked up with the
growing group consciousness of the dark-peoples and is gradually

learning their common interests. As one of our writers has recently put it: "It is imperative that we understand the white world in its relations to the non-white world." As with the Jew, persecution is making the Negro international.

As a world phenomenon this wider race consciousness is a different thing from the much asserted rising tide of color. Its inevitable causes are not of our making. The consequences are not necessarily damaging to the best interests of civilization. Whether it actually brings into being new Armadas of conflict or argosies of cultural exchange and enlightenment can only be decided by the attitude of the dominant races in an era of critical change. With the American Negro his new internationalism is primarily an effort to recapture contact with the scattered peoples of African derivation. Garveyism may be a transient, if spectacular, phenomenon, but the possible role of the American Negro in the future development of Africa is one of the most constructive and universally helpful missions that any modern people can lay claim to.

Constructive participation in such causes cannot help giving the Negro valuable group incentives, as well as increased prestige at home and abroad. Our greatest rehabilitation may possibly come through such channels, but for the present, more immediate hope rests in the revaluation by white and black alike of the Negro in terms of his artistic endowments and cultural contributions, past and prospective. It may be increasingly recognized that the Negro has aleady made very substantial contributions, not only in his folk-art, music especially, which has always found appreciation, but in larger, though humbler and less acknowledged ways. For generations the Negro has been the peasant matrix of that section of America which has most undervalued him, and here he has contributed not only materially in labor and in social patience, but spiritually as well. The South has unconsciously absorbed the gift of his folk-temperament. In less than half a generation it will be easier to recognize this, but the fact remains that a leaven of humor, sentiment, imagination and tropic nonchalance has gone into the making of the South from a humble, unacknowledged source. A second crop of the Negro's gifts promises still more largely. He now becomes a conscious contributor and lays aside the status of a beneficiary and ward for that of a collaborator and participant in American civilization. The great social gain in this is the releasing of our talented group from the arid fields of controversy and debate to the productive fields of creative expression. The especially cultural recognition they win should in turn prove the key to that revaluation of the Negro which must precede or accompany any considerable further betterment of race relationships. But whatever the general effect, the present generation will have added the motives of self-expression and spiritual development to the old and still unfinished task of making material headway and progress. No one who understandingly faces the situation with its substantial accomplishment or views the new scene with its still more abundant promise can be entirely without hope. And certainly, if in our lifetime the Negro should not be able to celebrate his full initiation into American democracy, he can at least, on the warrant of these things, celebrate the attainment of a significant and satisfying new phase of group development, and with it a spiritual Coming of Age.

*George S. Schuyler was a significant black journalist in the 1920's. His caustic wit earned him the nickname "the black Mencken." The following article and exchange with Langston Hughes aptly illustrate a major division of opinion among black intellectuals about black culture.*

# The Negro-Art Hokum

### *By George S. Schuyler*

NEGRO ART "made in America" is as non-existent as the widely advertised profundity of Cal Coolidge, the "seven years of progress" of Mayor Hylan, or the reported sophistication of New Yorkers. Negro art there has been, is, and will be among the numerous black nations of Africa, but to suggest the possibility of any such development among the ten million colored people in this republic is self-evident foolishness. Eager apostles from Greenwich Village, Harlem, and environs proclaimed a great renaissance of Negro art just around the corner waiting to be ushered on the scene by those whose hobby is taking races, nations, peoples, and movements under their wing. New art forms expressing the "peculiar" psychology of the Negro were about to flood the market. In short, the art of Homo Africanus was about to electrify the waiting world. Skeptics patiently waited. They still wait.

True, from dark-skinned sources have come those slave songs based on Protestant hymns and Biblical texts known as the spirituals, work songs and secular songs of sorrow and tough luck known as the blues, that outgrowth of rag-time known as jazz (in the development of which whites have assisted), and the Charleston, an eccentric dance invented by the gamins around the public market-place in Charleston, S. C. No one can or does deny this. But these are contributions of a caste in a certain section of the country. They are foreign to Northern Negroes, West Indian Negroes, and African Negroes. They are no more expressive or characteristic of the Negro race than the music and dancing of the Appalachian highlanders or the Dalmatian

From *Nation,* CXXII (June 16, 1926), 662–663.

peasantry are expressive or characteristic of the Caucasian race. If one wishes to speak of the musical contributions of the peasantry of the South, very well. Any group under similar circumstances would have produced something similar. It is merely a coincidence that this peasant class happens to be of a darker hue than the other inhabitants of the land. One recalls the remarkable likeness of the minor strains of the Russian mujiks to those of the Southern Negro.

As for the literature, painting, and sculpture of Aframericans— such as there is—it is identical in kind with the literature, painting, and sculpture of white Americans: that is, it shows more or less evidence of European influence. In the field of drama little of any merit has been written by and about Negroes that could not have been written by whites. The dean of the Aframerican literati is W. E. B. DuBois, a product of Harvard and German universities; the foremost Aframerican sculptor is Meta Warwick Fuller, a graduate of leading American art schools and former student of Rodin; while the most noted Aframerican painter, Henry Ossawa Turner, is dean of American painters in Paris and has been decorated by the French Government. Now the work of these artists is no more "expressive of the Negro soul"—as the gushers put it—than are the scribblings of Octavus Cohen or Hugh Wilers.

This, of course, is easily understood if one stops to realize that the Aframerican is merely a lampblackened Anglo-Saxon. If the European immigrant after two or three generations of exposure to our schools, politics, advertising, moral crusades, and restaurants becomes indistinguishable from the mass of Americans of the older stock (despite the influence of the foreign-language press), how much truer must it be of the sons of Ham who have been subjected to what the uplifters call Americanism for the last three hundred years. Aside from his color, which ranges from very dark brown to pink, your American Negro is just plain American. Negroes and whites from the same localities in this country talk, think, and act about the same. Because a few writers with a paucity of themes have seized upon imbecilities of the Negro rustics and clowns and palmed them off as authentic and characteristic Aframerican behavior, the common notion that the black American is so "different" from his white neighbor has gained wide currency. The mere mention of the word "Negro" conjures up in the average white American's mind a composite stereotype of Bert Williams, Aunt Jemima, Uncle Tom, Jack Johnson, Florian Slappey, and the various monstrosities scrawled by the cartoonists. Your average Aframerican no more resembles this stereotype than the average American resembles a composite of Andy Gump, Jim Jeffries, and a cartoon by Rube Goldberg.

Again, the Aframerican is subject to the same economic and social forces that mold the actions and thoughts of the white Americans. He is not living in a different world as some whites and a few Negroes would have us believe. When the jangling of his Connecticut alarm clock gets him out of his Grand Rapids bed to a breakfast similar to that eaten by his white brother across the street; when he toils at the same or similar work in mills, mines, factories, and commerce alongside the descendants of Spartacus, Robin Hood, and Erik the Red; when he wears similar clothing and speaks the same language with the same degree of perfection; when he reads the same Bible and belongs to the Baptist, Methodist, Episcopal, or Catholic church; when his fraternal affiliations also include the Elks, Masons, and Knights of Pythias; when he gets the same or similar schooling, lives in the same kind of houses, owns the same makes of cars (or rides in them), and nightly sees the same Hollywood version of life on the screen; when he smokes the same brands of tobacco and avidly peruses the same puerile periodicals; in short, when he responds to the same political, social, moral, and economic stimuli in precisely the same manner as his white neighbor, it is sheer nonsense to talk about "racial differences" as between the American black man and the American white man. Glance over a Negro newspaper (it is printed in good Americanese) and you will find the usual quota of crime news, scandal, personals, and uplift to be found in the average white newspaper—which, by the way, is more widely read by the Negroes than is the Negro press. In order to satisfy the cravings of an inferiority complex engendered by the colorphobia of the mob, the readers of the Negro newspaper are given a slight dash of racialistic seasoning. In the homes of the black and white Americans of the same cultural and economic level one finds similar furniture, literature, and conversation. How, then, can the black American be expected to produce art and literature dissimilar to that of the white American?

Consider Coleridge-Taylor, Edward Wilmot Blyden, and Claude McKay, the Englishmen; Pushkin, the Russian; Bridgewater, the Pole; Antar, the Arabian; Latino, the Spaniard; Dumas, *père* and *fils*, the Frenchmen; and Paul Laurence Dunbar, Charles W. Chesnutt, and James Weldon Johnson, the Americans. All Negroes; yet their

work shows the impress of nationality rather than race. They all reveal the psychology and culture of their environment—their color is
incidental. Why should Negro artists of America vary from the national artistic norm when Negro artists in other countries have not
done so? If we can foresee what kind of white citizens will inhabit
this neck of the woods in the next generation by studying the sort of
education and environment the children are exposed to now, it should
not be difficult to reason that the adults of today are what they are
because of the education and environment they were exposed to a
generation ago. And that education and environment were about the
same for blacks and whites. One contemplates the popularity of the
Negro-art hokum and murmurs, "How come?"

This nonsense is probably the last stand of the old myth palmed
off by Negrophobists for all these many years, and recently rehashed
by the sainted Harding, that there are "fundamental, eternal, and
inescapable differences" between white and black Americans. That
there are Negroes who will lend this myth a helping hand need occasion no surprise. It has been broadcast all over the world by the
vociferous scions of slaveholders, "scientists" like Madison Grant and
Lothrop Stoddard, and the patriots who flood the treasury of the Ku
Klux Klan; and it is believed, even today, by the majority of free,
white citizens. On this baseless premise, so flattering to the white
mob, that the blackamoor is inferior and fundamentally different, is
erected the postulate that he must needs be peculiar; and when he
attempts to portray life through the medium of art, it must of necessity be a peculiar art. While such reasoning may seem conclusive to
the majority of Americans, it must be rejected with a loud guffaw by
intelligent people.

*Langston Hughes, often referred to as the "Poet Laureate of Harlem," is possibly the best-known black poet of America. His poetry won him numerous awards and, at the time of his death in 1967, twelve volumes of his poetry had been published. In the following article, he rebuts George Schuyler's view of black culture.*

# The Negro Artist and the Racial Mountain

## By Langston Hughes

ONE OF THE most promising of the young Negro poets said to me once, "I want to be a poet—not a Negro poet," meaning, I believe, "I want to write like a white poet"; meaning subconsciously, "I would like to be a white poet"; meaning behind that, "I would like to be white." And I was sorry the young man said that, for no great poet has ever been afraid of being himself. And I doubted then that, with his desire to run away spiritually from his race, this boy would ever be a great poet. But this is the mountain standing in the way of any true Negro art in America—this urge within the race toward whiteness, the desire to pour racial individuality into the mold of American standardization, and to be as little Negro and as much American as possible.

But let us look at the immediate background of this young poet. His family is of what I suppose one would call the Negro middle class: people who are by no means rich yet never uncomfortable nor hungry—smug, contented, respectable folk, members of the Baptist church. The father goes to work every morning. He is a chief steward at a large white club. The mother sometimes does fancy sewing or supervises parties for the rich families of the town. The children go to a mixed school. In the home they read white papers and magazines. And the mother often says "Don't be like niggers" when the children are bad. A frequent phrase from the father is, "Look how well a white man does things." And so the word white comes to be unconsciously a symbol of all the virtues. It holds for the children

From *Nation,* CXXII (June 23, 1926), 692–694.

beauty, morality, and money. The whisper of "I want to be white"
runs silently through their minds. This young poet's home is, I believe, a fairly typical home of the colored middle class. One sees
immediately how difficult it would be for an artist born in such a
home to interest himself in interpreting the beauty of his own people.
He is never taught to see that beauty. He is taught rather not to see
it, or if he does, to be ashamed of it when it is not according to Caucasian patterns.

For racial culture the home of a self-styled "high-class" Negro has
nothing better to offer. Instead there will perhaps be more aping
of things white than in a less cultured or less wealthy home. The
father is perhaps a doctor, lawyer, landowner, or politician. The
mother may be a social worker, or a teacher, or she may do nothing
and have a maid. Father is often dark but he has usually married the
lightest woman he could find. The family attend a fashionable church
where few really colored faces are to be found. And they themselves
draw a color line. In the North they go to white theatres and white
movies. And in the South they have at least two cars and a house
"like white folks." Nordic manners, Nordic faces, Nordic hair, Nordic
art (if any), and an Episcopal heaven. A very high mountain indeed
for the would-be racial artist to climb in order to discover himself and
his people.

But then there are the low-down folks, the so-called common element, and they are the majority—may the Lord be praised! The
people who have their nip of gin on Saturday nights and are not too
important to themselves or the community, or too well fed, or too
learned to watch the lazy world go round. They live on Seventh Street
in Washington or State Street in Chicago and they do not particularly
care whether they are like white folks or anybody else. Their joy runs,
bang! into ecstasy. Their religion soars to a shout. Work maybe a little
today, rest a little tomorrow. Play awhile. Sing awhile. O, let's dance!
These common people are not afraid of spirituals, as for a long time
their more intellectual brethren were, and jazz is their child. They
furnish a wealth of colorful, distinctive material for any artist because
they still hold their own individuality in the face of American stan-
dardizations. And perhaps these common people will give to the
world its truly great Negro artist, the one who is not afraid to be
himself. Whereas the better-class Negro would tell the artist what to
do, the people at least let him alone when he does appear. And they
are not ashamed of him—if they know he exists at all. And they accept
what beauty is their own without question.

Certainly there is, for the American Negro artist who can escape
the restrictions the more advanced among his own group would put
upon him, a great field of unused material ready for his art. Without
going outside his race, and even among the better classes with their
"white" culture and conscious American manners, but still Negro
enough to be different, there is sufficient matter to furnish a black
artist with a lifetime of creative work. And when he chooses to touch
on the relations between Negroes and whites in this country with
their innumerable overtones and undertones, surely, and especially
for literature and the drama, there is an inexhaustible supply of
themes at hand. To these the Negro artist can give his racial individuality, his heritage of rhythm and warmth, and his incongruous
humor that so often, as in the Blues, becomes ironic laughter mixed
with tears. But let us look again at the mountain.

A prominent Negro clubwoman in Philadelphia paid eleven dollars
to hear Raquel Meller sing Andalusian popular songs. But she told
me a few weeks before she would not think of going to hear "that
woman," Clara Smith, a great black artist, sing Negro folksongs. And
many an upper-class Negro church, even now, would not dream of
employing a spiritual in its services. The drab melodies in white
folks' hymnbooks are much to be preferred. "We want to worship
the Lord correctly and quietly. We don't believe in 'shouting.' Let's
be dull like the Nordics," they say, in effect.

The road for the serious black artist, then, who would produce a
racial art is most certainly rocky and the mountain is high. Until
recently he received almost no encouragement for his work from
either white or colored people. The fine novels of Chesnutt go out
of print with neither race noticing their passing. The quaint charm
and humor of Dunbar's dialect verse brought to him, in his day,
largely the same kind of encouragement one would give a side-show
freak (A colored man writing poetry! How odd!) or a clown (How
amusing!).

The present vogue in things Negro, although it may do as much
harm as good for the budding colored artist, has at least done this:
it has brought him forcibly to the attention of his own people among
whom for so long, unless the other race had noticed him beforehand,
he was a prophet with little honor. I understand that Charles Gilpin
acted for years in Negro theaters without any special acclaim from his
own, but when Broadway gave him eight curtain calls, Negroes, too,
began to beat a tin pan in his honor. I know a young colored writer,
a manual worker by day, who had been writing well for the colored

magazines for some years, but it was not until he recently broke into the white publications and his first book was accepted by a prominent New York publisher that the "best" Negroes in his city took the trouble to discover that he lived there. Then almost immediately they decided to give a grand dinner for him. But the society ladies were careful to whisper to his mother that perhaps she'd better not come. They were not sure she would have an evening gown.

The Negro artist works against an undertow of sharp criticism and misunderstanding from his own group and unintentional bribes from the whites. "O, be respectable, write about nice people, show how good we are," say the Negroes. "Be stereotyped, don't go too far, don't shatter our illusions about you, don't amuse us too seriously. We will pay you," say the whites. Both would have told Jean Toomer not to write "Cane." The colored people did not praise it. The white people did not buy it. Most of the colored people who did read "Cane" hate it. They are afraid of it. Although the critics gave it good reviews the public remained indifferent. Yet (excepting the work of DuBois) "Cane" contains the finest prose written by a Negro in America. And like the singing of Robeson, it is truly racial.

But in spite of the Nordicized Negro intelligentsia and the desires of some white editors we have an honest American Negro literature already with us. Now I await the rise of the Negro theater. Our folk music, having achieved world-wide fame, offers itself to the genius of the great individual American Negro composer who is to come. And within the next decade I expect to see the work of a growing school of colored artists who paint and model the beauty of dark faces and create with new technique the expressions of their own soul-world. And the Negro dancers who will dance like flame and the singers who will continue to carry our songs to all who listen— they will be with us in even greater numbers tomorrow.

Most of my own poems are racial in theme and treatment, derived from the life I know. In many of them I try to grasp and hold some of the meanings and rhythms of jazz. I am sincere as I know how to be in these poems and yet after every reading I answer questions like these from my own people: Do you think Negroes should always write about Negroes? I wish you wouldn't read some of your poems to white folks. How do you find anything interesting in a place like a cabaret? Why do you write about black people? You aren't black. What makes you do so many jazz poems?

But jazz to me is one of the inherent expressions of Negro life in

America: the eternal tom-tom beating in the Negro soul—the tom-tom of revolt against weariness in a white world, a world of subway trains, and work, work, work; the tom-tom of joy and laughter, and pain swallowed in a smile. Yet the Philadelphia clubwoman is ashamed to say that her race created it and she does not like me to write about it. The old subconscious "white is best" runs through her mind. Years of study under white teachers, a lifetime of white books, pictures, and papers, and white manners, morals, and Puritan standards made her dislike the spirituals. And now she turns up her nose at jazz and all its manifestations—likewise almost everything else distinctly racial. She doesn't care for the Winold Reiss portraits of Negroes because they are "too Negro." She does not want a true picture of herself from anybody. She wants the artist to flatter her, to make the white world believe that all Negroes are as smug and as near white in soul as she wants to be. But, to my mind, it is the duty of the younger Negro artist, if he accepts any duties at all from outsiders, to change through the force of his art that old whispering "I want to be white," hidden in the aspirations of his people, to "Why should I want to be white? I am a Negro—and beautiful!"

So I am ashamed for the black poet who says, "I want to be a poet, not a Negro poet," as though his own racial world were not as interesting as any other world. I am ashamed, too, for the colored artist who runs from the painting of Negro faces to the painting of sunsets after the manner of the academicians because he fears the strange un-whiteness of his own features. An artist must be free to choose what he does, certainly, but he must also never be afraid to do what he might choose.

Let the blare of Negro jazz bands and the bellowing voice of Bessie Smith singing Blues penetrate the closed ears of the colored near-intellectuals until they listen and perhaps understand. Let Paul Robeson singing Water Boy, and Rudolph Fisher writing about the streets of Harlem, and Jean Toomer holding the heart of Georgia in his hands, and Aaron Douglas drawing strange black fantasies cause the smug Negro middle class to turn from their white, respectable, ordinary books and papers to catch a glimmer of their own beauty. We younger Negro artists who create now intend to express our individual dark-skinned selves without fear or shame. If white people are pleased we are glad. If they are not, it doesn't matter. We know we are beautiful. And ugly too. The tom-tom cries and the tom-tom laughs. If colored people are pleased we are glad. If they are not, their displeasure doesn't matter either. We build our temples for tomorrow, strong as we know how, and we stand on top of the mountain, free within ourselves.

## Correspondence: Negroes and Artists

To THE EDITOR OF THE NATION:

SIR: Langston Hughes, defending racial art in America, forgets that the Negro masses he describes are no different from the white masses we are all familiar with. Both "watch the lazy world go round" and "have their nip of gin on Saturday nights" (love of strong liquors is supposed to be a Nordic characteristic). If there is anything "racial" about the spirituals and the blues, then there should be immediate ability to catch the intricate rhythm on the part of Negroes from Jamaica, Zanzibar, and Sierra Leone. Such is not the case, and we must conclude that they are the products of a certain American environment: the South. They are American folk-songs, built around Anglo-Saxon religious concepts.

An artist, it seems to me, is one who, able to see life about him, and, struck by its quick interchange of comedy, drama, and tragedy, attempts to portray it or interpret it in music, poetry, or prose, on canvas or in stone. He can only use the equipment furnished him by education and environment. Consequently his creation will be French, British, German, Russian, Zulu, or Chinese, depending on where he lives. The work of the artist raised and educated in this country must necessarily be American.

It is the Aframerican masses who consume several millions' worth of hair-straightener and skin-whitener per annum in an effort to reach the American standard in pigmentation and hair-texture. This does not look as if they did not care whether they were like white folks or not. Negro propaganda-art, even when glorifying the "primitiveness" of the American Negro masses, is hardly more than a protest against a feeling of inferiority, and such a psychology seldom produces art.

*Atlanta, Georgia, June 21*                    GEORGE S. SCHUYLER


To THE EDITOR OF THE NATION:

SIR: For Mr. Schuyler to say that "the Negro masses . . . are no different from the white masses" in America seems to me obviously absurd. Fundamentally, perhaps, all people are the same. But as long as the Negro remains a segregated group in this country he must reflect certain racial and environmental differences which are his own. The very fact that Negroes do straighten their hair and try to forget their racial background makes them different from white people. If they were exactly like the dominant class they would not have to try so hard to imitate them. Again it seems quite as absurd to say that spirituals and blues are not Negro as it is to say that cowboy songs are not cowboy songs or that the folk-ballads of Scotland do not belong to Scotland. The spirituals and blues are American, certainly, but they are also very much American Negro. And if one can say that some of my poems have no racial distinctiveness about them or that "Cane" is not Negro one can say with equal truth that "Nize Baby" is purely American.

From an economic and sociological viewpoint it may be entirely desirable that the Negro become as much like his white American brother as possible. Surely colored people want all the opportunities and advantages that anybody else possesses here in our country. But until America has completely absorbed the Negro and until segregation and racial self-consciousness have entirely disappeared, the true work of art from the Negro artist is bound, if it have any color and distinctiveness at all, to reflect his racial background and his racial environment.

*New York, June 14*                                          LANGSTON HUGHES

*Eugene Gordon was a frequent contributor to the pop-
ular magazines. His major interest was the classes within
black society, a subject white audiences knew little about.*

# Negro Society

## By Eugene Gordon

LAST SUMMER a friend of mine who is in the real estate business gave
his charming daughter, teacher in a Boston graded school, in marriage to a youth who held a Phi Beta Kappa key and an A.B. from
Dartmouth and a diploma from the Harvard Medical School. The
wedding took place one evening in a beautifully furnished cottage-
like house near Boston, and everybody concerned owed allegiance to
Afro-America. I noticed among the hundred or more guests lawyers
of large and prosperous clienteles, physicians and surgeons whose
fees support these gentlemen in affluence, a waiter from the Parker
House, a brilliant young pianist, two commercial artists, a chauffeur
for a white business man; students and graduates of Harvard, Welles-
ley, Tufts, Radcliffe, Dartmouth, Fisk, Howard, and Simmons; a red
cap from the South Station, a Pullman porter and his dowager wife,
two stenographers, several girls of flapper type employed in the civil
service, an ex-policeman's wife, a cook for a family of North Shore
Nordics, a half-dozen school-teachers, two officers of the National
Guard, a newspaper editor, a banker, and a miscellany of post-office
workers. Everyone was dressed, of course, strictly à la mode. The
conversation was appropriate to the occasion. And the presents,
which filled a small room upstairs, were typical of those usually given
newlyweds. In short, the scene was a representative one in to-day's
Afro-American society. More important, it was representative too of
scenes rapidly ceasing to exist. Negro society is becoming more discriminating of those who compose it.

Like the whites' the colored man's society is grounded in family
and occupation. Unlike the whites the greater number of colored folk
are unable to boast of family traditions. Some of them can—and do.
The descendants of free Negroes who held slaves have as much to

From *Scribner's Magazine*, LXXXVIII (August 1930), 134–142.

brag about as most of their white compatriots. These will be found in many sections of Virginia, Maryland, South Carolina, and one or two other Southern States. But the masses of colored folk have no such boast. The portion of their family trees that they esteem sprouted since the Civil War, If a black man's grandfather was a senator or a congressman during the Reconstruction, he naturally has more to boast of than the man whose grandfather was a slave, whose father was an illiterate tenant-farmer, and whose mother was a cook in the big house. He, himself, in the third generation since the Civil War, may be a graduate of Harvard, a $60,000-a-year lawyer, an Odd Fellow, an Elk, and an Episcopalian, but he remains non-communicative on matters anent family trees.

There being few who can adorn family trees with pretty tales, the colored folk have had to employ the white man's secondary measurement of social eminence, occupation. There are a few Negro bankers scattered across the country, and some are men of consequence in American affairs. There are also the insurance heads, newspaper owners and publishers, writers, musicians, college professors, school-teachers, civil-service workers, and menials (including domestic servants). There being but a few Afro-Americans of the type that would automatically become one with the highest stratum of Caucasian society, if a miracle wrought such a merger, the black blue-bloods find themselves incapable of outdistancing the climbers.

The observation is frequently made that in Negro society one may find the barber seated beside the bank-president. This is true, but the reason is obvious and near at hand. The most exalted men and women in these colored United States represent individual achievement—save in a very few instances. A black banker is not such through inheritance, but through personal achievement. His father was not a banker but a butler, while his mother scrubbed to help out. That is why, in any large gathering of Afro-American élite, the sheep are found rubbing noses with the goats. The reason the goats are there is that they could not be separated from the sheep. The goat just happens to be the big ram's father or brother or some other close relative.

## II

But the situation is rapidly changing. Class distinctions within the race are multiplying and are being recognized by those affected. Not only that, but class distinctions within the race are being taken as a matter of course.

I have a room in a studio building in Copley Square, Boston. There

I go occasionally to conduct a class in English composition. Descending in the elevator one evening, I was conscious of the frank stare of the only other passenger, white. He stepped out ahead of me, and the black elevator-boy touched my arm.

"Wait a minute, Mr. Gordon," he said. "I want to tell you something."

When the other man was beyond hearing, the boy said indignantly: "See that white fellow that rode down just now?"

"Yes."

"Well, what do you think he asked me up-stairs?"

"Don't know. What?"

"Well, he was lookin' for the freight-elevator man, and he seen you go in the studio, and he started after you. See? And I says to him, I says, 'Say, mister, wait a minute,' I says. 'That ain't the man you want,' I tells him. He stops and looks at me, and he says: 'Isn't that Jimmy?' I says: 'No, that's not Jimmy.' And he says: 'Well, it doesn't matter; he'll do.' He wanted somebody to bring out a box of books and put 'em on the freight-elevator, you know. Now, can you imagine that!"

"What did you say?" I asked.

At the memory of it he spluttered with anger. "What I said? Y'ought to of heard me. I says to him, I says, 'Just because a man's colored he don't have to be nobody's servant,' I says to him. 'That man,' I says, 'is a teacher just like you.' You talk about a dumfounded white man! Why, just because we're colored they think we got to be equals. Believe me, every time I gets a chance I tells 'em. . . ."

Not long ago there was current among certain Nordics a fable to the general purport that the most rarefied of black society would joyfully and without question accept any white woman who condescended to present herself. If ever it was true, it is true no longer. A white face without character or accomplishment to recommend it is without a chance in the best black circles.

In spite of these evidences of tendencies toward class separatism in Afro-America, many whites as well as a considerable number of blacks refuse to recognize the distinctions. So advanced a woman as Marcet Haldeman-Julius wrote the following in the Kansas City *Call,* a colored news-sheet:

"Personally, I have had a great deal to do with Negroes. When I was a child I had a Negro nurse—a real mammy type she was. Her husband tended our yard and furnace. . . . Both of them lived with us until they died, and Mammy Gooch's death was my first real sorrow. I had a colored woman as nurse for my youngest child, Henry. She was from Alabama and could neither read nor write. My cook at this moment is her antithesis—a well-educated, capable, executive-type of woman, and a local leader among her race."

There is no disputing that Mrs. Haldeman-Julius is better informed of the personal qualities of her cook than I am, yet I challenge her allegation that her cook is "a well-educated, capable, executive-type of woman, and a local leader among her race." I agree that the woman may have capability—alone. I admit that she may be well-educated. And I grant her executive ability—alone. But I refuse to accept her *in toto* as presented by her mistress.

Such a woman would without doubt be a leader. She would probably be more than merely "a local leader among her race." But she would not be Mrs. Haldeman-Julius's cook. Instead, she would be a luminary in Kansas City's colored society. She would probably be, with her education and executive ability, head of a hair-straightening manufactory or some like enterprise. And she would *hire* a cook instead of being hired. Of course the reason Mrs. Haldeman-Julius and the man in the studio building entertained their point of view lies in their lack of real acquaintanceship with Negro life.

There are some colored folk with a similar point of view. They know the truth but refuse to accept it. In the first place, they insist, there is no such thing as colored society. Who ever heard of such nonsense? they demand. In the second place, even if there were, what of it? The non-conforming black man will not retreat from the position that he is as good as any other black man alive. Being black, he declares, places them all on the same level. He despises blacks who "think they're white" and "imitate" white society. In Boston recently a colored house-girl refused to accept employment in the home of William H. Lewis, formerly Assistant Attorney-General of the United States, when she learned that he was colored. "I'm just as good as he is," she maintained, demanding return of her fee by the employment bureau.

There are a few of this persisting type, but only a few. The greater number are accepting class separatism as an inevitable corollary of our present social order. And strange, too, the conformists are not illiterates, but of the type of Mrs. Haldeman-Julius's cook.

### III

But, if there be discrimination between the menials and the "leaders," there is little enough discrimination between the various grades of those who compose the leadership. Here the progress of class distinction has been retarded. And the reason is apparent. A line must be drawn somewhere; so it may as well be drawn between the menials, as of the top of the lowest stratum, and the clerks, postmen, and other such workers, as of the bottom of the highest stratum. Thus do the postmen, policemen, clerks, stenographers, schoolteachers, college professors, college presidents, heads of business concerns, bankers, writers, publishers, and professional men compose society. The upper layers of the crust have begun to withdraw into themselves, so that soon there will be several strata instead of, as now, only two. That time will come when the number of wealthy will have increased and when, after several generations, family trees in Afro-America will be sturdier than now.

The accusation that Negro society is patterned upon the white, in imitation of the latter, is only partially true. The average black man of wealth and education has as extensive a background of American civilization as the average white man of wealth and education. Neither knows any other civilization or culture. Both being schooled in American institutions, there is nothing for either to do but conform. There remains for the black man, as for the white, nothing but to assimilate the American culture and to be assimilated into the general scheme. This being true, accusing the Negro of imitation seems to be overlooking important circumstances. Perhaps they will explain how an indigenous growth can be imitative of its own soil. The same sets of circumstances that produce white Babbits and Ku-Kluxers and Odd Fellows produce also their black antitypes; if not actually, then in spirit. Throughout the social columns of the Afro-American press this truth is repeatedly exemplified; as in the following excerpts.

From Chicago:

"Mr. and Mrs. Robert S. Abbott were host and hostess to the fashionable Paramount Club on Saturday last. A full club attendance, except for the Charles S. Thompsons, was out. Prize-winners were Judge and Mrs. Albert B. George, Dr. Bousfield, Theodore Jones, and Mrs. Charles Dodson. The Abbotts were, as usual, most gracious in their rôles, and all present spent a most enjoyable evening."

The Abbotts, incidentally, are owners of the Chicago *Defender*, most widely circulated news-sheet in Afro-America. They live in a fine mansion in an "exclusive" neighborhood of whites. The gentleman, it is said, owns a Rolls-Royce touring-car and his wife a Pierce-Arrow roadster. They entertained the President of Haiti and Madame

Borno when the head of the Caribbean republic visited this country last year. They are undisputed leaders of Chicago colored society; and, because of the prestige that usually attends a wealthy newspaper-publisher, the Abbotts are top-liners in society wherever they go in these colored United States. . . .

Cleveland presents this:

"A. L. Bryant, foreman of E. Ramsay's tonsorial parlor, Cedar Avenue at 101st Street, was all smiles Friday. The 'stork special' arrived at the Maternity Hospital of Western Reserve University and left a fine bouncing baby son, A. L., Jr. Mother and son are doing fine. Mrs. Bryant was formerly Miss Dot Rose, of Columbus, but more recently stenographer in the office of Chandler and White, attorneys."

And, finally, from Boston:

"The Blue Birds Social Club held a chitterling and pigs'-feet supper in the vestry of the Halleluiah Baptist Church last Friday night. Among the guests were Rev. Smitten, Brother John Ball, Red Caps William Johns and Bently Turner, and the ever-popular proprietor of the Star Pressing Club, 'Jokesmith' Blue."

IV

Where, if anywhere, is the social capital of these colored United States? Harlem claims the honor; Washington challenges the claim. Chicago presents some stalwart arguments, and so do Pittsburgh and Philadelphia. Boston does not say very much. Washington's challenge is thrust into the face of Harlem by the social arbiter of Howard University, Professor Kelly Miller:

"Washington is the social capital of the Negro race. Social celebrities from all over the country find fulfilment of their highest ambition to shine at some great function in the national capital. Every four years a President of the United States is inaugurated. The occasion is usually featured by an inaugural ball. Although the Negroes may have little cause for jubilation over the incoming administration, they usually have two or three inaugural balls, whereas the whites are satisfied with one. . . . The capital city furnishes the best opportunity and facilities for the expression of the Negro's innate gaiety of soul. Washington is still the Negro's heaven, and it will be many a moon before Harlem will be able to take away the sceptre."

Harlem refuses to argue the question at length, for there is no community in the world more self-satisfied, more self-sufficient, more self-sustaining. And no challenger knows this better than Washington.

Harlem is letting her actions speak for her. And they *do* speak—eloquently. Visit a fashion show at Rockland Palace, or drop in on one of the dinner-parties given by the daughter and heiress of the late Madame Walker, of hair-grower fame, or get invited to James Weldon Johnson's flat and sit on the floor in the midst of weighty intellects, or—Washington, Harlem, Chicago, Pittsburgh, Atlanta; Hop Toad, Texas; Norfolk; Assbray, Ga.; and Braggadocio, S. C., have each a social circle which each thinks supreme.

v

The chief difference, as pointed out already, between the whites' and the blacks' society of the upper reaches lies in the *omnium-gatherum* composition of the blacks'. Effort is being made from the top, and observed with tolerant unconcern from the bottom, to make lines between social classes more sharply distinct. But the consummation of this effort, aimless and wavering as it is, is afar off. The occupational diversions of Afro-America are too conglomerate, reaching from the sewer to the cathedral spire, as they do, and being connected by blood-ties, as they are, to permit of indiscriminate discrimination. Thus, at an exclusive dinner-party, it often happens that the roster of guests represents an *olla podrida* of Afro-Americana. Beside a bishop of the African Methodist Episcopal Church sits a lady whose delicate hands daily manipulate the kink-remover pliers. The good bishop may have an opinion about such promiscuity, but he is both a gentleman and a man of sense. He says not a word. There being no social register, it is left to the hostess's intuition and rather doubtful sense of values to determine who shall and who shall not grace her board. No one with so much as three thousand dollars in cash, regardless as to how this fabulous sum was accumulated, may be ignored. In a case of this sort there is no alternative. And some manipulators of the hair-iron are ladies of wealth and power. Besides, you've got to let *somebody* in. It is all right, perhaps, to exclude the truck-driver, if you want to be nastily snobbish, and the ashman, and the offal-cart attendant; but, good Lord, use discretion! Besides, the hair-dresser's son may be a professor at Howard, her daughter a graduate of Radcliffe, with a Ph.D. from the Sorbonne, and her husband an editor of an influential journal. Not only has she three thousand dollars in her own right, but she has achieved spiritually—if you get the meaning; and achievement, no matter how futile it may seem to the complacent Caucasian, is fittingly esteemed in these colored United States. Granting Washington to be typical of the best, let us consider her.

In Washington the top cream of colored society—as in most other places—is a thick layer of doctors and lawyers, with a somewhat thinner layer of Howard University officials, a still thinner and less important layer of teachers in the public schools, and a somewhat watery sediment of government workers. The top of the cream is tacitly acknowledged to be the doctors and the lawyers. No one ever disputes that. If anyone did he would be suspected of all kinds of depravity. Some of the social notes printed in the *Tribune* and the *Eagle* of that fair city read like rosters from medical and law school reviews.

The houses these aristocrats occupy are well built and imposing, but old. Inside, examination would reveal most of them to be over-run with cockroaches and mice. Not one of this gentry owns a house built for his own use. They are all content merely to chase out the ha-rassed Nordic and to grab what he leaves. Some of the most moneyed of these folk are becoming more so through real estate operations. Many lawyers and some doctors are turning realtors, but they are not losing caste thereby. They purchase the deserted mansions lately occupied by Klansmen's families and sell them for double and treble their worth to such of their own race as will pay the prices.

Most of the matrons of the Washington set are ludicrously snob-bish—but so are the men. A majority of the women too possess Caucasian exteriors. To be able to "pass" is almost a requisite. It is an invaluable asset in a town where rests the centre of government of all the people, and where the congressmen and the senators spend their overtime thinking up new ways to humiliate the uppish darkies. So the matron of the smart colored set, with her fair skin and her in-variably beautiful face, sits beside the gentleman from Arkansas in Keith's or dines opposite him at the Mayflower, or even relieves him of his seat in a trolley, since these gentlemen will not under any circumstances see a "white" woman stand in a public conveyance. The experiences encountered thus by the Afro-American elite serve as morsels for gossip at many a five-hundred party, or bridge game, or informal luncheon.

Some of the most conspicuous of the male members of society are conspicuous because of the contrast they make beside their fair-skinned ladies. It is not nearly so important that the man be "passable" as that the woman be so. A black man, as a rule, if he be any-body at all, may climb to the very top of the social ladder; this is seldom true with respect to the woman. The woman in every racial group, apparently, is socially more ambitious than the man. In this country the dominating group has set a standard of beauty, and it is the steadfast conviction of every woman, be she white or non-white, that she must conform to it. And that accounts for the almost pathetic attempt of the darker women to bleach the skin and to straighten the hair. Submerged in a group of a hundred million, the colored woman feels that her salvation lies in being as nearly as possible like the women for whom fashions are designed and beauty cults main-tained. It is a question of survival, not one of simple imitation; as a matter of fact, it is not imitation at all, but conformity with the customs of their country.

An important ingredient of the Afro-American social melange in Washington is the coterie of lawyers holding public office. In former years these have included the Register of the Treasury; to-day they are the recorder of deeds of the District of Columbia, a judge of the municipal court, and an assistant to the attorney-general. The acknowledged leaders of colored society in Washington now are Congressman and Mrs. Oscar De Priest, of Chicago.

It might be supposed that the Haitian minister to the United States would be a ringleader in Washington colored society; most em-phatically he is not. Not that he would not be welcomed; society has more than once made invitatory gestures in his direction. But, being observant of the situation that obtains between black and white in the Land of the Free, the Haitian minister knows that if he ever crossed the social line into Afro-America he would find difficulty in returning. This is so, despite the ugly truth that the cultural level of Washington's colored society is flush with that to which the Haitian minister and his family are accredited. Therefore, that gentleman steers clear, accepting invitations from colored Washington only when the occasion is publicly in the open, like the inauguration, for example, of Howard University's colored president. The Haitian minister was present at that event; but so were the Secretary of War and the Secretary of the Interior.

About twelve years ago Maurice Menos, son of the dark-skinned Solon Menos, at that time minister from Haiti, eloped to Baltimore and was married to the daughter of a socially ambitious white family from Virginia. Colored Washington gasped; clasped its hands and waited to see what would happen. Nothing happened beyond the usual when a member of the diplomatic corps takes an American wife. The couple got the usual amount of newspaper space, and the young woman got into the "Social Register." The point is that colored Washington considered it a sort of personal triumph; but, of course, it was nothing of the sort. If young Menos bore toward colored Washington anything other than indifference, no one saw it.

Below the doctors and the lawyers come the school-teachers. Some of the most beautiful women of the country are undoubtedly to be found teaching in Washington's schools; and I refer to alleged Negro women. Of a lower social order, many of them graduate into the upper strata by getting married to doctors and lawyers. They make excellent matrons and dowagers, often completely eclipsing the pretty *dumm belles* whom the society gentlemen married because they *were* pretty.

The government workers and the menials are the mainstay of the upper crusts, the former, of course, being away out of sight above the latter. As for the washerwomen, the cart-drivers, the elevator-operators, and the other essential but thoroughly snubbed multitudes, they go their way in sweet contentment. They have few if any complaints to make. Now and then their ire may be stirred by the supercilious behavior of an erstwhile associate who, being pretty, has captured a doctor or a lawyer. But they soon forgive her and rejoice in her good fortune. It means progress when even one succeeds in scaling the heights. It means that the "culud fo'ks is gittin' mo' lak de w'ite fo'ks evah day," and that, I assure you, in a world where white is the badge of the redeemed and black that of the damned, where snobbery and class distinctions and tinsel riches are the new Baal to be fearfully worshipped—that, I say, is something to aspire to! And as goes Washington so goes the rest of it.

# ECONOMICS

*George Edmund Haynes received his Ph.D. in sociology
from Columbia University in 1912. He developed a department of sociology at Fisk University where he was
a professor from 1910 to 1920. His extensive research into
Negro migration eventually led to the creation of the
National Urban League, an organization devoted to aid-
ing black migrants to Northern industrial cities.*

# Conditions Among Negroes in the Cities

By *George Edmund Haynes*

### THE ECONOMIC SEQUEL

THREE FACTS should be placed in the foreground in looking at the
economic conditions of the segregated Negro in the city. First, the
masses of those who have migrated to town are unprepared to meet
the exacting requirements of organized industry, and the keen competition of more efficient laborers. Second, organized facilities for
training these inefficient, groping seekers for something better are
next to nothing in practically all the cities to which they are flock-
ing. They, therefore, drift hit or miss into any occupations which
are held out to their unskilled hands and untutored brains. Natural
aptitude enables many to "pick up" some skill, and these succeed
in gaining a stable place. But the thousands work from day to day
with that weak tenure and frequent change of place from which
all unskilled, unorganized laborers suffer under modern industry and
trade.

The third fact of prime importance is the prejudice of the white
industrial world, which the Negro must enter to earn his food, shelter
and raiment. This prejudice, when displayed by employers, is partly
due to the inefficiency indicated above and the failure to discriminate between the efficient individual and this untrained throng.
When exhibited by fellow wage-earners, it is partly due to fear of
probable successful competitors and to the belief that the Negro

From *Annals of the American Academy of Political and Social Science*, XLIX (September
1913), 112–114.

has "his place" fixed by a previous condition of servitude. But in the cases of many employers and employees, as shown in numbers of instances carefully investigated, the opposition to the Negro in industrial pursuits is due to a whimsical dislike of any workman who is not white and especially of one who is black!

The general result of this inefficiency, of this lack of facilities and guidance for occupational training which would overcome the defect, and of this dwarfing prejudice is far-reaching. In both Northern and Southern cities the result is a serious limitation of the occupational field for Negroes, thus robbing them of better income and depriving the community of a large supply of valuable potential labor. Examination of occupational statistics for Northern cities shows that from about three-fourths to about nine-tenths of Negro males engaged in gainful occupations are employed in domestic and personal service. Workmen in industries requiring skill are so well organized in the North that Negroes in any numbers must enter the trades through union portals. Only in late years, and frequently at the time of strikes, as in the building trades' strike of 1900, the stockyards' strike of 1904, and the teamsters' strike of 1905 in Chicago, has the Negro been recognized as a fellow-workman whose interests are common with the cause of organized labor. A large assortment of testimony lately gathered by Atlanta University from artisans and union officials in all parts of the country gives firm ground for the conclusion that, except in some occupations, largely the building and mining trades, white union men are yet a long distance from heartily receiving Negro workmen on equal terms.

In Southern cities Negro labor is the main dependence and manual labor is slow to lose the badge of servitude. But for selected occupations in Southern cities between 1890 and 1900 the rate of increase in domestic and personal service occupations among Negroes was greater than those in manufacturing and mechanical pursuits, and than those in trade and transportation, if draymen, hackmen, and teamsters are omitted from the last classification. The occupations of barbering, whitewashing, laundering, etc., are being absorbed by white men. The white firemen of the Georgia Railroad and Queen and Crescent Railway struck because these companies insisted upon giving Negro firemen employment on desirable trains. These are indications of a possible condition when the desire of white men for places held by Negroes becomes a matter of keen competition. An able writer on the Negro problem has asserted that in the South the Negroes can get any work "under the sun." But since an in-creasing proportion of modern industry is conducted in the shade, the Southern city Negro of tomorrow may find it as difficult to wedge his way into the better paid occupations as does his black brother in the North now.

When it comes to the question of business experience and oppor-tunity, the sea is still thicker with reefs and shoals. A Negro who wants training and experience in some line of business so that he may begin some enterprise of his own, finds, except in very rare cases, the avenues to positions in white establishments which would give him this experience closed. The deadline of his desire is a messen-ger's place or a porter's job. How can a porter learn to run a mer-cantile establishment or a messenger understand how to manage a bank? His only alternative, inexperienced as he may be, is to risk his meager savings in venturing upon an unsounded sea. Shipwreck is necessarily the rule, and successful voyage the exception.

The successes, however, in both industry and trade are multi-plying, and with substantial encouragement may change the rule to exception in the teeth of excessive handicaps. There was an in-crease between 1890 and 1900 of 11.6 per cent of Negroes engaged in selected skilled and semi-skilled occupations in Southern cities. In 1910 the executive council of the American Federation of Labor unan-imously passed a resolution inviting Negroes, along with other races, into its ranks. Some of its affiliated bodies have shown active sym-pathy with this sentiment, and have taken steps in different cities to bring in Negro workmen. All of eleven Negro inventors of 1911 were city dwellers. The "Freedmen's Bank," which had branches in about thirty-five cities and towns, failed in 1873. During its exis-tence it held deposits of over $50,000,000 of savings of the freedmen. Although the confidence of the freedmen was shaken to its founda-tion, they have rallied and in 1911 there were 64 private Negro banks in the towns and cities of the country. Many of these are thriving institutions. There is no means of knowing the number and importance of other Negro business enterprises. But judging from studies of Negro business enterprises made in Philadelphia and in New York City, and from the widespread attendance upon the annual meetings of the National Negro Business League, sub-stantial progress is triumphing over unusual obstacles.

*The following unsigned article typifies the Southern Workman's interest in publishing examples of black Horatio Alger stories.*

# An Upward Climb

THE STORY of the growth and success of the *Chicago Defender* reads almost like fiction. A few years ago its circulation was of such a size that the entire weekly output could be—and was—carried under the arm of its owner and publisher, Robert S. Abbott, LL.B. To-day the circulation has reached 175,000 and is still growing.

Robert S. Abbott was born in Savannah, Georgia. He is a graduate in the class of '96 of Hampton Institute, where he obtained his knowledge of printing. Following his graduation he accepted a position in a large printing office in Chicago at a salary of $25 per week. He later took a course at the Kent College of Law in Chicago, from which he received the degree of Bachelor of Law.

Mr. Abbott saw the need in the great city of Chicago of an up-to-date progressive newspaper for the colored people, and although without capital, he started the *Chicago Defender* in 1905. His progress was slow in the extreme. There were but few who seemed to sympathize with his ideas and efforts, and week after week he found it a desperate struggle to raise sufficient money to bring out the current issue. At the end of five years, the weekly had gained a circulation of 5000, and the office force consisted of two girls and a boy, the latter being Phil A. Jones, who is to-day general manager of the Robert S. Abbott Publishing Company, Inc. By 1917 the *Defender* had outgrown its offices until the entire two floors of its original home, where it started in one back room, were utilized. The circulation mounted higher and higher until the present mark of 175,000 was reached.

Mr. Abbott has recently bought a large building in Indiana Avenue, and has had it remodeled to suit his purposes. Equipment of the latest and best kind was installed. The editorial and departmental rooms were well furnished, and the entire plant is estimated to be worth $200,000. Its equipment includes four linotype machines, each one equipped with two magazines geared to cast seven lines per minute. A stereotype department makes the plates ready for the press at the rate of a page every three minutes. The press on which the *Defender* is printed is a 32-page and color machine, made by the celebrated Goss Printing Press Company of Chicago. It is driven by a 30 H. P. motor and six men are required for its operation. It prints, folds, and counts the papers all in one operation, at a speed of 35,000 copies per hour.

That Robert S. Abbott is a man of keen perception and force is admitted by all who are acquainted with his methods. He is gifted with the ability to select the right individuals for the heads of his various departments, many of whom have literally grown up with the *Chicago Defender* and are to-day sharing its prosperity. Mr. Abbott considers his efficient staff largely responsible for his success.

The loyal support given the *Defender* by people of every section is a fine tribute to its publisher, whose sacrifices during the early stages of his career show the caliber of the man. He faced conditions which would have discouraged ninety-nine men out of every hundred, and his life should be considered an object lesson for all who are willing to strive against adverse conditions in order to reach the top.

Mr. Abbott has always been a most loyal alumnus of Hampton Institute, and has recently contributed $1000 towards the athletic field which Hampton graduates propose to present to their alma mater.

*With the aid of expert sociological information, the Urban League, under Executive Secretary Eugene Kinckle Jones, developed a number of studies demonstrating the problems and progress of Southern blacks who migrated to the North.*

# Negroes, North and South—A Contrast

## By Eugene Kinckle Jones

So ACCUSTOMED are we to accepting generalizations upon the condition of the Negro North and the Negro South that the whole truth is rarely, if ever, known. The picture of the North, painted by early migrants to their friends who stayed in the South, as "a land of plenty," one of "full manhood privileges," of "unbounded opportunities" was and still is in large measure an illusion. So the South is misunderstood by men who have never lived there and have fed only on tales of its horrors. In both sections there are advantages, counterbalanced and frequently nullified by handicaps.

There are, however, certain very definite units by which the status of the Negro North and the Negro South stand out in striking contrast. The usual figures supporting this contrast are familiar to the average reader. Better educational facilities, compulsory education and longer school terms have reduced illiteracy and lifted the average intelligence wherever applied. Naturally $66 per capita spent in 1920 in New York City for the education of its children produces a higher grade of intelligence in the Negro children of New York than does the $1.25 per capita per year spent in South Carolina for Negro education. In home ownership, the Negroes of the South would compare more favorably. In farm ownership no real comparison between North and South is possible for 77.4 per cent of the Negroes in the North live in cities while about 79 per cent of those in the South live in rural districts. Except in such cases as southern New Jersey, southern Illinois and southern Ohio, and certain of the midwestern States such as Kansas and Missouri wholly or in part south-

From *Missionary Review of the World*, XLV (June 1922), 479–482.

ern, the Negro farm owner, like the Negro farmer in the North, is a rarity.

Business development among Negroes in the South has far exceeded that of those in the North. We see this in the growth of life and fire insurance companies and banks and trust companies and building construction by Negro contractors. Negroes in northern cities have concentrated instead of spreading out over the smaller communities. This has tended to enlarge the Negro's business opportunities among his own people. In the South, the urge to economic development has been mainly prejudice which inspired discourtesies, and in frequent cases absolute refusal to serve Negroes. In the North race prejudice was not so conspicuous. The development of real estate concerns, theatrical ventures and insurance companies has had its stimulus more largely in the secondary factor of race pride and in the normal desire of many Negroes to enter business as a vocation, playing upon the factor of race pride and relying upon a Negro market and custom for support.

In the North the Negro possesses the ballot which gives him the usual air of independence that men possessed of suffrage have everywhere. The lack of the ballot in the South keeps the Negro forever "within the veil."

### EXPLODED THEORIES

Some years ago, Negroes who came to the North to live, seeking to improve their lot from an economic and social point of view, were considered by their southern Negro friends as well as by southern whites as deliberately risking their lives because of their supposed inability to acclimate themselves to the rigors of the northern winters. Yet today, we find the Negro death rate in cities like New York, and Springfield, Mass., lower than the Negro death rate in the cities of the South. The difference is more significant because the migrant population in the North is heavily centered around the more advanced age groups where normally the death rate begins to increase. Infant mortality among Negroes in northern cities is lower than in cities of the South.

Ten years ago, the great proportion of Negroes in the North were employed in domestic and personal service. In the South a much larger proportion of Negroes were skilled and able to work at their trades. Following the increase of nearly a million Negroes in the North during the five years of the migration there has come an unprecedented expansion in industry and the professions. The number of doctors, lawyers and clergymen has almost doubled and, of particular significance in contrasting the two sections, they are able when once an opening has been made to advance higher in northern than in southern fields. There are now managers of dressmaking establishments; foremen and forewomen in factories; teachers in the public schools; stenographers and bookkeepers in large business establishments; electrical, mechanical and civil engineers. Many of these occupations are regarded as entirely without the Negroes' sphere in the South. Openings in many of these lines may be said to be due in large measure to the ceaseless effort and educational propaganda both by the Negroes themselves and by sympathetic and farsighted white people.

This change in the northern situation has affected the Southern attitude towards the Negro. At first the South took an attitude of indifference, then of alarm and finally of serious meditation and discussion of the questions involved. Just prior to America's participation in the world's war, when Negroes first began to come from the South, articles frequently appeared in southern dailies to the effect that this increase in migration would rather relieve the South of some of the "problem" and would place on the North a little of the "burden" which the North was wont to accuse the South of handling ineffectually. Later, employment agents representing northern industries were arrested because of their efforts to secure southern Negro workers for northern plants. Prepaid tickets were not delivered to Negroes to whom the railroads were directed to deliver them and trickery was resorted to to prevent Negroes who already had paid for their tickets leaving the South for northern points.

Then followed the rapid growth of the Ku Klux Klan and the development of a counteracting force in the form of inter-racial committees which have labored to establish a better feeling between the two races and for the encouragement of social justice, fairer play and a more equable division between the racial elements in the South of the fruits of progress. This same period has tended to unite the northern and southern elements of the Negro population in a spirit of comradeship.

Some years ago it was not unusual to hear heated discussions among the older Negro families of the North as to the proper treatment of southern Negroes who came North. Any Negro who happened to have seen the light of day north of the Mason and Dixon line considered himself superior to any Negro born in the South no matter what his attainments may have been. Booker T. Washington was considered, especially by many northern Negroes, an enemy of the race because he dared to speak in northern communities in favor of industrial training for Negroes even in the South. This feeling of opposition continued in a measure even after many municipalities of the North had established systems of vocational training for the northern white public school children. Today we see a new situation. One finds the same language used among the intelligent Negroes of Richmond or Atlanta or Jacksonville in regard to Negro aspirations and rights as in the drawing-rooms of the most cultured Negroes of Boston or Chicago. Of course this sectional feeling among Negroes has not entirely disappeared. A few days ago, a young colored woman of good education and progressive ideas, born and reared in New England by parents who came from the South, vehemently stated in my presence, "I just do not like southern colored people. There are only a few that I care anything about!" She thinks that southern Negroes are slothful, indolent and lazy and that these undesirable qualities introduced by southern Negro migrants tend to lower the estimate placed by the community on Negroes already in the North. Here, incidentally, is an evidence of the fact that the propaganda intended for white consumption had had its effect even on the Negro's mind.

It is interesting to note the nativity of some of the leaders of national public thought among Negroes. W. E. B. DuBois, editor of the "Crisis," is a native of Great Barrington, Mass.; James Weldon Johnson, secretary of the National Association for the Advancement of Colored People—Jacksonville, Fla.; George Cleveland Hall, prominent physician and public welfare worker of Chicago—Ypsilanti, Mich.; Dr. E. P. Roberts, former member of the Board of Education, New York City—North Carolina; Dr. W. G. Alexander, member of New Jersey State Legislature—Lynchburg, Va.; Robert S. Abbott, publisher of the "Chicago Defender"—Savannah, Ga.; William H. Lewis, former U. S. Assistant Attorney General—Portsmouth, Va.; Ferdinand Q. Morton, member New York City Civil Service Commission—Mississippi; Mrs. Mary Talbert, former president of the Federation of Colored Women's Clubs—Oberlin, Ohio.

The colored people of America no longer ask a man for information concerning his birthplace. They ask only whether he wishes all manhood rights for his Negro brothers and whether he will be fair and truthful in making representation for the race in high places and in conferences where the masses cannot speak for themselves.

Considerable discussion has been indulged in recently over the question as to whether separate colored schools, especially high schools, would be desirable in the North on the ground that colored teachers would give more encouragement to Negro pupils. The good effects of such a system some have sought to prove by referring to the larger percentage of colored children in attendance at high schools in such border cities as Louisville, Washington, Kansas City, St. Louis, and Baltimore as compared with cities in the North where the students are not separated according to race. While no careful analysis of this question has yet been made—most writers on the subject relying upon observation as a guide—it is significant that in the high schools of Hartford, Connecticut, the colored pupils comprise 2.2 per cent of the school population while the Negro population is only 1.8 per cent. It should be noted that Hartford's migrant Negro population has been mainly adult and therefore has had but slight effect on the high school population.

While the white people of the North and of the South have approached an understanding on sectional matters, the northern and southern Negroes have also come to a better understanding and the Negro population has distributed itself so widely over the country that the Negro has gained admission to discussions on race adjustments where white people from the South and from the North were both present. Time is a great solver of problems and we have lived to see the day when these four groups are represented at common meeting places where mutual problems are discussed and programs worked out. The adjustments are not to be made in a shorter time than it required to work out the theory of race relations. The theories are yet to be universally applied, and the adjustments will take considerable time. But the "way out" is clear.

*This news report effectively illustrates how the subject was treated in popular magazines. It also conveys the general viewpoint of white America toward Negro business.*

# The Negro as a Businessman

IT IS A SIGN of growing race tolerance that the city of Tulsa, Oklahoma, best known by many as the scene of race war, riot, and house-burning in 1921, invited the National Negro Business League to come there for its annual meeting this summer. Dr. Moton, of Tuskegee, in his address, expressed his pleasure that both races joined in the invitation and the welcome, and his pride that with indomitable pluck and determination Tulsa whites and Negroes had joined in restoring the damage done when passion and prejudice ran riot.

This address showed an encouraging, even surprising, advance in the business resources and activity of the colored people. Thus, the seventy-three banks they own and run have since 1918 raised their capitalization from two and a half to six and a quarter million dollars; their own insurance companies have policies in force amounting to a quarter of a billion dollars; the estimated value of property owned by Negroes in America to-day is over $1,800,000,000.

One curious situation in regard to Negro wealth was brought out when Dr. Moton said: "At this moment I am thinking of the vast opportunities in the hands of our people represented by the holdings in oil lands which they possess in Oklahoma, in Texas, in Arkansas, and in Louisiana. What a blessing it would be to our entire race if the boys and girls who are now the legal heirs of this wealth could be developed and trained for its wise direction when they come to maturity. Here alone is sufficient capital to develop many lines of business which Negroes are now prepared to operate."

An example of what can be done by a single hard-working colored man is recalled by the death last month of the "Negro potato king," Julius C. Groves, of Kansas. Born a slave, he died the richest Negro in Kansas. He began to work at forty cents a day; in time, aided

From *Outlook*, CXLI (September 2, 1925), 6.

by his seven sons, he raised and sold in one year 72,150 bushels of potatoes.

But with all the expansion in finance, business, and in the professions, Dr. Moton repeated and emphasized the words of Booker Washington that "the ultimate seat of power in a democracy is with those who own the land." Accordingly, Dr. Moton advised his people to save money, buy land, and raise intelligent families. He is as urgent as was Dr. Washington that passion and agitation for theoretical recognition should be discouraged and effort for improvement and intelligence take their place. As to what the Negro in America wants Dr. Moton said:

> Thoughtful Negroes, whether North or South, in the last analysis, want an equal chance with other American citizens, whether in banking, merchandising, business in general, and even in religious matters. They want for themselves and their children an absolutely equal chance for life, liberty, and the pursuit of happiness unhampered by creed or color, and judged only by the merits of the individual or group. They, like other Americans, want to be dealt with by constituted legal authority. Mobs, lynchings, and burnings have never solved any problem; they have rather aggravated and intensified the feeling of bitterness and hatred.

The spirit of Tuskegee and Hampton is doing much to make the colored race patiently persistent and ambitious to improve morally and intellectually and to become useful citizens.

*Here is another good example of reports dealing with economic progress of black Americans.*

# Your Cab Company

### By Camille Cohen-Jones

OUT IN Oberlin, Ohio, in the seventies, Henry Lee, a colored man, owned and operated for thirty-five years a livery stable with seventy-five horses and two acres of stables. Also he and Martha Moals, whom he married, had thirteen children—six boys and seven girls. One of the boys, Walter, was born January 25, 1871, at Oberlin. From the age of seven years he assisted his father in his business, coming home from school and getting right into the heart of the business.

At the age of sixteen, Walter left school and took full charge of his father's business. Finally, when his father decided to sell out and give each child his share, Walter Howard refused to be given anything. There were too many brothers and sisters and Walter had plans of his own. He had determined to conquer Chicago.

First of all, at the age of twenty-five, Walter married Ella Nora Massey. Then he came to Chicago. After looking the field over he decided on the coal business. He opened up a wholesale and retail coal business and began to do well. But white men did not want this colored competitor and began making it hard for him to buy coal. He found he could no longer order the coal in the car loads as he needed it to meet competition. There was still some money to be made in coal and hundreds of colored men had followed him in that business when he had paved the way for them. But Walter Howard Lee wanted to do bigger business and since the way to grow here was closed, he left the coal business and became the pioneer colored ice man. He opened a wholesale and retail ice business which he managed profitably for some time until again white competitors cut off his supply in the wholesale market. Here again he left behind him a trail of colored ice men who had followed in his footsteps and were doing small but successful business; but Walter Howard Lee wanted

From *The Crisis*, XXXIV (March 1927), 5–6.

bigger business and left the ice business to the men who were satisfied to carry on meagre profits.

That brings us then to the year of 1921 when Frank Gillespie, the Founder-President of the Liberty Life Insurance Company, had his dream and vision. He had no more enthusiastic listener than Walter Howard Lee. When the foundation for the company was laid, Lee went out as an agent and sold $45,000 of the $100,000 stock necessary to begin operating. He worked up from an agent to the position of treasurer, which he still holds in the Liberty Life Insurance Company.

Lee now began some hard thinking because he was not a mere business man: he was a Dreamer in Business, a Prophet of Profits. He wanted to find and open gates instead of sitting down before shut doors. Said Lee to himself: "Now, I have helped to form this big Insurance Company—but it takes employment to keep it up; in order for colored people to be in a position to pay their insurance premiums, they must have work. I have bought stock in the Binga State and the Douglas National Banks but people can not save money unless they have some way of making it. It is up to me to find some more means for colored people in Chicago to earn money." After thinking along these lines, Walter Lee, as a liveryman's son, thought he saw possibilities in the transportation problem of a large city like Chicago. He watched the Yellow Cab and its progress and he wondered why it was that he saw such a great number of Yellow Cabs with white drivers and white owners placed on the South Side where the colored people did the riding. Then too, the Yellow Cab Company served black Chicago when it got ready. It was often too busy.

After much deliberation, Lee decided he would go to the Yellow Cab owners who had a monopoly on making cabs and have a talk with them about starting a colored cab company. He was discouraged from the beginning. They told him that the colored boys could not drive the cabs—unreliable, poor mechanics, etc. In every way they tried to discourage him. Finally, seeing that he still persisted in his plan, they decided to give him a chance. Consequently, he formed a stock company with a few friends the latter part of July, 1923, and placed on the South Side ten maroon colored cabs labeled *"Your Cab Company";* they were well equipped taxis, with colored chauffeurs in uniform, who were courteous in every way. From that day to this the *Your Cab Company* and Walter Howard Lee have been the marvels of Chicago. When you say "Your Cab" you think of Walter Howard Lee; and when you say Walter Lee you think of "Your Cab."

Mr. Lee went deeply into debt in order to prove that a colored cab company could succeed. He did not make a stock campaign—those who believed in him came to him of their own accord; but from the day he placed those ten cabs on the streets of the South Side of Chicago, the business began to pick up. First, the stock was sold for ten dollars a share, par value, paying a dividend of seven per cent on the preferred and paying that dividend right off the reel after operating the first year and every year since.

After having kept his word as to dividends he started to pay off his indebtedness to the companies with which he dealt. This he did from the daily earnings of the cabs. When he placed the first ten cabs, he employed twenty-five persons and they were the real people behind the guns when the success of the *Your Cab Company* is mentioned. Salaries were paid promptly, all claims paid promptly and all notes met promptly.

It is only natural that a company with a man at the head of it with the bull-dog-tenacity-for-the-success-of-the-business should succeed. Today the *Your Cab Company* has a paid capital of $200,000; runs eighty cabs and employs over 250 persons. It has recently gone into its own new Garage and Office Building at 415-21 East Pershing Road and has a weekly pay roll of over $3,500.

Walter Howard Lee still has a vision of more good things. He sees the opening of a *Your Cab Cafeteria*—so the employees will not have to go out to buy their lunches; they will buy right there in the building. A sales force is being organized to sell "*Your Cab*" stock. Another of his visions is the opening of a *Your Cab Tailor Shop:* he has to pay to have the uniforms of the chauffeurs made and that could just as well be done about the place thus giving employment to perhaps fifty or one hundred more boys and girls; there is pressing and repairing to be considered and the chauffeurs' shoes to be looked after; why not right here, under one roof? Best of all, why not here under one roof and all by colored boys and girls, men and women? See the wonderful possibilities of the visions of Walter Howard Lee?

Let us go further with him right now: he has visions of an automobile insurance company—it costs the *Your Cab Company* in the neighborhood of $20,000 per year to keep passengers safe. Why could it not have a company of its own, the premiums going back to it, along with the other cars insured, thus giving employment to more? Then, last but not least, he has in mind, after having completed all other things, to form an investment company—a company owned and operated by the *Your Cab Company* for the purpose of helping the little fellows get into this business in other cities—the little fellows who have visions and no money. And when he has finally completed this and given employment and assistance to thousands in Chicago, then it is possible that the Chicago colored people will let him go and organize along the same lines for other cities; they do not mean to be selfish.

# AMERICAN VALUES

*Booker T. Washington was the most popular and best
known of black leaders from the 1880's until his death in
1915. He was a self-made man who graduated from
Hampton Institute and formed Tuskegee Institute in
Alabama in order to continue his aim of educating black
men for agricultural and vocational work.*

# Signs of Progress Among the Negroes

*By Booker T. Washington*

IN ADDITION to the problem of educating eight million negroes in our
Southern States and ingrafting them into American citizenship, we
now have the additional responsibility, either directly or indirectly,
of educating and elevating about eight hundred thousand others of
African descent in Cuba and Porto Rico, to say nothing of the white
people of these islands, many of whom are in a condition about as
deplorable as that of the negroes. We have, however, one advantage
in approaching the question of the education of our new neighbors.

The experience that we have passed through in the Southern States
during the last thirty years in the education of my race, whose history
and needs are not very different from the history and needs of the
Cubans and Porto Ricans, will prove most valuable in elevating the
blacks of the West Indian Islands. To tell what has already been
accomplished in the South under most difficult circumstances is to
tell what may be done in Cuba and Porto Rico.

To this end let me tell a story.

In what is known as the black belt of the South—that is, where the
negroes outnumber the whites—there lived before the Civil War a
white man who owned some two hundred slaves, and was prosperous.
At the close of the war he found his fortune gone, except that which
was represented in land, of which he owned several thousand acres.
Of the two hundred slaves a large proportion decided, after their
freedom, to continue on the plantation of their former owner.

Some years after the war a young black boy, who seemed to have

From *Century*, LIX (January 1900), 472–478.

"rained down," was discovered on the plantation by Mr. S——, the owner. In daily rides through the plantation Mr. S—— saw this boy sitting by the roadside, and his condition awakened his pity, for, from want of care, he was covered from head to foot with sores, and Mr. S—— soon grew into the habit of tossing him a nickel or a dime as he rode by. In some way this boy heard of the Tuskegee Normal and Industrial Institute in Alabama, and of the advantages which it offered poor but deserving colored men and women to secure an education through their own labor while taking the course of study. This boy, whose name was William, made known to the plantation hands his wish to go to the Tuskegee school. By each one "chipping in," and through the efforts of the boy himself, a few decent pieces of clothing were secured, and a little money, but not enough to pay his railroad fare, so the boy resolved to walk to Tuskegee, a distance of about one hundred and fifty miles. Strange to say, he made the long distance with an expenditure of only twenty cents in cash. He frankly told every one with whom he came in contact where he was going and what he was seeking. Both white and colored people along the route gave him food and a place to sleep free of cost, and even the usually exacting ferrymen were so impressed with the young negro's desire for an education that, except in one case, he was given free ferriage across the creeks and rivers.

One can easily imagine his appearance when he first arrived at Tuskegee, with his blistered feet and small white bundle, which contained all the clothing he possessed.

On being shown into my office his first words were: "I 's come. S'pose you been lookin' for me, but I didn't come on de railroad." Looking up the records, it was found that this young man had been given permission to come several months ago, but the correspondence had long since been forgotten.

After being sent to the bath-room and provided with a tooth-brush, —for the tooth-brush at Tuskegee is the emblem of civilization,— William was assigned to a room, and was given work on the school farm of fourteen hundred acres, seven hundred of which are cultivated by student labor. During his first year at Tuskegee William worked on the farm during the day, where he soon learned to take a deep interest in all that the school was doing to teach the students the best and most improved methods of farming, and studied for two hours at night in the class-room after his hard day's work was over. At first he seemed drowsy and dull in the night-school, and would now and then fall asleep while trying to study; but he did not grow discouraged. The new machinery that he was compelled to use on the farm interested him because it taught him that the farm work could be stripped of much of the old-time drudgery and toil, and seemed to awaken his sleeping intellect. Soon he began asking the farm-instructors such questions as where the Jersey and Holstein cattle came from, and why they produced more milk and butter than the common long-tailed and long-horned cows that he had seen at home.

His night-school teachers found that he ceased to sleep in school, and began asking questions about his lessons, and was soon able to calculate the number of square yards in an acre and to tell the number of peach-trees required to plant an acre of land. After he had been at Tuskegee two or three months the farm-manager came into my office on a cold, rainy day, and said that William was virtually bare-footed, the soles of his shoes having separated from the uppers, though William had fastened them together as best he could with bits of wire. In this condition the farm-instructor found him plowing without a word of complaint. A pair of second-hand shoes was secured for him, and he was soon very happy.

I will not take this part of the story further except to say that at the end of his first year at Tuskegee this young man, having made a start in his books, and having saved a small sum of money above the cost of his board, which was credited to his account, entered the next year our regular day-classes, though still dividing his time between the class-room and work on the farm.

Toward the end of the year he found himself in need of money with which to buy books, clothing, etc., and so wrote a carefully worded letter to Mr. S——, the white man on whose plantation he had lived, and who had been, in slavery, the owner of his mother.

In the letter he told Mr. S—— how he got to Tuskegee, what he was doing, and what his needs were, and asked Mr. S—— to lend him fifteen dollars. Before receiving this letter Mr. S—— had not thought once about the boy during his two years' absence; in fact, did not know that he had left the plantation.

Mr. S—— was a good deal shocked, as well as amused, over such a request from such a source. The letter went to the waste-basket without being answered. A few weeks later William sent a second letter, in which he took it for granted that the first letter had not been received. The second letter shared the same fate as the first. A third letter reached Mr. S—— in a few weeks, making the same request.

In answer to the third letter Mr. S—— told me that, moved by some impulse which he himself never understood, he sent William the fifteen dollars.

Two or three years passed, and Mr. S—— had about forgotten William and the fifteen dollars, but one morning while he was sitting upon his porch a bright young colored man walked up and introduced himself as William, the boy to whom he used to toss small pieces of money, and the one to whom he had sent fifteen dollars.

William paid Mr. S—— the fifteen dollars with interest, which he had earned while teaching school after leaving Tuskegee.

This simple experience with this young colored man made a new and different person of Mr. S——, so far as the negro was concerned.

He began to think. He thought of the long past, but he thought most of the future, and of his duty towards the hundreds of colored people on his plantation and in his community. After careful thought he asked William Edwards to open a school on his plantation in a vacant log cabin. That was seven years ago. On this same plantation at Snow Hill, Wilcox County, Alabama, a county where, according to the last census, there are twenty-four thousand colored people and about six thousand whites, there is now a school with two hundred pupils, five teachers from Tuskegee, and three school buildings. The school has forty acres of land. In addition to the text-book lessons, the boys are taught farming and carpentry, and the girls sewing and general house-keeping, and the school is now in the act of starting a blacksmith and wheelwright department. This school owes its existence almost wholly to Mr. S——, who gave to the trustees the forty acres of land, and has contributed liberally to the building fund, as well as to the pay of the teachers. Gifts from a few friends in the North have been received, and the colored people have given their labor and small sums in cash. When the people cannot find money to give, they have often given corn, chickens, and eggs. The school has grown so popular that almost every leading white man in the community is willing to make a small gift toward its maintenance.

In addition to the work done directly in the school for the children, the teachers in the Snow Hill school have organized a kind of university extension movement. The farmers are organized into conferences, which hold meetings each month. In these meetings they are taught better methods of agriculture, how to buy land, how to economize and keep out of debt, how to stop mortgaging, how to build school-houses and dwelling-houses with more than one room, how to bring about a higher moral and religious standing, and are warned against buying cheap jewelry, snuff, and whisky.

No one is a more interested visitor at these meetings than Mr. S—— himself. The matter does not end in mere talk and advice. The women teachers go right into the cabins of the people and show them how to keep them clean, how to dust, sweep, and cook.

When William Edwards left this community a few years ago for the Tuskegee school, he left the larger proportion in debt, mortgaging their crops every year for the food on which to live. Most of them were living on rented land in small one-room log cabins, and attempting to pay an enormous rate of interest on the value of their food advances. As one old colored man expressed it, "I ain't got but six feet of land, and I is got to die to git dat." The little school taught in a cabin lasted only three or four months in the year. The religion was largely a matter of the emotions, with almost no practical ideas of morality. It was the white man for himself and the negro for himself, each in too many cases trying to take advantage of the other. The situation was pretty well described by a black man who said to me: "I tells you how we votes. We always watches de white man, and we keeps watchin' de white man. De nearer it gits to 'lection-time de more we watches de white man. We keeps watchin' de white man till we find out which way he gwine to vote; den we votes 'zactly de odder way. Den we knows we is right."

Now how changed is all at Snow Hill, and how it is gradually changing each year! Instead of the hopelessness and dejection that were there a few years ago, there are now light and buoyancy in the countenances and movements of the people. The negroes are getting out of debt and buying land, ceasing to mortgage their crops, building houses with two or three rooms, and a higher moral and religious standard has been established.

Last May, on the day that the school had its closing exercises, there were present, besides the hundreds of colored people, about fifty of the leading white men and women of the county, and these white people seemed as much interested in the work of the school as the people of my own race.

Only a few years ago in the State of Alabama the law in reference to the education of the negro read as follows: "Any person or persons who shall attempt to teach any free person of color or slave to spell, read, or write shall, upon conviction thereof by indictment, be fined in a sum not less than two hundred and fifty dollars nor more than five hundred dollars."

Within half a dozen years I have heard Dr. J. L. M. Curry, a brave, honest ex-Confederate officer, in addressing both the Alabama and Georgia State legislatures, say to those bodies in the most emphatic manner that it was as much the duty of the State to educate the negro children as the white children, and in each case Dr. Curry's words were cheered.

Here at Snow Hill is the foundation for the solution of the legal and political difficulties that exist in the South, and the improvement of the industrial condition of the negro in Cuba and Porto Rico. This solution will not come all at once, but gradually. The foundation must exist in the commercial and industrial development of the people of my race in the South and in the West Indian Islands.

The most intelligent whites are beginning to realize that they cannot go much higher than they lift the negro at the same time. When a black man owns and cultivates the best farm to be found in his county he will have the confidence and respect of most of the white people in that county. When a black man is the largest taxpayer in his community his white neighbor will not object very long to his voting, and having that vote honestly counted. Even now a black man who has five hundred dollars to lend has no trouble in finding a white man who is willing to borrow his money. The negro who is a large stockholder in a railroad company will always be treated with justice on that railroad.

Many of the most intelligent colored people are learning that while there are many bad white men in the South, there are Southern whites who have the highest interests of the negro just as closely at heart as have any other people in any part of the country. Many of the negroes are learning that it is folly not to cultivate in every honorable way the friendship of the white man who is their next-door neighbor.

To describe the work being done in connection with the public schools by graduates of Tuskegee and other institutions in the South, at such places as Mount Meigs, under Miss Cornelia Bowen; Denmark, South Carolina; Abbeville and Newville, Alabama; Christiansburg, Virginia, and numbers of other places in the Gulf States, would be only to repeat in a larger or smaller degree what I have said of Snow Hill. . . .

But such forces as I have described—forces that are gradually regenerating the entire South and will regenerate Cuba and Porto Rico

—are not started and kept in motion without a central plant—a power-house, where the power is generated. I cannot describe all these places of power. Perhaps the whole South and the whole country are most indebted to the Hampton Institute in Virginia. Then there is Fisk University at Nashville, Tennessee; Talladega College at Talladega, Alabama; Spelman Seminary, Atlanta University, and Atlanta Baptist College at Atlanta; Biddle University in North Carolina; Claflin University at Orangeburg, South Carolina; and Knoxville College at Knoxville, Tennessee. Some of these do a different grade of work, but one much needed.

At Tuskegee, Alabama, starting fifteen years ago in a little shanty with one teacher and thirty students, with no property, there has grown up an industrial and educational village where the ideas that I have referred to are put into the heads, hearts, and hands of an army of colored men and women, with the purpose of having them become centers of light and civilization in every part of the South. One visiting the Tuskegee Normal and Industrial Institute to-day will find eight hundred and fifty students gathered from twenty-four States, with eighty-eight teachers and officers training these students in literary, religious, and industrial work.

Counting the students and the families of the instructors, the visitor will find a black village of about twelve hundred people. Instead of the old, worn-out plantation that was there fifteen years ago, there is a modern farm of seven hundred acres cultivated by student labor. There are Jersey and Holstein cows and Berkshire pigs, and the butter used is made by the most modern process. . . .

When the student is through with his course of training he goes out feeling that it is just as honorable to labor with the hand as with the head, and instead of his having to look for a place, the place usually seeks him, because he has to give that which the South wants. One other thing should not be overlooked in our efforts to develop the black man. As bad as slavery was, almost every large plantation in the South during that time was, in a measure, an industrial school. It had its farming department, its blacksmith, wheelwright, brick-making, carpentry, and sewing departments. Thus at the close of the war our people were in possession of all the common and skilled labor in the South. For nearly twenty years after the war we overlooked the value of the ante-bellum training, and no one was trained to replace these skilled men and women who were soon to pass away; and now, as skilled laborers from foreign countries, with not only educated hands but trained brains, begin to come into the South and take these positions once held by us, we are gradually waking up to the fact that we must compete with the white man in the industrial world if we would hold our own. No one understands his value in the labor world better than the old colored man. Recently, when a convention was held in the South by the white people for the purpose of inducing white settlers from the North and West to settle in the South, one of these colored men said to the president of the convention: " 'Fore de Lord, boss, we 's got as many white people down here now as we niggers can support."

The negro in the South has another advantage. While there is prejudice against him along certain lines,—in the matter of business in general, and the trades especially,—there is virtually no prejudice so far as the native Southern white man is concerned. White men and black men work at the same carpenter's bench and on the same brick wall. Sometimes the white man is the "boss," sometimes the black man is the boss. . . .

The negro will find his way up as a man just in proportion as he makes himself valuable, possesses something that a white man wants, can do something as well as, or better than, a white man.

I would not have my readers get the thought that the problem in the South is settled, that there is nothing else to be done; far from this. Long years of patient, hard work will be required for the betterment of the condition of the negro in the South, as well as for the betterment of the condition of the negro in the West Indies.

There are bright spots here and there that point the way. Perhaps the most that we have accomplished in the last thirty years is to show the North and the South how the fourteen slaves landed a few hundred years ago at Jamestown, Virginia,—now nearly eight millions of freemen in the South alone,—are to be made a safe and useful part of our democratic and Christian institutions.

The main thing that is now needed to bring about a solution of the difficulties in the South is money in large sums, to be used largely for Christian, technical, and industrial education.

For more than thirty years we have been trying to solve one of the most serious problems in the history of the world largely by passing around a hat in the North. Out of their poverty the Southern States have done well in assisting; many more millions are needed, and these millions will have to come before the question as to the negro in the South is settled.

There never was a greater opportunity for men of wealth to place a few million dollars where they could be used in lifting up and regenerating a whole race; and let it always be borne in mind that every dollar given for the proper education of the negro in the South is almost as much help to the Southern white man as to the negro himself. So long as the whites in the South are surrounded by a race that is, in a large measure, in ignorance and poverty, so long will this ignorance and poverty of the negro in a score of ways prevent the highest development of the white man.

The problem of lifting up the negro in Cuba and Porto Rico is an easier one in one respect, even if it proves more difficult in others. It will be less difficult, because there is the absence of that higher degree of race feeling which exists in many parts of the United States. Both the white Cuban and the white Spaniard have treated the people of African descent, in civil, political, military, and business matters, very much as they have treated others of their own race. Oppression has not cowed and unmanned the Cuban negro in certain respects as it has the American negro.

In only a few instances is the color-line drawn. How Americans will treat the negro Cuban, and what will be the tendency of American influences in the matter of the relation of the races, remains an interesting and open question. Certainly it will place this country in an awkward position to have gone to war to free a people from Spanish cruelty, and then as soon as it gets them within its power to treat a large proportion of the population worse than did even Spain herself, simply on account of color.

While in the matter of the relations of the races the problem before us in the West Indies is easier, in respect to the industrial, moral, and religious sides it is more difficult. The negroes on these islands are largely an agricultural people, and for this reason, in addition to a higher degree of mental and religious training, they need the same agricultural, mechanical, and domestic training that is fast helping the negroes in our Southern States. Industrial training will not only help them to the ownership of property, habits of thrift and economy, but the acquiring of these elements of strength will go further than anything else in improving the moral and religious condition of the masses, just as has been and is true of my people in the Southern States.

With the idea of getting the methods of industrial education pursued at Hampton and Tuskegee permanently and rightly started in

Cuba and Porto Rico, a few of the most promising men and women from these islands have been brought to the Tuskegee Normal and Industrial Institute, and educated with the view of having them return and take the lead in affording industrial training on these islands, where the training can best be given to the masses.

The emphasis that I have placed upon an industrial education does not mean that the negro is to be excluded from the higher interests of life, but it does mean that in proportion as the negro gets the foundation,—the useful before the ornamental,—in the same proportion will he accelerate his progress in acquiring those elements which do not pertain directly to the utilitarian.

Phillips Brooks once said, "One generation gathers the material, and the next builds the palaces." Very largely this must be the material-gathering generation of black people, but in due time the palaces will come if we are patient.

*DuBois wrote the following article while he was still a professor of economics and history at Atlanta University. A few years later he would leave Atlanta and become active in civil rights work in New York City with the NAACP.*

# The Training of Negroes for Social Power

## By W. E. B. DuBois

THE RESPONSIBILITY for their own social regeneration ought to be placed squarely upon the shoulders of the negro people. But such responsibility must carry with it a grant of power; responsibility without power is a mockery and a farce. If, therefore, the American people are sincerely anxious that the negro shall put forth his best efforts to help himself, they must see to it that he is not deprived of the freedom and power to strive. The responsibility for dispelling their own ignorance implies that the power to overcome ignorance is to be placed in black men's hands; the lessening of poverty calls for the power of effective work; and the responsibility for lessening crime calls for control over social forces which produce crime.

Such social power means, assuredly, the growth of initiative among negroes, the spread of independent thought, the expanding consciousness of manhood; and these things to-day are looked upon by many with apprehension and distrust, and there is systematic and determined effort to avoid this inevitable corollary of the fixing of social responsibility. Men openly declare their design to train these millions as a subject caste, as men to be thought for, but not to think; to be led, but not to lead themselves.

Those who advocate these things forget that such a solution flings them squarely on the other horn of the dilemma: such a subject child-race could never be held accountable for its own misdeeds and shortcomings; its ignorance would be part of the Nation's design, its poverty would arise partly from the direct oppression of the strong and partly from thriftlessness which such oppression breeds; and,

From *Outlook*, LXXV (October 17, 1903), 409–414.

above all, its crime would be the legitimate child of that lack of self-respect which caste systems engender. Such a solution of the negro problem is not one which the saner sense of the Nation for a moment contemplates; it is utterly foreign to American institutions, and is unthinkable as a future for any self-respecting race of men. The sound afterthought of the American people must come to realize that the responsibility for dispelling ignorance and poverty and up-rooting crime among negroes cannot be put upon their own shoulders unless they are given such independent leadership in intelligence, skill, and morality as will inevitably lead to an independent manhood which cannot and will not rest in bonds.

Let me illustrate my meaning particularly in the matter of educating negro youth.

The negro problem, it has often been said, is largely a problem of ignorance—not simply of illiteracy, but a deeper ignorance of the world and its ways, of the thought and experience of men; an ignorance of self and the possibilities of human souls. This can be gotten rid of only by training; and primarily such training must take the form of that sort of social leadership which we call education. To apply such leadership to themselves, and to profit by it, means that negroes would have among themselves men of careful training and broad culture, as teachers and teachers of teachers. There are always periods of educational evolution when it is deemed quite proper for pupils in the fourth reader to teach those in the third. But such a method, wasteful and ineffective at all times, is peculiarly dangerous when ignorance is widespread and when there are few homes and public institutions to supplement the work of the school. It is, there-fore, of crying necessity among negroes that the heads of their edu-cational system—the teachers in the normal schools, the heads of high schools, the principals of public systems, should be unusually well trained men; men trained not simply in common-school branches, not simply in the technique of school management and normal methods, but trained beyond this, broadly and carefully, into the meaning of the age whose civilization it is their peculiar duty to in-terpret to the youth of a new race, to the minds of untrained people. Such educational leaders should be prepared by long and rigorous courses of study similar to those which the world over have been designed to strengthen the intellectual powers, fortify character, and facilitate the transmission from age to age of the stores of the world's knowledge.

Not all men—indeed, not the majority of men, only the exceptional few among American negroes or among any other people—are adapted to this higher training, as, indeed, only the exceptional few are adapted to higher training in any line; but the significance of such men is not to be measured by their numbers, but rather by the numbers of their pupils and followers who are destined to see the world through their eyes, hear it through their trained ears, and speak to it through the music of their words.

Such men, teachers of teachers and leaders of the untaught, Atlanta University and similar colleges seek to train. We seek to do our work thoroughly and carefully. We have no predilections or prejudices as to particular studies or methods, but we do cling to those time-honored sorts of discipline which the experience of the world has long since proven to be of especial value. We sift as carefully as possible the student material which offers itself, and we try by every conscientious method to give to students who have character and ability such years of discipline as shall make them stronger, keener, and better for their peculiar mission. The history of civilization seems to prove that no group or nation which seeks advancement and true development can despise or neglect the power of well-trained minds; and this power of intellectual leadership must be given to the talented tenth among American negroes before this race can seriously be asked to assume the responsibility of dispelling its own ignorance. Upon the foundation-stone of a few well equipped negro colleges of high and honest standards can be built a proper system of free common schools in the South for the masses of the negro people; any attempt to found a system of public schools on anything less than this—on narrow ideals, limited or merely technical training—is to call blind leaders for the blind.

The very first step toward the settlement of the negro problem is the spread of intelligence. The first step toward wider intelligence is a free public-school system; and the first and most important step toward a public-school system is the equipment and adequate support of a sufficient number of negro colleges. These are first steps, and they involve great movements: first, the best of the existent colleges must not be abandoned to slow atrophy and death, as the tendency is to-day; secondly, systematic attempt must be made to organize secondary education. Below the colleges and connected with them must come the normal and high schools, judiciously distributed and carefully manned. In no essential particular should this system of common and secondary schools differ from educational systems the world over. Their chief function is the quickening and training of human intelligence; they can do much in the teaching of morals and manners incidentally, but they cannot and ought not to replace the home as the chief moral teacher; they can teach valuable lessons as to the meaning of work in the world, but they cannot replace technical schools and apprenticeship in actual life, which are the real schools of work. Manual training can and ought to be used in these schools, but as a means and not as an end—to quicken intelligence and self-knowledge and not to teach carpentry; just as arithmetic is used to train minds and not skilled accountants.

Whence, now, is the money coming for this educational system? For the common schools the support should come from local communities, the State governments, and the United States Government; for secondary education, support should come from local and State governments and private philanthropy; for the colleges, from private philanthropy and the United States Government. I make no apology for bringing the United States Government in thus conspicuously. The General Government must give aid to Southern education if illiteracy and ignorance are to cease threatening the very foundations of civilization within any reasonable time. Aid to common-school education could be appropriated to the different States on the basis of illiteracy. The fund could be administered by State officials, and the results and needs reported upon by United States educational inspectors under the Bureau of Education. The States could easily distribute the funds so as to encourage local taxation and enterprise and not result in pauperizing the communities. As to higher training, it must be remembered that the cost of a single battle-ship like the Massachusetts would endow all the distinctively college work necessary for negroes during the next half-century; and it is without doubt true that the unpaid balance from bounties withheld from negroes in the Civil War would, with interest, easily supply this sum.

But spread of intelligence alone will not solve the negro problem. If this problem is largely a question of ignorance, it is also scarcely less a problem of poverty. If negroes are to assume the responsibility of raising the standards of living among themselves, the power of intelligent work and leadership toward proper industrial ideals must be placed in their hands. Economic efficiency depends on intelligence, skill, and thrift. The public-school system is designed to furnish the necessary intelligence for the ordinary worker, the secondary school for the more gifted workers, and the college for the exceptional few. Technical knowledge and manual dexterity in learning branches of the world's work are taught by industrial and trade schools, and such schools are of prime importance in the training of colored children. Trade-teaching cannot be effectively combined with the work of the common schools because the primary curriculum is already too crowded, and thorough common-school training should precede trade-teaching. It is, however, quite possible to combine some of the work of the secondary schools with purely technical training, the necessary limitations being matters of time and cost: the question whether the boy can afford to stay in school long enough to add parts of a high-school course to the trade course, and particularly the question whether the school can afford or ought to afford to give trade-training to high-school students who do not intend to become artisans. A system of trade-schools, therefore, supported by State and private aid, should be added to the secondary school system.

An industrial school, however, does not merely teach technique. It is also a school—a center of moral influence and of mental discipline. As such it has peculiar problems in securing the proper teaching force. It demands broadly trained men: the teacher of carpentry must be more than a carpenter, and the teacher of domestic arts more than a cook; for such teachers must instruct, not simply in manual dexterity, but in mental quickness and moral habits. In other words, they must be teachers as well as artisans. It thus happens that college-bred men and men from other high schools have always been in demand in technical schools, and it has been the high privilege of Atlanta University to furnish during the thirty-six years of its existence a part of the teaching force of nearly every negro industrial school in the United States, and to-day our graduates are teaching in more than twenty such institutions. The same might be said of Fisk University and other higher schools. If the college graduates were to-day withdrawn from the teaching force of the chief negro industrial schools, nearly every one of them would have to close its doors. These facts are forgotten by such advocates of industrial training as oppose the higher schools. Strong as the argument for industrial schools is—and its strength is undeniable—its cogency simply increases the urgency of the plea for higher training-schools and colleges to furnish broadly educated teachers.

But intelligence and skill alone will not solve the Southern problem of poverty. With these must go that combination of homely habits and virtues which we may loosely call thrift. Something of thrift may be taught in school, more must be taught at home; but both these agencies are helpless when organized economic society denies to workers the just rewards of thrift and efficiency. And this has been true of black laborers in the South from the time of slavery down through the scandal of the Freedmen's Bank to the peonage and crop-lien system of to-day. If the Southern negro is shiftless, it is primarily because over large areas a shiftless negro can get on in the world about as well as an industrious black man. This is not universally true in the South, but it is true to so large an extent as to discourage striving in precisely that class of negroes who most need encouragement. What is the remedy? Intelligence—not simply the ability to read and write or to sew—but the intelligence of a society permeated by that larger vision of life and broader tolerance which are fostered by the college and university. Not that all men must be college-bred, but that some men, black and white, must be, to leaven the ideals of the lump. Can any serious student of the economic South doubt that this to-day is her crying need?

Ignorance and poverty are the vastest of the negro problems. But to these later years have added a third—the problem of negro crime. That a great problem of social morality must have become eventually the central problem of emancipation is as clear as day to any student of history. In its grosser form as a problem of serious crime it is already upon us. Of course it is false and silly to represent that white women in the South are in daily danger of black assaulters. On the contrary, white womanhood in the South is absolutely safe in the hands of ninety-five per cent of the black men—ten times safer than black womanhood is in the hands of white men. Nevertheless, there is a large and dangerous class of negro criminals, paupers, and outcasts. The existence and growth of such a class, far from causing surprise, should be recognized as the natural result of that social disease called the negro problem; nearly every untoward circumstance known to human experience has united to increase negro crime: the slavery of the past, the sudden emancipation, the narrowing of economic opportunity, the lawless environment of wide regions, the stifling of natural ambition, the curtailment of political privilege, the disregard of the sanctity of black men's homes, and, above all, a system of treatment for criminals calculated to breed crime far faster than all other available agencies could repress it. Such a combination of circumstances is as sure to increase the numbers of the vicious and outcast as the rain is to wet the earth. The phenomenon calls for no delicately drawn theories of race differences; it is a plain case of cause and effect.

But, plain as the causes may be, the results are just as deplorable, and repeatedly to-day the criticism is made that negroes do not recognize sufficiently their responsibility in this matter. Such critics forget how little power to-day negroes have over their own lower classes. Before the black murderer who strikes his victim to-day, the average black man stands far more helpless than the average white, and, too, suffers ten times more from the effects of the deed. The white man has political power, accumulated wealth, and knowledge of social forces; the black man is practically disfranchised, poor, and unable to discriminate between the criminal and the martyr. The negro needs the defense of the ballot, the conserving power of property, and, above all, the ability to cope intelligently with such vast questions of social regeneration and moral reform as confront him. If social reform among negroes be without organization or trained leadership from within, if the administration of law is always for the avenging of the white victim and seldom for the reformation of the black criminal, if ignorant black men misunderstand the functions of government because they have had no decent instruction, and intelligent black men are denied a voice in government because they are black—under such circumstances to hold negroes responsible for the suppression of crime among themselves is the cruelest of mockeries.

On the other hand, a sincere desire among the American people to help the negroes undertake their own social regeneration means, first, that the negro be given the ballot on the same terms as other men, to protect him against injustice and to safeguard his interests in the administration of law; secondly, that through education and social organization he be trained to work, and save, and earn a decent living. But these are not all: wealth is not the only thing worth accumulating; experience and knowledge can be accumulated and handed down, and no people can be truly rich without them. Can the negro do without these? Can this training in work and thrift be truly effective without the guidance of trained intelligence and deep knowledge—without that same efficiency which has enabled modern peoples to grapple so successfully with the problems of the Submerged Tenth? There must surely be among negro leaders the philanthropic impulse, the uprightness of character and strength of purpose, but there must be more than these; philanthropy and purpose among blacks as well as among whites must be guided and curbed by knowledge and mental discipline—knowledge of the forces of civilization that make for survival, ability to organize and guide those forces, and realization of the true meaning of those broader ideals of human betterment which may in time bring heaven and earth a little nearer. This is social power—it is gotten in many ways by experience, by social contact, by what we loosely call the chances of life. But the systematic method of acquiring and imparting it is by the training of youth to thought, power, and knowledge in the school and college. And that group of people whose mental grasp is by heredity weakest, and whose knowledge of the past is for historic reasons most imperfect, that group is the very one which needs above all, for the talented of its youth, this severe and careful course of training; especially if they are expected to take immediate part in modern competitive life, if they are to hasten the slower courses of human development, and if the responsibility for this is to be in their own hands.

Three things American slavery gave the negro—the habit of work, the English language, and the Christian religion; but one priceless thing it debauched, destroyed, and took away from him, and that was the organized home. For the sake of intelligence and thrift, for the sake of work and morality, this home-life must be restored and regenerated with newer ideals. How? The normal method would be by actual contact with a higher home-life among his neighbors, but this method the social separation of white and black precludes. A proposed method is by schools of domestic arts, but, valuable as these are, they are but subsidiary aids to the establishment of homes; for real homes are primarily centers of ideals and teaching and only incidentally centers of cooking. The restoration and raising of home ideals must, then, come from social life among negroes themselves; and does that social life need no leadership? It needs the best possible leadership of pure hearts and trained heads; the highest leadership of carefully trained men.

Such are the arguments for the negro college, and such is the work that Atlanta University and a few similar institutions seek to do. We believe that a rationally arranged college course of study for men and women able to pursue it is the best and only method of putting into the world negroes with ability to use the social forces of their race so as to stamp out crime, strengthen the home, eliminate degenerates, and inspire and encourage the higher tendencies of the race not only in thought and aspiration but in every-day toil. And we believe this, not simply because we have argued that such training ought to have these effects, or merely because we hope for such results in some dim future, but because already for years we have seen in the work of our graduates precisely such results as I have mentioned: successful teachers of teachers, intelligent and upright ministers, skilled physicians, principals of industrial schools, business men, and, above all, makers of model homes and leaders of social groups, out from which radiate subtle but tangible forces of uplift and inspiration. The proof of this lies scattered in every State of the South, and, above all, in the half-unwilling testimony of men disposed to decry our work.

Between the negro college and industrial school there are the strongest grounds for co-operation and unity. It is not a matter of mere emphasis, for we would be glad to see ten industrial schools to every college. It is not a fact that there are to-day too few negro colleges, but rather that there are too many institutions attempting to do college work. But the danger lies in the fact that the best of the negro colleges are poorly equipped and are to-day losing support and countenance, and that, unless the Nation awakens to its duty, ten years will see the annihilation of higher negro training in the South. We need a few strong, well-equipped negro colleges, and we need them now, not to-morrow; unless we can have them and have them decently supported, negro education in the South, both common-school and industrial, is doomed to failure, and the forces of social regeneration will be fatally weakened, for the college to-day among negroes is, just as truly as it was yesterday among whites, the beginning and not the end of human training, the foundation and not the capstone of popular education.

Strange, is it not, my brothers, how often in America those great watchwords of human energy—"Be strong!" "Know thyself!" "Hitch your wagon to a star!"—how often these die away into dim whispers when we face these seething millions of black men? And yet do they not belong to them? Are they not their heritage as well as yours? Can they bear burdens without strength, know without learning, and aspire without ideals? Are you afraid to let them try? Fear rather, in this our common fatherland, lest we live to lose those great watchwords of Liberty and Opportunity which yonder in the eternal hills their fathers fought with your fathers to preserve.

*Booker T. Washington, Kelly Miller, and others acted as vigorous propagandists for black opportunity. Their articles, mainly directed to white audiences, continually emphasized the progress made by blacks to help themselves.*

# The Negro's Place in American Life

## By Booker T. Washington

ONE OF THE most striking and interesting things about the American Negro, and one which has impressed itself upon my mind more and more in the course of the preparation of these articles, is the extent to which the black man has intertwined his life with that of the people of the white race about him. While it is true that hardly any other race of people that has come to this country has remained in certain aspects so separate and distinct a part of the population as the Negro, it is also true that no race that has come to this country has so woven its life into the life of the people about it. No race has shared to a greater extent in the work and activities of the original settlers of the country, or has been more closely related to them in interest, in sympathy, and in sentiment than the Negro race.

In fact, there is scarcely any enterprise of any moment that has been undertaken by a member of the white race in which the Negro has not had some part. In all the great pioneer work of clearing forests and preparing the way for civilization the Negro, as I have tried to point out, has had his part. In all the difficult and dangerous work of exploration of the country the Negro has invariably been the faithful companion and helper of the white man.

Negroes seem to have accompanied nearly all the early Spanish explorers. Indeed, it has even been conjectured that Negroes came to America before Columbus, carried hither by trade winds and ocean currents, coming from the west coast of Africa. At any rate, one of the early historians, Peter Martyr, mentions "a region in the Darien district of South America where Balboa, the illustrious discoverer of the Pacific Ocean, found a race of black men who were con-

From *Outlook*, XCIII (November 13, 1909), 579–585.

jectured to have come from Africa and to have been shipwrecked on this coast."

It is said that the first ship built along the Atlantic coast was constructed by the slaves of Vasquez de Ayllon, who, one hundred years before the English landed there, attempted to found a Spanish settlement on the site of what was later Jamestown, Virginia. There were thirty Negroes with the Spanish discoverer Balboa, and they assisted him in building the first ship that was constructed on the Pacific coast of America. Cortez, the conqueror of Mexico, had three hundred Negro slaves with him in 1522, the year in which he was chosen Captain-General of New Spain, as Mexico was then called; and it is asserted that the town of Santiago del Principe was founded by Negro slaves who had risen in insurrection against their Spanish masters.

In the chronicles of the ill-starred Coronado expedition of 1540, which made its way from Mexico as far north as Kansas and Nebraska, it is mentioned that a Negro slave of Hernando de Alarcon was the only member of the party who would undertake to carry a message from the Rio Grande across the country to the Zuñis in New Mexico, where Alarcon hoped to find Coronado and open communication with him.

I have referred elsewhere to the story of Estevan, "little Steve," a companion of Panfilo Narvaez in his exploration of Florida in 1527, who afterward went in search of the seven fabulous cities which were supposed to be located somewhere in the present State of Arizona, and discovered the Zuñi Indians.

Negroes accompanied De Soto on his march through Alabama in 1540. One of these Negroes seems to have liked the country, for he remained and settled among the Indians not far from Tuskegee, and became in this way the first settler of Alabama. Coming down to a later date, a Negro servant accompanied William Clark, of the Lewis and Clark expedition, which in 1804 explored the sources of the Missouri River and gained for the United States the Oregon country. Negroes were among the first adventurers who went to look for gold in California; and when John C. Fremont, in 1848, made his desperate and disastrous attempt to find a pathway across the Rockies, he was accompanied by a Negro servant named Saunders. . . .

One reason why the Negro is found so closely associated with the white man in all his labors and adventures is that, with all his faults, the Negro seldom betrays a specific trust. Even the individual who does not always clearly distinguish between his own property and that of his neighbor, when a definite thing of value is intrusted to him, in nine cases out of ten will not betray that trust. This is a trait that characterizes the Negro wherever he is found. I have heard Sir Harry H. Johnston, the African explorer, use almost exactly the same words, for example, in describing the characteristics of the native African. . . .

I have already referred to the part that the Negro took in the wars which were fought to establish, defend, and maintain the United States. One of the soldiers of the Revolutionary War who afterward distinguished himself in a remarkable way was the Rev. Lemuel Haynes, and, as I have not mentioned him elsewhere, I will do so here. Lemuel Haynes was born in West Hartford, Connecticut, in 1753. In 1775 he joined the Colonial army, as a minuteman, at Roxbury, Massachusetts, having volunteered for the Ticonderoga expedition. At the close of the war he settled in Granville, New York, where he worked on a farm, meanwhile studying for the ministry. By some means or other he succeeded in securing an exceptionally good education. In 1785 he was offered a position as a minister to a white congregation in Torrington, Connecticut. As there was objection from some members of the congregation on account of his color, he removed to Rutland, Vermont, where he served as a minister from 1787 to 1817. In 1818 he went to Manchester, New Hampshire. It was while there that he made himself famous by opposing the execution of the Boone brothers, who had been condemned to death for murdering an insane man. He visited the brothers in the prison, and, having listened to their story, became convinced of their innocence, whereupon he took up their defense in the face of violent opposition. In spite of his efforts, they were convicted, but a few days before their execution the man they were supposed to have killed, Louis Calvin, returned alive to his home. At that time people generally believed it was the colored minister's prayers that brought him back.

In 1822 Mr. Haynes returned to his former home at Granville, where he continued to preach until his death. He is most widely known for his "sermon against Universalism," which he preached in opposition to Hosea Ballou. This sermon, which was preached impromptu and without notes, created a great impression. It was afterward published and circulated widely all over the United States and in some parts of Europe. Lemuel Haynes died in Granville in 1832. He was, so far as I know, the first colored Congregational minister.

During the Civil War there were several Negro officers appointed to take charge of the Negro troops, and immediately after the war several Negroes were admitted to West Point. Three of these were graduated. The only one of these now in the service is First Lieutenant Charles Young, who was Major of the Ninth Ohio Battalion, United States Volunteers, in the Spanish-American War.

Negro soldiers took a more prominent part in the Spanish-American War than in any previous war of the United States. In the first battle in Cuba the Tenth Cavalry played an important part in coming to the support, at a critical moment, of the Rough Riders under Colonel Theodore Roosevelt, at the battle of Las Guasimas.

The Twenty-fifth Infantry took a prominent part in the battle of El Caney. It is claimed by Lieutenant-Colonel A. D. Daggett that the Twenty-fifth Regiment caused the surrender of the stone fort at El Caney, which was the key to all the other positions in that battle for the possession of San Juan. Eight men of this regiment were given certificates of gallantry for their part in the battle of San Juan Hill. The other Negro regiments which took part in these battles were the Ninth Cavalry and the Twenty-fourth Infantry, both of which did heroic service in the famous battle for the crest of San Juan Hill.

What impresses me still more, however, is the part which these black soldiers played after the battle was over, when they were called to remain and nurse the sick and wounded in the malarial-haunted camp at Siboney, at a time when the yellow fever had broken out in the army. . . .

The Negro must, at all hazard and in all times and places, avoid crossing the color line. It is a little difficult, however, sometimes to determine upon what principle this line is drawn. For instance, customs differ in different parts of the same town, as well as in different parts of the country at large. In one part of a town a Negro may be able to get a meal at a public lunch-counter, but in another part of the same town he cannot do so. Conditions differ widely in the different States. In Virginia a Negro is expected to ride in a separate railway coach; in West Virginia he can ride in the same coach with the white people. In one Southern city Negroes can enter the depot, as they usually do, by the main entrance; in another Southern city there is a separate entrance for colored people. While in one Southern city the Negro is allowed to take his seat in the main waiting-room, he will be compelled at another depot in the same city to go into a separate waiting-room. In some cities the Negro is allowed to go without question into the theater; in other cities he either cannot enter the theater at all or he has a separate place assigned to him. In all these different situations, somehow or other, the Negro manages to comport himself so as rarely to excite comment or cause trouble.

He often hears the opinion expressed that the Negro should keep his place or that he is "all right in his place." People who make use of these expressions seldom understand how difficult it is, considering the different customs in different parts of the country, to find out just what his place is. I might give further illustrations of this fact. In the Southern States the Negro is rarely allowed to enter a public library. In certain parts of the United States the Negro is allowed to enter the public high school, but he is forbidden to enter the grammar school where white children are taught. In one city the Negro may sit anywhere he pleases in the street car; in another city, perhaps not more than twenty miles away, he is assigned to special and separate seats. In one part of the country the Negro may vote freely; in another part of the country, perhaps across the border of another State, he is not expected to vote at all.

As illustrating the ability of the Negro to avoid the rocks and shoals which he is likely to meet in traveling about the country and still manage to get what he wants, I recall an experience of a colored man with whom I was traveling through South Carolina some time ago. This man was very anxious to reach the railway train, and had only a few minutes in which to do so. He hailed, naturally enough, the first hackman he saw, who happened to be a white man. The white man told him that it was not his custom to carry Negroes in his carriage. The colored man, not in the least disturbed, at once replied: "That's all right, we will fix that; you get in the carriage and I'll take the front seat and drive you." This was done, and in a few minutes they reached the depot, in time to catch the train. The colored man handed the white man twenty-five cents and departed. Both were satisfied, and the color line was preserved.

The facts I have detailed serve to illustrate some of the difficulties that the colored man has in the North as well as in the South, with the present unsettled conditions as to his position in the community. The Negro suffers some other disadvantages living in the midst of a people from whom he is so different, with whom he is so intimately associated, and from whom he is, at the same time, so distinctly separate.

In living in the midst of seventy millions of the most highly civilized people of the world the Negro has the opportunity to learn much that he could not learn in a community where the people were less enlightened and less progressive. On the other hand, it is a disadvantage to him that his progress is constantly compared to the progress of a people who have the advantage of many centuries of civilization, while the Negro has for only a little more than forty years been a free man. If the American Negro, with his present degree of advancement, were living in the midst of a civilization such as exists to-day in Asia or in the south of Europe, the gap between him and the people by whom he is surrounded would not then be so wide, and he would receive credit for the progress that he has already made. . . .

The story of the American Negro has been one of progress from the first. While there have been times when it seemed the race was going backward, this backward movement has been temporal, local, or merely apparent. On the whole, the Negro has been and is moving forward everywhere and in every direction.

In speaking of his experiences in the South, Mr. Ray Stannard Baker, whose articles on Southern conditions are in many respects the best and most informing that have been written since Olmsted's famous "Journey in the Seaboard Slave States," said that before he came into the South he had been told that in many sections of the country the Negro was relapsing into barbarism. He, of course, was very anxious to find these places and see for himself to what extent the Negro had actually gone backward. Before leaving New York he was told that he would find the best example of this condition in the lowlands and rice-fields of South Carolina and Georgia. He visited these sections of South Carolina and Georgia, but he did not find any traces of the barbarism that he expected to see. He did find, however, that colored people in that part of the country were, on the whole, making progress. This progress was slow, but it was in a direction away from and not toward barbarism.

In South Carolina he was told that the people in that part of the country had not gone back into barbarism, but if he would go to the sugar-cane regions of Louisiana he would find the conditions among the Negroes as bad as in any other part of the United States. He went to Louisiana, and again he found, not barbarism, but progress. There he was told that he would find what he was looking for in the Yazoo Delta of the Mississippi. In Mississippi he was told that if he went into Arkansas he would not be disappointed. He went to Arkansas, but there, also, he found the colored people engaged in buying land, building churches and schools, and trying to improve themselves. After that he came to the conclusion that the Negro was not relapsing into barbarism.

The Negro is making progress at the present time as he made progress in slavery times. There is, however, this difference: In slavery the progress of the Negro was a menace to the white man. The security of the white master depended upon the ignorance of the black slave. In freedom the security and happiness of each race depend, to a very large extent, on the education and the progress of the other. The problem of slavery was to keep the Negro down; the problem of freedom is to raise him up.

The story of the Negro, in the last analysis, is simply the story of the man who is farthest down; as he raises himself he raises every other man who is above him.

In concluding this narrative I ought to say, perhaps, that if in what I have written I seem to have emphasized the successes of the Negro rather than his failures, and to have said more about his achievements than about his hardships, it is because I am convinced that these things are more interesting and more important. To me the history of the Negro people in America seems like the story of a great adventure in which, for my own part, I am glad to have had a share. So far from being a misfortune, it seems to me that it is a rare privilege to have part in the struggles, the plans, and the ambitions of ten millions of people who are making their way from slavery to freedom.

At the present time the Negro race is, so to speak, engaged in hewing its path through the wilderness. In spite of its difficulties there are a novelty and a zest as well as an inspiration in this task that few who have not shared it can appreciate. In America the Negro race, for the first time, is face to face with the problem of learning to till the land intelligently; of planning and building permanent and beautiful homes; of erecting school-houses and extending school terms; of experimenting with methods of instruction and adapting them to the needs of the Negro people; of organizing churches, building houses of worship, and preparing ministers. In short, the Negro in America to-day is face to face with all the fundamental problems of modern civilization, and for each of these problems he has, to some extent, to find a solution of his own. The fact that in his case this is peculiarly difficult only serves to make the problem peculiarly interesting.

We have hard problems, it is true, but instead of despairing in the face of the difficulties we should, as a race, thank God that we have a problem. As an individual I would rather belong to a race that has a great and difficult task to perform than be a part of a race whose pathway is strewn with flowers. It is only by meeting and facing manfully hard, stubborn, and difficult problems that races, like individuals, are in the highest degree made strong.

*Oswald Garrison Villard, publisher of the New York Evening Post and the Nation, was a leading white spokesman for the cause of black Americans. He too was a founder of the NAACP and became the first chairman of its executive committee.*

# The Objects of the National Association for the Advancement of Colored People

## By Oswald Garrison Villard

THE OBJECTS of the National Association for the Advancement of Colored People may be put into a single sentence: This society exists in order to combat the spirit of persecution and prejudice which confronts the colored people of this land, and to assure to them every right, privilege and opportunity to which every citizen of the United States is entitled. That it exists at all is in itself an indictment of our American democracy. For it asks no favors, no privileges, no special advantages or benefits for those disadvantaged ones, whose fathers and mothers but fifty years ago to-day were still being sold upon the auction block as so much livestock. It does not, of course, ask that financial reparation be made to them for what their race suffered under the monstrous aggregation of wrongdoing which went by the name of slavery; the colored people themselves never demanded any such damages in the courts of law, or of public opinion. It does not even ask special indulgence for any of their shortcomings or beg for them unusual economic and educational opportunities because of their disadvantages and the frightful inheritance of vice and ignorance which was the chief bequest of slavery. It merely asks equality of opportunity, equality at the ballot box, equality in the courts of the land.

Surely this is a simple enough platform—a reasonable enough demand. Theoretically, all but those most imbued with race prejudice grant the justness of our contentions. Theoretically, everybody in this country throws his cap in the air each day and asserts that all men are born free and equal and fit to govern themselves. And yet there are many persons interested in the welfare of the Negro who look with suspicion upon our simple platform and hold aloof from our work, for there are two schools of thought even among those who feel that the Negro is at all times grievously wronged and at times shockingly maltreated. The difference between the two schools is chiefly one of method. There are, for instance, those prominent in the educational work among the Negroes of the South, both white and black, who feel that it is a mistake to dwell upon injuries and wrongs, outrages and persecution, because, in their belief, the cure can only come through the slow education of all the people, and with the lapse of an indefinite amount of time. It does not worry them that during the past decades no effective protest was made against disfranchisement; one State after another has deprived the black man of his vote and discriminated against him in a hundred different ways. They believed, at the time, like many an honest Southerner, that the disfranchisement laws were blessings in disguise because, first, they would incite the Negro to educate himself and his children that he might qualify as a voter, so far as the educational test is concerned; and, secondly, that with the removal of the Negro from politics he would find himself free to develop materially and socially; in fact, along every other line save the political one. They are not daunted to-day by the fact that their forecasts have proved incorrect, that the Negro is still in politics in the South, that his way upward from slavery is barred by many a barrier, and hindered by many a needless obstacle—by prejudice, by the caste feeling, by the malicious spirit of persecution, which, in some instances of late, finds its satiation only in burning women alive. Still the cry with them is "Time and patience." This association they deem too radical. Like the old abolition societies, this is believed to be a mischief maker, because it is willing in season and out of season to lay unpleasant facts before the public. Its organ of opinion, THE CRISIS, is not always optimistic, but usually pessimistic, if that adjective covers properly its monthly chronicle of crimes against the race and against the law, the mocking of the courts, the passing of segregation ordinances that would make ghettos in each one of our Southern cities, and other reactionary happenings of the same kind. With these reformers the cry is, to paraphrase the French philosopher: "Patience, patience—it is the most beautiful thing in the world." They are silent in the face of all this wrongdoing unless at times and places where it is safe to speak out against the growing lynching habit. They look with ill-concealed un-easiness upon those who would make each single wrongdoing as a fire bell in the night to alarm the conscience of the people. Their duty as they see it is to serve, but not to protect; to sit silent if need be in the presence of sin, with their eyes fixed only upon the numer-ous and encouraging signs that this republic will in the long run not tolerate injustice against a class or race among its citizens.

For this opinion, honestly held, particularly when advocated by those in the educational field, one can have the fullest respect if it is consistently adhered to, but that is not the policy of this association. It is not content to sit idly by and see wrong done, even though cer-tain at heart that in the long run righteousness will prevail, that the mills of the gods grind exceedingly fine, however slowly. While see-ing nothing in the history of the last one hundred years, but a steady progress toward true democracy; reading this in the story of all Europe, of England, of France, Germany and Italy, and latterly even in Turkey and Persia, Japan and China, as well as in the development of the woman suffrage movement in this country and abroad and in the rise of the progressive movement in the United States and its purpose to strike at special privilege, the members of the association still feel as much entitled to point out our national wrongdoing and to strike at intrenched privilege as the Abolitionists felt at liberty to assail every citadel garrisoned by slaveholders or their sympathizers. Ours, too, is a battle for democracy, pure and undefiled. It is not for us to compromise, however much others may feel the necessity of doing so. It is not for us to withhold our scorn and indignation when we see colored men and women outraged, robbed, maimed or burned in Pennsylvania or in Illinois, in Mississippi or in Georgia. On the con-trary, it is our duty to speak out that everyone may know and hear.

Observing the situation carefully, what do the members of this association behold in the country at large? That abstract justice ap-peals to us all is plain. The nation boasts of this as it does of that alleged equality of opportunity by which the humblest rail splitter of them all may rise to the White House. Then it makes a prompt ex-ception to the rule and says that the colored man may rise, not ac-cording to his industry, or his merit, or his talents, but only so far as his white fellows will let him. He may not live in the White House; he may not even take a meal there. Thus abstract justice loses consid-erable of its abstractness, and those of the white skin who sit in judg-ment upon the Negro are as much outraged by the idea that he may

know a little bit better what he needs and what is good for him than
anybody else, as were the lords of England in 1775 upset by the
theory that the Colonists of America were the best judges of what
made for their happiness and welfare. We hear on all sides in this
year of our lord 1912 much to the effect that the people shall rule;
that direct government is what we need to cure all our political ills;
that the people may be trusted with complete control of legislation
and of the executive offices of city and State as well as of the judiciary
—but not the colored man. For his benefit the country waives aside
every one of these doctrines so warmly espoused and connives at the
Negro's disfranchisement by the hundred thousand on the ground
that it is for his own good. The violation of the Constitution which
this procedure involves affects them not at all. The magic powers
with which the initiative, referendum and recall have been endowed
are, it appears, potent only when these devices of government are
availed of by white men; they cease to operate for the communal
advantage if colored men vote and desire to evoke their aid.

Again we learn that the affectionate term "God's Country," applied
by so many to our land, is interchangeable with "White Man's Country," and that this term is again synonymous with trickery and wrongdoing; yes, even wholesale murder and a denial of the courts of
justice, if necessary, to black men—on all which proceeding the God,
who owns this country, looks down, it is confidently asserted, with
complete satisfaction. Thus, the color line does more than to set apart
the sheep and the goats among us; more even than to throw out of
gear this new political machinery upon which so many of our fellow
citizens base their hope of a future democracy. Fundamental political
actions and principles go by the board when it is asserted that they
apply only in a community in which the whites are in a comfortable
majority. The law of gravitation remains unchanged under all circumstances, so does the multiplication table when those who con it
are black; but when a community largely Negroid begins to chant
the sacred fundamental truths that government rests only on the consent of the governed; that, as Lincoln put it—"No man is good
enough to govern another without that other's consent"—then we
learn that these truisms upon which our whole structure of government rests are truisms only when they apply to men of white blood.
It is just as if we declared that the teachings of Christianity itself
apply only to the white man, and cease to be effective or binding or
to provide a sound chart of life for those inhabitants of this universe
who have a drop of Negro blood in their veins.

That is what the slogan of "White Man's Country" means, the giving the lie to every political principle, to every democratic belief, to every article of American faith, to every tenet of religion. Should we not be wickedly recreant to those principles and doctrines if there were not some Americans ready to band together to declare with all the strength that comes with union in an unselfish cause, that our treatment of the colored people of to-day tarnishes the country's good name, mocks and flouts our republican institutions and makes a hypocrite of the nation for which we are ready to give our lives?

It was three years ago that the need became so clear as to bring this organization into being. Three years ago marked the centennial of the birth of Abraham Lincoln, surely the most fitting time of all to found such an undertaking. From small beginnings it has grown rapidly. Its organ of public opinion, THE CRISIS, reaches more than 22,000 readers. Branches have been organized in Boston, Chicago, Baltimore, Washington and New York, and there is a host of applications for branches elsewhere on file in our main office. Meetings have been held in great numbers. The association's centenary celebrations of Sumner, Phillips and Harriet Beecher Stowe have done not a little to keep alive the spirit of the abolition times. The work of legal redress is going on apace; there is being undertaken at the present time a careful investigation of one of the most terrible of lynchings, one of more than one hundred which took place during the year 1911. In every direction the effort is being made to obtain the truth about the progress of the colored people, and to put the facts in their case before the public.

*James Weldon Johnson was a versatile man—an able writer and poet as well as an administrator. During much of the twenties, he participated in the cultural life of the Harlem Renaissance while working as secretary of the NAACP. The following article was the commencement speech at Hampton Institute in June 1923.*

# The Larger Success

## By James Weldon Johnson

MEN MAY be divided into any number of classes—rich and poor, educated and ignorant, successful and unsuccessful, and so on; but none of these classifications is fundamental. A more vital classification or division of men would be those who live only in the present and those who live both in the present and the future. Having or lacking the power to project oneself into the future is what primarily divides men who move forward and upward from those who remain stationary or slip back.

There is a homely illustration often given to mark this dividing line. It is the difference between a man who plants a tree and a man to whom such an act would never appeal. The man who plants a tree performs an act in the spirit of the Great Creator. He serves not only himself but future generations unknown to him, who will enjoy its fruit and its shade.

To realize in life the deeper meanings of success one's vision cannot be limited by the circumscribed horizon of the present. It must transcend those bounds and take in the future. This comprehension of the future involves the spirit of altruism, the divine spirit of service to others, and embraces all men and all generations; but it carries not only these abstract and, perhaps to some, vague principles of altruism, but also a very concrete and individual value. For, contrary to the general notion, there is a future which is neither hazy nor unknown. There is a definitely known future, a future which it is possible to know as well as the past is known. This is the future

From *Southern Workman*, LII (September 1923), 427–436.

in which those who are today going out from this institution are now probably most interested.

The future is commonly regarded as a mystery in the hands of soothsayers and fortune-tellers. We may grant that this is true of the insignificant details of the future. If a young man is curious to know whether he will marry a girl with light hair and gray eyes or dark hair and brown eyes, let him go to a fortune-teller; but if he desires to know if the sum total of life for him will be a success or a failure, he can find out for himself. For the fundamental and vital facts about the future are subject to governing laws—laws that are as fixed as those we call the laws of nature. No man, unless insane, would jump off the Woolworth Tower and expect to go up. He would know that there is a law called gravitation which never fails to operate. Nor would any scientist put one part of hydrogen with two parts of oxygen and expect to get anything but water.

Following these same principles one may observe himself or others and, depending upon whether he finds diligence or indolence, thrift or shiftlessness, sincerity or hypocrisy, the wasting of time or the improving of opportunities, courage or cowardice, be able to prophesy, and without the aid of a fortune-teller, whether there will be success or failure in life. Here we are reduced to commonplace platitudes, but when we get down to the fundamentals of life, what is there, after all, to stand upon but these same moral platitudes? It is these platitudes, so often sneered at, that contain the wisdom of the human race, proven through ages of experience.

We can foretell the future when we know and understand the past. The future of individuals and nations is all plainly written in history. What man was there familiar with the science of history who could not have foretold the Great War from which the world has not yet recovered? In fact, a number of men did foretell it. The nations of Europe had been doing what nations have done over and over again since the beginning of recorded history, and their acts were followed by precisely the same results.

And so, along these fundamental lines, anyone can tell whether, in the deeper sense, his life is to be a failure or a success. But here I should add that defeat must not be confounded with failure. Many have gone down for the sake of principle and truth. They have been defeated but they have not failed. The crucified Christ on the cross has become the greatest spiritual force in the world.

And now we come back to the larger sense of the future—that

sense of the future which comprehends not only the greatest service to self but the greatest service to others, that sense of the future which involves success in its deepest and highest meaning, that which brings not only self-gratification and self-satisfaction but also gratification and satisfaction to our fellows. This is the success to which I wish to point you, and I wish at the same time to impress upon you that this larger success contains within itself the smaller and more concrete success. It is through service in pursuit of the larger success that the smaller success comes unsought.

And what an incentive there is for you into whose faces I am looking for service in the pursuit of the larger success! Millions are waiting upon you—you who are trained and inspired—to bring them light, to bring them hope, to bring them help. You have before you the opportunity to take part in a fight for common humanity and common justice, to have a pioneer's share in building for the future greatness of a race, the opportunity to help in the making of our common country, in deed as well as in name, the greatest democracy under which men have ever lived. These constitute an incentive for service which the white youth of America might well envy you.

And are you familiar with the wonderful background of those you are called upon particularly to serve? Do you realize that you are sprung from and belong to a great race—a race great in numbers, great in physical strength and stamina; and numerical strength and physical strength are prime essentials of racial greatness? And do you also realize that this race from which you are sprung is endowed with many wonderful qualities and gifts: that its historic and prehistoric background is something of which you have no reason to be ashamed and of which you have many reasons to be intensely proud?

Popular opinion has it that the Negro in Africa has been from time immemorial a savage. This is far from the truth. Such an opinion is possible only because there has been and still is an historical conspiracy against Africa which has successfully stripped the Negro race of all credit for what it contributed in past ages to the birth and growth of civilization. Makers of history have taught the world that from the beginning of time the Negro has never been anything but a race of savages and slaves. Anyone who is willing to dig out the truth can learn that civilization was born in the upper reaches of the River Nile: that, in the misty ages of the past, pure black men in Africa were observing the stars, were turning human speech into

song, were discovering religious truths, were laying the foundations
of government, were utilizing the metals, developing agriculture,
inventing primitive tools; in fact, giving the impulse which started
man on his upward climb.

The truth is that the torch of civilization was lighted on the banks
of the Nile; and we can trace the course of that torch, sometimes
flaming, sometimes flickering, and at times all but extinguished,—
we can trace it up through Egypt, around the borders of the Medi-
terranean, through Greece and Italy and Spain, on into Northern
Europe. In the hands of each people that held it the torch of civilization has grown brighter and brighter and then died down until it
was passed on to other hands. The fact that dark ages fell upon Africa
and her people is no more of a discredit than the fact that dark ages
fell upon the buried empires of Asia Minor or Asia or ancient Greece.
Races and peoples have in their turn carried this torch of civilization
to a certain height and then sunk back under the weight of their own
exertions.

It seems that there is more truth than mythology in the story of
Antæus and Hercules. Hercules, in wrestling with Antæus, found
that each time the giant was thrown he arose stronger. The secret
lay in the fact that the earth was his mother, and each time he came
in contact with her he gained renewed strength. Hercules then resorted to the stratagem of holding him off the earth until his strength
was exhausted. So with races and peoples. It seems that after they
have climbed to a certain height they must fall back and lie for a
period close to Mother Earth. And this reminds us of the truth that
all things in the universe move in cycles; so who knows but that, in
the whirl of God's great wheel, the torch may not again flame in the
upper valley of the Nile?

Nor need you go so far to find a background which will give you
confidence and justifiable pride. The record of the Negro in this
country constitutes one of the most wonderful pages in American
history. Brought here against his will, cut off entirely from the moor-
ings of his native culture, however primitive it may have been,
he has, in spite of obstacles, never turned his back to the light.
Whatever may be his shortcomings, however slow may have been
his progress, however disappointing may have been his achievements, he has never consciously sought the downward path. He has
always kept his face to the light and has continued to struggle
forward and upward, making his humble contribution to the com-

mon prosperity and glory of our land. He has woven himself into the woof and warp of the nation. First setting foot upon the soil of this very State, before the landing of the Pilgrim Fathers, he has, in language, in customs, in mode of thought, and in religion, become thoroughly American.

When this country was plunged into the great World War and we were startled by the thought that perhaps after all we were not a nation but merely a conglomeration of groups assembled here under one flag; and when there was distrust and suspicion and even panic, there came the realization that side by side with the original American stocks that landed at Jamestown and at Plymouth stood the American Negro. Indeed, he has every right to say:—

> This land is ours by right of birth,
>     This land is ours by right of toil;
> We helped to turn its virgin earth,
>     Our sweat is in its fruitful soil.
>
> Where once the tangled forest stood,—
>     Where flourished once rank weed and thorn,—
> Behold the path-traced, peaceful wood,
>     The cotton white, the yellow corn.
>
> To gain these fruits that have been earned,
>     To hold these fields that have been won,
> Our arms have strained, our backs have burned,
>     Bent bare beneath a ruthless sun.
>
> That banner which is now the type
>     Of victory on field and flood—
> Remember, its first crimson stripe
>     Was dyed by Attucks' willing blood.
>
> And never yet has come the cry—
>     When that fair flag has been assailed—
> For men to do, for men to die,
>     That we have faltered or have failed.
>
> We've helped to bear it, rent and torn,
>     Through many a hot-breath'd battle breeze;
> Held in our hands, it has been borne
>     And planted far across the seas.
>
> And never yet—O haughty Land,
>     Let us, at least, for this be praised—
> Has one black, treason-guided hand
>     Ever against that flag been raised.
>
> Then should we speak but servile words,
>     Or shall we hang our heads in shame?
> Stand back of new-come foreign hordes,
>     And fear our heritage to claim?

No! stand erect and without fear,
And for our foes let this suffice—
We've bought a rightful sonship here,
And we have more than paid the price.

And not only has the American Negro served America, but he has made his contribution to her civilization, especially in art. He has given to America her only great body of folklore and he has likewise given to her her only great body of folk music, that wonderful mass of music which will some day furnish material to Negro composers through which they will voice, not only the soul of their race, but the soul of America.

I have always been glad of the fact that Hampton has made itself the home of that music, that here it has been nurtured and taught and spread, that here your own Nathaniel Dett has developed it in a way to attract the attention of the musicians of the world. This has been an important work because, under a misconception, there has at times been a tendency among Negroes themselves to be ashamed of their greatest contribution to American art. This great gift has sometimes been regarded as a kind of sideshow, something for occasional exhibition, when it is the touchstone, it is the magic thing, it is that by which the Negro can bridge all chasms. No persons, however hostile, can listen to the Negro's singing of this wonderful music without having their hostility melted down.

It is a race with this creditable and even glorious background, with these wonderful potentialities, that you are called upon to serve. This background and these potentialities you ought to study, and from that study you will learn that it is not dead and hopeless material that you have to work with but material waiting to be moulded into an essential element of the future American civilization.

This service has a definite end in view. It is the securing for yourselves and those for whom and among whom you will specifically work the status of full and unlimited American citizenship. I shall not here take the time to re-state the problem of the struggle that is before you. You know the conditions, and evidently you have a knowledge of the favorable and opposing forces that are at work. I shall only say that the problem which is commonly called the Negro Problem but which is, in fact, the American Problem, is not simple; it is complex. It is at the same time economic, social, and sexual. It is complicated by the diverse attitudes taken toward it by white people of various groups. It is further complicated by the fact that for the Negro himself it is compound, in that it is both an individual problem and a group problem.

The compound phase of this question for the Negro is of vital importance because it is the least understood phase of the whole problem, and because it is compound it resolves itself into the two following propositions:—

(1) The Negro must fit himself to the very best of his ability for all the rights and privileges of American citizenship.

(2) He must also find a way to compel a recognition of those rights and privileges when he has fitted himself.

The first proposition is comparatively easy, for it rests almost entirely with the individual and is dependent almost wholly upon his own determination. Thousands and hundreds of thousands of Negroes have achieved individual fitness, but individual fitness, as may be seen at a glance, is not the solution of the whole problem. Study of this first proposition ought to teach us not to make the easy error of believing that our status is due entirely to outside conditions. We must searchingly study ourselves and learn wherein we ourselves fall short, see how much of the blame is our own. One of the first discoveries we shall make is that we are not fully using the powers we already possess.

Perhaps our greatest God-given endowment is our emotionalism, the over-soul in us. But this greatest power in our possession is being recklessly dissipated in loud laughter, boisterous dancing, and a general good time. A pill box of gas with sufficient pressure removed will expand to fill the universe. Steam floating around in the air is no more effective than a whiff of cigarette smoke, but confined in a cylinder is a giant. When we have learned to channel down our emotional power, to run it through a cylinder, it will be transformed into great music, poetry, literature, and drama. It will become an irresistible force in battering down many of the obstacles that now confront us.

I spoke of our wonderful music as being the touchstone, the magic thing, by which the Negro can bridge all chasms. Let me expand that thought. It is through the arts that we may find the easiest approach to the solution of some of the most vital phases of our problem. It is the path of least friction. It is the plane on which all men are willing to meet and stand with us. We might argue in the abstract that the Negro possesses intellect, that he has high ideals, that his soul is sensitive to the most delicate nuances of spiritual reactions, and yet not convince those with whom we argue. But the production of sublime music, of moving poetry, of noble literature, is that which was to be demonstrated. There is no argument about it.

A people may become great through many means, but there is only one measure by which its greatness is recognized and acknowledged. The final measure of the greatness of all peoples is the amount and standard of literature and art they have produced. The world does not know that a people is great until that people produces great literature or art; and, conversely, no people that has produced great literature or art has ever been looked upon by the world as distinctly inferior.

The status of the Negro in the United States is more a question of mental attitude toward the race than it is a question of actual conditions. This attitude is based upon a generally accepted estimate of innate intellectual inferiority. There is nothing that will do more to change this mental attitude and raise the status of the Negro than a demonstration by him of intellectual and esthetic parity through the production of literature and art. And, luckily, his artistic endowment outweighs all his other gifts.

The second proposition of compelling the recognition of rights and privileges which correspond to fitness for them is a far more difficult problem. It takes group action to solve it. No amount of individual effort has much effect upon it. We must be able to correlate all of the forces within the group—economic, intellectual, moral, and political—in order to break down the barriers that will not give way to individual effort. These forces can be made to operate effectively only through an adequate machine and that machine is a national organization for this specific purpose. And the effort which this will take is in no sense selfish; it is in no sense for the exclusive advantage of the Negro. It is, indeed, for the benefit of true democracy in America. The Negro stands today demanding of America:—

> How would you have us, as we are—
> Or sinking 'neath the load we bear?
> Our eyes fixed forward on a star—
> Or gazing empty at despair?
> Rising or falling? Men or things?
> With dragging pace or footsteps fleet?
> Strong, willing sinews in your wings?
> Or tightening chains about your feet?

It is upon the answer to these questions that there hangs the fulfillment or the failure of democracy in America. It is for yourselves, and for your particular group, and for your native land, that you are called upon to see that these questions are answered right.

I say to you, stand firm and unequivocal in your claim for every right common to American citizenship. Do not surrender or abdicate a single one. Assert your claim with courage and determination. Make those who withhold these rights feel constantly that they are committing an injustice. Do not allow their consciences to go asleep. Because our future in this country holds only two choices—full and unlimited American citizenship, or a permanent secondary status —we must rise to the one or fall to the other. It may be a long time before some of these rights are accorded, but if we keep our courage we must surely win, for we have God and right on our side. The only danger is that we acquiesce, that we surrender, that we abdicate. If we ever become Jim-Crowed in our own souls, God Himself will not be able to save us. But let me here warn you that for those who serve in this cause there is a pit into which many may have fallen. It is the pit of selfishness, the pit of narrow ambitions. This pit is filled with many a man who has conspired with himself to be a leader of his fellows rather than a server. Such a one is always doomed to disappointment. Such a one must learn that only to him who serves well will the mass some day say, "This man serves well: let us follow him." Sooner or later it is always found that nothing endures but the truth, that nothing succeeds but service.

And let me here add one other word of warning. It is a sad confession to make that some who have had the advantage of trained minds have used that advantage for the exploitation of their less fortunate fellows. They have preyed upon mass ignorance and trustfulness for their own selfish gain. I cannot believe that anyone who has been imbued with the Hampton spirit will be guilty of such practice, but you must make it your duty to crush out these vultures wherever you find them. Do it without fear and without mercy.

And now to those who are today to receive their diplomas from this institution and leave its doors as students: I want you to take deep into your hearts this truth—the greatest of all problems lies within yourself, the problem transcending all differences of race or color or creed or condition, the problem of your own spiritual and moral development. Just how the world will look to you, just what the world will mean to you,—these lie entirely within yourself. This is the problem which no one can prevent you from working out successfully. Its correct solution depends entirely upon yourself. It is the problem beside which all others sink into insignificance. It is the problem of life itself.

Do you remember those lines in Walt Whitman's "Song of Occupations" in which he makes us understand and feel this fundamental truth? The platitudinarian would say, "Life is what you make it." Whitman in his magic poetry says:—

> All architecture is what you do to it
>    when you look upon it.
> (Did you think it was in the white or
>    gray stone? or in the lines of arches
>    and cornices?)
> All music is what awakes in you when you
>    are reminded by the instruments.
> It is not the violins and the cornets;
>    it is not the oboe nor the beating
>    drums, nor the score of the baritone
>    singer singing his sweet romanza, nor
>    that of the men's chorus, nor that
>    of the women's chorus.
> It is nearer and farther than they.

I add one more thought to the main theme of these inadequate words which I have been pronouncing. I wish to leave you with a thought of service to God. Perhaps it may be a new thought, for it is common to think of God as all powerful and of service when praying for Him to help. In a degree this idea is erroneous. God is not all powerful and He often needs our help. There are some things which God Himself cannot do: and never yet in the history of the human race has He been able to do anything for any people unless He could find a human heart, a human head, or a human hand to do it through.

And so, whatever plans there may be in the mind of God for us in this land, He cannot realize them, He cannot bring them into being unless we make ourselves the willing instruments through which He may work.

*This is an excerpt from an address Mr. Jones delivered
at the dedication of the Community House of the Canton
Urban League.*

# The Negro's Opportunity Today

## By Eugene Kinckle Jones

IN AN APPRAISAL of the Negro's contribution to life in America and
his potentialities in that direction, the Negro race looms up the mystery race of mankind. Usually, the Chinese are considered the mystery race because of the mask-like face of the Oriental, whose inner
thoughts cannot be interpreted from pantomime or facial expression.
The Negro has been considered the most easily understood of racial
groups because of his frank, open face, his jovial nature and his extraordinary ability through pantomime to give expression to his
thoughts.

Much has been said concerning the ultimate place in the world at
which the Negro race will come into its own. We have had the "back
to Africa" movements, including the Liberian experience and the
Garvey bubble. One of our most widely read weekly newspapers at
one time carried a series of articles on Brazil, the Utopia of Negro
existence. The absolute lack of prejudice against persons of color in
France has been presented as a hope that under French authority
Negro life might come to perfect fruition.

But none of these ideas has proved practical when the tremendous
economic problems of modern day life have been considered as concomitant questions along with that of human association. It is one
thing to be tolerated or even desired as an associate and another to
be welcomed as an economic competitor. Even in America, the Negro brought in as a slave was not introduced into the economic life
of the country as a competitor to the white man, but as an aid. I doubt
whether any statesman of the periods in which Negroes were brought
to America as slaves would have continued the experiment if they
had known that 1865 would have recorded on American soil Negroes

From *Opportunity*, VI (January 1928), 10–12.

to the number of four million, eventually to become industrial competitors of white men.

The past history of the Negro in Africa is but little known. It is hidden in a labyrinth of uncertain channels of information which when followed up leave the historian more in doubt than ever. In Egyptian life there is evidence of Negro influence, as well as in the life of the mixed races of the northern African coast. It is fairly certain that seven-eighths of the Jews in the world come from stock which had contact some time in their past history with Negro life. Undoubtedly, the Negro in antiquity played an interesting and important role in the affairs of men.

In recent years, in the field of Art, African Negro sculptures of various periods between the 10th and 19th centuries have had the most potent influence of any known to the modern art world. In fact, according to Paul Guillaume, one of the leading French authorities on Art, Negro Art has caused a renaissance in Art and kept it from reaching a point of stagnation or inertia which threatened modern Art development. Mr. Guillaume makes the following statement:

> I have said that before 1905, art in France, and indeed in all of Europe, was menaced by extinction. Five years later, the enthusiasm, the joy of the painters, their fever of excitement, made it apparent that a new renaissance had taken place. Not less evident was it that the honor of this renaissance belonged to Negro art.
>
> In the work of Picasso there was a whole epoch named the "Negro epoch"; there was an entire literature, a whole school of music, which was, at first ironically, named after the Negroes—a name which they will keep, though the irony has long since disappeared. One may almost say that there was a form of feeling, an architecture of thought, a subtle expression of the most profound forces of life, which had been extracted from Negro civilization. For a time, the consciousness of Negro art was confined to the leaders of thought and feeling, the pioneers. The mass of the people knew it only at second-hand, and had no idea when they delighted in the brilliant decoration of the Russian Ballet, or felt the throbbing rhythms of Stravinsky, or were warmed by the new vitality in the poetry of their contemporaries, that so much of their life-giving art was born in tropical jungles many centuries ago. But soon people grew anxious to drink from this spring at its source. The world quickly learned of the vast and unsuspected wealth of spiritual inspiration bequeathed to modern times by unnamed artists of the black race, artists to whom it was then eager to do homage.

In the partitioning of Africa by the European countries, the natives have been denied their rights in the very lands which for centuries have been their own. While in many of the protectorates in Africa Negro tribes are given a chance to develop their own resources under the supervision or guidance of the powers holding mandates, in South Africa, Negroes are denied rights of property ownership in the cities and are corralled in compounds or "locations" which deprive them of their rights even of locomotion. In districts sparsely settled by the whites they are restricted to certain narrow areas and in some sections at night are not permitted to visit their friends and relatives on adjoining estates without the written consent of the white property owners.

For 250 years in America, the Negro was held in slavery and was considered as mere chattel possessed neither of his own body nor soul. The sixty years that have elapsed, however, since he gained his freedom, have proved the "golden age" of the American Negro and his progress has been greater than that of any similar number of Negroes anywhere on the globe. It is true that during these sixty years, his career of progress has been punctuated by a series of unjust and discouraging events which would have spelled disaster to any less hopeful race of people—lynchings, "grandfather" clauses, peonage, segregation laws, denial of rights before the bar of public opinion and the bar of justice.

These phases of the Negro's experience in America, however, have been only events that have tended to arrest the upward curve marking his progress. We could show without question various lines of group improvement in Negro life in America which would demonstrate beyond doubt that here in our native land is the most hopeful spot on the globe for a favorable social improvement experiment for the Negro which may serve as a model for Negro groups elsewhere in the world. The white race and the Negro race in America are each possessed of heritages and have had racial experience so vastly different. They are given an unusual opportunity to prove the possibilities of a true democracy where different races of mankind may live in peace and harmony, each one giving of his best to the welfare of all and to the glory of God and man.

In general health conditions among Negroes, the records show improvement. Unquestionably there have been years when the death rates among Negroes have risen a little, but these years usually have been followed by decreases and we find that in making a comparison of the Negro death rate with the death rate of the whites today, the Negroes are less than fifteen years behind the white population—

possessed of hundreds of years of unhindered opportunity in a favorable environment. In 1912, the Negro death rate was 22.9 per thousand. It is now less than 15.7 per thousand. The white death rate in 1900 was 17.1 per thousand.

In the matter of home ownership, the Negro has increased his holdings to a point where more than one-quarter of the Negro families in the United States are residing in houses to which they hold title. Negro wealth in America today is in excess of two billions of dollars. A side of the development of home ownership among Negroes more hopeful than that of material possession is the accompanying rise of the standards of home life due to pride of ownership, increased income and a higher grade of intelligence acquired through improved school facilities.

This leads to a brief discussion of the subject of occupations. Possibly, there is no phase of Negro life which has undergone a more marked change than his vocational experience during the past ten or twelve years. His occupations have improved in type and in remuneration; they have become more diversified. With the one million increase in the Negro population in the north between 1910 and the present, many new types of occupations have engaged the service of the Negroes, some of which the race's most optimistic leaders had little hope of his entering.

In New York City, which is typical of the most favored of the cities to which Negroes have migrated, the 1920 Census listed one or more Negroes in 316 of the 321 occupations recorded. This means that there were only five different types of work in the whole city in which there were no Negroes engaged. In each of 175 of these 321 occupations, there was a minimum of 50 Negroes listed.

The business development of the Negro has probably been the slowest. It requires more than just the ability to sell to conduct a successful business. One must be able to buy well, which means having many contacts and the development of credit. One must be satisfied with large numbers of small profits in lieu of a small number of large profits. One must appreciate the value of advertising and be possessed of the necessary capital to see it through. Competition in this line is keener for the Negro than in any professional or other vocation; but despite this consideration, business activity within the race is surely gaining headway. Developments in banks, fire and life insurance, real estate, electrical wiring, coal and wood retail operations, taxicab and garage service have recorded extraordinary successes. In science, letters and the arts, there has been a great awakening. General hospitals in some cities have opened their doors to Negro internes and to staff physicians. Hospitals for Negroes have been established. The biological sciences have been developed by such men as Dr. Just of Howard University and Professor Lewis of the University of Chicago; Dr. Carver of Tuskegee has transformed the lowly peanut and sweet potato into commercial products which have placed him in a class with Luther Burbank.

In letters, the race has developed W. E. B. Du Bois, whose English has been declared the purest of any Harvard graduate; Alain LeRoy Locke, former Rhodes Scholar whose *New Negro* has provoked much discussion recently and gained new respect for the race; Walter F. White, Jessie Fauset and Jean Toomer, whose novels have elicited much praise, and James Weldon Johnson, whose novels, poetry and other writings have gained for him an enviable reputation. In poetry, Countee Cullen and Langston Hughes have mastered the art of singing without music and have published two books rated as "best sellers" in the world of poetry.

Of course, every intelligent American knows of the successes in the musical world of Roland Hayes, and Harry Burleigh; and of Benjamin Tanner—the Negro American artist, dean of the American art colony in Paris. Florence Mills!

Success in life calls for thorough preparation. Success in American life today is fraught with keen competition. The Negro must compete not only with members of other races, but with those within his own race who have caught the vision of the new age and who are lured along by the attraction of success. The rank and file are dependent upon trained men and women for guidance and extraordinary service.

The higher types of pleasure which one gets out of life when he is performing unusual tasks is sufficient urge for the talented of the race to make the necessary sacrifices for thorough preparation, but the financial gain to be derived is a stimulus which the American youth of today cannot ignore.

Tabulations kept by a number of public school superintendents in some of our larger cities of the income of graduates of elementary and high schools have shown how rapidly the high school graduate's income approaches that of the elementary school graduate who finished four years ahead. In a few years, the high school graduate is receiving a higher wage than the elementary school graduate who left school to go to work four years earlier earned during the period that the high school student was in school, and the total income of the high school graduate very soon is far above that of his former school mate of lesser scholastic training. The same would hold true in regard to college graduates and those with special vocational training when compared with graduates from the general course in the high school.

It is not my thought that college training should be sought after by all persons who have had the equivalent of a secondary education, for there is much waste of time in the effort of persons whose minds are not fitted to assimilate and utilize collegiate training. It is more important that one develop his mind along his natural bent and talent than to seek some form of popular education which leaves the student ill-equipped and proceeding along blind occupational alleys.

By preparation for life, I mean securing that sort of scholastic training and practice which would best fit the individual for the work he can best do. The day of the self-educated man is past. First of all, it takes too long to educate oneself, and in the second place, the school of experience cannot half so well point out the difficulties and pitfalls of competitive economic life as can those persons who have acquired the necessary knowledge, through study and experience, of the difficulties to be met in life by the youth and who can impart it in our institutions of public instruction.

Before concluding, permit me to cite some examples of unusual success on the part of members of our race which should give encouragement and determination to all of us:

In some cases, I do not mention names, because the persons referred to are in positions to which they would prefer not to have public attention drawn. Mr. Alexander, a Negro civil engineer in Iowa, has built most of the largest bridges in the southern part and has been associate engineer on some very important engineering jobs. He has the contract for the new heating plant in his Alma Mater—Iowa University. He employs 289 men. He says his color is an asset to him. A Negro mechanical engineer is manager of the Pittsburgh office of a large Chicago manufacturing concern. The largest house-moving business in Ohio is that of Bryant in Columbus, Ohio. He has scores of auto trucks constantly busy. A colored physician, Louis Wright of New York City, is a member of the Presbyterian Hospital Board of Trustees, having been elected because of his medical record and in appreciation of his raising some twenty-odd thousand dollars among the colored citizens of New York in a recent campaign. Mrs. Eslanda Goode Robeson, wife of Paul Robeson, the actor, has for some years been on the laboratory staff of this hospital.

There are now over 600 public school teachers in New York City who are engaged all through the educational system of the Greater City. They are senior and junior high school teachers, supervisors of music, lecturers and special teachers, vocational guides, visiting teachers, an assistant principal, a retired principal. Negroes are employed on the engineering staff of the new subway construction in New York—ten years ago we were happy to get Negroes jobs as unskilled laborers on such construction work. Samuel A. Irving, a Negro, has the contract for building all the concrete moulds for the foundations of the new seven-million-dollar Columbia University–Presbyterian Hospital in New York. His contract is for more than $350,000. He employs over 125 carpenters in his work and a Negro civil engineer for all of his calculations. This engineer was for seven years employed on the engineering staff of English railroads and before this was a bridge engineer of the Michigan Central Railroad. He is a University of Pittsburgh graduate. The metallurgist of the Deuter-Hampden Watch Company in Canton, Ohio, is a Negro. In the Cleveland Hardware Company, the chief chemist is a Negro girl —a Fisk graduate. The metallurgist there is a Negro, as is the head of the die press room, and its fastest press hand is a colored woman. Her record shows 18,500 operations in eight hours—practically two every three seconds. Ferdinand Q. Morton, Civil Service Commissioner of New York; Edward H. Wright, Public Service Commissioner of Chicago; David Manson, manager of the Western office in Chicago of the Ohio Iron Works, are Negroes. I know of ten Negro members of City Councils; thirteen Negro members of State Legislatures and one State Senator; one member of the editorial staff of a metropolitan daily paper; three Negro Assistant U. S. District Attorneys, three Negro judges of municipal courts and hundreds of other colored men and women holding responsible positions in private and public institutions. There is a colored woman who is special case reader of a large charity organization society in one of the largest cities of the West. All cases come to her before final adjustment is made.

Until a little over a year ago, a colored man, Forrester B. Washington, was the Director of Research of the Detroit Community

Union, the Chest organization representing every recognized and approved charity of that great American city of a million inhabitants.

A colored man is a member of the National Conference of Social Work. He is now serving his second three-year term, having recently been re-elected to this Board of fifteen persons by a membership of 4,000 social workers—the overwhelming majority of whom are white.

These instances of success in many different fields prove conclusively that there can be no generalization made of the Negro's capacity and outlook and therefore no generalization of the type of training Negroes should receive. Mental tests, whether of racial groups or of classes of persons, white or black, from the north and from the south, have proved nothing except that environment and opportunity count most.

The Negro will come into his own in this country when he is recorded as a member of a creative group, contributing to the welfare of his country; who yet is not boastful of his accomplishments, and who is taking his rightful place—a great race among other great races, keeping step in the march of human progress.

# PART TWO

# *The American Nightmare*

WHILE WHITE children pledged allegiance to a nation that promised them freedom and liberty, black children grew up with the terrible knowledge that America failed to protect them from terror, discrimination, and lynching. For black Americans, the American Dream turned out to be a nightmare. From 1900 to 1922, there was an average of one race riot a year, with the number evenly divided between the North and the South. During those same years, more than fifteen hundred blacks were lynched; from 1918 to 1923, thirty-four blacks were burned alive at the stake. Jim Crow laws and political disfranchisement characterized the life of black Southerners. Any breach of the rigid white Southern code of conduct by a black man insured violent retaliation.

But life in the North, depicted as so desirable in many black newspapers, turned out to be equally disheartening and frustrating for those who moved up from the South. The first massive migration of Southern blacks to the North occurred during and after the First

World War. Instead of finding Northern cities friendly and responsive, black Southerners were shunned by labor unions and exploited as scabs by employers. Black organizations, such as the Urban League, helped to make the transition from a rural to an urban environment easier, but their task was a mighty one. Southern blacks were greeted with job discrimination, ghetto living, political corruption, and inferior educational facilities. A flourishing literature, music, and art developed in Harlem despite the fact that most New York blacks faced daily experiences of prejudice and misery.

The following articles, many of them personal accounts, accurately depict the nightmarish existence of black Americans. Most black writers, however, continued to display an enduring faith in the morality of white Americans and their willingness to correct unjust treatment.

*Mrs. Barnett, a leader in the fight against lynching, was head of the Anti-Lynching Bureau of the Afro-American Council.*

# The Negro's Case in Equity

### By Ida B. Wells Barnett

THE *Independent* published an earnest appeal to negro editors, preachers and teachers "to tell their people to defend the laws and their own rights even to blood, but never, never to take guilty participation in lynching white man or black." This advice is given by way of comment on the double lynching in Virginia the other day. Theoretically the advice is all right, but viewed in the light of circumstances and conditions it seems like giving a stone when we ask for bread.

For twenty years past the negro has done nothing else but defend the law and appeal to public sentiment for defense *by* the law. He has seen hundreds of men of his race murdered in cold blood by connivance of officers of the law, from the governors of the States down to sheriffs of counties, as in this Virginia case, and that upon the unsupported word of some white man or woman. He has seen his women and children stripped and strung up to trees or riddled with bullets for the gratification of spite, as in the case of Postmaster Baker's family two years ago, and in that in Alabama a few weeks ago, when an entire family was wiped out of existence because a white man had been murdered.

The negro has seen scores of his race, absolutely innocent of any charge whatever, used as scapegoats for some white man's crime, as in the case of C. J. Miller, lynched in Bardwell, Ky., in 1893, and John Peterson, of Denmark, S.C., the same year. Miller was stripped, hung with a log chain to a telegraph pole, riddled with bullets, then burned, since which proceeding he was found to have suffered for a crime committed by a white man. Peterson had sought protection from Governor (now Senator) Tillman, but was given over to the

From the *Independent*, LII (April 26, 1900), 1010–1011.

mob, and altho the girl in the case said he was not the man, yet the lynchers, led by a State Senator, said a crime had been committed and somebody had to hang for it; so Peterson was strung up and five hundred bullets fired into his body. . . .

All this and more the negro has seen and suffered without taking the law into his hands for, lo, these many years. There have been no Nat Turner insurrections and San Domingan horrors in retaliation for all the wrongs he has suffered. When the negro has appealed to the Christian and moral forces of the country—asking them to create a sentiment against this lawlessness and unspeakable barbarism; demanding justice and the protection of the law for every human being regardless of color—that demand has been met with general indifference or entirely ignored. Where this is not true he has been told that these same forces upon which he confidently depends refuse to make the demand for justice, because they believe the story of the mob that negroes are lynched because they commit unspeakable crimes against white women. For this reason the Christian and moral forces are silent in the presence of the horrible barbarities alleged to be done in the name of woman. . . .

Again and again, during the present session of Congress, in both the House and Senate, the negro has been attacked and this foul slander against his good name made in several speeches and sent broadcast. Except a brief rejoinder by Congressman George White, there was no attempt at refutation or rebuke in Congress or out by any of the champions of truth and justice. . . .

Who, if not the negro preachers, editors and teachers, are to be credited with the fact that there are few, if any, instances of negroes who have had "guilty participation in lynching white men or black?" . . .

For the seven years the negro has been agitating against lynching he has made this appeal to the leaders of thought and action among the white race. If they will do their duty in this respect the negroes will soon have no bad examples of the lynching kind set, which in their desperation they may be tempted to follow.

As matters now stand, the negroes down in Virginia the other day would have fared badly had they attempted to defend the law in either case. A band of negroes prevented a lynching in Jacksonville, Fla., in the summer of 1892 by guarding the jail, tho not a shot was fired. The man who led the band has been an exile from his home ever since. He was indicted for "conspiracy" and about to be sent to the penitentiary for preventing white men from lynching a negro, when he forfeited his bond by leaving home and sacrificing his property. Only last summer the same thing happened in Darien, Ga. A white woman gave birth to a negro child, and the mob prepared to lynch the father for the "usual crime." The negroes got wind of it, guarded the jail and prevented the lynching. They were all indicted for that "conspiracy" and lodged in jail. John Delegal, who helped guard his father when the mob was after him, lived in the country. The posse went after him as a "conspirator," broke open his house and entered firing. He returned the fire, killing the leader instantly. Those negroes have all been tried since by a jury of the kind of men who tried to lynch Delegal's father, found guilty of "conspiracy," and are now doing time in the penitentiary. John was sent up for life. In the present apathetic condition of public sentiment, North and South, this is what the negro gets who attempts to "defend the law and his rights." Not until the white editors, preachers and teachers of the country join with him in his fight for justice and protection by law can there be any hope of success.

*Daniel Webster Davis was a lesser-known black poet who wrote in the latter part of the nineteenth century and contributed to a short-lived magazine called* The Voice of the Negro, *the same title as the following poem from which it is reprinted.*

## The Voice of the Negro

*By Daniel Webster Davis*

Stop! O, Nation, stop and listen!
Listen with your heart and brain,
Hear the weird Voice of the Negro,
Coming up from Southern p'ain:
From the brakes of Louisiana,
From the fields of whit'ning grain,
From the lees of Mississippi,
Listen, as it comes again.

Not for social recognition,
Not for alms this Voice is rife.
For this, and only this 'tis pleading,—
A man's chance in the race of life.
For an equal chance to labor,
And honest pay for honest toil;
Give this, and by the God who made us,
We'll win success on Southern soil.

We still have hope, tho' darkness lowers,
And thunders spread their dread alarms;
Faith in the best blood of the Southland,
Faith in the strength of our own arms,
Faith in the truth, tho' crushed and bleeding;
That justice in man's heart still dwells,
We'll kiss the rod, then rise and labor,
God reigns above, and all is well.

From *The Voice of the Negro* (February 1904), p. 66.

*A week before this article appeared, a race riot had oc-
curred in Ohio. In order to describe the race problem,
the* Independent *began a series of three articles—one by
a Southern black woman, a second by a Southern white
woman, and a third by a Northern white woman living in
the South.*

---

# The Race Problem—An Autobiography

## *By a Southern Colored Woman*

MY FATHER was slave in name only, his father and master being the
same. He lived on a large plantation and knew many useful things.
The blacksmith shop was the place he liked best, and he was allowed
to go there and make little tools as a child. He became an expert
blacksmith before he was grown. Before the war closed he had married and was the father of one child. When his father wanted him to
remain on the plantation after the war, he refused because the wages
offered were too small. The old man would not even promise an increase later; so my father left in a wagon he had made with his own
hands, drawn by a horse he had bought from a passing horse drover
with his own money.

He had in his wagon his wife and baby, some blacksmith tools he
had made from time to time, bedding, their clothing, some food, and
twenty dollars in his pocket. As he drove by the house he got out of
the wagon to bid his father good-by. The old man came down the
steps and, pointing in the direction of the gate, said: "Joseph, when
you get on the outside of that gate—stay." Turning to my mother, he
said: "When you get hungry and need clothes for yourself and the
baby, as you are sure to do, come to me," and he pitched a bag of
silver in her lap, which my father immediately took and placed at his
father's feet on the steps and said, "I am going to feed and clothe
them and I can do it on a bare rock." My father drove twenty-five
miles to the largest town in the State, where he succeeded in renting
a small house.

From *The Independent*, LVI (March 17, 1904), 586–589.

The next day he went out to buy something to eat. On his way home a lady offered him fifty cents for a string of fish for which he had only paid twenty cents. That gave him an idea. Why not buy fish every day and sell them? He had thought to get work at his trade, but here was money to be made and quickly. So from buying a few strings of fish he soon saved enough to buy a wagon load of fish.

My mother was very helpless, never having done anything in her life except needlework. She was unfitted for the hard work, and most of this my father did. He taught my mother to cook, and he would wash and iron himself at night.

Many discouraging things happened to them—often sales were slow and fish would spoil; many would not buy of him because he was colored; another baby was born and died, and my father came very near losing his life for whipping a white man who insulted my mother. He got out of the affair finally, but had to take on a heavy debt, besides giving up all of his hard earned savings.

My father said after the war his ambition was first to educate himself and family, then to own a white house with green blinds, as much like his father's as possible, and to support his family by his own efforts; never to allow his wife and daughters to be thrown in contact with Southern white men in their homes. He succeeded.

The American Missionary Association had opened schools by this time, and my father went to night school and sent his wife and child to school in the day.

By hard work and strict economy two years after he left his father's plantation he gave two hundred dollars for a large plot of ground on a high hill on the outskirts of the town.

Three years later I was born in my father's own home, in his coveted white house with green blinds—his father's house in miniature. Here my father kept a small store, was burned out once and had other trials, but finally he had a large grocery store and feed store attached.

I have never lived in a rented house except for one year since I've been grown. I have never gone to a public school in my life, my parents preferring the teaching of the patient "New England school-marm" to the Southern "poor white," who thought it little better than a disgrace to teach colored children—so much of a disgrace that she taught her pupils not to speak to her on the streets. My mother and her children never performed any labor outside of my father's and their own homes.

To-day I have the same feeling my parents had. There is no sacrifice I would not make, no hardship I would not undergo rather
than allow my daughters to go in service where they would be
thrown constantly in contact with Southern white men, for they
consider the colored girl their special prey.

It is commonly said that no girl or woman receives a certain kind
of insult unless she invites it. That does not apply to a colored girl
and woman in the South. The color of her face alone is sufficient
invitation to the Southern white man—these same men who profess
horror that a white gentleman can entertain a colored one at his table.
Out of sight of their own women they are willing and anxious to
entertain colored women in various ways. Few colored girls reach
the age of sixteen without receiving advances from them—maybe
from a young "upstart," and often from a man old enough to be their
father, a white haired veteran of sin. Yes, and men high in position,
whose wives and daughters are leaders of society. I have had a clerk
in a store hold my hand as I gave him the money for some purchase
and utter some vile request; a shoe man to take liberties, a man in a
crowd to place his hands on my person, others to follow me to my
very door, a school director to assure me a position if I did his bidding.

It is true these particular men never insulted me but once; but
there are others. I might write more along this line and worse things
—how a white man of high standing will systematically set out to
entrap a colored girl—but my identification would be assured in
some quarters. My husband was also educated in an American Missionary Association school (God bless the name!), and after graduat-
ing took a course in medicine in another school. He has practiced
medicine now for over ten years. By most frugal living and strict
economy he saved enough to buy for a home a house of four rooms,
which has since been increased to eight. Since our marriage we have
bought and paid for two other places, which we rent. My husband's
collections average one hundred dollars a month. We have an iron-
bound rule that we must save at least fifty dollars a month. Some
months we lay by more, but never less. We do not find this very
hard to do with the rent from our places, and as I do all of my work
except the washing and ironing.

We have three children, two old enough for school. I try to be a
good and useful neighbor and friend to those who will allow me. I
would be contented and happy if I, an American citizen, could say
as Axel Jarlson (the Swedish emigrant, whose story appeared in The
Independent of January 8th, 1903) says, "There are no aristocrats to

push him down and say that he is not worthy because his father was poor." There are "aristocrats" to push me and mine down and say we are not worthy because we are colored. The Chinaman, Lee Chew, ends his article in THE INDEPENDENT of February 19th, 1903, by saying, "Under the circumstances how can I call this my home, and how can any one blame me if I take my money and go back to my village in China?"

Happy Chinaman! Fortunate Lee Chew! You can go back to your village and enjoy your money. This is my village, my home, yet am I an outcast. See what an outcast! Not long since I visited a Southern city where the "Jim Crow" car law is enforced. I did not know of this law, and on boarding an electric car took the most convenient seat. The conductor yelled, "What do you mean? Niggers don't sit with white folks down here. You must have come from 'way up yonder. I'm not Roosevelt. We don't sit with niggers, much less eat with them."

I was astonished and said, "I am a stranger and did not know of your law." His answer was: "Well, no back talk now; that's what I'm here for—to tell niggers their places when they don't know them."

Every white man, woman, and child was in a titter of laughter by this time at what they considered the conductor's wit.

These Southern men and women, who pride themselves on their fine sense of feeling, had no feeling for my embarrassment and unmerited insult, and when I asked the conductor to stop the car that I might get off, one woman said in a loud voice, "These niggers get more impudent every day; she doesn't want to sit where she belongs."

No one of them thought that I was embarrassed, wounded, and outraged by the loud, brutal talk of the conductor and the sneering, contemptuous expressions on their own faces. They considered me "impudent" when I only wanted to be alone that I might conquer my emotion. I was nervous and blinded by tears of mortification which will account for my second insult on this same day.

I walked downtown to attend to some business and had to take an elevator in an office building. I stood waiting for the elevator, and when the others, all of whom were white, got in I made a move to go in also, and the boy shut the cage door in my face. I thought the elevator was too crowded and waited; the same thing happened the second time. I would have walked up, but I was going to the fifth story, and my long walk downtown had tired me. The third time the elevator came down the boy pointed to a sign and said, "I guess you can't read; but niggers don't ride in this elevator; we're white folks here, we are. Go to the back and you'll find an elevator for freight and niggers."

The occupants of the elevator also enjoyed themselves at my expense. This second insult in one day seemed more than I could bear. I could transact no business in my frame of mind, so I slowly took the long walk back to the suburbs of the city, where I was stopping.

My feelings were doubly crushed and in my heart, I fear, I rebelled not only against man but God. I have been humiliated and insulted often, but I never get used to it; it is new each time, and stings and hurts more and more.

The very first humiliation I received I remember very distinctly to this day. It was when I was very young. A little girl playmate said to me: "I like to come over to your house to play, we have such good times, and your ma has such good preserves; but don't you tell my ma I eat over here. My ma says you all are nice, clean folks and she'd rather live by you than the white people we moved away from; for you don't borrow things. I know she would whip me if I ate with you, tho, because you are colored, you know."

I was very angry and forgot she was my guest, but told her to go home and bring my ma's sugar home her ma borrowed, and the rice they were always wanting a cup of.

After she had gone home I threw myself upon the ground and cried, for I liked the little girl, and until then I did not know that being "colored" made a difference. I am not sure I knew anything about "colored." I was very young and I know now I had been shielded from all unpleasantness.

My mother found me in tears and I asked her why was I colored, and couldn't little girls eat with me and let their mothers know it.

My mother got the whole story from me, but she couldn't satisfy me with her explanation—or, rather, lack of explanation. The little girl came often to play with me after that and we were little friends again, but we never had any more play dinners. I could not reconcile the fact that she and her people could borrow and eat our rice in their own house and not sit at my table and eat my mother's good, sweet preserves.

The second shock I received was horrible to me at the time. I had not gotten used to real horrible things then. The history of Christian men selling helpless men and women's children to far distant States was unknown to me; a number of men burning another chained to a post an impossibility, the whipping of a grown woman by a strong man unthought of. I was only a child, but I remember to this day what a shock I received. A young colored woman of a lovely disposition and character had just died. She was a teacher in the Sunday school I attended—a self-sacrificing, noble young woman who had been loved by many. Her coffin, room, hall, and even the porch of her house were filled with flowers sent by her friends. There were lovely designs sent by the more prosperous and simple bouquets made by untrained, childish hands. I was on my way with my own last offering of love, when I was met by quite a number of white boys and girls. A girl of about fifteen years said to me, "More flowers for that dead nigger? I never saw such a to-do made over a dead nigger before. Why, there must be thousands of roses alone in that house. I've been standing out here for hours and there has been a continual stream of niggers carrying flowers, and beautiful ones, too, and what makes me madder than anything else, those Yankee teachers carried flowers, too!" I, a little girl, with my heart full of sadness for the death of my friend, could make no answer to these big, heartless boys and girls, who threw stones after me as I ran from them.

When I reached home I could not talk for emotion. My mother was astonished when I found voice to tell her I was not crying because of the death of Miss W., but because I could not do something, anything, to avenge the insult to her dead body. I remember the strongest feeling I had was one of revenge. I wanted even to kill that particular girl or do something to hurt her. I was unhappy for days. I was told that they were heartless, but that I was even worse, and that Miss W. would be the first to condemn me could she speak.

That one encounter made a deep impression on my childish heart; it has been with me throughout the years. I have known real horrors since, but none left a greater impression on me.

My mother used to tell me if I were a good little girl everybody would love me, and if I always used nice manners it would make others show the same to me.

I believed that literally until I entered school, when the many encounters I had with white boys and girls going to and from school made me seriously doubt that goodness and manners were needed in this world. The white children I knew grew meaner as they grew older—more capable of saying things that cut and wound.

I was often told by white children whose parents rented houses: "You think you are white because your folks own their own home;

but you ain't, you're a nigger just the same, and my pa says if he had his rights he would own niggers like you, and your home, too."

A child's feelings are easily wounded, and day after day I carried a sad heart. To-day I carry a sad heart on account of my children. What is to become of them? The Southern whites dislike more and more the educated colored man. They hate the intelligent colored man who is accumulating something. The respectable, intelligent colored people are "carefully unknown"; their good traits and virtues are never mentioned. On the other hand, the ignorant and vicious are carefully known and all of their traits cried aloud.

In the natural order of things our children will be better educated than we, they will have our accumulations and their own. With the added dislike and hatred of the white man, I shudder to think of the outcome.

In this part of the country, where the Golden Rule is obsolete, the commandment, "Love thy neighbor as thyself" is forgotten; anything is possible.

I dread to see my children grow. I know not their fate. Where the white girl has one temptation, mine will have many. Where the white boy has every opportunity and protection, mine will have few opportunities and no protection. It does not matter how good or wise my children may be, they are colored. When I have said that, all is said. Everything is forgiven in the South but color.

*The following exchange presents three different points of view about the Atlanta Riot of 1906—the South's most sensational race riot to that date. The white writer, A. J. McKelway, was one of two assistant secretaries of the National Child Labor Committee. Mrs. Carrie Clifford was honorary president of the Ohio Federation of Colored Women's Clubs. Edward Ware was a faculty member of Atlanta University.*

## The Atlanta Riots
## I—A Southern White Point of View

### By A. J. McKelway

I HAVE NOT been a citizen of Atlanta long enough to feel any passion of partisanship in defending the good name of the city. I was out of town during the period of the rioting, from Friday night until Wednesday morning, and so neither shared the universal feeling of the white people on Saturday that something had to be done nor had my sensibilities shocked by the actual spectacle of the murder of innocent and inoffensive negroes by the mob. The Outlook was good enough to credit my story of the "Wilmington Revolution," eight years ago, and to take a position on that subject that has added greatly to the influence of the magazine in the South. I crave a word which will be of the nature of a reply to the editorial comment of September 29 entitled "An American Kishinev."

The only parallel that can be drawn between Kishinev and Atlanta is that there was race antagonism in both instances. There was no religious fanaticism, as at Kishinev. There was no sympathy with the mob by civil or military authorities, as The Outlook admits. The Jews are a law-abiding and inoffensive people. The negroes are our criminal class. There had been no outrages inflicted by Jewish criminals upon the Russian women or men as the incentive to the Kishinev massacre. But the fact that there was such race antagonism as resulted in an indiscriminate slaughter of negroes by whites because

From *Outlook*, LXXXIV (November 3, 1906), 557–566.

they were negroes is something to be emphasized rather than denied, and its cause or causes patiently and calmly inquired into.

The Outlook says that Atlanta is not a typical Southern city. I have found it intensely Southern, and with a most hospitable attitude toward settlers from other sections. Ninety-five per cent of the people are of Southern birth. It has quite a large population of skilled laborers from the North and West, but it should be said that organized labor here is distinctly friendly to the negro laborers, while there may be some of the prejudice, which is still rather foreign to the South, against the negro who has a job that the white man might fill, and this feeling may have found expression in the murder of a telegraph messenger and the two barbers. I am disposed also to question the statement that the race feeling is acuter in Atlanta than in almost any other Southern city. I have thought rather the contrary to be true until the events of the last few weeks occurred.

But the fact remains that for the first time in the history of Southern crime there was an indiscriminate lynching of negroes by a mob. The mob has heretofore been after the negro criminal and anxious to avoid a mistake for the very desire that the criminal should be punished. We have read of such assaults upon negroes in the two Springfields, and there have been anti-negro riots in New York. But Southern cities have been free from this particular form of mob violence, the race wars being in all other cases clashes between armed bodies of whites and negroes.

Nor do I consider plausible The Outlook's theory that the political issue of negro disfranchisement has had much to do with the trouble. If it did, its settlement in favor of the negro would have been the more dangerous thing for peace between the races. If it did, it was because of the division of the white people on that question and the apparent "backing" given to the political claims of the negroes. The quality that makes the negro regiment with white officers efficient in war will make the negro dare much with the possession or the fancy of white sympathy and encouragement. But if The Outlook's theory is correct, we hark back to race antagonism excited in the breasts of the negroes, for there was nothing in the campaign or its results to kindle resentment or antipathy in the hearts of white people.

If there had been no assaults upon white women in and near Atlanta, there would have been no mobs and no riots. That is a truism. A brief history of these assaults within the year, with their cumulative frequency within the last few weeks, will help to determine the cause of this unique experience in a Southern city—the wholesale murder of innocent negroes by the mob.

On October 26, 1905, Mrs. M., a respectable white woman, fifty-five years of age, was most brutally assaulted by a negro, a railroad hand, who escaped immediately after the crime, was captured in a distant city on November 9, after the arrest of several negroes on suspicion, whom Mrs. M. pronounced not the guilty one, was brought back to Atlanta, fully identified, was protected from the threat of mob violence, confessed his guilt to so many people that his attorneys were powerless, pleaded guilty, and was sentenced to death and hanged, the execution taking place on December 8. The law had acted with certainty and without delay.

In March, 1906, the negro janitor of one of the public schools made an insulting proposal to a white school-girl and laid his hands on her person. He bore a good character to which several white people testified, and while there was no shaking the testimony of the little girl, it was his word against hers, and he was convicted of a minor crime and sentenced to twelve months on the roads.

On July 31 there was an assault by a negro upon a young girl, Miss P., in one of the suburbs of Atlanta. It should be understood, and will be from these recitals, that every neighbor of an outraged family turns out at once to help in hunting down the criminal, and that, with a city like Atlanta near, he generally escapes. A number of neighbors helped the county police in searching for this negro, found him, with the evidences of his crime, took him before the girl, who unhesitatingly identified him, and instantly he was shot by some of the citizens who had caught him, the bullets wounding the two white men who were holding him, and this was done just before the county police arrived. His dead body was brought to Atlanta, and the effort to discover the men who shot him was futile. This is the only lynching of a criminal that has occurred.

On July 20 a negro boy assaulted a negro girl one day, and a white girl, a mere child, the next, in the country, some thirty miles from Atlanta. He confessed to the first crime and was brought to the jail in Atlanta for safe-keeping, "the Tower," as it is called, being impregnable to the attacks of a mob.

On August 15 Mrs. H. was criminally assaulted by a negro, who escaped capture, those arrested on suspicion not having been identified.

On August 20 there was a brutal assault, in another suburb of Atlanta, upon Misses M. and E. L., the former a visitor from England,

and the latter a mere child. Both were terribly injured in the struggle. It is believed that, after weeks of search, the right negro has been taken. There were threats of lynching one or two suspects. The negro captured is confined in the Tower and has been indicted by the Grand Jury.

On August 26 the number of county police was trebled, being increased from twelve to thirty-six, and it was agreed to add forty policemen to the city force on the first of October—which was too late.

On August 24 Miss W., a schoolteacher, went to a spring on private property and was accosted and pursued by a negro, but escaped his clutches. He also escaped arrest.

On September 20, Thursday afternoon preceding the riot, Mrs. K. was assaulted near Fort McPherson, and, with the rumors of the gathering of a mob, Governor Terrell left the dinner that was given in honor of Mr. Bryan's visit, and called out the military, who conducted the negro arrested for this crime from Fort McPherson to the jail in Atlanta. Mrs. K. failed to identify the one arrested.

The same night a half-clad negro, who was probably intoxicated, but who had hidden his clothing for disguising himself afterward, entered a house in the heart of the city, attacked a mother and her two daughters, who successfully defended themselves, and was captured by the neighbors and landed in jail.

Friday evening a negro who was delivering ice was shown where to put it by a young white girl when he seized her by the hand and kissed her. He was caught and lodged in jail.

Saturday, September 22, a negro came to the home of Mrs. C. in another suburb, was ordered away, and then hid in the barn, whence he issued later and pursued Mrs. C. to her house, when she caught up an unloaded gun and drove him off.

The same afternoon Mrs. A., in another suburb, was attacked on the rear porch of her home by a negro, her husband being away. But she had persuaded her brother to stay at the house that evening, and her screams brought him to her aid. A negro suspect was arrested for this crime during Sunday of the riot, and while being brought to town in a buggy managed to pull the reins so that the buggy was overturned by a streetcar, and so he escaped.

The same evening, Saturday, Miss A., eighteen years of age, was attacked on the back porch of her home by a negro, who threw her to the floor. Her screams also brought help, but the negro escaped.

At eight o'clock that night Mrs. H. went to the window to close the blinds, and saw a negro at the window, according to her account. But by this time there was a shadow of dread on every home in the city, and it may have been her imagination.

I believe this to be an entirely accurate account of the crimes and attempted crimes that struck terror to the hearts of the white women, and of every man who had to leave his womankind at all unprotected. Men with families to protect went early to their homes Saturday evening, leaving to the negroes and the white hoodlums largely the possession of the streets.

May I suggest here a comparison? The population of Atlanta is, in round numbers, a hundred thousand; of New York, four millions. Multiply everything by forty. Suppose in New York City there had been, say, four hundred and eighty assaults, or attempted assaults, upon white women of your city, by Chinese brutes—two hundred and forty in three days, one hundred and sixty in one afternoon; that the New York papers, yellow or otherwise, had published extras describing these assaults; that the police, with the best will in the world, had succeeded in arresting only a small number of these criminals, compared with those who escaped; and that the whole white population of the city had come to believe that the different Chinese quarters of the city were hiding and protecting these criminals of their own race, successfully baffling detection of the guilty: what would the New York mob have done under those circumstances? What could have prevented their indiscriminate slaughter of the Chinese?

And this is the heart of the matter of the race antagonism. Individual and sporadic cases of assault would have been, as they always have been heretofore in the South, ascribed to the individual. But the unheard-of frequency of the crimes in two months, with the cumulative aggravation of the last three days, made it a race matter; while the failure to find the guilty, and the absolute indifference of the negroes to the punishment of the criminal, to say the most charitable thing, arrayed white against black, as it was believed that black had already been arrayed against white, and in a matter that has been the distinction of the Saxon race since Tacitus wrote of it—its jealousy of the honor of its women. Certainly there was the appearance of conspiracy, of the many or the few. There was the universal suspicion that the criminals were known to the negroes, and there was never the slightest effort on the part of any negro to bring any of them to justice. The excuse generally given is that the criminals would have been lynched. But why is the negro race so determined for the rule of law and order in this one particular, unless there is racial sympathy with the criminal? In the only trial for assault that I ever witnessed, the criminal was as evidently the hero of the occasion to the negro half of the audience in the court-house as he was the villain to the white spectators.

The story of the riots, whose disgrace Atlanta keenly feels, has been made even worse than it was by the stories sent out from Atlanta for the papers. The beginnings of the riot were apparently insignificant. Peachtree Street is crossed, in the heart of the city, by another street, called on the east side Decatur and on the west Marietta. Within the open triangular square at this point all the street-cars of the city come for the transfer of passengers. Saturday night it is always full of people passing to and fro, and a crowd can be gathered in five minutes. The news of the four assaults that had been attempted that afternoon and evening, published in night extras by one of the papers, was enough to block the streets and the open space. At the same time the police were conducting a raid upon the negro dives on Decatur Street, two or three blocks away. This attracted a crowd in that direction. A negro girl was shot in a negro row and killed, early in the evening. The negroes had resisted their capture by the police in the raid. There were but fifty-seven police on duty that night. Presently the news was brought that two white boys had been held up and robbed by a gang of negro toughs on the outskirts of the city, and doubtless the rumor grew as it passed from mouth to mouth. Then, with the police occupied in the raid, a crowd of boys and young hoodlums began chasing the negroes on Decatur Street. Finally, on the corner of Peachtree and Decatur Street, a negro snatched a pocketbook from a woman, and a white man sprang upon him. Two negroes came to their comrade's aid, and they were at once attacked by several white people, while a negro telegraph messenger was also set upon. The four negroes got away, but the telegraph messenger presently returned, was recognized by his former assailants, and was brutally killed by the crowd that had now become a mob. The mob started toward Decatur Street, and were held back by the police until the fire department came to the rescue and turned the hose on them, when the mob separated into smaller mobs. Then the street-cars began coming to the crossing, and the mob, having already tasted blood, began dragging the negroes from the cars and beating them with sticks. Some of these were killed, though the most escaped without serious injury. By this time, say half-past ten, the character of the mob had been changed by the emptying of the bar-rooms, which close at ten o'clock. It is estimated that there were seven thousand in the mob that now crowded Peachtree, Decatur, and Marietta Streets at their crossing. It overflowed into side streets, attacked two negro barbers and killed one of them, and attacked the porters in a Pullman car near by. In all, there were eight negroes killed Saturday night, including the girl who was shot by negroes.

Either the Mayor, the Sheriff, or the Governor could have called out the military. In the face of the provocation given to mischief by a mob, the delay in this matter is inexcusable. All should have been on the alert. Atlanta has recently elected a new Mayor and Georgia a new Governor, from whom better things are expected. But a member of the State militia called up Colonel Clifford Anderson, commander of the regiment, and told him of the mob and asked if he should turn in the riot alarm. Colonel Anderson asked him to find the Mayor at once and get a request from him. The Mayor had tried moral suasion and cold water, but it was a time for the cold steel. After an hour's delay the Mayor communicated with Colonel Anderson, who in the meantime had communicated with the Governor, but it was a quarter to twelve before the request for the military reached Colonel Anderson, and, as he lived two miles from the center of the city, it was a quarter past twelve when he reached the armory. By that time some seventy-five men of the three hundred State militia of Atlanta had reached the armory, and Colonel Anderson put himself at their head and stopped the progress of a mob of two hundred men that came down the streets. The loading with ball cartridges and the fixing of bayonets dispersed this mob, and it never assembled in any large proportions during the three following days while the military, reinforced by companies from other cities, were in possession of the city.

At the breaking out of the riot the hardware stores sold out their stock of firearms in a few minutes, and the mob broke into the pawnshops on Decatur Street in the search for pistols and guns. But there was no more killing of negroes after the first attack already described. The negroes had taken the alarm and gone, some to their homes, but thousands to the homes of the white people on whom they had some claim as old servants or friends. The case of the woman who protected a negro man from the mob that was pursuing him was typical. And this is one bright spot in the dark story. Any Southern man would protect an innocent negro who appealed to him for help, with his own life if necessary.

Sunday was a trying day for the military. Little roving bands of hoodlums would appear first in one part and then in another of the city. Sunday night one negro was chased into the Aragon Hotel and was supposed to have been killed by a pistol shot, but he escaped. Another negro was badly wounded and sent to the Grady Hospital. Street-cars carrying negroes were attacked, but no injury was done beyond putting the negroes off the cars in some instances. Street-cars with white passengers, passing through negro settlements, were fired into by the negroes, and windows were broken with stones. But it was hoped that Monday morning would see the last of the rioting.

Atlanta is inclosed by a semicircle of colleges for negroes, but their fall terms had not opened and there were few students in the settlements. Beginning with Atlanta University, co-educational, there come next the Atlanta Baptist College for men, and Spelman Seminary for women. Then come Clark University, Gammon Theological Seminary, and the Morris Brown College. A fruitful subject of consideration would be the real influence for good upon the negro race exerted for a generation by the kind of education that has been given the pupils. But this by the way. Adjoining the grounds of Clark University is the negro settlement called Brownsville. During the year a part of the village was destroyed by fire, and an appeal was made upon the citizens by the Mayor for contributions for rebuilding it, which I understand was quite liberally answered. On Monday whites and blacks had both been ordered to disarm, so far as parading the streets was concerned. The law against carrying concealed weapons was of course in force. Monday night it was learned that the Brownsville settlement was arming for retaliation. It has always been a center of disturbance. But a very direct and circumstantial telephone message came for protection against a threatening mob of white men from a house in Brownsville, accurately describing the location and appealing for help. A squad of the county police, six or eight men, was sent out in answer to this call. On reaching Brownsville they arrested several armed negroes, and left them guarded by two of their number while the others went to the place where the trouble had appeared. This little squad of men, sent for the protection of the negroes, walked into a trap, carefully laid. They marched down a wide street with houses on both sides. At the end of the street a body of armed negroes was waiting. One of them gave a signal in a loud voice, "Number One," and the squad was fired upon from the front, both sides, and the rear. Officer James Heard was instantly killed, and three of his men wounded. Yet they returned the fire and killed six negroes and wounded four more who were found by the military next day. The news of this encounter, sent back to town, created excitement anew, and the mob formed again, and, meeting a street-car with two negro prisoners from Brownsville, chased them onto the front porch of a white resident and shot them to death. This occasioned the death by fright of a white woman who witnessed the scene. After the attack on the county police a cordon of the military was thrown around Brownsville in order to arrest the guilty parties the next day. Tuesday every house in the town was entered by the soldiers, and some two hundred and fifty negroes temporarily held, while the search was proceeding and inquiries being made. They were all disarmed, and those with concealed weapons, or under suspicion of having been in the party firing on the police, were sent to jail. Two negroes were shot by the soldiers in this encounter with the Brownsville population. Those wounded the night before were sent to the hospital, and the others, about forty in number, were sent to jail.

This was the end of the disturbance.

On the side of law and order, there might be mentioned the splendid conduct of the State militia, the meeting of citizens calling for the punishment of the rioters, the arrest by the police and the military of twoscore rioters, the action of the City Recorder in giving heavy penalties to those brought before him and requiring heavy bonds on appeal, the charge to the Grand Jury by Judge Pendleton—which was all that could be desired—and the probable verdicts by the petty juries in punishment of the white rioters at Atlanta and the negro rioters at Brownsville.

But while deploring and denouncing the action of the rioters, and feeling the disgrace that has come to the city, suffering also from the loss of business that has come through the interruption of trade, the white people of Atlanta breathe more freely, when thinking of their own homes, than they have done for weeks. It is a universal feeling that the thunder-storm has cleared the atmosphere, and that a long era of peace between the races has begun. The altered demeanor of the negroes has been very noticeable. What a writer in the October Century calls the negro's "bumptiousness" is gone. The thousand appeals for protection have created new sympathy for this child-race among us; and it would be uncandid to deny that the negroes have been taught a needed lesson, even by the indiscriminate violence of the mob. It is this:

For the first time the negroes have been impressed with the truth that the individual criminal who lays his hand upon a white woman is a menace to the mass. The first resolutions denouncing the crime of assault, of which the sincerity was evident, have been passed by the Atlanta negroes since the riots. The negro criminal will have little sympathy from his own race in Atlanta for some time to come. The negro of slavery days or war times who would have attempted such a crime would have been torn to pieces by his fellow-slaves. If now the law of self-preservation shall lead the negroes sincerely to condemn this crime, to aid in the detection of the criminal and his delivery to justice, the crime itself may at last become sporadic and infrequent.

And if the Northern press were to remember the illogical processes of the negro's mind, how he perverts the denunciation of lynching into an approval of the provocative crime, it would leave the lynching to be attended to by Southern opinion and warn the negroes of their danger in its committal.

And, as a friend of the negro, I would deprecate more than anything else such advice as he has received in certain quarters to make retaliation and thus protect himself. There has been but one white man killed in Atlanta. There was none in Wilmington. In anything like a race war the negro has everything to lose. It means for him, not battle, but extermination.

One other question our people are considering—whether, in accordance with the precedent of prohibiting the sale of liquor to Indians, and, by international agreement, its prohibition in certain isles of the Pacific, a local law preventing the sale of rum to negroes, with exceptions in cases of sickness, or a State law to the same effect, would be a violation of the Fourteenth Amendment. Does that amendment allow us to protect the negro from what has caused the destruction of the weaker races everywhere?

# II—A Northern Black Point of View

*By Carrie W. Clifford*

You will, of course, be able to realize that the terrible outburst of race hatred at Atlanta a little over two weeks ago has deeply stirred the colored people of the North. I confess I have been stirred to the depths, and have eagerly read everything I could obtain bearing upon the situation. I was genuinely pleased with your very just utterances in the editorial comment in The Outlook of September 30. How-

ever, in the article of October 6 entitled "Racial Self-Restraint," I
believe you have in the more important features reasoned from wrong
premises, and that, perhaps unconsciously, you have let your own
prejudiced feeling color your conclusions.

I fully agree with you that "although the trouble is, for the present,
ended, the danger of its recurrence there or elsewhere is not removed." I also agree that "this is an evil for which all Americans can
unite in seeking a cure"; and that "if the conditions can be understood, a way to a remedy can be found."

The way to a remedy is self-evident, and I am astonished that you
do not seem to know it! It consists in living up to the Golden Rule.
The "condition" is the result of "man's inhumanity to man." Change
that, and the remedy will have been found.

Our black ancestors were savages. The God we serve is the God
revealed to us by you. It is the white man who has brought us this
message of salvation; it is he who has put this inspired Word of God,
the Holy Bible, into our hands; and it is he who has taught us to
read it, not only in the translation, but in the original Hebrew and
Greek. To me, then, comes the burning question, "If this be true, as
you profess to believe, how can it be possible that your profession
and your actions so ill accord? If you believe that not one jot or tittle
of his Word shall fail, and if you believe that your neighbor is the
man spoken of in the parable, and if you believe that you must love
your neighbor as yourself, the question of how the negro should be
treated is as clear as the noonday sun."

I feel very sure that this obvious and simple remedy will not be
tried; that the white Christians of America are not, in the main, willing to do unto the black millions exactly as they would that men
should do to them.

Well, then, let us pass on! You say, "The black and white races
are distinct. In this condition no change is desirable and no change
possible." Then you point out that this very isolation of the negro,
which you say renders him practically an alien, makes him irresponsible. That, it seems to me, is the very reason why he should not be
left distinct, isolated, and alien. And your statement that no change
is possible is dogmatically stated as a fact wholly unsupported by
reason.

Further you say, "When he sees privileges, denied him on account
of race, granted to those whom he regards as inferiors, his contempt
is changed to enmity." This is only half of the truth, only one side of
the question. When the poor whites who have all their lives been

taught to hate and despise the negro see him take heart and look up, and watch him as he rubs elbows with them as together they struggle up the ladder of progress, the hatred of these poor whites for the negro is increased and intensified.

It is true that "in Atlanta there is an unusually large number of cultivated negroes, many with college education." True also that "they have little to do with the poorer, less educated negroes"; but the reason you allege is far, far from the truth. It is not because of "their social separation from the great body of the race," but because to come into frequent contact with them they must undergo the most degrading humiliations, discriminations, and insults—things impossible for men of spirit to bear with equanimity. The negro is willing that these lines of discrimination be drawn on any other ground than race or color.

You say, "Furthermore, they are too much concerned about certain rights and too little appreciative of their opportunities." Do you think it possible for men to be too much concerned about the right to be treated as men? Is there to you, a son of that old Puritan stock that loved liberty better than life, anything dearer than the *right* to life, liberty, and the pursuit of happiness?

And will you be so kind as to point out a single opportunity for the negro in Atlanta?

Mail-carriers in the discharge of their duty are insulted and molested. During the recent riot colored barbers were dragged out of their shops and mobbed. The postmaster and storekeeper at South Atlanta was thrown in jail for no offense, and the arrest of Dr. J. W. E. Bowen, of Gammon Theological Seminary, and Dr. Coogman, President of Clark University (the very flower and culture of our manhood), shows all too clearly that the riot was not directed at the vicious negro so much as at the progressive negro. One way for you to get even faintly some idea of the ignominy which a negro suffers is to strive with all the power of your imagination to "put yourself in his place." Better still, masquerade as a negro in Georgia for the space of one little month!

I agree with what you say of a "Georgia political campaign reinforced by unscrupulous journalistic methods," only of course with greater emphasis.

I come now to the point where we disagree utterly.

"The idea that it [the race] might be removed by assimilation is *not* open to argument." And pray why not? My ancestors were as much white as black, and family tradition says there were the Governors of two States among the number. Personally, assimilation is as distasteful to me as I surmise it is to you. Nevertheless, I recognize the right of any man, black or white, to make his own choice in the matter of the marital relationship.

"There remains but one cure: some method of requiring the black race to exercise self-control." This should be amended to read, "some method of requiring *both* races to exercise self-control."

Thomas Nelson Page's suggestion might possibly be a good thing, provided the idea of negro policemen obtained throughout the whole régime. I mean if there were also negro judges, lawyers, and juries to try negro lawbreakers arrested by negro police. Nothing could be worse than the present system; for if you know aught of these things in the South, you know that for a negro to get justice is almost impossible.

The best way for the people, not only of Atlanta but of the United States, to do is to treat the negro as a citizen of this Republic, with rights which all are bound to respect. Grant him no farms, give him no special privileges. Give him his just deserts, but let him have justice.

One last word regarding self-restraint. When it is generally conceded that the newly elected Governor of Georgia, one of the thirteen original States of our glorious Republic, secured his election through his superior ability to stir up race hatred and the lowest animal passions—and he, be it remembered, a member of the superior white race; and when for three days a white mob had control of Atlanta, attacking, maiming, and killing whomsoever it wished, provided only his face was black—I say that when this is the spectacle presented by the proud white race to a gaping world, a lecture to blacks on self-restraint becomes indeed a roaring farce!

## III—From the Point of View of a Missionary College

### By Edward T. Ware

In your recent editorial regarding "Racial Self-Restraint" the charge is brought against the cultivated negroes of Atlanta that they have little to do with the poorer, less educated negroes, and therefore have little restraining influence over them. This charge seems to me unjust in view of what is actually being done through the efforts of these very people. Some time ago your representative who was studying the churches in the South reported that, of all the churches he had visited, the First Congregational Church of Atlanta, whose pastor is the Rev. H. H. Proctor, was one of the best organized for work. As the result of the earnest and unceasing effort of this negro pastor, two of the worst negro "dives" in the city were closed long before the recent outbreak between the races occurred. His church maintains several missions in the city, in which negroes who have had the opportunities of education come into sympathetic touch with the less fortunate. Several other of the negro churches and the negro Young Men's Christian Association afford occasions for the cultivated people of this race to meet and help the poorer and less educated.

Perhaps the most general recent movement in this direction was the organization of the Gate City Free Kindergarten Association about two years ago. By means of this Association last year two free kindergartens were established and maintained in poorer parts of the city for the little waifs of this race. Through the Mothers' Meetings many of the families were also reached and helped. Almost all of the negro churches and schools in the city contribute to the support of this association. A third kindergarten has been opened this fall, and plans for a fourth are under way.

It must be remembered, too, that the public schools for the negroes afford an opportunity for the best-educated negroes, from whom the teachers are chosen, to come constantly into touch with some of the most ignorant, whose children are among their pupils. Many of these young teachers, trained as they are in Christian schools, show more than professional interest in their pupils. Entirely apart from church organization or school system, a great amount of genuine Christian service is done by individual negroes, simply out of the largeness of their hearts.

There is, no doubt, need for a great deal more of the sort of work suggested; but we should take into consideration the fact that the negroes, even the most well-to-do, have little surplus either of money or of time to use in service of the less fortunate. The opportunity for making money and saving money is not as good for colored people as it is for white. And, since the riots, the incentive to save and invest in business or homes in Atlanta is even less than it was before, so that many substantial negro men are making plans to sell what they own and go elsewhere to live. Few of the negro mothers have servants with whom they may leave their children and the cares of the household while they turn their attention to the needs of the less fortunate.

Many of them even have to work as teachers, or helping their husbands in store or office, in order to eke out a respectable living for their families. The problem of providing daily bread is much more immediate in the case of the educated negroes of Atlanta than in the case of people of similar culture and attainments and standards of living among those of another race. Considering their limitations in financial resources and in ability to command their time, it seems to me that the educated negroes of Atlanta are doing much for their less fortunate neighbors, and that the charge that they have little to do with them is unjust.

In some form this charge of having nothing to do with the ignorant of their race is often brought against the educated negroes, and frequently with an inconsistency that ill conceals the source of the charge. A young man recently said, "The Mississippi negroes are a worthless, low-down set." When asked about the educated negroes, he answered, "They are spoiled; they think themselves above the others of their race." Is it a strange thing, or is it wrong, that men and women who have had the advantages of education and culture do not care to fraternize with or consider themselves "exactly like" those who are still in the gutter? Nobody accuses the residents in Fifth Avenue of being unduly exalted because they do not fraternize with the denizens of Hell's Kitchen. If the cultured negroes choose for their companions and friends people like themselves in interests and attainments, are they to be blamed? If most of them attend the one or two churches in the city where they hear a man with like education with themselves preach, and do not go to hear some ignorant man exhort and shout in the real old-fashioned darky manner, are they to be blamed or counted too good for their race or station in life?

As it appears to me, the source of the charge of the aloofness of educated negroes from the masses is in most cases as follows: The evident fact that such negroes are in some genuine qualities different from and better than the masses of their people is irritating to those who are not in sympathy with the progress of the negro race. Thus many qualities which in a white man are regarded with favor are in a negro regarded with disfavor. What in a white man is evidence of self-respect is in a negro evidence of arrogance or insolence; and what in a white man is simply seeking congenial companions is in a negro considering himself better than his people—in short, trying to raise himself out of the station of inferiority where some men dare to say he is destined to remain forever by the decree of God.

*One of the many letters to the editor regarding the At-
lanta Riot was from Mary White Ovington, a leading
board member of the NAACP.*

# A Letter from Mary White Ovington

THE OUTLOOK has been generous in the space which it has given to
a consideration of the Atlanta riots; and to ask for a further word on
the matter must seem inconsiderate. But Mr. McKelway, in his paper
written from the Southern white man's point of view, emphasizes so
strongly the matter of assault upon women as the cause of the riot
that, as a woman, I would ask to be permitted to say a word upon the
matter from a somewhat different standpoint.

Fifteen assaults or attempts at assault within a year are given by
Mr. McKelway as the cause of the Atlanta outbreak. We must realize
that these accounts are given by white people, not by negroes. To
touch a woman in Georgia is a crime, and the negro janitor who was
sentenced for a year, according to his story, was only helping the
girl who complained against him to find her hat-pin, pushing her
aside as he knelt on the floor and saying, "Let me look, honey." Fear
exaggerates crime, and white women to-day everywhere are being
trained to fear colored men; but, making allowance for all this, there
would seem to have been a number of attacks by Africans upon
women of the Caucasian race.

The negroes, Mr. McKelway says, are our criminal class. But if
assault is a crime, especially assault upon women, then the negro is
not the only criminal class. For every charge of assault that the white
man brings against the black man, the black man can bring an equally
important one against the white man. I knew myself of two very
brutal attacks, horrible in their details, that were made upon little
colored girls by white men this summer in Atlanta. Brutal rudeness,
such as some of the Atlanta cases appear to be, has been experienced
by virtuous colored women of the city.

Now change the words "white" to aristocrat and "colored" to
proletariat, and you have a condition that is not uncommon over all

From *Outlook*, LXXXIV (November 17, 1906), 684.

233

this Christian world. The chivalry of men is often extended only to women of their own class. It would be well if more of us should hear the story that many an Irish girl could tell us of her experience in domestic service. Taking the first position that she can secure, she may find a home where her womanhood is not respected. She escapes or overcomes by her indomitable pluck, but there are no headlines in the evening papers, and the man who has sought her ruin goes unpunished. Yet this same man stands ready to protect his own women with his life. I remember, after a winter of unusually happy times in a college town, hearing an older girl say to a younger one in a working-girls' club, "Don't have anything to do with the college fellows. A decent girl keeps away from them." My own class, that brought me companionship and safety, was known to her as a danger.

When Javert brought Fantine before Jean Valjean, the Mayor, he presented the case as that of a prostitute insulting a property-owner. No matter that the evidence showed that the man had first struck the girl between her naked shoulders; she was an outcast and he a respected citizen. Jean Valjean saw a deeper justice, as we do at times; but we are still all too ready to protect our own class, to gloss our own sins. And this is more true when the sinner is a man than a woman. The citizen who has been well born, who has had education and opportunity, may assault a helpless, unprotected woman, and never be brought to justice; he does not belong to the criminal class; but the untrained, unlettered man, whose school has been the dirty alley or the chain-gang, is fortunate if his foul deed leads him to the gallows, not to the stake. Those of us who wish to understand what is in the heart of the negro as well as of the white man in Atlanta must recognize that there are these two kinds of justice in the city; and it should not be difficult for us to understand this, as the same situation, in a less exaggerated form, is present wherever we find a marked division between the moneyed and the working class.

*The editor of the* Independent *noted, in a parenthetical
statement, that the author of the following piece was a
woman of "much culture and recognized standing." Her
experiences in the nation's capital illustrate the tragic gap
between American rhetoric and American practice.*

## What It Means To Be Colored in the Capital of the United States

WASHINGTON, D. C., has been called "The Colored Man's Paradise."
Whether this sobriquet was given to the national capital in bitter
irony by a member of the handicapped race, as he reviewed some
of his own persecutions and rebuffs, or whether it was given immediately after the war by an ex-slave-holder who for the first time in
his life saw colored people walking about like freemen, minus the
overseer and his whip, history saith not. It is certain that it would be
difficult to find a worse misnomer for Washington than "The Colored
Man's Paradise" if so prosaic a consideration as veracity is to determine the appropriateness of a name.

For fifteen years I have resided in Washington, and while it was far
from being a paradise for colored people when I first touched these
shores, it has been doing its level best ever since to make conditions
for us intolerable. As a colored woman I might enter Washington any
night, a stranger in a strange land, and walk miles without finding a
place to lay my head. Unless I happened to know colored people who
live here or ran across a chance acquaintance who could recommend
a colored boarding-house to me, I should be obliged to spend the
entire night wandering about. Indians, Chinamen, Filipinos, Japanese
and representatives of any other dark race can find hotel accommodations, if they can pay for them. The colored man alone is thrust
out of the hotels of the national capital like a leper.

As a colored woman I may walk from the Capitol to the White
House, ravenously hungry and abundantly supplied with money
with which to purchase a meal, without finding a single restaurant in

From *Independent*, LXII (January 24, 1907), 181–186.

which I would be permitted to take a morsel of food, if it was patronized by white people, unless I were willing to sit behind a screen. As a colored woman I cannot visit the tomb of the Father of this country, which owes its very existence to the love of freedom in the human heart and which stands for equal opportunity to all, without being forced to sit in the Jim Crow section of an electric car which starts from the very heart of the city—midway between the Capitol and the White House. If I refuse thus to be humiliated, I am cast into jail and forced to pay a fine for violating the Virginia laws. Every hour in the day Jim Crow cars filled with colored people, many of whom are intelligent and well to do, enter and leave the national capital.

As a colored woman I may enter more than one white church in Washington without receiving that welcome which as a human being I have a right to expect in the sanctuary of God. Sometimes the color blindness of the usher takes on that peculiar form which prevents a dark face from making any impression whatsoever upon his retina, so that it is impossible for him to see colored people at all. If he is not so afflicted, after keeping a colored man or woman waiting a long time, he will ungraciously show these dusky Christians who have had the temerity to thrust themselves into a temple where only the fair of face are expected to worship God to a seat in the rear, which is named in honor of a certain personage, well known in this country, and commonly called Jim Crow.

Unless I am willing to engage in a few menial occupations, in which the pay for my services would be very poor, there is no way for me to earn an honest living, if I am not a trained nurse or a dress-maker or can secure a position as teacher in the public schools, which is exceedingly difficult to do. It matters not what my intellectual attainments may be or how great is the need of the services of a competent person, if I try to enter many of the numerous vocations in which my white sisters are allowed to engage, the door is shut in my face.

From one Washington theater I am excluded altogether. In the remainder certain seats are set aside for colored people, and it is almost impossible to secure others. I once telephoned to the ticket seller just before a matinee and asked if a neat-appearing colored nurse would be allowed to sit in the parquet with her little white charge, and the answer rushed quickly and positively thru the receiver—NO. When I remonstrated a bit and told him that in some of the theaters colored nurses were allowed to sit with the white children for whom they cared, the ticket seller told me that in Washington it was very poor policy to employ colored nurses, for they were excluded from many places where white girls would be allowed to take children for pleasure.

If I possess artistic talent, there is not a single art school of repute which will admit me. A few years ago a colored woman who possessed great talent submitted some drawings to the Corcoran Art School, of Washington, which were accepted by the committee of awards, who sent her a ticket entitling her to a course in this school. But when the committee discovered that the young woman was colored they declined to admit her, and told her that if they had suspected that her drawings had been made by a colored woman they would not have examined them at all. The efforts of Frederick Douglass and a lawyer of great repute who took a keen interest in the affair were unavailing. In order to cultivate her talent this young woman was forced to leave her comfortable home in Washington and incur the expense of going to New York. Having entered the Woman's Art School of Cooper Union, she graduated with honor, and then went to Paris to continue her studies, where she achieved signal success and was complimented by some of the greatest living artists in France.

With the exception of the Catholic University, there is not a single white college in the national capital to which colored people are admitted, no matter how great their ability, how lofty their ambition, how unexceptionable their character or how great their thirst for knowledge may be.

A few years ago the Columbian Law School admitted colored students, but in deference to the Southern white students the authorities have decided to exclude them altogether. . . .

Another young friend had an experience which, for some reasons, was still more disheartening and bitter than the one just mentioned. In order to secure lucrative employment she left Washington and went to New York. There she worked her way up in one of the largest dry goods stores till she was placed as saleswoman in the cloak department. Tired of being separated from her family she decided to return to Washington, feeling sure that, with her experience and her fine recommendation from the New York firm, she could easily secure employment. Nor was she overconfident, for the proprietor of one of the largest dry goods stores in her native city was glad to secure the services of a young woman who brought such hearty credentials from New York. She had not been in this store very long, however, before she called upon me one day and asked me to intercede with the proprietor in her behalf, saying that she had been discharged that afternoon because it had been discovered that she was colored. When I called upon my young friend's employer he made no effort to avoid the issue, as I feared he would. He did not say he had discharged the young saleswoman because she had not given satisfaction, as he might easily have done. On the contrary, he admitted without the slightest hesitation that the young woman he had just discharged was one of the best clerks he had ever had. In the cloak department, where she had been assigned, she had been a brilliant success, he said. "But I cannot keep Miss Smith in my employ," he concluded. "Are you not master of your own store?" I ventured to inquire. The proprietor of this store was a Jew, and I felt that it was particularly cruel, unnatural and cold-blooded for the representative of one oppressed and persecuted race to deal so harshly and unjustly with a member of another. I had intended to make this point when I decided to intercede for my young friend, but when I thought how a reference to the persecution of his own race would wound his feelings, the words froze on my lips. "When I first heard your friend was colored," he explained, "I did not believe it and said so to the clerks who made the statement. Finally, the girls who had been most pronounced in their opposition to working in a store with a colored girl came to me in a body and threatened to strike. 'Strike away,' said I, 'your places will be easily filled.' Then they started on another tack. Delegation after delegation began to file down to my office, some of the women my very best customers, to protest against my employing a colored girl. Moreover, they threatened to boycott my store if I did not discharge her at once. Then it became a question of bread and butter and I yielded to the inevitable—that's all. Now," said he, concluding, "if I lived in a great, cosmopolitan city like New York, I should do as I pleased, and refuse to discharge a girl simply because she was colored." But I thought of a similar incident that happened in New York. I remembered that a colored woman, as fair as a lily and as beautiful as a Madonna, who was the head saleswoman in a large department store in New York, had been discharged, after she had held this position for years, when the proprietor accidentally discovered that a fatal drop of African blood was percolating somewhere thru her veins.

Not only can colored women secure no employment in the Washington stores, department and otherwise, except as menials, and such positions, of course, are few, but even as customers they are not infrequently treated with discourtesy both by the clerks and the proprietor himself. Following the trend of the times, the senior partner of the largest and best department store in Washington, who originally hailed from Boston, once the home of Wm. Lloyd Garrison, Wendell Phillips and Charles Sumner, if my memory serves me right, decided to open a restaurant in his store. Tired and hungry after her morning's shopping a colored school teacher, whose relation to her African progenitors is so remote as scarcely to be discernible to the naked eye, took a seat at one of the tables in the restaurant of this Boston store. After sitting unnoticed a long time the colored teacher asked a waiter who passed her by if he would not take her order. She was quickly informed that colored people could not be served in that restaurant and was obliged to leave in confusion and shame, much to the amusement of the waiters and the guests who had noticed the incident. Shortly after that a teacher in Howard University, one of the best schools for colored youth in the country, was similarly insulted in the restaurant of the same store. . . .

Not long ago one of my little daughter's bosom friends figured in one of the most pathetic instances of which I have ever heard. A gentleman who is very fond of children promised to take six little girls in his neighborhood to a matinee. It happened that he himself and five of his little friends were so fair that they easily passed muster, as they stood in judgment before the ticket seller and the ticket taker. Three of the little girls were sisters, two of whom were very fair and the other a bit brown. Just as this little girl, who happened to be first in the procession, went by the ticket taker, that argus-eyed sophisticated gentleman detected something which caused a deep, dark frown to mantle his brow and he did not allow her to pass. "I guess you have made a mistake," he called to the host of this theater party. "Those little girls," pointing to the fair ones, "may be admitted, but this one," designating the brown one, "can't." But the colored man was quite equal to the emergency. Fairly frothing at the mouth with anger he asked the ticket taker what he meant, what he was trying to insinuate about that particular little girl. "Do you mean to tell me," he shouted in rage, "that I must go clear to the Philippine Islands to bring this child to the United States and then I can't take her to the theatre in the National Capital?" The little ruse succeeded brilliantly, as he knew it would. "Beg your pardon," said the ticket taker, "don't know what I was thinking about. Of course she can go in."

"What was the matter with me this afternoon, mother?" asked the little brown girl innocently, when she mentioned the affair at home. "Why did the man at the theater let my two sisters and the other girls in and try to keep me out?" In relating this incident, the child's mother told me her little girl's question, which showed such blissful ignorance of the depressing, cruel conditions which confronted her, completely unnerved her for a time.

Altho white and colored teachers are under the same Board of Education and the system for the children of both races is said to be uniform, prejudice against the colored teachers in the public schools is manifested in a variety of ways. From 1870 to 1900 there was a colored superintendent at the head of the colored schools. During all that time the directors of the cooking, sewing, physical culture, manual training, music and art departments were colored people. Six years ago a change was inaugurated. The colored superintendent was legislated out of office and the directorships, without a single exception, were taken from colored teachers and given to the whites. There was no complaint about the work done by the colored directors any more than is heard about every officer in every school. The directors of the art and physical culture departments were particularly fine. Now, no matter how competent or superior the colored teachers in our public schools may be, they know that they can never rise to the height of a directorship, can never hope to be more than an assistant and receive the meager salary therefor, unless the present regime is radically changed. . . .

Strenuous efforts are being made to run Jim Crow street cars in the national capital. "Resolved, that a Jim Crow law should be adopted and enforced in the District of Columbia," was the subject of a discussion engaged in last January by the Columbian Debating Society of the George Washington University in our national capital, and the decision was rendered in favor of the affirmative. Representative Heflin, of Alabama, who introduced a bill providing for Jim Crow street cars in the District of Columbia last winter, has just received a letter from the president of the East Brookland Citizens' Association "indorsing the movement for separate street cars and sincerely hoping that you will be successful in getting this enacted into a law as soon as possible." Brookland is a suburb of Washington.

The colored laborer's path to a decent livelihood is by no means smooth. Into some of the trades unions here he is admitted, while from others he is excluded altogether. By the union men this is denied, altho I am personally acquainted with skilled workmen who tell me they are not admitted into the unions because they are colored. But even when they are allowed to join the unions they frequently derive little benefit, owing to certain tricks of the trade. When the word passes round that help is needed and colored laborers apply, they are often told by the union officials that they have secured all the men they needed, because the places are reserved for white men, until they have been provided with jobs, and colored men must remain idle, unless the supply of white men is too small. . . .

And so I might go on citing instance after instance to show the variety of ways in which our people are sacrificed on the altar of prejudice in the Capital of the United States and how almost insurmountable are the obstacles which block their path to success. Early in life many a colored youth is so appalled by the helplessness and the hopelessness of his situation in this country that in a sort of stoical despair he resigns himself to his fate. "What is the good of our trying to acquire an education? We can't all be preachers, teachers, doctors and lawyers. Besides those professions there is almost nothing for colored people to do but engage in the most menial occupations, and we do not need an education for that." More than once such remarks, uttered by young men and women in our public schools who possess brilliant intellects, have wrung my heart.

It is impossible for any white person in the United States, no matter how sympathetic and broad, to realize what life would mean to him if his incentive to effort were suddenly snatched away. To the lack of incentive to effort, which is the awful shadow under which we live, may be traced the wreck and ruin of scores of colored youth. And surely nowhere in the world do oppression and persecution based solely on the color of the skin appear more hateful and hideous than in the capital of the United States, because the chasm between the principles upon which this Government was founded, in which it still professes to believe, and those which are daily practiced under the protection of the flag, yawns so wide and deep.

*James David Corrothers was considered by DuBois, as well as other critics, to be one of the best early black poets. He wrote frequently for magazines such as* Century *and* The Crisis.

# At the Closed Gate of Justice

### By James D. Corrothers

To be a Negro in a day like this
  Demands forgiveness. Bruised with blow on blow,
Betrayed, like him whose woe-dimmed eyes gave bliss,
  Still must one succor those who brought one low,
To be a Negro in a day like this.

To be a Negro in a day like this
  Demands rare patience—patience that can wait
In utter darkness. 'T is the path to miss,
  And knock, unheeded, at an iron gate,
To be a Negro in a day like this.

To be a Negro in a day like this
  Demands strange loyalty. We serve a flag
Which is to us white freedom's emphasis.
  Ah! one must love when truth and justice lag,
To be a Negro in a day like this.

To be a Negro in a day like this—
  Alas! Lord God, what evil have we done?
Still shines the gate, all gold and amethyst,
  But I pass by, the glorious goal unwon,
"Merely a Negro"—in a day like *this!*

From *Century*, LXXXVI (June 1913), 272.

*Herbert Seligmann, a journalist, wrote a book entitled*
The Negro Faces America *(1920). He became the director
of public relations for the NAACP in the mid-1920's.*

# Democracy and Jim-Crowism

## *By Herbert J. Seligmann*

THE NEGRO, we have been told, is an inferior race. Challenged, his
critics have insisted that his achievements belong in the lower intellectual reaches. His sense of rhythm which produced ragtime, his
patience and docility, have been made into weapons by his critics.
But remarkably little investigation worthy of the name of science
has been conducted to show how, if at all, the Negro race is inferior.
Sir Sidney Olivier has more than suggested that the Negro's lack
of adaptability to certain industrial processes is in itself a criticism
of the white man's submission to modern civilization.

That civilization in its recent phases has challenged the Negro.
The Negro has replied by posing a question which it will take centuries perhaps to answer. Civilization called upon the Negro to learn
to die—not in despair, not as a matter of course, but militant in defense of a concept all too abstract from his own existence. More
particularly, the United States government called upon the Negro
to die for democracy. It spent enormous effort in making that concept a reality to men who were to offer themselves in sacrifice to it.
And although the Negro has fought in every American war from
the pre-Revolutionary campaigns against aboriginal Americans, this
latest war was most distinctively educative. In it the Negro was
called upon as a citizen and as a member of a race to do what all
other citizens had to do. Responding under the special stimulus of
the disabilities attached to his color, he learned his lesson better,
perhaps, than did his comrades. He learned what war so anomal-
ously teaches: that civilization is built upon the preference of general and abstract concepts to individual impulses and individual
lives. That lesson is most destructive of caste and caste privileges.

From *New Republic*, XX (September 3, 1919), 151–152.

The war was not only an education, it proved to be an opportunity. Of the half million Negroes who by conservative estimate came North, many merely took the occasion industry offered to leave the South. Labor agents from industrial centres deprived of European immigration induced some Negroes to come North. Some came without solicitation other than the lure of higher wages and better living. But many had long wanted to leave the South because they had found life intolerable there. How these elements were distributed it is impossible to say. In any event, the migrant Negroes were leaving a civilization in which caste, a passionate defense of "racial purity" by white men, reenforced by terrorism and violence or threats, kept them a source of easily exploitable labor. The kindly and paternal attitude of many white men, so often mentioned in extenuation, does not alter the essential facts.

The consequences of the migration were manifold. Special problems of all sorts were created in the North. For the first time in the past few years the question of segregation of white and colored people in residence districts and of their children in schools was presented in northern industrial cities like Chicago. Acute conflict as in East St. Louis came about between labor unions of white men and the, for the most part, unorganized migrant Negroes. But these local conditions were incidental. Everywhere the Negro was increasing his stakes in American life. Wages went up for him in the South as much by reason of the war service and migration of white men as by circumstances affecting Negroes only. The South was aghast at losing its chief labor—an ironic reversal of the feeling in post–Civil War days when the states looked with distrust and disfavor upon the presence within their borders of free men of color. This change of status created resentment in the South. Animus was directed especially against the Negro soldier, embodiment of the joint guardianship of and participation in that abstract democracy for which the Negro was giving his life and buying bonds. Negro soldiers were accused of having consorted with white women in France and the entire race was charged with manifestation of a new intractable spirit of aggression and independence. Lynching flourished during the war and especially after the armistice. The resentment so engendered found its easiest expression in charges of criminality against the Negro race.

This has long been the excuse for the treatment accorded the Negro in certain sections of the South. A newspaper propaganda featuring the word Negro in the headlines reporting crimes was responsible for the Atlanta riots some thirteen years ago. The same sort of propaganda occasioned the attacks upon Negroes in Washington. If the Washington race riots were of the passional type not directly traceable to economic causes, the Chicago disorders were directly traceable to industrial circumstances. In Washington it was a case of "teaching the damned nigger his place." In Chicago primitive hatred for the unfamiliar was stimulated by real estate manipulations, corrupt policing and political alliances, and resentment of white union workers in the stockyards against non-union Negroes. One race riot was southern in type, the other northern. The Washington riots were like those of Atlanta. Chicago's resembled those of East St. Louis. With this important difference, however: both in Washington and in Chicago the Negro fought back. He was armed, and in his own district, despite the police, he protected himself. To some extent, as the casualty lists show, he retaliated. Much of the fighting, most of it in fact, was occasioned by white hoodlums and was deprecated by sober citizens. Still, the Negro had an unsympathetic environment and an inequitable administration of the law and of the police to contend with. The measures he took for defense were not entirely unnecessary.

Although the fighting in Chicago was preceded by bombing of Negro residences, was occasioned by the unprovoked murder of a Negro boy by a white man at a bathing beach, and although white mobs burned Negro houses and brutally murdered unoffending Negroes, the Chicago Grand Jury found it necessary to protest against proceedings begun exclusively against Negroes. They found it necessary to call to the attention of officers of the law the fact that if Negroes alone were prosecuted and no white men, dangerous tension might be renewed between white and colored citizens.

The press, as always, recklessly prejudiced the public safety. When a disastrous fire burned eighty houses of Poles and Lithuanians near the stockyards, the Chicago Daily Journal and the Chicago Evening Post carried stories, news articles and headlines imputing the blaze to Negro incendiaries animated by race hatred. A white man was subsequently arrested and charged with having set the fire. The immediate consequence of this newspaper outcry was a movement to deprive Negroes of their jobs at the stockyards. The packing houses actually had to postpone for three days reemploying their colored workmen. When the Negro stockyard employees did return to work, it was only under a heavy militia guard and white workers made their objection to the guard a pretext for threatening a general strike against the employment of Negroes. Meanwhile a number of hotels and other places of employment announced they had replaced their Negro employees with white men.

Coincident with the economic retribution the race riots put upon the Negro came numerous suggestions that the North must adopt the southern policy of Jim-Crowism. Of Jim-Crowism in the North there seems to be slight danger. The Negro's struggle here will be in the field of industry. He will have the difficulty, so long as he remains unorganized, of any group of workers permanently distinguished by superficial characteristics from their fellows. The American Federation of Labor has begun to recognize the danger of this division and its possible uses against labor. It was this, probably, that motivated President Gompers at Atlantic City. Despite industrial troubles, the Negro will continue to come North as his manhood rebels against the position of inferiority in every sense which is forced upon him in the South.

The question, then, which the Negro has posed, arises from a caste civilization in the South, which, as soon as the war furnished occasion, extended its problems to the entire nation. That question is: What place is there in a democracy for permanently distinct racial groups who accept that democracy on its own terms? In the growth of his determination to die if necessary in this country in defense of democracy, the Negro has shown his readiness to maintain it. The problem becomes one of ways and means. It demands study and investigation rather than passion and obscurantism.

*William Pickens was a Yale graduate, an educator and
writer, and field secretary of the NAACP.*

# The Woman Voter Hits the Color Line

## By William Pickens

THE NINETEENTH Amendment has become the law of the land and
it is constitutionally possible for twenty-five million women to vote.
How many of these will actually vote? Three million are colored, and
more than three-fourths of them live below Mason and Dixon's Line.
There the colored man has been cheated out of nine-tenths of his
votes, and only a small proportion of the white men vote because
of the indirect reaction of this political dishonesty. Will the colored
women of the South be similarly shut out?

The recent registration of voters in South Carolina may be taken
as a fair example, as this State has been ever representative of the
South. In common with other Southern States, it has, by administration and manipulation of suffrage laws, practically nullified the
Fourteenth and Fifteenth amendments, which enfranchised colored
men. The black race slightly outnumbers the white in South Carolina, and colored women outnumber colored men. The colored
woman is accordingly the largest class in the State, and her right to
vote gives a new concern to the maintainers of "white supremacy."

What of the colored women? They have shown themselves in
every sense and in every emergency good citizens. In the war their
auxiliaries were second to none in efficient service. As the State Federation of Colored Women's Clubs in Alabama founded a reform
school for colored boys long before the State would adopt the work,
so now the colored women of South Carolina are supporting an Industrial School for Wayward Colored Girls to which they gave
$9,000 last year. A colored woman owns and operates the best hos-
pital for her race anywhere in the State, and it is patronized by
white physicians.

While colored people predominate in numbers in the whole State,

From *Nation,* CXI (October 6, 1920), 372–373.

in the city of Columbia, with 37,500 inhabitants, they number about one-third. Let us observe the attempt of colored women to register in this capital city. The registrars are white men, sometimes but half-educated. One can register either as tax-payer on a stated minimum value of taxable property or under the "educational qualification." On the first day of the registration in September the colored women who presented themselves evidently took the registrars by surprise, as the latter seemed to have no concerted plan for dealing with colored women except to register them like the white women; and this they were doing without any test or question whatsoever save such necessary inquiries as to name, age and residence. The registrars had evidently believed that few colored women would have the nerve to attempt to register, and there was visible disappointment when many colored women, bright and intelligent, in some cases armed with the necessary tax receipt, appeared the first day. While there was apparently no preconcerted plan not to register them, one ready-made discrimination of the South was freely used, that of "white people first." The registrars would keep numbers of colored women standing for hours while they registered every white person in sight, man or woman, even the late-comers. A registrar was sometimes observed to break off right in the middle of registering a colored woman, and turn to some white new-comer. To the credit of the instinctive fairness of white women it should be said that they at first manifested a disposition merely to fall in line and await their turn until interfered with by the white officers who would call them arbitrarily from behind a group of colored applicants. Yet many of these colored women bravely stayed and patiently stood from 11:30 in the morning till 8:00 at night in order to register to vote! The attitude and the disappointed calculation of the white men can be best expressed by quoting one of them: "Who stirred up all these colored women to come up here and register?" Such persistent courage, however, was too ominous to the white registrars, the guardians of racial supremacy and party success; for although they seemed to have no plan of repulse for the first day, they evidently held a council of war at night—and things looked different on the morrow.

Consider how the law itself is made the vehicle of injustice and oppression in its administration. One can register if one pays taxes on at least three hundred dollars' worth of property, or can read from the State or the Federal Constitution some passage selected by the registrar. It would seem the purpose of such a law merely to determine the general fitness and intelligence of the candidate, or to make a bona fide test of his literacy. But although all women were registered without tests the first day, and white women without test or question throughout the registration, colored women after the first day, in addition to being tortured by long standing, were greeted with scowls, rough voices and insulting demeanor. They were made to read and even to explain long passages from the constitutions and from various civil and criminal codes, although there is no law requiring such an inquisition. On the second day the registrars were assisted by a lawyer, apparently for the special business of quizzing, cross-questioning and harassing the colored women, in the manner of opposing counsel in court. He asked questions about all sorts of things from all sorts of documents—questions which he could not himself answer and about which lawyers wrangle every day in court. It was the evident purpose to send back to the colored population so discouraging a report that others would not even try to register. Indeed the Columbia *State*, the morning paper, had suggested that the colored women were manifesting "very little interest," and that "very few" were expected to register.

Well educated colored women were denied the right to register. Some of the questions actually put to the inexperienced colored applicant were: "Explain a *mandamus*." "Define civil code." "How would you appeal a case?" "If presidential votes are tied, how would you break the tie?" "How much revenue did the State hospital pay the State last year?" "How much revenue does the Baptist Church pay the State?"

South Carolina law requires only that one shall *read*, and not the passing of any examination in law or civil government. If a colored woman mispronounced a word in the *opinion* of the half-educated registrar, she was disqualified. In one of the county registration places a colored man was threatened with disfranchisement because he accented the word "municipal" on the antepenult, where the accent belongs, and not "muni*ci*pal" as the registrar insisted it should be.

There was not only injustice but rank insult. A colored man was thrown out of the room for speaking with one of the waiting colored women, for fear that he was coaching or prompting her in the manner of primary school discipline. As one colored woman was reading with ease the passage set before her, the registrar blurted out: "Heah, girl, yo' mispononced two words. Yo' git out o' here! Yo' cain't vote—yo' ain't got sense enough to vote!" A graduate of the State College for Negroes was rejected because she "mispronounced a word"—always in the mere opinion of the registrar, with never an appeal to Webster. Some of the colored teachers of Columbia, licensed by the State to teach colored children, were denied the right to register, as being insufficiently educated to read a ballot!

There was not only insult but threatened and actual violence. On the second day when the number of colored people in the room had grown large because the registrars had compelled them to wait while they registered white people out of turn, the "high sheriff" came in and shouted: "Yo' niggahs git out o' de way, git out an' let de whahte people register—an' stay out! An' if yo' don' stay out, dey'll be some buckshot to keep yo' out."—And still the colored people came. The women especially defied all opposition.

By Friday of the registration week more than twenty of the better educated colored women who had been rejected had signed an affidavit against the registrars. Contrary to calculations, some colored women were even stimulated to go and assert their right to register because they heard that others of their race had been unjustly turned away. They decided either to register or to put the responsibility on the officers of the law. No discouragement, no "test," no petty insult stopped them. Nothing availed against them save the arbitrary will of the tyrants who sat as registrars. The women's suit will be based on the Nineteenth Amendment, to open the way for appeal to federal courts. The colored women of South Carolina may thus play a leading role in the judicial establishment of the enfranchisement of her race and her sex.

According to the press many colored women in Richmond have been denied the right of registration in the same manner and there are similar reports from other localities. Does this mean that the South will resort to the methods to keep Negro women from voting that have been employed to keep the men from the polls? These methods have included every means of trickery and brutality from vague statutes to shot guns. The "white primary" of the dominant and majority party of the South practically ousts the whole colored race from any share in government. There is no trouble in keeping ignorant and shiftless black men from voting—most of them do not want to vote. But the "educational qualification" clauses are chiefly employed to keep industrious and intelligent colored men from the polls, and some have been disfranchised who were graduates of

European universities, in addition to Yale or Harvard. A Norfolk daily paper recently said in an editorial that a law should be enacted by the legislature of Virginia against the passage of the woman suffrage amendment which could be so manipulated as to allow any white man to vote "unless he were an idiot" and to prevent any Negro from voting even if he were "a graduate of Harvard." Every method has been employed against the colored man, up to "red shirt," "Ku Klux" campaigns and less picturesque but equally forceful terrorism. In some districts a colored man seals his death warrant by even attempting to register. Nothing in the code of "Southern chivalry" will prevent similar treatment of colored women. Will the women of the United States who know something at least of disfranchisement tolerate such methods to prevent intelligent colored women from voting?

# The Lynching Industry—1920

## By M. G. Allison

DURING THE year 1920 there were 69 persons lynched in the United States; of these lynchings 60 were Negroes, of whom one was a woman, and 9 were white men. Compared with the year 1919 this record shows a decrease of 17 among Negroes and an increase of 5 among white people.

The record for 1920 follows:

January 14—Florala, Ala., Jack Waters, shot; attacking woman.

February 5—Pine Bluff, Ark., unknown Negro; murder.

February 5—Osceola, Ark., W. E. Hansel (white); burned by unidentified robbers.

March 4—Pike City, Ga., Cornelius Alexander.

March 11—Montgomery County, Ala., William Smith, shot; attacking girl.

March 30—Maysville, Ky., Grant Smith; attacking girl.

April 1—Laurens, S. C., George Robertson; cutting boys in dispute.

April 8—Laurens, S. C., James Steward; injuring men in fight.

April 20—Pittsburg, Kan., Albert Evans; assault.

May 8—Tampa, Fla., M. Scott, shot; insulting woman.

From *The Crisis*, XXI (February 1921), 160.

May 8—Beaumont, Tex., Charles Arling, flogged to death; threatening man.

June 15—Duluth, Minn., Isaac McGhee, Elmer Jackson, Nat Green; attacking girl.

June 21—Rincon, Ga., Philip Gaithers, shot; murder.

June 30—Wharton, Tex., Washington Giles and brother, shot, and Jodie Gordan and Elijah Anderson, hanged; murder.

July 2—Paris, Tex., Irving and Herman Arthur, burned; murder.

*During the summer of 1919, the nation was rent by race
riots. One of the worst occurred in Chicago at the end of
July: thirty-eight people were killed and 537 injured. A
commission was created to investigate causes and recommend measures to prevent riots. DuBois, in the following
piece, comments on the work of the commission.*

# Chicago

## By W. E. B. DuBois

WE WOULD advise our Chicago friends to watch narrowly the work
and forthcoming report of the Inter-racial Commission appointed
by the Governor of Illinois after the late riot. The Commission consists of colored men who apparently have a much too complacent
trust in their white friends; of white men who are too busy to know;
and of enemies of the Negro race who under the guise of impartiality
and good will are pushing insidiously but unswervingly a program
of racial segregation. They have, for instance, sent a "questionnaire" to prominent colored men, consisting of 15 questions, which
with all their surface frankness and innocence seek to betray black
folk by means of the logical dilemma of "segregation" and "racial
solidarity." By subtle suggestion these queries say: If you believe
in colored churches, why not in colored ghettos? Does not Negro
advancement increase anti-Negro hatred? Are not Negroes prejudiced against whites? Are not the mistakes of Negro leaders manifest? And so on.

Indeed if a professed enemy of black folk and their progress had
set out to start a controversy so as to divide the Negroes and their
friends in counsel and throw the whole burden of such nasty out-
breaks of race hate as the East St. Louis, Washington and Chicago
riots upon them, he would have framed just such a questionnaire as
has been sent out by this Commission.

From *The Crisis*, XXI (January 1921), 102.

*Dr. Ossian Sweet, a black physician, ran into trouble with his white neighbors after he bought a home in a white neighborhood in Detroit. In the following article, Walter White describes his case and the trial against him after a riot and murder ensued outside his home.*

# The Sweet Trial

## By Walter White

AT HALF-PAST three in the afternoon of the day before Thanksgiving, Judge Frank Murphy of the Recorder's Court of Detroit finished reading his charge to the jury and turned over to that body for decision the now famous case of The People of the State of Michigan vs. Ossian H. Sweet *et al.*

Seldom in any court has a more impartial, learned or complete charge to a jury been heard. As was evidenced throughout the case, Judge Murphy was exerting every effort at his command to assure to the eleven defendants a completely fair trial. His charge to the jury reached its dramatic climax when in a voice filled with emotion and sincerity, he declared:

> "Dr. Sweet has the same right under the law to purchase and occupy the dwelling house on Garland Avenue as any other man. Under the law, a man's house is his castle. It is his castle, whether he is white or black, and no man has the right to assail or invade it. The Negro is now by the Constitution of the United States given full citizenship with the white man and all the rights and privileges of citizenship attend him wherever he goes."

The jury retired. All afternoon and far into the night anxious crowds thronged the court room and the corridors without. From the jury room could be heard the muffled voices of the jury raised in anger but the door remained closed. Shortly after midnight, a message was sent to Judge Murphy asking for further instructions. Out came the jury with haggard faces and listened to Judge Murphy as he re-read the parts of his charge referring to justifiable self-defense.

From *The Crisis*, XXXI (January 1926), 125–129.

Back into the jury room filed the twelve men. Again voices were heard in argument. At 2:15 Thanksgiving morning, Judge Murphy summoned the jury to permit them to go to bed. The court room was so crowded that court attendants had to use force in getting enough space in front of the judge's dais to permit the jury to stand. Ninety-five per cent of the crowd was composed of Negroes, hope and fear and apprehension and questioning in their faces, asking if justice could be secured for eleven black defendants in a white man's court and at the hands of a white judge and a white jury.

Early on Thanksgiving morning, the jury resumed its deliberations. All day long the court room remained full, hundreds of people going without Thanksgiving dinner for fear that the jury's verdict might be rendered when they were away eating. Towards midnight of the second day, the jury, yet deadlocked, was allowed to retire.

At 1:30 in the afternoon of November 27th, the jury sent word again to Judge Murphy that there was no hope of their reaching a decision. At the end of forty-six hours of deliberation, Judge Murphy declared a mistrial and thanked and dismissed the jurors.

Thus ended the first trial of the case which has stirred Negro America as no other case has ever moved it. Within fifteen years, the Negro population of Detroit has been multiplied by ten, jumping from eight thousand in 1911 to 81,831 by 1925 as a result of the stoppage of immigration from Europe and increased activity on the part of Northern industries. Negroes during and after the war worked in the plants of Detroit, made money and saved it. As has been said many times, it is obvious that eighty-one thousand people cannot live in the homes which housed eight thousand people thirteen years ago. Since 1916 there has been gradual and necessary penetration by Negro home buyers of neighborhoods which hitherto have been occupied by white people. There has been practically no trouble attendant upon these so-called "invasions" until the last year or two. People in Detroit have been so busy earning money that they have not had time to nourish and develop racial or other prejudices. With the exception of a few minor clashes, Detroit has been without doubt one of the fairest cities in the country so far as its treatment of Negroes is concerned.

About two years ago, the Ku Klux Klan started a campaign to capture control of Detroit. This was a part of the movement to gain control of that city and, that purpose gained, make similar efforts to gain control of other Northern cities based upon success in Detroit. Whether a part of that campaign or not, fully ninety per cent of the policemen who have gained positions on the Detroit police force during the past two years have been Southern whites. Charles Bowles, an obscure attorney, was put up as the Klan candidate for Mayor. A little more than a year ago, he secured as the result of Klan support approximately one hundred thousands votes in a mayoralty primary, his name being written in on the ballots. In 1925, he was again a candidate, running against the present incumbent, John W. Smith, who is a Catholic. In the campaign which ended in November, out of approximately a quarter of a million votes, Bowles was defeated by Smith by a narrow margin of about thirty thousand votes.

In order to gain this strength, the Klan has capitalized on and stirred up bitter racial and religious animosities. Early in 1925 there began a series of attacks on the homes of Negroes which reached its most serious stage up to that time in the attack last June upon the home of Dr. A. L. Turner, a respected Negro physician of Detroit. Dr. Turner was driven out of his house, forced to sign an agreement to sell his newly acquired home on Spokane Avenue, his furniture smashed, and he and Mrs. Turner attacked by the mob as they drove away. Practically nothing was done by the police to prevent this attack.

Dr. Ossian H. Sweet, a young Negro physician who is a graduate of Wilberforce and Howard Universities and who has done postgraduate work in pediatrics and gynecology at the Universities of Vienna and Paris, bought a home on Garland Avenue last May. Because of threats against him, Dr. Sweet deferred moving into his new house for two months and a half. He did move in on September 8th, the day after Labor Day. That night a mob gathered but no attack was made on the house. The following evening a larger crowd gathered and stoned the house. In the excitement shots were fired and one member of the mob fell dead and one was wounded.

Police officers, including a deputy superintendent of police, an inspector, a lieutenant, a sergeant, and eight officers, were galvanized into action. They rushed into the house, arrested Dr. Sweet, his wife, Mrs. Gladys B. Sweet, mother of a fourteen months old baby, and nine other occupants of the house. In September, the eleven defendants were given a preliminary hearing before the late Judge John Faust. All were held without bail charged with murder in the first degree.

After remaining in jail for a month, Mrs. Sweet was finally released on bail. In her early twenties, weighing but little more than a hundred pounds, a well educated and intelligent young woman, certain elements in Detroit felt that she was so grave a menace to society that a number of threats were made against the judge for releasing her on bail. From this may be learned the intensity of feeling against the eleven defendants.

The N. A. A. C. P., realizing the very great issue involved and feeling that this case represented the dramatic high point of the nationwide issue of segregation, entered the case, throwing all of its resources without stint into the defense. If the right of a Negro to defend his home against a mob is to be denied him, the N. A. A. C. P. felt that very grave consequences would follow. It was felt also that a successful defense would serve notice upon members of other mobs that decent white and colored people throughout the country had determined to put an end to the unwarranted attacks which had been made with impunity by other mobs upon the persons and property of Negroes. Again, a completely fair trial to Dr. and Mrs. Sweet and their co-defendants would give hope to Negroes throughout the country that their lot was not as hopeless as it sometimes appears to be.

For these reasons, the N. A. A. C. P. retained the most eminent array of counsel which, according to the general consensus of opinion, had ever been engaged for a trial in any Michigan court. Clarence Darrow of Chicago, generally regarded as the greatest criminal lawyer in America and perhaps in the world, was secured as chief counsel. Mr. Darrow, because of his great interest in the case and because of his broad humanitarianism, agreed to serve at a fee which was approximately one-tenth of what he would ordinarily receive in a case of this magnitude. Mr. Arthur Garfield Hays of New York, one of the eminent criminal attorneys of America who was associated with Mr. Darrow in the famous Evolution Case at Dayton, Tennessee, agreed also to enter the case at a nominal fee. Other attorneys secured were Mr. Walter M. Nelson, a prominent white attorney of Detroit, and Messrs. Julian Perry, Cecil Rowlette and Charles Mahoney, colored attorneys of Detroit. Mr. Herbert J. Friedman of Chicago volunteered his services and assisted in the trial without fee.

The trial began on October 30th. At the very outset, Mr. Hays demanded and secured a Bill of Particulars. Prosecutor Robert M. Toms thereupon filed a Bill which particularized as follows:

The theory of the people in this case is that the defendants premeditatedly and with malice aforethought, banded themselves together and armed themselves with the common understanding and agreement that one or more of them would shoot to kill, in the event, first, of threatened or actual trespass on the property wherein they were assembled, or, second, of the infliction of any damage, real or threatened, however slight, to the persons or property of them or any of them. Further, that deceased came to his death by a bullet fired by one of the defendants, aided and abetted by all of the others, in furtherance of their common understanding as above set forth. Further, that such understanding and agreement was to commit an unlawful act, to wit, to shoot to kill without legal justification or excuse.

The purpose in demanding this Bill of Particulars was to force the State to confine its testimony to the proving of a specific thing rather than permit the State to maintain at the conclusion of the trial that it had set out to prove whatever it had happened to prove during the trial.

Through nearly three weeks the State put on its witnesses. Man after man, woman after woman, went on the stand and declared that there were only twelve or fifteen people around the Sweet home on the night of September 9th. The contentions of these witnesses as to the number of persons actually present was somewhat amusing inasmuch as the State in filing names and addresses of the witnesses it intended to call listed seventy-one eye-witnesses to the shooting. The purpose of the testimony giving the figures of bystanders at so low a figure can be understood from the fact that Michigan law provides that a mob consists of "twelve or more persons armed with clubs or other dangerous weapons or of thirty or more persons armed or unarmed."

The State's case began to crumble under the cross-examination of Mr. Darrow and Mr. Hays. For example, Dwight Morrow, a prosecution witness, was asked by Mr. Toms what he saw at Garland and Charlevoix Avenue on the night of September 9th. Morrow answered: "Well, there were—a great number of people and the officers—I won't say a great number—there were a large—there were a few people there and the officers—"

Under cross-examination by Mr. Darrow, this statement was recalled to Morrow's attention. Mr. Darrow asked Morrow:

Q. "You kind of forgot you were to say a few people, didn't you when you started in?"

A. "Yes, Sir." . . .

Again, Norton Schuknecht, Inspector of Police in charge of the Fifth Precinct, testified that he on the night of September 9th was standing at the corner of Charlevoix and Garland Avenues which location was in his precinct. Inspector Schuknecht testified there were no crowds congregated nor any disturbance but that there were around seventy-five people near Dr. Sweet's house, but he also declared that he had found it necessary to station two traffic officers near the house to divert traffic. Several days later, Deputy Superintendent of Police Sprott testified that he was present also on September 9th, that there were no people around the house, that there were four traffic officers and that *he* had stationed them there. These are but a few of the many contradictions on the part of prosecution witnesses which were brought out through cross-examination by the defense attorneys. By the time that the prosecution's testimony was in, it was clearly evident that there was a large crowd present and the prosecution itself introduced a number of stones which were taken from the inside and the roof of the Sweet home.

At the close of the prosecution's case, a motion was made by the defense for a directed verdict inasmuch as the State had wholly failed to prove the conspiracy which it had set forth to prove according to its Bill of Particulars. Judge Murphy denied the motion but granted the right to the defense to renew the motion at the conclusion of the presentation of the defense testimony.

Defense witnesses were then placed on the stand. A number of them told of the threats made against Dr. Sweet and Mrs. Smith from whom Dr. Sweet had purchased the house and of the actual attack upon the house. Four colored witnesses, who happened to be driving in the vicinity of the Sweet home on the night in question and who were attacked and beaten by the mob when they unwittingly drove near the Sweet home, told of their experiences.

The dramatic climax of the trial was reached when Dr. Ossian H. Sweet himself was placed on the stand. Over the objection of the prosecution, the entire background of Dr. Sweet was entered into the record. He told of his birth in a small Florida town, of his leaving home at the age of fourteen to go to Wilberforce University, of his arrival there only to find that the Scholarship Fund through which he had hoped to get an education had been exhausted. Simply, directly and convincingly, Dr. Sweet told of his efforts to gain an education. He told of the years he had worked as a bell boy, shovelling snow, waiting table, firing furnaces and at the same time carry-

ing on his studies until he had finished the academic and college
courses at Wilberforce. He then related how he had worked his way
through Howard University Medical School and, though he was
without funds, he had determined to go to Europe and there pursue
his studies at the Universities of Vienna and Paris.

He told, too, how during a campaign for funds by the American
Hospital at Paris he had given what he could to that hospital—some
three hundred francs—a gift which meant certain privations for himself and wife; and then later when he made application for Mrs.
Sweet to enter that hospital to give birth to a daughter, how she had
been denied admission because of the colored blood within her veins.

Then there were brought out the things which had most definitely
influenced Dr. Sweet's mind in its reactions toward American mobs.
A race riot a few years ago at Orlando, Florida, where Dr. Sweet was
born, in which several colored people were killed and the homes of a
number of Negroes burned; of the Tulsa riot in 1921 when Dr. Jackson, eminent Negro surgeon, was shot and killed in cold blood after
he had been guaranteed protection by the police force; of the Phillips
County, Arkansas, Riots in 1919 when the four Johnson brothers, one
of them a physician and another a dentist, had been ambushed
through treachery and killed; of the Washington race riots in 1919
when Dr. Sweet had seen a colored man dragged from a street car
and beaten to death; of the Chicago race riots of that same year when
a cousin of Mrs. Sweet, a police officer, had been forced to go to trial
when he in clear self-defense had killed a member of the mob which
was attacking him; of the terrible riots at East St. Louis in 1917. All
of these things were brought out through adroit questioning to show
the state of mind of the eleven Negroes within the house on the night
of September 9th at 2905 Garland Avenue, Detroit. As Mr. Darrow
pointed out convincingly to the court, the theory of a reasonable man
as propounded by the State could not possibly mean in this case the
attitude of a white man but must necessarily be that of a Negro with
a white mob outside and in the Negro's brain a picture of what similar mobs have done to Negroes during the last sixty years in America.

By the time the case was ready to go to the jury, it was freely predicted throughout Detroit that the case could not possibly end in
anything other than acquittal for all eleven defendants. The newspapers of Detroit gave full and impartial reports of the trial, for thirty
days featuring the story on the front page. As a result of this impartial
reporting, the decent and fair minded element in Detroit had been

informed to such an extent that sympathy had swung definitely toward the defendants—a very marked contrast to feeling in the city prior to the entry of the N. A. A. C. P. and Mr. Darrow into the case.

On the other hand, the anti-Negro sentiment, and especially that represented by such organizations as the Ku Klux Klan and the Waterworks Park Improvement Association which had been formed for the purpose of keeping Dr. Sweet from occupying his home, definitely became very bitter as the case went on. Because of the feeling on the part of the two groups just mentioned, it is reasonably certain that all eleven defendants would have been convicted had it not been for the work of the attorneys engaged and the efforts of the N. A. A. C. P. both in retaining these attorneys and in conducting the case and in the efforts of the N. A. A. C. P. in placing before the people of Detroit the actual facts in the case to displace the half truths and untruths which had stirred such hostility against the defendants.

The case has cost the N. A. A. C. P. upwards of $20,000. A new trial has been set for the first week in January. Mr. Darrow announced to the court that it was probable that the defense would ask for separate trials for the eleven defendants. With renewed vigor, the N. A. A. C. P. is going into the case again determined to see it through to the end and to secure complete justice for the defendants.

After the mistrial, Messrs. Darrow and Hays made a motion for the admission to bail of the defendants. Eight of them were freed on bail of $5,500 each while three others, Dr. Ossian H. Sweet, Henry Sweet and Leonard C. Morse, were freed on bail of $10,000 each. This bail has been almost entirely furnished by Negro property owners of Detroit.

# PART THREE

# *The Irony of the Dream*

As SUGGESTED in the introduction to this book, imaginative writers in the black community often treated the American Dream ironically. How could it be otherwise? The chasm between the beauty and purity of American rhetoric and the ugliness of the black American's reality made such an approach inevitable. The selections in this part offer many poetic examples of how American themes were discussed and described by leading black poets such as Langston Hughes and Claude McKay. Writing primarily during the 1920's in Harlem, these poets found a growing audience of blacks and whites who were interested in the authentic African past of the black American and who also believed that a harmony could be worked out between the uniqueness of the black man's cultural past and the legal, political, and socio-economic institutions of modern America. Much of the literature of the period addresses itself to this theme: the earnest desire of black Americans for an equal chance in American life at the same time they preserve their original heritage.

Some ironic personal accounts are also included in this section, particularly the articles "Our White Folks" by George Schuyler and "The Joys of Being a Negro" by Edward E. Wilson. Schuyler has been called the black H. L. Mencken. His icy tone and satiric treatment of the race problem made him a famous critic in the twenties. Wilson's essay is equally powerful in this respect.

*In quietly sardonic tones, Wilson shows the terrible
dilemma faced by black Americans in the land of ultimate
opportunity.*

# The Joys of Being a Negro

## By Edward E. Wilson

SOME TIME AGO I received a beautifully engraved card inviting me to
spend my winter at a certain aristocratic Southern hotel. In I know
not what way—perhaps because I was duly enrolled among the
lawyers of a Northern city—my name had drifted with a few others
into the hands of the proprietor of this hostelry. I am sure there was
no intention either on my part or on the part of my name to impose
on anyone. In America one may have whatever name he chooses,
and mine was of the plainest kind; it was neither parted in the middle
nor preceded by *de* or *von;* it had, indeed, an absolute and hopeless
democracy in sound and meaning.

But to the point. When I received the above invitation, flinging off
realities for a moment, I yielded to my fancy and began forthwith to
imagine myself, after collecting from every conceivable source over-
due fees, and after such extensive borrowing as my credit would allow,
going to this exclusive winter resort and offering myself as a guest
thereof. Fancy was not so extravagant, however, as to allow me to
ride thither in a Pullman, because not even fancy could evade certain
laws enacted by fastidious legislators preventing persons of my ancestry from so traveling. Nor, as being beneath the dignity of a select
resorter, did I care to try the delights of a ride in a freight car;
although such a ride was most ingratiatingly recommended by a
writer in the *Atlantic* a short time since. Arrived, in imagination, at
my destination, I look up the broad shrubbery-fringed esplanade
leading to the hotel; but I see no black servitor with shining ivories
hastening to meet me. As I enter the hotel I am sensible of an excitement—the mixture of curiosity and consternation—created by my
coming; the factotums of my own race about the hotel gaze at me

From *Atlantic Monthly*, XCVII (February 1906), 245–250.

in speechless wonder, or else whisper meaningly to one another; as I stalk to the clerk's desk and ask to register, I gorgonize that hitherto unabashed individual; the loungers, amazed, sit upright like statues in the Hall of Silence. Imagination picturing true, I will not dwell upon what happens thereafter. Suffice to say, that if I escape unbruised and unarrested, and can make my way with the aid of a freight car or any other vehicle through the dark and tortuous ways of a hostile country to that city of the North whence I came, I shall ever afterwards recall my safe return with soul-sincere thanksgiving.

Now I ask in all seriousness, what member of any other race could have such a thrilling experience in his imagination, from the mere imaginary acceptance of an invitation duly directed and solemnly sent to him?

Such an experience in reality at a Northern hotel or in a Northern Young Men's Christian Association would, in some quarters, call forth a deal of gratuitous sympathy. An idea has unfortunately got abroad that being a Negro is like being in solitary confinement,—away from the rest of the world. It is thought, indeed, that there could be no place chosen so gloomy or so hopeless in which to be born as among this race composed to some extent of descendants of Ham. Yet the whole question depends—as all other things do in life—on the point of view and the state of mind. I can never forget how near I came once, at a certain institution of learning, to rustication, because I insisted, in the face of frequent and emphatic asseverations of the Professor of Philosophy to the contrary, that objects were objects and things existed outside of the mind. Since then I have seen how cheerful was the view of the good professor, and how a Negro adopting it can experience joys such as no white man can ever know.

Worn as is the saying that life's happiness lies in anticipation, it is a truism that perfectly fits the Negro's case. So much lies before him, the things he can hope to achieve are so much more numerous than those which Aryans can look forward to, that his pleasures of hope are endless. And why should he end them? why seek disillusion in attainment? Was Sancho Panza happier when he was hoping for, or when he had come into his government? With the Negro it is but seldom that delights grow stale by being transformed from the imaginary to the real. He may have suffered here and there such disillusioning, but not enough to render him cynical. He had faith, it is true, that the coming of his freedom would solve all questions for him; yet he found it but broadened his field of anticipation. He as firmly believed that his advance in education would help him, but this merely served to show the measureless distance between him and satiety. He is in position to pity the self-extolled Aryan who, if American, thinks himself nearing the limits of perfection.

In fact the Negro is the rustic of America. Of the doings of this great and busy nation he is but a spectator. He stands as the procession passes, with mouth agape. He imagines that ever new wonders are to arrive, and his fancy creates a veritable *Arabian Nights*. What is common to others is a source of admiration to him.

One who basks in the sunshine of adulation, who is constantly told or constantly telling himself that he is the very climax of civilization, the heir of all the ages, knows not what it is to feel the heart beat quickly at a word of praise. Heap abuse upon one, however, misrepresent his every action, call his assertion of his ordinary rights insolence, scoff at his efforts at deference and politeness as servility, and then a kind word to him is as a grateful palm in the midst of a desert. . . .

But all things have their recompense. Does a theatre refuse to sell me a first class seat? or rather, not refusing because of the law, falsely pretend that all such seats are sold? Does a heartless real estate dealer decline to sell me a house outside of the slums?—I simply call on a white Negro to buy one for me, and go off, gloating over the fact that the proud Aryan has put it in my power to triumph over his unrighteous exclusiveness. More than once Negroes have, because of what is known as their "white reinforcement," moved along in intimate relations side by side with those the very breath of whose lives was the hatred of anything African. Now I challenge the world to show me an Aryan who can successfully pass for a Negro.

Moreover, it is a great wonder that the blacks have so little haughtiness when they find themselves the topic for magazine and newspaper articles, the inspiration for many marvelous songs, the subject of innumerable discussions in the very Congress of the United States, and not seldom the moving spirit in those latter-day gems of literature,—race novels.

Many have thought the common belief that all Negroes are alike was a fact much to be deplored; but here again is an almost universal mistake. The surprise, the pleasant shock, that the Aryan gets when now and again he finds this belief upset, in no small measure atones for any injury done to the less fortunate race. I remember once upon a time meeting on a railroad train an elderly gentleman full of good intentions toward the heathen and downtrodden, and somewhat officious withal. I had in my hand a score of the opera *Rigoletto,* which had been sung in my city the night before. A book in the hands of a Negro quickly attracted the benevolent gentleman's attention. He then perused me from head to foot, as though I was the strangest of creatures. I could see condescension oozing from every pore. "Young man," he said, "I see you are trying to elevate yourself. This is a glorious country, where every man has a chance. The nation shed its blood for you. What book have you there?" I meekly showed it to him. "Ah, music—opera—you enjoy that! You are different from the rest of your people. My family was at that opera. I know very little about music myself." Not less than the writer; but here was my chance for revenge. I dragged forth and criticised out of hand musician after musician (my knowledge of them having been obtained much after the manner of Pendennis's acquaintance with things while working with Warrington on the *Pall Mall Gazette*),—Wagner, Verdi, Bach, Bizet, Strauss, Donizetti, Gounod, and such others as my ransacked memory afforded. My new-found acquaintance was the very picture of amazement,—began to retreat when I appealed to him to decide whether the world was most indebted to Mozart or Wagner for dramatic music; but I was unrelenting, and, pursuing, poured upon him such volleys of "counterpoint," "arias," "ensembles," "phrasings," that he dropped into his seat mute and helpless. Should any one object that I was guilty of pretentiousness, even of deception, I admit it, but plead self-defense, which justifies extreme measures,—even to the taking of human life. What right had he to assume because I had a book in my hand that I was a prodigy, and to affront me by telling me so? . . .

In negroes' working for themselves alone, there would, from a larger view, be something of selfishness. Yet they can fairly claim to have lightened the burdens of myriads, and to have furnished amusement to countless thousands who could not, perhaps, have been otherwise entertained. One often wonders what would become of the cheap cartoonist and outlandish dialect-writer if the Negro were suddenly removed from American life; what untimely fate would overtake the melon joke and the chicken joke. As one contemplates the matter a real alarm is created; for what would become of certain heavy magazine writers, sensational novelists, and numberless Lilliputians in newspaper offices? How many words of detraction would

lie unused and rusting in the lexicon! How, here and there, philanthropy itself would droop and die!

Giving joy to another is a joy in itself. To keep another in a state
of complacency amounts to the same thing. Of how much just pride
the Aryan would be divested if he no longer had the lowly Negro to
measure himself by, we can never know. Could there be nobility
without commons? Could there be princes without subjects? Could
there be an indomitable Aryan race, whose matchless courage, virtue,
and heroism conquered the American wilderness and overcame its
savages, were there no Negro here clamoring for his share in American life? Not so; without the Negro as a foil, Americans would be
nothing more than plain white men.

If the satisfaction furnished the superior race sometimes causes
the less fortunate pain, the latter should remember that what benefits the majority makes for the good of the whole, and that nothing
is nobler than vicarious suffering. The frogs were foolish when they
cried out to the boys, "What is fun for you is death to us." The very
wrongs of the oppressed have more than once called out the finest
qualities in their oppressors, which might have, for the want of in-
citement, lain dormant forever. In compensation for injustice at home
a deal of commiseration may be scattered abroad. Who can tell but
that certain small, sporadic iniquities wrought against the blacks in
America have so softened the consciences both of the people and
of our ruling powers that they have been led to sympathize with the
oppressed of all the foreign world, and to utter tearful protests against
Armenian outrages and Kishinev massacres?

In this age where all is doubt, and every statement outside vera-
cious newspapers is picked to pieces by original investigation, one
may, without being liable to the charge of heresy, stick at accepting
the theory that he who enjoys the highest things alone enjoys existence. It would not be fair to presume that, because one leads a
lowly and unlettered life, he in his own way has not as much solid
enjoyment as the greatest of philosophers, poets, or artists. The
youngster, swallowing with eager gulps the contents of a detective
story in which are recounted the hairbreadth escapes of some matchless sleuth, will, even though raised in after life above such literature,
confess, if ingenuous, that he enjoyed his *Old Thunderbolt* as much
as the *Adam Bede* of his later life. And what has brought more real
joy to the soul of the sentimental maiden than, say, *When Armor Was
in Fashion?* It would be many a long year before she would prefer

*Henry Esmond* to it. There is no aristocracy of enjoyment. Those who tell us that there is no music but Wagner's, and that the love of melody is an infallible sign of a vicious taste; no poetry but Browning's,—at least that part of him that must be guessed at,—thrive by assumption alone. It is impossible that any considerable portion of the human race shall be elevated to the level where these alleged highest pleasures are; and to the many,—the common people have some rights,—those things they comprehend and delight in give as true gratification as the elect enjoy.

If this be true, the Negro, presumed by the thoughtless majority, because of his environment, to be the most joyless of creatures, has a much larger share of happiness than many who outwardly appear more fortunate. (Here we speak of the typical Negro, not the late, revised, Aryanized one.) First of all he has what satisfaction there is in knowing that the theory of things is right. In theory he has whatever any other man has; just as in theory all men are created equal, —the law is impartially administered,—we are a Christian nation. Though the Negro is actually excluded from the social, political, and industrial life of America, there is comfort in the fact that he is not the least of the non-Aryans in this country. He has been theoretically placed on equal footing with the great white man by the great white man himself. Mongolians cannot become citizens of the United States, while the African from any part of the world and his descendants have this glorious privilege. It is interesting to note that members of the race that has so lately flung the proud Aryan into the dust in the Far East have, on several occasions, once in enlightened Massachusetts (*In Re Saito*, 62 Fed. Rep. 126), been refused the citizenship which a Negro may have for the asking. But after all, such discrimination as is practiced against him gives him leisure to develop, undisturbed by outside cares, those things in him worth cultivating. While the German, Irishman, Frenchman, and even the proud Englishman, who comes to this country, pools each his individuality in Americanism, the Negro, developing independence, stands aloof, with a determination to yield only when longer resistance would be criminal folly.

The negative pleasures of the Negro are not few. He has none of the burdens of governing, being relieved therefrom by his altruistic Aryan fellow-citizens. He has none of the troubles and temptations of millionaires; he expects but little and hence is seldom disappointed. He carries no revenges concealed in his bosom. He forgives his enemies easily. Do him a grievous injury, and a modicum of kindness removes resentment therefor. Bastinado his sensibilities to-day; he will salve them with biblical quotations, and to-morrow go on his way rejoicing.

From the Bible, indeed, the Negro draws no small portion of his philosophy of life; and while he may take a passage here and there too literally, yet he derives such satisfaction from this book that he would probably assail more truculently an enemy thereof than one who had done him personal wrong. "Take no thought for the morrow"; "The Lord will provide"; "Lay ye not up treasures on earth"; "Consider the lilies how they grow, they toil not neither do they spin"; "Man that is born of woman is of few days and full of trouble,"— these and such passages are unction to his soul.

From the Bible, likewise, the Negro draws justification for his failure to be actively resentful of his wrongs. And who best represents the Christian spirit, the Aryan raging over the loss of a tooth, demanding a tooth in return and refusing to be comforted without it, or the humble black who, hardly smitten on one cheek, meekly presents the other to the smiter? In the lowliness of the Founder of his faith the Negro finds comfort for his own poverty. He is not so engrossed with earthly things, but he has a constant eye on Paradise. He believes that like Lazarus he will recline on Abraham's bosom; while those who enjoyed without stint this world's goods squirm amidst brimstone with no drop of water to cool their quenchless thirst.

The contemplation of death, which brings terror to many and to almost all men sadness, brings to the Negro the idea of rest from labor and surcease of sorrow. Hence one finds more preparation by him for that fatal last event than for living, moving, and having his being on earth. Death, too, is a certain vindicator of equality; not that the Negro is glad when an Aryan, though a hostile one, goes to the land of darkness; but he points significantly and with melancholy satisfaction to the fact that poor Mose, who died a social pariah only yesterday, occupies as much of his mother earth as the dead colonel who lorded it over him so haughtily but a short fortnight ago.

Through all his vicissitudes hope is the black man's priceless asset. This he never loses, how gloomy soever the way. For him there is always something in the future, no matter how distant. A negro of uncommon ability, the advocate of a new education for Negroes, has told them that in a thousand years they would be fitted to partake of the things the Aryan now enjoys, and this promise of remote enjoyment the blacks hail with enthusiasm. Was there ever sublimer faith? The very heart-wailings of the Negro speak of a brighter beyond. Of joy he cannot be bereft: his buoyancy overtops any sorrow. Pessimism seldom knows him. One miracle of deliverance has been performed for him, and he is confidently expecting another.

Should any question my authority to speak as above for the Negro, I reply that I became a Negro about thirty years ago; and, being initiated into all the mysterious rites of the race, have remained one ever since.

*Both James Corrothers and Fenton Johnson were minor poets who wrote in the early decades of the century. Both experimented with poetic forms as well as content.*

# Up! Sing the Song

### By James D. Corrothers

I am a Negro, but I sing and sing,
    Burning with kiss divine that made
        me so.
O brother mortal, likest to the snow,
Turn not in coldness from the song I bring,
But listen to my lyre's low murmuring,
        where down the cypresses I sadly go,
    Through deepening twilight, lest the faint
        winds know
The secret of some tender little thing

That haunts and haunts me, and they tell
        it all—
    All, all my sorrows and ambitions, too!
For these o'ercome me; these, through dreamy
        fall,
    Keep calling, calling; beckoning, as to
        you:
"Up! Sing the song! Men shall forget
        your race,
Nor blush to keep the image of your face."

From *The Crisis*, VI (May 1913), 39.

# Children of the Sun

### *By Fenton Johnson*

### I.

We are children of the sun,
   Rising sun!
Weaving Southern destiny,
Waiting for the mighty hour
When our Shiloh shall appear
With the flaming sword of right,
With the steel of brotherhood,
And emboss in crimson die
   *Fraternity!*

### II.

We are the star-dust folk,
   Striving folk!
Sorrow songs have lulled to rest;
Seething passions wrought
   through wrongs,
Led us where the moon rays dip
In the night of dull despair,
Showed us where the star
   gleams shine,
And the mystic symbols glow—
*Liberty! Fraternity!*

### III.

We have come through cloud and mist,
   Mighty men!
Dusk has kissed our sleep-born eyes,
Reared for us a mystic throne
In the splendor of the skies,
That shall always be for us,
Children of the Nazarene,
Children who shall ever sing
*Liberty! Fraternity!*

*The following two poetic examples demonstrate Corrothers' consistent concern with the meaning of democracy in America.*

# An Indignation Dinner

### By James D. Corrothers

Dey was hard times jes 'fo' Christmas
    round our neighborhood one year;
So we held a secret meetin', whah de
    white folks could n't hear,
To 'scuss de situation, an' to see whut
    could be done
Towa'd a fust-class Christmas dinneh an'
    a little Christmas fun.

Rufus Green, who called de meetin', ris'
    an' said: "In dis here town,
An' throughout de land, de white folks
    is a-tryin' to keep us down."
S' 'e: "Dey 's bought us, sold us, beat us;
    now dey 'buse us 'ca'se we 's free;
But when dey tech my *stomach*, dey 's
    done gone too fur foh *me!*

"Is I right?" "You sho is, Rufus!" roared
    a dozen hungry throats.
"Ef you 'd keep a mule a-wo'kin', don't
    you tamper wid his oats.
Dat 's sense," continued Rufus. "But
    dese white folks nowadays
Has done got so close an' stingy you can't
    live on whut dey pays.

"Here 't is Christmas-time, an', folkses,
    I 's indignant 'nough to choke.

From *Century,* XCI (December 1915), 320.

Whah 's our Christmas dinneh comin'
  when we 's 'mos' completely broke?
I can't hahdly 'fo'd a toothpick an' a
  glass o' water. Mad?
Say, I 'm desp'ut! Dey jes better treat
  me nice, dese white folks had!"

Well, dey 'bused de white folks scan'lous,
  till old Pappy Simmons ris',
Leanin' on his cane to spote him, on
  account his rheumatis',
An' s' 'e: "Chilun, whut 's dat wintry
  wind a-sighin' th'ough de street
'Bout yo' wasted summeh wages? But,
  no matteh, we mus' *eat*.

"Now, I seed a beau'fuh tuhkey on a
  certain gemmun's fahm.
He 's a-growin' fat an' sassy, an'
  a-struttin' to a chahm.
Chickens, sheeps, hogs, sweet pertaters—
  all de craps is fine dis year;
All we needs is a *committee* foh to vote
  de goodies here."

Well, we lit right in an' voted dat it was
  a gran' idee,
An' de dinneh we had Christmas was
  worth trabblin' miles to see;
An' we eat a full an' plenty, big an'
  little, great an' small,
*Not* beca'se we was dishonest, but
  *indignant*, sah. Dat 's all.


# In the Matter of Two Men

*By James D. Corrothers*


One does such work as one will not,
  And well each knows the right;

Though the white storm howls, or the sun is hot,
   The black must serve the white.
And it's, oh, for the white man's softening flesh,
   While the black man's muscles grow!
Well, I know which grows the mightier,
   *I* know; full well I know.

The white man seeks the soft, fat place ,
   And he moves and he works by rule.
Ingenious grows the humbler race
   In Oppression's prodding school.
And it's, oh, for a white man gone to seed,
   While the Negro struggles so!
And I know which race develops most,
   I know; yes, well I know.

The white man rides in a palace car,
   And the Negro rides "Jim Crow."
To damn the other with bolt and bar,
   One creepeth so low; so low!
And it's, oh, for a master's nose in the mire,
   While the humbled hearts o'erflow!
Well, I know whose soul grows big at this,
   And whose grows small; *I know!*

The white man leases out his land,
   And the Negro tills the same.
One works; one loafs and takes command,
   But I know who wins the game!
And it's, oh, for the white man's shrinking soil,
   As the black's rich acres grow!
Well, I know how the signs point out at last,
   I know; ah, well I know.

The white man votes for his color's sake,
   While the black, for his is barred;
(Though "ignorance" is the charge they make),
   But the black man studies hard.
And it's, oh, for the white man's sad neglect,
   For the power of his light let go!
So, I know which man must win at last,
   I know! Ah, Friend, I know!

*In a speech in Birmingham, Alabama, on October 26,
1921, President Warren G. Harding asserted that the
black man's equality did not extend to social spheres.
The following editorial in the* Nation *responds to this
point of view.*

# President Harding and Social Equality

FIND FAULT with the President after he has gone straight into Southern territory and come out plump for the Negro's political and economic rights, and the necessity of giving him an education equal to
the white man's? To many that will seem like base ingratitude, for, as
we said last week, his was in the main a brave and noble statement.
Nothing compelled Mr. Harding to make it; no public emergency
necessitated his taking up an issue which Mr. Wilson for eight years
refused to face. There were personal reasons to keep him from it.
Since the colored vote is now more than ever attached to the Republican Party, Mr. Harding could have had no other motive at this time
than a sincere desire to aid ten millions of colored Americans who,
disfranchised and in economic servitude, are constantly suffering the
most galling discriminations by reason of the color of their skins. To
millions of these Mr. Harding today appears a veritable Sir Gala-
had. By the "grapevine telegraph" whose amazing speed and thor-
oughness in disseminating news to our black plantation workers
throughout the South filled Booker T. Washington with awe and
amazement, it is unquestionably known in every Negro cabin today
that there is a President in the White House who has pleaded the
cause of the black man before the nation.

Why then cavil at any single phrase of the President? Why not
overlook his one unfortunate utterance in order to bestow upon him
unqualified praise? Because that one reference to social equality—
"men of both races may well stand uncompromisingly against every
suggestion of social equality"—fell like a lash upon every thoughtful
Negro and offset much of the good Mr. Harding did. Even in far-off
Buenos Aires it called forth protests; the national Argentine Socialist

From *Nation*, CXIII (November 16, 1921), 561.

convention at once interpreted Mr. Harding as meaning that the condition of "the ten millions of Negro population in the great republic will be eternally one of inferiority and subordination," and emphatically protested against it. True, the phrase quoted sweetened the rest of the dose for the South and saved the President from endless coarse abuse and fanatical denunciation as a "nigger lover" and from the charge of "insulting the South." Yet it would have been far better had he never uttered it, for by it he played into the hands of all who justify any discrimination against the Negro.

At least he should have defined just what he meant by social equality. It he had in mind intermarriage only, he should, in justice to himself and to the Negro, have said so. Unfortunately the phrase covers a multitude of sins. It is the excuse for endless aggression and wrongdoing by the "superior race." In the final analysis in the South social equality invariably whittles down to the relations of black men with white women, and in order to prevent them multitudes of our white Americans in the South honestly think themselves justified in resorting to any measures down to torture and burning. So certain are they that this must not be tolerated that they seek to prevent any approach to it by even forbidding colored people the use of public libraries, to say nothing of public carriers. Hardly an hour goes by in the life of a black adult without there being driven in upon his consciousness a realization that in a republic which hypocritically boasts of the freedom of all its citizens and their equality of opportunity he bears upon his brow the badge of shame and of deliberately classified inferiority.

So President Harding ought to have informed us whether he meant by his words on social equality to approve of the Jim Crow car, the denial of all cultural opportunities in theaters, in concert and lecture halls to colored people, and the unending discrimination against them in restaurants and hotels and in practically every walk of life. He has not even stated that he is opposed to that precious bit of Wilson wrongdoing, the segregation of the Negro in the departments at Washington. Until Mr. Harding does speak out on these questions, which mean more to the Negro than anything else, which daily bend his back, scarify his soul, and make every educated Negro mother look upon her children and ask whether she can justify to them their being called into existence, he cannot have thought through the problem nor can he render the full service which we believe he desires to render, which we honor him for seeking to render.

280 The Irony of the Dream

Without in the least urging intermarriage we must protest against the President's propaganda of "fundamental, eternal, and inescapable race differences." We have no quarrel whatever with those of either race who urge what they call racial purity. But the true method of control in this matter is by a sound social public opinion and not by laws, nor by the branding iron, nor that slow fire which in the Middle Ages was relied upon to prevent the spread of Protestantism. These measures are as ineffective as they are cruel and debasing.

The laws against intermarriage in the South are the most effective promoters of immorality and of concubinage and they place the black woman at the mercy of the white man without redress. As a matter of fact, statistics prove that where marriage is permitted the amount of it is negligible. We may rest assured that if racial intermarriage is socially unwise and racially destructive, nature herself will take a hand and control it without men's having to resort to crime to check it. But in the last analysis anyone who believes in individual freedom and liberty must believe in the right of every sound individual to seek his mate where he will and if necessary to pay the price for his deed in social ostracism to which there is no need of adding legal penalties. Once more we repeat that if racial admixture is not prevented by the instinctive disinclination of the races, it will not effectually be prevented by denying to one of them the ordinary courtesies which individuals earn by their conduct or deserve by their essential humanity.

What Mr. Harding has yet to see is that if the Negro obtains the economic freedom, the political freedom, and the boon of education which he craves for him this whole question of race relationship will at once adjust itself on a far nobler and better basis; that as long as the question of social equality is made the excuse for abuse, ill treatment, and the denial of rights sacredly guaranteed by the Constitution it works infinite harm to the whites who thus make of their republic an hypocrisy and defile their own souls by sponsoring injustice and wrong. There is something sadly wrong with a racial integrity which must be preserved in that manner. Moreover, if there are "fundamental, eternal, and inescapable race differences" they will take care of the situation themselves. But whether they do or not, no President is true to America who does not insist that every American citizen shall have the freest social opportunity without barriers of class or race or color, and political freedom as well.

*Eric D. Walrond was a West Indian who migrated to the United States and became a major participant in the Harlem Renaissance. His* Tropic Death *(1926) was considered one of the most realistic and colorful descriptions of West Indian life produced during the period. He contributed frequently to the magazines of the day.*

# On Being Black

## By Eric D. Walrond

I GO TO an optician and ask for a pair of goggles. My eyes are getting bad and my wife insists upon my getting them. For a long time I have hesitated to do so. I hated to be literary—that is, to look literary. It is a fad, I believe. On an afterthought I am convinced she is right; I need them. My eyes are paining me. Moreover, the lights in the subway are blindingly dark, and head swirling. Again, the glitter of spring sends needles through my skull. I need the things badly. I decide to go to the optician's. I go. It is a Jewish place. Elderly is the salesman. I put my cards on the table. . . . "Fine day, isn't it?" He rubs and twists his pigmy fingers and ambles back to the rear. A moment later he returns. With him is a tray of jewelry—lenses and gold rims, diamonds and silver frames. Fine, dainty, effeminate things.

"Here is a nice one," chirps the old gentleman in a sing-song tone, as he tries to fit it on to my nose. "Just the right kind of goggles to keep the dust from going into your eyes. Only the other day I sold—"

At first I feel as if it is one of these confounded new fangled things. Overnight they come, these new styles. Ideas! Here, I whisper to myself, is a new one on me. But I look again. It has a perforated bit of tin on either side of it, like the black star-eyed guard on a horse's blinker.

"Oh, I can show you others, if you don't like that one. Want one with a bigger dust piece? I have others back here. Don't be afraid, I'll fix you up. All the colored chauffeurs on Cumberland Street buy their glasses here."

From *New Republic*, XXXII (November 1, 1922), 244–246.

"But I am not a chauffeur," I reply softly. Were it a Negro store, I might have said it with a great deal of emphasis, of vehemence. But being what it is, and knowing that the moment I raise my voice I am accused of "uppishness," I take pains—oh such pains, to be discreet. I wanted to bellow into his ears, "Don't think every Negro you see is a chauffeur." But the man is overwhelmingly amused. His snow-white head is bent—bent over the tray of precious gold, and I can see his face wrinkle in an atrociously cynical smile. But I cannot stand it—that smile. I walk out.

## II

I am a stenographer. I am in need of a job. I try the employment agencies. I battle with anaemic youngsters and giggling flappers. I am at the tail end of a long line—only to be told the job is already filled. I am ignorantly optimistic. America is a big place; I feel it is only a question of time and perseverance. Encouraged, I go into the tall office buildings on Lower Broadway. I try everyone of them. Not a firm is missed. I walk in and offer my services. I am black, foreign-looking and a curio. My name is taken. I shall be sent for, certainly, in case of need. "Oh, don't mention it, sir. . . . Glad you came in. . . . Good morning." I am smiled out. I never hear from them again.

Eventually I am told that that is not the way it is done here. What typewriter do I use? Oh, ——. Well, go to the firm that makes them. It maintains an employment bureau, for the benefit of users of its machine. There is no discrimination there; go and see them. Before I go I write stating my experience and so forth. Are there any vacancies? In reply I get a flattering letter asking me to call. I do so.

The place is crowded. A sea of feminine faces disarms me. But I am no longer sensitive. I've got over that—long since. I grind my teeth and confidently take my seat with the mob. At the desk the clerks are busy telephoning and making out cards. I am sure they do not see me. I am just one of the crowd. One by one the girls, and men, too, are sent out after jobs. It has been raining and the air is frowsy. The Jewish girls are sweating in their war-paint. At last they get around to me. It is my turn.

I am sitting away down at the front. In order to get to me the lady is obliged to do a lot of detouring. At first I thought she was about to go out, to go past me. But I am mistaken. She takes a seat right in front of me, a smile on her wrinkled old-maidish face. I am sure she is the head of the department. It is a situation that requires a strong diplo-

matic hand. She does not send one of the girls. She comes herself.
She is from Ohio, I can see that. She tries to make me feel at home by
smiling broadly in my face.

"Are you Mr. ——?"

"Yes."

"That's nice. Now how much experience you say you've had?"
She is about to write.

"I stated all that in the letter, I think. I've had five years. I worked
for—"

"Oh yes, I have it right here. Used to be secretary to Dr. ——. Then
you worked for an export house, and a soap manufacturer. Also as a
shorthand reporter on a South American paper. That is interesting;
quite an experience for a young man, isn't it?"

I murmur unintelligibly.

"Well," continues the lady, "we haven't anything at present—"

"But I thought you said in your letter that there is a job vacant.
I've got it here in my pocket. I hope I haven't left it at home—"

"That won't suit you. You see it—it—is a post that requires banking experience. One of the biggest banks in the city. Secretary to the
vice-president. Ah, by the way; come to think of it, you're just the
man for it. You know Mr. —— of Lenox Avenue? You do! I think
the number is—— Yes, here it is. Also one of his cards. Well, if I
were you I would go and see him. Good day."

Dusk is on the horizon. I am once more on Broadway. I am not
going to see the man on Lenox Avenue. It won't do any good. The
man she is sending me to is a pupil of mine!

### III

My wife's health is not very good and I think of sending her to the
tropics. I write to the steamship company and in reply I receive a
sheaf of booklets telling me all about the blueness of the Caribbean,
the beauty of Montega Bay, and the fine a la carte service at the
Myrtle Bank Hotel. I am intrigued—I think that is the word—by a
three months' cruise at a special rate of $150.00. I telephone the com-
pany in an effort to get some information as to sailing dates, reservations, and so forth.

"I understand," I say to the young man who answers the telephone,
"I understand that you have a ship sailing on the tenth. I would like
to reserve a berth at the $150.00 you are presently offering."

"White or colored?"

"Colored."

Evidently the clerk is consulting someone. But his hand is over the mouthpiece and I can not hear what he is saying. Presently—

"Better come in the office and make reservations."

"What time do you close?"

"Five o'clock."

"What time is it now, please?"

"Ten to."

"Good," I hurry, "I am at Park Place now. Do you think if I hop on a Broadway trolley I can make it before five?"

"I don't know," unconcernedly.

I am at the booking desk. It is three minutes to five. The clerks, tall, lean, light-haired youths, are ready to go home. As I enter a dozen pairs of eyes are fastened upon me. Murmuring. Only a nigger. Again the wheels of life grind on. Lots are cast—I am not speaking metaphorically. The joke is on the Latin. Down in Panama he is a government clerk. Over in Caracas, a tinterillo, and in Mexico, a scientifico. I know the type. Coming to New York, he shuns the society of Spanish-Americans. On the subway at night he reads the New York Journal instead of La Prensa. And on wintry evenings, you can always find him around Seventy-second Street and Broadway. The lad before me is dark, has crystal brown eyes, and straight black hair.

"I would like," I begin, "to reserve a passage for my wife on one of your steamers to Kingston. I want to get it at the $150.00 rate."

"Well, it is this way." I am positive he is from Guayaquil. "It will cost you $178.00."

"Why $178.00?"

"You see, the passage alone is $170.00—"

"A hundred and seventy dollars! Why, this booklet here says $150.00 round trip. You must have made a mistake."

"You see, this $150.00 rate is for three in a room, and all the rooms on the ship sailing on the tenth are already taken up."

"All right," I decide, "the date is inconsequential. What I want is the $150.00 rate. Reserve a berth for me on any ship that is not already filled up. I don't care how late in the summer it is. I have brought a deposit along with me—"

I am not truculent. Everything I say I strive to say softly, unoffensively—especially when in the midst of a color-ordeal!

"Well, you'd have to get two persons to go with her." The Peruvian is independent. "There are only three berths in a stateroom, and if your wife wants to take advantage of the $150.00 rate, she will have to get two other colored persons to go with her."

"I s-e-e!" I mutter dreamily. And I did see!

"Come in tomorrow and pay a deposit on it, if you want to. It is five o'clock and—"

I am out on the street again. From across the Hudson a gurgling wind brings dust to my nostrils. I am limp, static, emotionless. There is only one line to Jamaica, and I am going to send her by it. It is the only thing to do. Tomorrow I am going back, with the $178.00. It pays to be black.

*The following article by Gustavus Steward offers a per-
sonal, intimate portrait of the agony of black Americans,
written in terms of the authentic experiences of ordinary
black people.*

# Elizabeth Goes to School

### By Gustavus Adolphus Steward

ELIZABETH IS OUR first-born. Her six years on earth are powerless to
render her of the earth. She lives in a childhood land of dolls, cut-
outs, ring games, nursery rhymes, fairy tales, and glorious "pretend-
like" adventures from which even an occasional spanking utterly fails
to drag her.

Early in the spring school became a vital subject to Elizabeth. The
neighbors' children played school on the front steps, and Elizabeth
with her smaller sister was initiated into the pedagogical mysteries
through the door of make-believe. And although the play school was
more taken up with being sent to the principal, staying in at recess,
and scoldings for being tardy than with lessons, still it all fitted har-
moniously into her enchanted land.

Hence, when the day actually arrived, Elizabeth was eager for
the real adventure. She was talkative to her smaller sister, and fidgety
as her mother prepared her for the great occasion. With every detail
complete from shoes to hair-bow, after the final maternal inspection
she slipped her hand into mine, and, with little sister's tears to bless
her, departed. What was in her head as she trudged beside me I have
no means of knowing. I have no analogous experience of my own by
which even to conjecture. I know, however, that she walked as tri-
umphantly and as importantly as a hen just emerging from her first
period of incubation with one poor, wobbly chick. And thus she
entered school.

I left her there, not without misgiving. Certain forebodings disturbed my return trip. They hung about the family table every day.
Momentarily we expected their horrid realization. But day followed

From *Nation*, CXV (December 6, 1922), 601–604.

day and nothing occurred. Elizabeth came and went, always impatient to leave in the morning, always bubbling over with some new achievement, some new adventure in the evening. She learned new games and rhymes to teach her sister. She brought home a primer which was too precious for her sister to touch, and proudly exhibited her breathless facility in "reading." She regaled us excitedly with what Tom or Helen did at school to earn the teacher's rebuke. Teacher became a goddess or fairy, grand, beautiful, and correct. School was an extension of that delightful bowerland, forever unfolding new wonders.

And then it happened. It was only a very small thing, an ordinary childish question put to her mother. But it was realization of the entire train of tragic foreboding that had haunted the household every hour since Elizabeth entered school. "Mother," she asked one day, "why doesn't the teacher let me march with Dorothy any more, but always makes me march with Lucy?" Now, that seems a simple question. But two words complicate it. Two words change this whole story, and bring to the fore an ugly facet of the great many-sided lie which besmirches American democracy.

Elizabeth and Lucy are brown. Dorothy is white. Brown and white —those two little words—and the forebodings are realized. The teacher was true to form when she introduced Elizabeth to the American race problem at the age of six. Hereafter she marches with brown Lucy, not with white Dorothy, until the end of time. What the resultant ignorance of white and brown, each of the other's way, will produce in misunderstanding, prejudice, and hate is a consideration which apparently disturbs no one much, least of all Elizabeth.

Family councils have not revealed what reply was returned to Elizabeth. Inquiry, however, disclosed the fact that all the little brown children in the beginner's room, as elsewhere in the school, were seated together in the rear of the room. Again, painfully true to form in the separation of Negroes and whites with inference of inferiority by seating the brown children in the rear. And this to six-year-olds! The thought of deluging Elizabeth with these American horrors intensified the bitterness which I cannot avoid when I think of the Negro's place in America. Why not begin teaching this doctrine of race superiority in the nursery? Why not have the babies so indoctrinated before they reach the first grade that they will avoid the brown Elizabeths on sight? Is it not the parents' duty to give the child proper home training and cooperate with the teacher? Why doesn't the "great and growing city of Columbus," as one booster sign has it, why doesn't the great State of Ohio, boasted haven of fugitive slaves, famous port of underground railroad refugees, proud mother of Presidents, self-constituted guardian of democracy, public acclaimer of justice and equal rights, preacher of fair dealing to all races—why do not Ohio and its capital city come out as boldly for race segregation as Georgia, and cease this everlasting lying? There is a certain compelling admiration for the crook who admits his crookedness frankly and glories in it. It is the gentleman crook who is repulsive. Georgia's frankness is to be preferred to Ohio's insincerity.

With thoughts like these I went back to the school. I found Elizabeth's teacher agreeable, courteous, cultured, cheerful. She ushered me into her room with a warm welcome. The advanced section of beginners (that is, those who began in the middle of last term and are five months ahead of those like Elizabeth who began last month) was reading. They were seated in a semi-circle about the teacher. Two little brown boys were sitting close together at one extremity of the semi-circle, while a little brown girl sat alone behind the others. In the other section Elizabeth was seated in the rear with a group of little brown children. I wonder if the teacher had some inner revelation of my feeling as I looked at the brown children? At any rate, she chose for me the subtlest form of flattery, calling Elizabeth to prompt an advanced boy and commending her when she did so correctly. I waited for a few moments and then asked:

"Is there any reason why all the little colored children should sit together in the rear? Is it a rule of the principal, the Board of Education, or the State?"

"Why no," she said. "But don't you think it's nice for all the little colored ones to sit together?"—in a tone of pained surprise.

When I told her that I did not think it nice, she asked my objection. Upon my telling her she excused herself by saying that she was only one, and asked what she should do if she had "objections from the other side," meaning from white parents, I suppose. I suggested that she seat the children alphabetically, and she then began to explain, irrelevantly, that the seats were all filled, and finding herself floundering—I really was disturbing her recitation—she advised that I see the principal.

I found the principal cool, polite, and impenetrable. To all my objections concerning the marching and the seating she repeated "I don't understand." I tried to state my case. Once or twice I thought

I had made an impression as she nervously fumbled the key to her desk, or dawdled with the beads dangling from her neck, but she only returned, "I really don't understand." She reminded me that all such minor matters were left to the teachers, and I then wondered why the teacher had advised me to come to the principal.

I hazard the guess, however, that this practice of separating brown and white, universally accepted in that school, is tacitly approved, if not ordered, by the principal. I told her that such separation taught hate, that it taught children that they were different, that the inference of inferiority was intended for colored children, that separated the two races grew up in ignorance of each other, that such ignorance led to misunderstanding, and that misunderstanding was the first step to hate. She repeated, "I do not understand," and she could not see that her failure to understand was the very result of the separation she defended. She denied that there was a particle of hate in her school, seemed fearful of what she implied was my antagonistic attitude, stressed the beautiful spirit of her school, enlightened me as to how long she had been there without any unhappiness, praised her numerous colored friends, injected a little soothing syrup into the interview by referring delicately and commendingly to my "type of educated man," graciously suggested that I might be a great somebody in the colored race, announced that after all she and I were quite different, and was altogether a charming person receiving a rather misguided, unhappy, and unfortunately notional parent.

I went to the school sorry for Elizabeth because of this heartless and unnecessary forcing upon her a glimpse of what inevitably lies ahead of her. But Elizabeth lives in an enchanted land unruffled by thoughts of the future. I think I am now sorry for that principal. She lives in a hard shell of preconceptions. No consideration of the daily mounting powder-pile of hate America is building for some mad-cap to fire, nor of her own part and responsibility in the hideous enterprise remotely aroused her consciousness. The shell was impenetrable. She did not understand.

*The following five poems by Langston Hughes deal with the explicit theme of America, her ideals, and her treatment of Black Americans.*

# The White Ones

### By Langston Hughes

I don't hate you,
For your faces are beautiful, too;
I don't hate you,
Your faces are whirling lights of loveliness and
splendor, too;
Yet why do you torture me,
O, white strong ones,
Why do you torture me?

From *Opportunity*, II (March 1924), 68.

# America

### By Langston Hughes

Little dark baby,
Little Jew baby,
Little outcast
America is seeking the stars,
America is seeking tomorrow.
You are America.
I am America
America—the dream,
America—the vision.
America—the star-seeking I.
Out of yesterday
The chains of slavery;
Out of yesterday,
The ghettos of Europe;

Out of yesterday,
The poverty and pain of the old, old world,
The building and struggle of this new one,
We come
You and I,
Seeking the stars.
You and I,
You of the blue eyes
And the blond hair,
I of the dark eyes
And the crinkly hair.
You and I
Offering hands
Being brothers,
Being one,
Being America.
You and I.
And I?

Who am I?
You know me:
I am Crispus Attucks at the Boston Tea Party;
Jimmy Jones in the ranks of the last black troops
    marching for democracy.
I am Sojourner Truth preaching and praying
    for the goodness of this wide, wide land;
Today's black mother bearing tomorrow's America.
Who am I?
You know me,
Dream of my dreams,
I am America.
I am America seeking the stars.
America—
Hoping, praying,
Fighting, dreaming.
Knowing
There are stains
On the beauty of my democracy,
I want to be clean.
I want to grovel
No longer in the mire.

I want to reach always
After stars.
Who am I?
I am the ghetto child,
I am the dark baby,
I am you
And the blond tomorrow
And yet
I am my one sole self,
America seeking the stars.

From *Opportunity*, III (June 1925), 175.

# Liars

### *By Langston Hughes*

It is we who are liars:
The Pretenders-to-be who are not
And the Pretenders-to-be who are.
It is we who use words
As screens for thoughts
And weave dark garments
To cover the naked body
Of the too white Truth.
It is we with the civilized souls
      Who are liars.

From *Opportunity*, III (March 1925), 90.

# I, Too

### *By Langston Hughes*

I, too, sing America.

I am the darker brother.
They send me to eat in the kitchen
When company comes.
But I laugh,

And eat well,
And grow strong.

Tomorrow
I'll sit at the table
When company comes
Nobody 'll dare
Say to me,
"Eat in the kitchen"
Then.

Besides, they'll see how beautiful I am
And be ashamed,—

I, too, am America.

From *Survey*, LIII (March 1, 1925), 678, 683.

# Our Land

### By Langston Hughes

We should have a land of sun,
Of gorgeous sun,
And a land of fragrant water
Where the twilight is a soft bandanna handkerchief
Of rose and gold,
And not this land
Where life is cold.

We should have a land of trees,
Of tall thick trees,
Bowed down with chattering parrots
Brilliant as the day,
And not this land where birds are gray.

Ah, we should have a land of joy,
Of love and joy and wine and song,
And not this land where joy is wrong.

From *Survey*, LIII (March 1, 1925), 683.

*The five-line poem that follows succinctly captures a basic irony.*

---

## To Negroes

*By Howard J. Young*

You who carry
   The lance of laughter and the sword of song,
Let this be blazoned on your pennons:
Whatever the color of man,
The shadow must always be black.

From *Opportunity*, IV (January 1926), 15.

Claude McKay was born in Jamaica and came to the United States in 1912. After a short time at Tuskegee Institute, he came to Harlem. McKay became a familiar figure in black and white intellectual circles both in Harlem and Greenwich Village. His poetry, short stories, and essays were well known. In 1922 he traveled to Russia and elsewhere, returning to America in 1928 to write and publish.

# My House

### By Claude McKay

For this peculiar tint that paints my house
Peculiar in an alien atmosphere
Where other houses wear a kindred hue,
I have a stirring always very rare
And romance-making in my ardent blood,
That channels through my body like a flood.

I know the dark delight of being strange,
The penalty of difference in the crowd,
The loneliness of wisdom among fools,
Yet never have I felt but very proud,
Though I have suffered agonies of hell,
Of living in my own peculiar cell.

There is an exaltation of man's life,
His hidden life, that he alone can feel.
The blended fires that heat his veins within,
Shaping his metals into finest steel,
Are elements from his own native earth,
That the wise gods bestowed on him at birth.

Oh each man's mind contains an unknown realm
Walled in from other men however near,

And unimagined in their highest flights
Of comprehension or of vision clear;
A realm where he withdraws to contemplate
Infinity and his own finite state.

Thence he may sometimes catch a god-like glimpse
Of mysteries that seem beyond life's bar;
Thence he may hurl his little shaft at heaven
And bring down accidentally a star,
And drink its foamy dust like sparkling wine
And echo accents of the laugh divine.

Then he may fall into a drunken sleep
And wake up in his same house painted blue
Or white or green or red or brown or black—
His house, his own, whatever be the hue.
But things for him will not be what they seem
To average men since he has dreamt his dream!

From *Opportunity*, IV (November 1926), 342.

# America in Retrospect

### By Claude McKay

Like vivid scene stamped on a keen child's mind,
Your gorgeous pageants entertain my view;
I see your great all-sweeping lights that blind
Your vision to the Shadow over you.
My thoughts of you are memories of a child,
A healthy child that soon forgets its hurt;
Wistful, I feel no hatred deep and wild,
For you made me a stoic introvert,
I fight with time but for a longer lease
Of those creative hours severe and stern,
Those hours in which I see my purpose plain,
That I may write in freedom and in peace
The accumulations of the years that burn,
White forge-like fires within my haunted brain.

From *Opportunity*, IV (November 1926), 342.

*This poem by Langston Hughes is followed by one by Countee Cullen, a more traditional black poet and contemporary of Hughes. The contrast in style is evident. Cullen was highly regarded as a productive contributor to the broad and diverse writings of the twenties. A graduate of New York University, with an M.A. from Harvard, he was also associate editor of* Opportunity *in the mid-twenties.*

---

# Lincoln Monument

### (Washington)

### *By Langston Hughes*

Let's go see old Abe
Sitting in the marble and the moonlight,
Sitting lonely in the marble and the moonlight,
Quiet for ten thousand centuries, old Abe.
Quiet for a million, million centuries.
Quiet,—and yet a voice forever
Against the timeless walls of time,
Old Abe.

From *Opportunity*, IV (March 1927), 85.

# A Thorn Forever in the Breast

### *By Countee Cullen*

A hungry cancer will not let him rest
Whose heart is loyal to the least of dreams;
There is a thorn forever in his breast
Who cannot take his world for what it seems.
Aloof and lonely must he ever walk,
Plying a strange and unaccustomed tongue,

An alien to the daily round of talk,
Mute when the sordid songs of earth are sung.

This is the certain end his dream achieves:
To sweat his blood and prayers while others sleep,
To shoulder his own coffin up the steep,
Incredulous summit that shapes his doom
Between two wretched dying men, of whom
One doubts, and one for pity's sake believes.

From *Opportunity*, V (August 1927), 225.

*George S. Schuyler's caustic wit was well known in Harlem as well as in black communities throughout the country. He became a columnist for the* Pittsburgh Courier *at the end of the twenties after having been a staff member of the* Messenger, *a radical New York black magazine, from 1922 to 1928.*

# Our White Folks

## By George S. Schuyler

NUMEROUS AND ponderous tomes have been written about Negroes by white folks. With a pontifical air they rush into print on the slightest provocation to tell the world all about the blackamoor. These writings range all the way from alarmist gabble about the Black Menace or the tragedy of the dark brethren suffocating in the midst of white civilization to sloppy sentimentalities by the lunatic fringe of Liberals and the mooney scions of Southern slaveholders who deplore the passing of Uncle Tom and Aunt Beckie, who knew how to "act properly" and did not offend them by being self-respecting or intelligent. This fervent scribbling has been going on for a dozen decades or more, until today the libraries and attics of the country are crammed with more books and papers on the Negro than on any other American group. With so much evidence of what the Nordic thinks of his black brother, no one need remain ignorant on the subject. And if one doesn't read one may learn his attitude and opinion by observing the various Jim-crow laws and other such exhibits throughout this glorious land.

We Ethiops, one gathers from this mass of evidence, are a childish, shiftless, immoral, primitive, incurably religious, genially incompetent, incredibly odoriferous, inherently musical, chronically excitable, mentally inferior people with pronounced homicidal tendencies. We are incapable of self-government or self-restraint, and irresponsible except when led by white folks. We possess a penchant for assaulting white females and an inordinate appetite

From *American Mercury*, XII (December 1927), 385–392.

for chicken, gin, and watermelon. While it is finally and reluctantly admitted that we belong to the human race, we are accorded only the lowest position in the species, a notch or two above the great apes. We make good domestics but hopeless executives. Even at this late date, all coons look alike to the great majority of Nordic Americans, and even the highest type of Negro is under no consideration to be accorded a higher position than the lowest type of white. In short, from examining the bulk of the evidence, the impartial investigator must conclude that the Negro has almost a monopoly of all the more discreditable characteristics of mankind. But at the same time one is effusively informed that he is deeply loved and thoroughly understood, especially by his pork-skinned friends of Southern derivation.

As a result of this attitude of his pale neighbors, the lowly moke has about ten times as many obstacles to hurdle in the race of life as the average peckerwood. It is difficult enough to survive and prosper in this world under the best of conditions, but when one must face such an attitude on the part of those who largely control the means of existence, the struggle is great indeed. Naturally there is deep resentment and bitterness among the more intelligent Negroes, and there always has been. Nothing else could be expected from a people who confront a continuous barrage of insult and calumny and discrimination from the cradle to the grave. There are Negroes, of course, who publicly claim to love the white folks, but privately the great majority of them sing another tune. Even the most liberal blacks are always suspicious, and have to be on the alert not to do or say anything that will offend the superior race. Such an atmosphere is not conducive to great affection, except perhaps on the part of halfwits.

Is it generally known that large numbers of Negroes, though they openly whooped it up for Uncle Sam, would have shed no tears in 1917–18 if the armies of the Kaiser had by some miracle suddenly swooped down upon such fair cities as Memphis, Tenn., Waycross, Ga., or Meridian, Miss.? The Negro upper class, in press and pulpit, roared and sweated to keep the dinges in line by telling them how much the white folks would do to improve their status after the war if they would only be loyal, but the more enlightened Ethiops were frankly skeptical, a skepticism justified later on. On several occasions during that struggle for democracy I sounded out individual Sambos here and there, and was somewhat surprised to find many of them holding the view that it made no difference to them who won the war, since the Germans could hardly treat them any worse than the Nordics of the U. S. A., and might treat them a lot better. Any number of intelligent Negroes expressed the opinion under the breath that a good beating would be an excellent thing for the soul of America. Even some of the actual black soldiers were observed on occasion to indulge in cynical smirks and sarcastic exclamations during the reading of tracts from Mr. Creel's propaganda mill.

## II

Of course the attitude of the Negro toward the Nordics varies with the locality he lives in, the conditions under which he lives, and the class to which he belongs. Traveling in the South, it is difficult to get the truth about race relations in a given community unless one is very painstaking. This is due to the fact that among both whites and blacks down there, there is a great deal of local patriotism, no matter how bad conditions may actually be. The whites will claim that their niggers are the best in the world and that those in all of the surrounding towns are gorillas, while the Ethiops will speak highly of their own white folks, but heap maledictions upon the heads of the crackers further down the line. It is always wise to let them talk themselves out of breath in praise of their particular community, and then inquire discreetly about the schools, the courts, the franchise, economic opportunities, civic improvements, health conditions, and so forth. As the Negroes discuss such things one begins to get an indication of their real feelings, which are seldom flattering to their townsfolk of paler hue.

Curiously enough, the majority of Nordics seem to believe that all Negroes look upon them as some sort of demigods—as paragons of intelligence, efficiency, refinement, and morality. No doubt they have arrived at this curious conclusion by observing how the blackamoors ape their appearance with skin whiteners and hair straighteners, and how they are given to disparaging the efforts and attainments of other Negroes. They have probably heard such Negroisms as "A nigger ain't nuthin," "What more can you expect from a nigger?" and "Why don't you be like white folks?"

The Negro, it is true, is cynical and skeptical about his own, and often his castigations of his brethren are more devastating than any administered by the white folks. In this respect, he resembles his Jewish brother. But the crow is equally critical of his red-necked comrades. Only infrequently do the white folks perceive that this indirect flattery is a sort of combination of protective coloration, group discipline, and feeling of annoyance and futility. It does not in the majority of cases mean that the individual Negro they see in front of them thinks that they are his superiors—except in power.

If the Southern white, as is his wont, can with any justification trumpet to the world that he knows the Negro, the Aframerican can with equal or greater truth claim to have the inside information on the cracker. Knowing him so intimately, the black brother has no illusions about either his intelligence, his industry, his efficiency, his honor, or his morals. The blacks haven't been working with and for the white folks all these decades and centuries for nothing. While the average Nordic knows nothing of how Negroes actually live and what they actually think, the Negroes know the Nordics intimately. Practically every member of the Negro aristocracy of physicians, dentists, lawyers, undertakers, and insurance men has worked at one time or another for white folks as a domestic, and observed with cynical detachment their orgies, obsessions, and imbecilities, while contact with the white proletariat has acquainted him thoroughly with their gross stupidity and often very evident inferiority.

Toward the white working classes, indeed, there is a great suspicion and ill-feeling among the Negroes of the United States, much to the discomfiture of labor organizers and radicals. The superior posture of the poor whites is based on nothing but the fortuitous circumstance that created them lighter in color. The Negro puts this down to mere ignorance and a fear of competition for jobs. He believes that the white workers would have nothing to lose by ditching their color prejudice and aligning themselves with him. Ever since the so-called Civil War, he has been attempting to make the white proletariat see the light, but the mudsill Caucasians are obdurate. They think far more of an empty color superiority than they do of labor solidarity. Even the Jewish working-people, of whom solidarity might be expected, are far from being free of color prejudice.

Quite naturally, the Negroes feel far more kindly toward the whites of wealth and influence. From them they have obtained quite a few favors and largesses, but they do not lose sight of the fact that in the face of a group crisis, such as a lynching or a race riot, they cannot depend upon these upper class Nordics, who invariably desert when the mob heaves into sight, if indeed they do not join it. Directing and controlling the social and economic life of the country,

they have allowed to go almost unquestioned all sorts of legislation
inimical to the Negro's advancement. Toward individual Negroes
they may be kindly and helpful, but except in the case of those who
support Negro colleges and schools, they do not seem to care a rap
about how the mass of blacks gets along. They allow gross inequalities
in the appropriation of school funds; they allow Negro residential
sections to go without adequate health inspection; they allow the
compulsory school laws to remain unenforced in so far as the blacks
are concerned; they make little or no protest against peonage and
the horrors of Southern prisons and chain-gangs; they allow petty
officials to make a mockery of the judicial system where Negroes
are involved; and they refuse to see to it that the Negro is given the
means to protect himself, if possible, through the franchise.

These upper class white folks contend that the workings of democracy prevent them from forcing the poor whites to toe the mark,
but the Negroes observe that when it is desired to put over anything
else that is deemed important, some way is always found. It seems
to the thinking black man that, even granting that the white ruling
class is incapable of assisting the masses of his people, they could at
least openly enlist themselves on the side of honesty, fairness, and
square dealing, and thereby set an example to the others. But in the
main they prefer to remain silent, and so leave the Negro to the
mercies of the white rabble. Is it any wonder that he views them
with distrust?

The attitude of the Northern white folks, in particular, puzzles
and incenses him. Very often he feels that they are more dangerous
to him than the Southerners. Here are folks who yawp continuously
about liberty, justice, equality, and democracy, and whoop with indignation every time a Senegambian is incinerated below the Poto-
mac or the Belgians burn another village in the Congo, but toward
the Negro in their midst they are quite as cruel as the Southern
crackers. They are wont to shout, in their liberal moments, that the
Negro is as good as they are—as if that were a compliment!—and
to swear by all the gods that they want to give him a square deal
and a chance in the world, but when he approaches them for a job
they offer him a mop and pail or a bellhop's uniform, no matter what
his education and training may be. And except in isolated instances
they see that he remains permanently in the lowly position they
have given him.

The majority of them are almost as prejudiced as their Southern brethren, as any Negro knows who has ever attempted to enter a public place or to attend their social gatherings. Unlike the crackers, they only grudgingly give him a chance to earn a living, even as a menial. The restriction of European immigration has helped the Negro in the North considerably in the field of industry, but in the marts of commerce there seems to be an impression that he is incapable of functioning in the field of general business. At present, in the city of New York, which is considered a heaven for Negroes, and the tolerance and liberality of which are widely advertised throughout the nation, it is harder for a capable young Negro to get a decent job in a business house than it is for a comely Negro girl to escape being approached by white men in a Southern town.

To the intelligent Aframerican, an individual who has color prejudice seems manifestly to belong in the same intellectual class as the Holy Rollers and the Ku Kluxers. To judge an individual solely on the basis of his skin color and hair texture is so obviously nonsensical that he cannot help classing the bulk of Nordics with the inmates of an insane asylum. He views with mingled amusement and resentment the stupid reactions of white folks to a black skin. It excites his bitter mirth to observe how his entrance into almost any public place is sufficient to spoil the evening of the majority of the proud Caucasians present, no matter how intelligent they may claim to be. Nor is this insanity restricted alone to Anglo-Saxons, for Jews, Irish, Greeks, Poles, Russians, Italians, and Germans, even those who know little of the American language and less of the national customs, grow quite as apoplectic at the sight of a sable countenance.

### III

Because the whites bellow so much about their efficiency and thrift, the Negro marvels that they go to the expense of a dual school system, Jim-crow railroad coaches and waiting-rooms, separate cemeteries, and segregated parks, libraries, and street cars, when the two peoples are so intimately associated all day, not to mention at night. Indeed, an examination of family trees will reveal that a large number of the whites and blacks are really related, especially in the land of cotton, where most of the hue and cry is raised about Anglo-Saxon purity. The South, the Negro does not fail to note, has actually retarded its own progress by maintaining this hypocritical double standard. And now it is threatening the standards of living in the New England mill towns and Northern coal fields by offering cheaper labor and lower taxes,—an offer that it can make only because of the ready acceptance of low living standards by the Southern white mob out of fear that Negroes will take its poorly paid jobs. Thus the results of the stupid system are felt in sections where hardly any Negroes live at all.

Almost every thoughtful Negro believes that the scrapping of the color caste system would not hinder but rather help the country. In their zeal to keep the black brother away from the pie counter, the whites are depriving the nation of thousands of individuals of extraordinary ability. The rigid training and discipline that the Negro has received since his arrival on these sacred shores has left him with a lower percentage of weaklings and incompetents than is shown by any other group. He has always had to be on the alert, ever the diplomat and skillful tactician, facing more trying situations in a week than the average white citizen faces in a year. This experience has certainly fitted him for a more important position than he now holds in the Republic. He is still imbued with the pioneering spirit that the bulk of the whites have had ironed out of them. He has energy and originality, the very qualities being sought today in business and government. Yet narrow bigotry and prejudice bar his way.

When the Southern white man asks the liberal Caucasian, "Do you want your daughter to marry a nigger?", he is probably hitting the nail on the head, for that is the crux of the entire color problem. Fear of economic and political competition is a factor, but above all it is the bogey of sex competition. Equality in one field will unquestionably lead to equality in the other. And yet there is no law compelling blacks and whites to intermarry, and if the natural aversion that the scientists shout of really exists there need be no fears on that score. The Anglo-Saxons will retain their polyglot purity if they wish to do so—and if they really find the Ethiops as repellant as the authorities on the subject allege.

But there is considerable doubt in the mind of the Negro as to whether this aversion actually exists, and whether the Anglo-Saxons actually *think* it exists. He tries to reconcile the theory that it does with the fact that nearly thirty States have laws prohibiting intermarriage between the so-called races, and with the additional fact that half of the Negroes in America obviously possess more or less Caucasian blood, thus being neither black nor white. The dark brother is convulsed with mirth over the famous one-drop theory, that distinctive American contribution to the science of anthropology which lists as Negroes all people having the remotest Negro ancestry, despite the fact that they may be, and often are, indistinguishable from the purest Nordic. He whoops with glee over the recent incident in Virginia, where the workings of the new Racial Integrity Law caused fifty white children to be barred from the white schools and ordered to attend Negro schools on the ground that they were Negroes, although no one knew it except the official genealogists, whereas all the while, in the States of Texas and Oklahoma, dark brown Mexicans and Indians were listed as white, and their children attended white schools. Knowing how much racial intermixture has been going on in this country since the Seventeenth Century, he is eager to see racial integrity laws passed in all of the States, as has been done in Georgia and Virginia, so that the genealogists may get busy on a national scale and thus increase the "Negro" population to at least four times its present number.

The Negro listens with a patient tolerance born of much knowledge and observations to the gabble of white gentlemen concerning the inferior morality of black women. These chivalrous folk, in some sections, do not hesitate to discuss these illicit amours within hearing of their Negro servitors, who boil within as they listen to the racy conversation of the advocates of racial separatism. The whites, of course, never hear the Negro's side of the story. Indeed, it is doubtful whether they realize that he *has* a side. For many and obvious reasons, he keeps his very interesting information to himself and grins along his way. He knows that no one group in this country monopolizes sex morality. Some day a black American Balzac is going to gather material for another volume of Droll Stories that will be quite as interesting and entertaining as the original.

The attitude of the whites toward the Negro's participation in politics seems very absurd to the contemplative dinge. He is a part of American life and he knows very well what is going on in politics. If his sooty brethren are not yet ready to be trusted with the ballot, neither for that matter are the ruck of peckerwoods. He has heard the yells and moans of the ex-Confederates about the alleged horrors of the Reconstruction period, when Negro legislators (who never controlled a single Southern State) are said to have indulged in graft on a great scale and squandered the public funds, but after careful investigation he has failed to learn of a single State or community in the whole country in which precisely the same thing is not true of white politicians. If Negroes sell their votes for a quart of corn liquor and two dollars, they are, he observes, by no means alone. Surely, he concludes, no Legislature composed of Negroes could pass more imbecile legislation than is the annual product of every legislative body in the land, not by any means excluding Congress. He concludes that he is barred from the ballot in the South only in order to keep capable Negroes from competing with broken-down Nordic lawyers for political sinecures. The excuse that his inability to use the ballot intelligently is the cause of his disfranchisement is highly amusing to him after a glance at the national scene.

The amazing ignorance of whites—even Southern whites—about Negroes is a constant source of amusement to all Aframericans. White men who claim to be intelligent and reasonable beings persist in registering surprise whenever they hear of or meet a Negro who has written a novel, a history, or a poem, or who can work a problem in calculus. Because of this naïveté, many mediocre Negroes are praised to the high heavens as geniuses of the first flight, and grow sleek and fat. Such fellows are frequently seized upon by gullible whites and labeled as leaders of the Negro race, without the Negroes being consulted on the matter. It seems incredible to most white folks that within the Negro group are social circles quite as cultured and refined as those existing among whites. I recall with amusement the story circulating the rounds of Aframerica concerning a wealthy white woman in a Southern city who asked her Negro maid if it was true that there were Negro homes in New York City such as those described by Carl Van Vechten in "Nigger Heaven," and who was quite astonished and incredulous when the girl informed her that not only were there such homes in New York but also in that town as well.

IV

Those Negroes who have entrée to white intellectual circles do not return to their own society with regret, but rather with relief, for they rightly observe that the bulk of the white intellectuals have more form than content; that they have a great deal of information but are not so long on common sense; and that they lack that sense of humor and gentle cynicism which one expects to find in the really civilized person, and which are the chief characteristics of even the most lowly and miserable Aframerican.

These so-called sophisticated whites leap from one fad to another, from mah jong to "Ask Me Another," with great facility, and are usually ready to embrace any cause that comes along thirsting for supporters. They are obsessed by sex and discuss it interminably, with long dissertations on their moods and reactions, complexes and sublimations. Life to them seems to be one perpetual psychoanalytical clinic. This appears to the Negro observer as a sure sign of sexual debility. The lusty, virile fellow, such as is the average shine, is too busy really living to moon overly much about the processes of life. It is difficult to imagine a group of intelligent Negroes sprawling around a drawing-room, consuming cigarettes and synthetic gin while discussing their complexes and inhibitions.

The Negroes have observed, too, that they know how to have a good time, despite all their troubles and difficulties, while the majority of white people certainly do not. Indeed, the frantic efforts of the crackers to amuse themselves is a never-ending source of amusement to the blacks. The Nordics take all amusements so seriously! They cannot swim without attempting to cross the English Channel or the Gulf of Mexico; they cannot dance without organizing a marathon to see which couple can dance the longest. They must have their Charleston contests, golf contests, coffee-drinking contests, frankfurter-eating contests. In short, they always go to extremes. The Negroes, on the other hand, have learned how to enjoy themselves without too much self-consciousness and exhibitionism.

The efforts of the Nordics to be carefree are grotesque; the so-called emancipated whites being the worst of the lot. No group of Negroes anywhere could be louder or rowdier than they are in their efforts to impress the neighborhood with the fact that they are having a good time. Look, for example, at their antics in Greenwich Village. It is not without reason that those white folks who want to enjoy themselves while in New York hustle for Harlem. The less emancipated ones go to the cabarets, where they can sit and watch Negroes dance and caper; the more sensible go to a Negro dance-hall, where they can participate in the fun. It is not uncommon to hear them say that the only time they thoroughly enjoy themselves is when they journey to the so-called Black Belt, where joy is not shackled or saddled.

This is probably the reason why, to the white brethren, the blacks are supposed to be happy-go-lucky children, with never a serious thought in their polls. But the Negro, recalling how the white folks swarm to hear such mountebanks as Billy Sunday, Krishnamurti, Conan Doyle, Imperial Wizard Evans, and William Hale Thompson, and eagerly swallow all of the hokum flowing through the Republic, concludes that the Sambos have no monopoly on intellectual infantilism.

The Negro is a sort of black Gulliver chained by white Lilliputians, a prisoner in a jail of color prejudice, a babe in a forest of bigotry, but withal a fellow philosophical and cynical enough to laugh at himself and his predicament. He has developed more than any other group, even more than the Jews, the capacity to see things as they are rather than as he would have them. He is a close student of the contradictory pretensions and practices of the ofay gentry, and it is this that makes him really intelligent in a republic of morons. It is only during the last few years that the cracker *intelligentsia* have begun to sniff suspiciously at the old Anglo-Saxon slogans and concepts of justice, democracy, chivalry, honor, fair play, and so forth. The Negro has always been skeptical about them, knowing that they were conditioned by skin color, social position, and economic wealth.

He is sick and tired of the holier-than-thou attitude of the white folks. On what, he inquires, do they base the contention that they are superior? He puts the history of the blacks down through the ages alongside that of the whites and is not ashamed of the comparison. He knows that there is as much evidence that black men founded human civilization as there is that white men did, and he doubts whether the occidental society of today is superior to the monarcho-communist society developed in Africa. He knows that neither intellectually nor physically is he inferior to the Caucasians. The fact is that in America conditions have made the average Negro more alert, more resourceful, more intelligent, and hence more interesting than the average Nordic. Certainly if the best measure of intelligence is ability to survive in a changing or hostile environment, and if one considers that the Negro is not only surviving but improving all the time in health, wealth, and culture, one must agree that he possesses a high degree of intelligence. In their efforts to fight off the ravages of color prejudice, the blacks have welded themselves into a homogeneity and developed a morale whose potentialities are not yet fully appreciated.

## v

They laugh to themselves when they hear white folks refer to them as ugly and black. Thanks to the whites who are always talking about racial purity, the Negroes possess within their group the most handsome people in the United States, with the greatest variety of color, hair, and features. Here is the real melting-pot, and a glorious sight it is to see. Ugly people there are, certainly, but the percentage of beautiful folk is unquestionably larger than among the ofay brethren. One has but to venture abroad in a crowd of whites and then go immediately to a fashionable Negro thoroughfare to be impressed with this fact. Black? Well, yes, but how beautiful! How well it blends with almost every color! How smooth the skin; how soft and rounded the features! But there are browns, chocolates, yellows, and pinks as well. Here in Aframerica one finds such an array of beauty that it even attracts Anglo-Saxons, despite their alleged color aversion.

The dark brother looks upon himself as an American, an integral part of this civilization. To him it is not a white civilization, but a white and black civilization. He rightly feels that it is partially his, because for three hundred years he toiled to make it possible. He wants no more than an equal break with everybody else, but he feels that he has much greater contributions to make to our national life than he has so far been allowed to make. There is hope among the more enlightened Negroes that the similar group among the Nordics can be educated to see the social value and necessity of removing the barriers that now hamper the black citizen. The country can lose nothing and may gain much by such a step. Strange as it may seem, many Negroes look to the enlightened Southern whites as the force that will help bring about the change. While these ofays do not understand the blacks as well as they think, they do at least know them fairly well, and there is, propaganda to the contrary, some good feeling between the two groups. This emerging group of Southern whites is gradually becoming strong enough to make its voice heard and respected, and in the years to come it will have more and more influence.

The Aframerican, being more tolerant than the Caucasian, is ready to admit that all white people are not the same, and it is not unusual to read or hear a warning from a Negro orator or editor against condemning all crackers as prejudiced asses, although agreeing that such a description fits the majority of them. The Ethiop is given to pointing out individual pinks who are exceptionally honorable, tolerant, and unprejudiced. In this respect, I venture to say, he rises several notches higher than the generality of ofays, to whom, even in this day and time, all coons look alike.

## PART FOUR

# *Other Dreams*

DURING THE first thirty years of the twentieth century, a small minority of voices wholeheartedly rejected the American dream as
viable or desirable for black Americans. Many of the harshest critics
of the dream wrote for radical periodicals such as the *Crusader* and
the better-known *Messenger,* or for radical newspapers with very
small circulations. Rarely did their words reach the larger audiences
of the popular magazines. Occasionally, however, the rumblings of
the radicals provoked national attention. This was especially true of
the most popular radical of the twenties, Marcus Garvey. Garvey, a
Jamaican émigré to New York in 1917, attracted a huge following
in Harlem and formed the Universal Negro Improvement Association
which had chapters all around the country. His message, delivered
with a great deal of pomp and ceremony, was that black people had
a superior culture, should remain separate from whites, and should
emigrate to Africa. Although his Back-to-Africa plan was never seriously considered by black Americans, his views on black power and
black pride were well received.

The socialist and communist critique of the race problem provided another alternative to black Americans. Rather than offering a color or race explanation of prejudice in America, the Marxists argued that the capitalistic structure was the root cause. As long as capitalists controlled the wealth and black men were largely laborers, there would be discrimination and bias. An economic revolution, one that would unite black and white workers against their common enemy, was the Marxist solution. A. Philip Randolph and Chandler Owen best represented the intellectual socialist position, while the American Negro Labor Congress represented the Communist party position. The communist philosophy did not gain many adherents during the 1920's. Even at the end of the decade, when a serious economic depression had already set in and the blacks were among the first casualties, communism was unable to attract large numbers of followers.

The final sentence in an editorial from the *Independent* of 1925, reprinted in this section, offers a prophetic view: "If the American negro becomes a radical it will be our fault, not Russia's." As Mordecai Wyatt Johnson notes in the last selection in the book, black Americans are Americans who have always seen their future within the physical and intellectual boundaries of the United States. The challenge and possible success of biracial harmony is up to white Americans.

# GARVEYISM

*Although DuBois is usually regarded as a severe critic of Marcus Garvey, the following two articles display DuBois' basic temperateness and fairness in his analysis of Garvey and his weak points.*

<hr/>

# Marcus Garvey

### By W. E. B. DuBois

MARCUS GARVEY was born at St. Ann's Bay, Jamaica, about 1885. He was educated at the public school and then for a short time attended the Church of England Grammar School, although he was a Roman Catholic by religion. On leaving school he learned the printing trade and followed it for many years. In Costa Rica he was associated with Marclam Taylor in publishing the *Bluefield's Messenger*. Later he was on the staff of *La Nacion*. He then returned to Jamaica and worked as a printer, being foreman of the printing department of P. Benjamin's Manufacturing Company of Kingston. Later he visited Europe and spent some time in England and France and while abroad conceived his scheme of organizing the Negro Improvement Society. This society was launched August 1, 1914, in Jamaica, with these general objects among others:

"To establish a Universal Confraternity among the race"; "to promote the spirit of race pride and love"; "to administer to and assist the needy"; "to strengthen the imperialism of independent African States"; "to conduct a world-wide commercial and industrial intercourse."

His first practical object was to be the establishment of a farm school. Meetings were held and the Roman Catholic Bishop, the Mayor of Kingston, and many others addressed them. Nevertheless the project did not succeed and Mr. Garvey was soon in financial difficulties. He therefore practically abandoned the Jamaica field and came to the United States. In the United States his movement for many years languished until at last with the increased migration from the West Indies during the war he succeeded in establishing a strong nucleus in the Harlem district of New York City.

From *The Crisis*, XXI (December 1920), 58–60; (January 1921), 112–115.

His program now enlarged and changed somewhat in emphasis. He began especially to emphasize the commercial development of the Negroes and as an islander familiar with the necessities of ship traffic he planned the "Black Star Line." The public for a long time regarded this as simply a scheme of exploitation, when they were startled by hearing that Garvey had bought a ship. This boat was a former coasting vessel, 32 years old, but it was put into commission with a black crew and a black captain and was announced as the first of a fleet of vessels which would trade between the colored peoples of America, the West Indies and Africa. With this beginning, the popularity and reputation of Mr. Garvey and his association increased quickly.

In addition to the *Yarmouth* he is said to have purchased two small boats, the *Shadyside,* a small excursion steamer which made daily excursions up the Hudson, and a yacht which was designed to cruise among the West Indies and collect cargo in some central spot for the *Yarmouth.* He had first announced the Black Star Line as a Five Million Dollar corporation, but in February, 1920, he announced that it was going to be a Ten Million Dollar corporation with shares selling at Five Dollars. To this he added in a few months the Negro Factories Corporation capitalized at One Million Dollars with two hundred thousand one dollar shares, and finally he announced the subscription of Five Million Dollars to free Liberia and Haiti from debt.

Early in 1920 he called a convention of Negroes to meet in New York City from the 1st to the 31st of August, "to outline a constructive plan and program for the uplifting of the Negroes and the redemption of Africa." He also took title to three apartment houses to be used as offices and purchased the foundation of an unfinished Baptist church which he covered over and used for meetings, calling it "Liberty Hall." In August, 1920, his convention met with representatives from various parts of the United States, several of the West India Islands and the Canal Zone and a few from Africa. The convention carried out its plan of a month's meetings and culminated with a mass meeting which filled Madison Square Garden. Finally the convention adopted a "Declaration of Independence" with 66 articles, a universal anthem and colors,—red, black and green—and elected Mr. Garvey as "His Excellency, the Provisional President of Africa," together with a number of various other leaders from the various parts of the Negro world. This in brief is the history of the Garvey movement.

The question comes (1) Is it an honest, sincere movement? (2) Are its industrial and commercial projects business like and effective? (3) Are its general objects plausible and capable of being carried out?

The central and dynamic force of the movement is Garvey. He has with singular success capitalized and made vocal the great and long suffering grievances and spirit of protest among the West Indian peasantry. Hitherto the black peasantry of the West Indies has been almost leaderless. Its natural leaders, both mulatto and black, have crossed the color line and practically obliterated social distinction and to some extent economic distinction, between them and the white English world on the Islands. This has left a peasantry with only the rudiments of education and with almost no economic chances, grovelling at the bottom. Their distress and needs gave Garvey his vision.

It is a little difficult to characterize the man Garvey. He has been charged with dishonesty and graft, but he seems to me essentially an honest and sincere man with a tremendous vision, great dynamic force, stubborn determination and unselfish desire to serve; but also he has very serious defects of temperament and training: he is dictatorial, domineering, inordinately vain and very suspicious. He cannot get on with his fellow-workers. His entourage has continually changed.* He has had endless law suits and some cases of fisticuffs with his subordinates and has even divorced the young wife whom he married with great fanfare of trumpets about a year ago. All these things militate against him and his reputation. Nevertheless I have not found the slightest proof that his objects were not sincere or that he was consciously diverting money to his own uses. The great difficulty with him is that he has absolutely no business sense, no *flair* for real organization and his general objects are so shot through with bombast and exaggeration that it is difficult to pin them down for careful examination.

On the other hand, Garvey is an extraordinary leader of men. Thousands of people believe in him. He is able to stir them with singular eloquence and the general run of his thought is of a high plane. He has become to thousands of people a sort of religion. He

---

* Of the 15 names of his fellow officers in 1914 not a single one appears in 1918; of the 18 names of officers published in 1918 only 6 survive in 1919; among the small list of principal officers published in 1920 I do not find a single name mentioned in 1919.

allows and encourages all sorts of personal adulation, even printing in his paper the addresses of some of the delegates who hailed him as "His Majesty." He dons on state occasions a costume consisting of an academic cap and gown flounced in red and green!

Of Garvey's curious credulity and suspicions one example will suffice: In March, 1919, he held a large mass meeting at Palace Casino which was presided over by Chandler Owen and addressed by himself and Phillip Randolph. Here he collected $204 in contributions on the plea that while in France, W. E. B. DuBois had interfered with the work of his "High Commissioner" by "defeating" his articles in the French press and "repudiating" his statements as to lynching and injustice in America! The truth was that Mr. DuBois never saw or heard of his "High Commissioner," never denied his nor anyone's statements of the wretched American conditions, did everything possible to arouse rather than quiet the French press and would have been delighted to welcome and co-operate with any colored fellow-worker.

WHEN IT COMES to Mr. Garvey's industrial and commercial enterprises there is more ground for doubt and misgiving than in the matter of his character. First of all, his enterprises are incorporated in Delaware, where the corporation laws are loose and where no financial statements are required.* So far as I can find, and I have searched with care, Mr. Garvey has never published a complete statement of the income and expenditures of the Negro Improvement Association or of the Black Star Line or of any of his enterprises, which really revealed his financial situation. A courteous letter of inquiry sent to him July 22, 1920, asking for such financial data as he was willing for the public to know, remains to this day unacknowledged and unanswered.

---

* Mr. Garvey boasts Feb. 14, 1920:

"This week I present you with the Black Star Line Steamship Corporation recapitalized at ten million dollars. They told us when we incorporated this corporation that we could not make it, but we are now gone from a $5,000,000 corporation to one of $10,000,000."

This sounds impressive, but means almost nothing. The fee for incorporating a $5,000,000 concern in Delaware is $350. By *paying $250 more the corporation may incorporate with* $10,000,000 *authorized capital without having a cent of capital actually paid in!* Cf. "General Corporation Laws of the State of Delaware," edition of 1917.

Now a refusal to publish a financial statement is no proof of dishonesty, but it *is* proof that either Garvey is ill-advised and unnecessarily courting suspicion, or that his industrial enterprises are not on a sound business basis; otherwise he is too good an advertiser not to use a promising balance-sheet for all it is worth.

There has been one balance sheet, published July 26, 1920, purporting to give the financial condition of the Black Star Line after one year of operation; neither profit or loss is shown, there is no way to tell the actual cash receipts or the true condition of the business. Nevertheless it does make some interesting revelations.

The total amount of stock subscribed for is $590,860. Of this $118,-153.28 is not yet paid for, leaving the actual amount of paid-in capital charged against the corporation, $472,706.72. Against this stands only $355,214.59 of assets (viz.: $21,985.21 in cash deposits and loans receivable; $12,975.01 in furniture and equipment, $288,515.37 which is the alleged value of his boats, $26,000 in real estate and $5,739 of insurance paid in advance). To offset the assets he has $152,264.14 of other liabilities (accrued salaries, $1,539.30; notes and accounts payable, $129,224.84; mortgages due $21,500). In other words, his capital stock of $472,706.72 is after a year's business impaired to such extent that he has only $202,950.45 to show for it.

Even this does not reveal the precariousness of his actual business condition. Banks before the war in lending their credit refused to recognize any business as safe unless for every dollar of current liabilities there were *two* dollars of current assets. Today, since the war, they require *three* dollars of current assets to every *one* of current liabilities. The Black Star Line had July 26, $16,485.21 in current assets and $130,764.14 in current liabilities, when recognition by any reputable bank called for $390,000 in current assets.

Moreover, another sinister admission appears in this statement: the cost of floating the Black Star Line to date has been $289,066.27. In other words, it has cost nearly $300,000 to collect a capital of less than half a million. Garvey has, in other words, spent more for advertisement than he has for his boats!

This is a serious situation, and even this does not tell the whole story: the real estate, furniture, etc., listed above, are probably valued correctly. But how about the boats? The *Yarmouth* is a wooden steamer of 1,452 gross tons, built in 1887. It is old and unseaworthy; it came near sinking a year ago and it has cost a great deal for repairs. It is said that it is now laid up for repairs with a large bill due.

Without doubt the inexperienced purchasers of this vessel paid far more than it is worth, and it will soon be utterly worthless unless rebuilt at a very high cost.

The cases of the *Kanawha* (or *Antonio Maceo*) and the *Shadyside* are puzzling. Neither of these boats is registered as belonging to the Black Star Line at all. The former is recorded as belonging to C. L. Dimon, and the latter to the North and East River Steamboat Company. Does the Black Star Line really own these boats, or is it buying them by installments, or only leasing them? We do not know the facts and have been unable to find out. Under the circumstances they look like dubious "assets."

The majority of the Black Star stock is apparently owned by the Universal Negro Improvement Association. There is no reason why this association, if it will and can, should not continue to pour money into its corporation. Let us therefore consider then Mr. Garvey's other resources.

Mr. Garvey's income consists of (a) dues from members of the U. N. I. Association; (b) shares in the Black Star Line and other enterprises, and (c) gifts and "loans" for specific objects. If the U. N. I. Association has "3,000,000 members" then the income from that source alone would be certainly over a million dollars a year. If, as is more likely, it has under 300,000 paying members, he may collect $150,000 annually from this source. Stock in the Black Star Line is still being sold. Garvey himself tells of one woman who had saved about four hundred dollars in gold: "She brought out all the gold and bought shares in the Black Star Line." Another man writes this touching letter from the Canal Zone: "I have sent twice to buy shares amounting to $125 (numbers of certificates 3752 and 9617). Now I am sending $35 for seven more shares. You might think I have money, but the truth, as I stated before, is that I have no money now. But if I'm to die of hunger it will be all right because I'm determined to do all that's in my power to better the conditions of my race."

In addition to this he has asked for special contributions. In the spring of 1920 he demanded for his coming convention in August, "a fund of two million dollars ($2,000,000) to capitalize this, the greatest of all conventions." In October he acknowledged a total of something over $16,000 in small contributions. Immediately he announced "a constructive loan" of $2,000,000, which he is presumably still seeking to raise.

From these sources of income Mr. Garvey has financed his enterprises and carried on a wide and determined propaganda, maintained a large staff of salaried officials, clerks and agents, and published a weekly newspaper. Notwithstanding this considerable income, there is no doubt that Garvey's expenditures are pressing hard on his income, and that his financial methods are so essentially unsound that unless he speedily revises them the investors will certainly get no dividends and worse may happen. He is apparently using the familiar method of "Kiting"—*i.e.*, the money which comes in as investment in stock is being used in current expenses, especially in heavy overhead costs, for clerk hire, interest and display. Even his boats are being used for advertisement more than for business—lying in harbors as exhibits, taking excursion parties, etc. These methods have necessitated mortgages on property and continually new and more grandiose schemes to collect larger and larger amounts of ready cash. Meantime, lacking business men of experience, his actual business ventures have brought in few returns, involved heavy expense and threatened him continually with disaster or legal complication.

On the other hand, full credit must be given Garvey for a bold effort and some success. He has at least put vessels manned and owned by black men on the seas and they have carried passengers and cargoes. The difficulty is that he does not know the shipping business, he does not understand the investment of capital, and he has few trained and staunch assistants.

The present financial plight of an inexperienced and headstrong promoter may therefore decide the fate of the whole movement. This would be a calamity. Garvey is the beloved leader of tens of thousands of poor and bewildered people who have been cheated all their lives. His failure would mean a blow to their faith, and a loss of their little savings, which it would take generations to undo.

Moreover, shorn of its bombast and exaggeration, the main lines of the Garvey plan are perfectly feasible. What he is trying to say and do is this: American Negroes can, by accumulating and ministering their own capital, organize industry, join the black centers of the south Atlantic by commercial enterprise and in this way ultimately redeem Africa as a fit and free home for black men. This is true. It is *feasible*. It is, in a sense, practical; but it will take for its accomplishment long years of painstaking, self-sacrificing effort. It will call for every ounce of ability, knowledge, experience and devotion in the whole

Negro race. It is not a task for one man or one organization, but for co-ordinate effort on the part of millions. The plan is not original with Garvey but he has popularized it, made it a living, vocal ideal and swept thousands with him with intense belief in the possible accomplishment of the ideal.

This is a great, human service; but when Garvey forges ahead and almost single-handed attempts to realize his dream in a few years, with large words and wild gestures, he grievously minimizes his task and endangers his cause.

To instance one illustrative fact: there is no doubt but what Garvey has sought to import to America and capitalize the antagonism between blacks and mulattoes in the West Indies. This has been the cause of the West Indian failures to gain headway against the whites. Yet Garvey imports it into a land where it has never had any substantial footing and where today, of all days, it is absolutely repudiated by every thinking Negro; Garvey capitalizes it, has sought to get the coöperation of men like R. R. Moton on this basis, and has aroused more bitter color enmity inside the race than has ever before existed. The whites are delighted at the prospect of a division of our solidifying phalanx, but their hopes are vain. American Negroes recognize no color line in or out of the race, and they will in the end punish the man who attempts to establish it.

Then too Garvey increases his difficulties in other directions. He is a British subject. He wants to trade in British territory. Why then does he needlessly antagonize and even insult Britain? He wants to unite all Negroes. Why then does he sneer at the work of the powerful group of his race in the United States where he finds asylum and sympathy? Particularly, why does he decry the excellent and rising business enterprises of Harlem—intimating that his schemes alone are honest and sound when the facts flatly contradict him? He proposes to settle his headquarters in Liberia—but has he asked permission of the Liberian government? Does he presume to usurp authority in a land which has successfully withstood England, France and the United States,—but is expected tamely to submit to Marcus Garvey? How long does Mr. Garvey think that President King would permit his anti-English propaganda on Liberian soil, when the government is straining every nerve to escape the Lion's Paw?

And, finally, without arms, money, effective organization or base of operations, Mr. Garvey openly and wildly talks of "Conquest" and of telling white Europeans in Africa to "get out!" and of becoming himself a black Napoleon!*

Suppose Mr. Garvey should drop from the clouds and concentrate on his industrial schemes as a practical first step toward his dreams: the first duty of a great commercial enterprise is to carry on effective commerce. A man who sees in industry the key to a situation must establish sufficient businesslike industries. Here Mr. Garvey has failed lamentably.

The *Yarmouth*, for instance, has not been a commercial success. Stories have been published alleging its dirty condition and the inexcusable conduct of its captain and crew. To this Mr. Garvey may reply that it was no easy matter to get efficient persons to run his boats and to keep a schedule. This is certainly true, but if it is difficult to secure one black boat crew, how much more difficult is it going to be to "build and operate factories in the big industrial centers of the United States, Central America, the West Indies and Africa to manufacture every marketable commodity"? and also "to purchase and build ships of larger tonnage for the African and South American trade"? and also to raise "Five Million Dollars to free Liberia" where "new buildings are to be erected, administrative buildings are to be built, colleges and universities are to be constructed"? and finally to accomplish what Mr. Garvey calls the "Conquest of Africa"!

To sum up: Garvey is a sincere, hard-working idealist; he is also a stubborn, domineering leader of the mass; he has worthy industrial and commercial schemes but he is an inexperienced business man. His dreams of Negro industry, commerce and the ultimate freedom of Africa are feasible; but his methods are bombastic, wasteful, illogical and ineffective and almost illegal. If he learns by experience, attracts strong and capable friends and helpers instead of making needless enemies; if he gives up secrecy and suspicion and substitutes open and frank reports as to his income and expenses, and above all if he is willing to be a co-worker and not a czar, he may yet in time succeed in at least starting some of his schemes toward accomplishment.

---

* He said in his "inaugural" address:

"The signal honor of being Provisional President of Africa is mine. It is a political job; it is a political calling for me to redeem Africa. It is like asking Napoleon to take the world. He took a certain portion of the world in his time. He failed and died at St. Helena. But may I not say that the lessons of Napoleon are but stepping stones by which we shall guide ourselves to African liberation?"

But unless he does these things and does them quickly he cannot escape failure.

Let the followers of Mr. Garvey insist that he get down to bed-rock business and make income and expense balance; let them gag Garvey's wilder words, and still preserve his wide power and influence. American Negro leaders are not jealous of Garvey—they are not envious of his success; they are simply afraid of his failure, for his failure would be theirs. He can have all the power and money that he can efficiently and honestly use, and if in addition he wants to prance down Broadway in a green shirt, let him—but do not let him foolishly overwhelm with bankruptcy and disaster one of the most interesting spiritual movements of the modern Negro world.

*William Pickens was an early supporter of the Garvey movement. Later, in the mid-twenties when Garvey's ties with the Ku Klux Klan became known, Pickens repudiated his support of Garvey.*

# Africa for the Africans—The Garvey Movement

## By William Pickens

*Marcus Garvey and his movement have been criticized, probably justly, for unsound methods of finance. They have been denounced by colored critics for failing to assert social equality and by radical critics for lack of economic understanding. They have been ridiculed by white men who do not see that the foibles of their own racial consciousness are reflected in this Negro movement. But the movement goes on—a vigorous proof that the Negro no longer answers to Mr. Dooley's definition of a "docile people easily lynched."*

THE VISITOR to the thriving Negro section of the Harlem district in New York any time during the month of August would have been aware that something unusual was going on. At the corners newsboys hawked the *Negro World*—"all about Marcus Garvey and the great convention." Cigar stores sold Marcus Garvey cigars. At certain hours parades drew thousands to the streets. A long one-story building, Liberty Hall, was filled all during the month with hundreds of delegates during business sessions and jammed to the doors every night. And this convention was an army with banners—red, black, and green—borne by delegates from three continents. Its leading functionaries on great occasions wore resplendent robes and at all times bore resounding titles: Potentate, Provisional President of Africa, Chaplain General, and the like. The man responsible for all this was Marcus Garvey, a West Indian Negro, not long in the United States, who asserts that in four years his Universal Negro Improvement Association has reached a membership of 4,500,000, about 45 per cent from the United States, the remainder from Africa,

From *Nation*, CXIII (December 28, 1921), 750–751.

Central and South America, the West Indies, Canada, and Europe. Reduce this high estimate as much as you like, yet it still remains an unprecedented fact that representatives of all the principal Negro groups of the world have come together in an organization which raises the cry of "Africa for the Africans!" and proposes to found a great Negro government, an African Republic, which they vow to realize if it takes five hundred years.

This is a new thing for Negroes, but in strict harmony with many a slogan old or new which white men have used. "Self-determination of all peoples," "a white Australia," "100-per-cent Americanism"— how are they different in principle from Garvey's cry "Africa, the self-governing home of the Negro race"? Any phenomenon among the colored population, like the U. N. I. A., white persons at first incline to regard as a huge joke, while the better-off colored people look upon it as something which they must shun in defense of their respectability. So there are educated and conscientious colored people who live within five minutes of Liberty Hall but have never been in it, and yet believe that the whole movement is disreputable, dishonest, and disgraceful to their race, and that Garvey, whom they have never heard, is a smart thief or a wild fanatic. But the stubborn fact remains that a man of a disadvantaged group, by his almost unsupported strength and personal magnetism, has founded so large a power in the English-speaking world as to add to the current vocabulary of that language a new word, "Garveyism."

And still honest people have honest doubts which we may consider under various heads:

1. Is a Republic of Africa, controlled by black people, possible? Friends of the movement say that the idea may unite the Negro groups of the world in large industrial cooperation and commercial enterprise, even if the dream of African empire is not realized for many generations. Colored people have similar problems wherever they live in large numbers among white people, and it will help them to have financial and economic strength such as the Jews have maintained throughout the world for centuries, even without territory and without sovereign or national power. As for the future, it is a very large assumption to deny the possibility of African freedom. Ten years ago it seemed impossible to get the Germans out of Africa. Something happened, unpredicted and unbelievable. Are the British and French empires less mortal than Germany seemed ten years ago? If ever the British Empire goes to pieces, the chances for a

Negro state will be good. And the longer that empire holds the better the chances for such a state when the empire does break up, for the culture of the native African will be more advanced.

2. Garvey's emphasis on racial consciousness as a bond to unite Negroes of all nations is not a retrograde movement. Possibly the idea of race may vanish in the future. But how far in the future? The comfort, convenience, and protection of hundreds of millions of Negroes cannot wait on that millennial jubilee. We might as well console a Negro who is about to be burned in Texas by prophesying to him that a thousand years from now his kind will not be burned because the constantly inflowing stream of white blood will have so lightened the skins of his group that nobody will know whom to burn. Race is now and will be for ages one of the deepest lines of human demarcation. And a race must have power and cohesion or perish. There is no such thing as the inalienable right of the individual against the established government, and when one race monopolizes the power and the functions of government, the other race or races are under the power of the governing race, even in the most advanced democracies and republics. And so interdependent are the interests of nations today that whenever any race holds power anywhere on earth the nationals and members of that race who live under the government of other races receive more respect and better treatment than the members of a race who have not the indirect backing of a racial government. That explains the queer fact that a brown-faced Japanese, who is regarded as a dangerous rival and almost feared as a potential enemy, can travel without Jim Crow in Mississippi and register at the best hotels of New York or Atlanta, while a native Negro who is a citizen and whose skin may be many shades lighter than that of the Japanese, but who has no appeal from the local white juries, will be jim-crowed in Mississippi, told that "all rooms are taken" in New York, and kicked out of the lobbies in Atlanta. And this same Negro can be drafted to fight that Japanese.

3. The parades, regalia, ceremonials, and rituals of the Garvey movement form the outside, the least important side, of his organization. The desire for them is primarily human, not Negro. The writer does not happen to share it, but he understands it. Garvey's ritual is infinitely less absurd than that of the Ku Klux Klan and is neither secret nor sinister. Garvey is a Britisher and frankly wishes to use British social institutions. He is President-General of the organization; there are also a High Potentate from Liberia, a leader for the

American Negro contingent, a head for the African Legion or military organization, and other high officers. What really troubles many white observers is not the ritual but the fact that in it the Negroes are striving to express their own racial pride rather than bow down to the white man. Formerly the Negro accepted the white and straighthaired God of the white man; when the white man wrote a prayer for the health of his own kind and the perpetuation of his own supremacy, the black Christian simply repeated, reinforced, and abetted the white man's supplications. But here come black Garvey and his followers praying for their own sovereignty, idealizing their own kind, pigmenting their God, and the thing sounds outrageous to some white men and ridiculous even to the Caucasianized section of the Negro race. But is not some such racial pride necessary to the strength of the race?

4. An expert in business procedure would doubtless find many weaknesses in Garvey's business methods, not because it is Garvey's movement, certainly not because the people are colored, but for the same reason that one would expect to find risk and waste and some unfit and misplaced officials in any new, very large, and fast-growing organization. These things are remediable if the head and heart of an organization are right. Nearly everyone who looks into the face and listens to the words of Marcus Garvey becomes convinced of his honesty and his utter sincerity, as I am. But colored Americans of large business experience have held aloof hitherto and have lent no aid toward systematizing this tremendous enterprise of their race, and its greatest need seems to be better talent in its management. Nobody knows this better than Mr. Garvey. All the more reason why the financial transactions of the movement and its various subdivisions should be above the very breath of suspicion.

The United Negro Improvement Association is a membership organization, and if it received not more than one dollar per member a year from one-tenth of the number claimed it would have about the largest net income of any Negro institution. The U. N. I. A. holds the majority of stock in the Black Star Line, which is said to own three vessels. The creation of a steamship line, even in embryo, is one of the greatest achievements of the twentieth century Negro. The U. N. I. A. is also the basis of various other business organizations, one of which is the African Communities League. I take it that this League is simply a legal device for doing business which could not be done under the charter of the U. N. I. A., especially under British law. There is also a Negro Factories Corporation. A safe development of these business enterprises will mean more to the Negroes of the Western Hemisphere for some generations to come than will the hope of the Republic of Africa.

5. It is a serious question whether a big international race movement like this Garvey movement will not have a harmful influence on the domestic struggle here, if only by sapping the energies and consuming the resources of American colored folk. Yet in so far as international race power grew, it would strengthen the Negroes in the United States and everywhere else. There is no essential antagonism between Negro civil rights in Texas and Negro political rights in West Africa. There is no reason why the same individual Negro may not have a membership in the Urban League, the National Association for the Advancement of Colored People, and the Universal Negro Improvement Association, and yet talk consistently in an "interracial congress" in Atlanta, Georgia.

6. Will the Garvey propaganda introduce a dangerous color division in the ranks of the colored American group itself? Garvey emphasizes and idealizes black; accepting the white man's challenge at its face value, he calls for black racial integrity and the preservation of "type." Now, it happens that what is called "the American Negro" consists of every shade and grade of human being from a white person with a drop of African blood in his veins to the full-blooded Negro. American race prejudice has welded this group into one. In the West Indies it is different: the British there have created a gulf between the light-skinned colored people and the darker ones, making both easier for the British to control. It is perhaps one of Garvey's mistakes that when he sees colored Americans contending for exact citizenship equality between the two races, he suspects them of trying to bring about amalgamation between whites and blacks. Amalgamation is hardly subject to group control; it is almost as independent of individual will as is the cooling of the sun. The leaders of the U. N. I. A., including Garvey himself, declare that the organization draws no distinction among the Negroes of the world.

Whatever may be said by way of criticism, this movement of the colored masses is anything but a joke. Neither Garvey nor any other human being could ever build up such a movement among the masses if it did not answer some longing of their souls. His particular movement may fail; the new racial consciousness of the Negro will endure. The deepest instincts of the scattered scions of the Negro race, like

330 Other Dreams: Garveyism

those of every race, call for group life, group propagation, and group power. That this is a white man's country, that other races must be kept out, or if already in must be kept in their place, is the viewpoint, the belief, and the will of nine-tenths of the native white people of the United States, even the most cultured and the most religious. It is but natural that such a pervasive feeling in their environment is answered in the soul of colored folk by a striving after self-preservation and self-perpetuation. And there is a *laissez-faire* majority in both races who are always worried and anxious enough, but who are willing only to "wait on the Lord" and see what will happen from decade to decade. And, of course, "nature and time" would gradually but very slowly and very wastefully solve this problem and all other earthly problems by the creeping processes of destroying and uniformizing. But the horrors of a thousand years while waiting on Nature would be a disgrace to human intellect and genius.

Out of the colored people must come their own salvation. They must be a race and a power. The preparation for it could never have started too early, and cannot start earlier than now. The earlier the start, the less waste and the fewer horrors. It may take a hundred years or five hundred, a thousand years or five thousand, but four hundred million people can never be expected either to perish or forever to renounce their right to self-direction.

*E. Franklin Frazier was a noted black sociologist whose urban studies of black communities such as Chicago remain classic accounts. His contemporary analysis of Garvey provides an important perspective on black thought during the twenties.*

# Garvey: A Mass Leader

## By E. Franklin Frazier

THE GARVEY movement is a crowd movement essentially different from any other social phenomenon among Negroes. For the most part American Negroes have sought self-magnification in fraternal orders and the church. But these organizations have failed to give that support to the Negro's ego-consciousness which the white masses find in membership in a political community, or on a smaller scale in Kiwanis clubs and the Ku Klux Klan. In a certain sense Garvey's followers form the black Klan of America.

The reason for Garvey's success in welding the Negroes into a crowd movement becomes apparent when we compare his methods and aims with those of other leaders. Take, for example, the leadership of Booker Washington. Washington could not be considered a leader of the masses of Negroes, for his program commended itself chiefly to white people and those Negroes who prided themselves on their opportunism. There was nothing popularly heroic or inspiring in his program to captivate the imagination of the average Negro. In fact the Negro was admonished to play an inglorious role. Certain other outstanding efforts among Negroes have failed to attract the masses because they have lacked the characteristics which have distinguished the Garvey movement. It is only necessary to mention such an organization as the National Urban League and its leadership to realize that so reasoned a program of social adjustment is lacking in everything that appeals to the crowd. The leadership of Dr. DuBois has been too intellectual to satisfy the mob. Even his glorification of the Negro has been in terms which escape the black masses. The

From *Nation*, CXXIII (August 18, 1926), 147–148.

Pan-African Congress which he has promoted, while supporting to some extent the boasted aims of Garvey, has failed to stir any considerable number of American Negroes. The National Association for the Advancement of Colored People, which has fought uncompromisingly for equality for the Negro, has never secured, except locally and occasionally, the support of the masses. It has lacked the dramatic element.

The status of Negroes in American life makes it easy for a crowd movement to be initiated among them. In America the Negro is repressed and an outcast. Some people are inclined to feel that this repression is only felt by cultured Negroes. As a matter of fact many of them can find satisfaction in the intellectual and spiritual things of life and do not need the support to their personalities that the average man requires. The average Negro, like other mediocre people, must be fed upon empty and silly fictions in order that life may be bearable. In the South the most insignificant white man is made of supreme worth simply by the fact of his color, not to mention the added support he receives from the Kiwanis or the Klan .

Garvey came to America at a time when all groups were asserting themselves. Many American Negroes have belittled his influence on the ground that he is a West Indian. It has been said that Garvey was only able to attract the support of his fellow-countrymen. The truth is that Garvey aroused the Negroes of Georgia as much as those of New York, except where the black preacher discouraged anything that threatened his income, or where white domination smothered every earthly hope. Moreover, this prejudice against the West Indian Negro loses sight of the contribution of the West Indian to the American Negro. The West Indian who has been ruled by a small minority instead of being oppressed by the majority, is more worldly in his outlook. He has been successful in business. He does not need the lodge, with its promise of an imposing funeral, or the church, with its hope of a heavenly abode as an escape from a sense of inferiority. By his example he has given the American Negro an earthly goal.

Garvey went even further. He not only promised the despised Negro a paradise on earth, but he made the Negro an important person in his immediate environment. He invented honors and social distinctions and converted every social invention to his use in his effort to make his followers feel important. While everyone was not a "Knight" or "Sir" all his followers were "Fellow-men of the Negro

Race." Even more concrete distinctions were open to all. The women were organized into Black Cross Nurses, and the men became uniformed members of the vanguard of the Great African Army. A uniformed member of a Negro lodge paled in significance beside a soldier of the Army of Africa. A Negro might be a porter during the day, taking his orders from white men, but he was an officer in the black army when it assembled at night in Liberty Hall. Many a Negro went about his work singing in his heart that he was a member of the great army marching to "heights of achievements." And even in basing his program upon fantastic claims of empire, Garvey always impressed his followers that his promise was more realistic than that of those who were constantly arguing for the theoretical rights of the Negro. In the *Negro World* for October 18, 1924, he warned his followers that

> Those who try to ridicule the idea that America is a white man's country are going to find themselves sadly disappointed one of these days, homeless, shelterless, and unprovided for. Some of us do harp on our constitutional rights, which sounds reasonable in the righteous interpretation thereof, but we are forgetting that righteousness is alien to the world and that sin and materialism now triumph, and for material glory and honor and selfishness man will slay his brother. And in the knowledge of this, is the Negro still so foolish as to believe that the majority of other races are going to be so unfair and unjust to themselves as to yield to weaker peoples that which they themselves desire?

And after all this is essentially what most Negroes believe in spite of the celebrated faith of the Negro in America.

A closer examination of the ideals and symbols which Garvey always held up before his followers shows his mastery of the technique of creating and holding crowds. The Negro group becomes idealized. Therefore he declares he is as strongly against race-intermixture as a Ku Kluxer. He believes in a "pure black race just as all self-respecting whites believe in a pure white race." According to Garvey, civilization is about to fall and the Negro is called upon "to evolve a national ideal, based upon freedom, human liberty, and true democracy." The "redemption of Africa" is the regaining of a lost paradise. It is always almost at hand.

This belief has served the same purpose as does the myth of the general strike in the syndicalist movement. Garvey, who is dealing with people imbued with religious feeling, endows the redemption of Africa with the mystery of the regeneration of mankind. He said on one occasion: "No one knows when the hour of Africa's redemption cometh. It is in the wind. It is coming one day like a storm. It will be here. When that day comes, all Africa will stand together."

Garvey gave the crowd that followed him victims to vent their hatred upon, just as the evangelist turns the hatred of his followers upon the Devil. Every rabble must find someone to blame for its woes. The Negro who is poor, ignorant, and weak naturally wants to place the blame on anything except his own incapacity. Therefore Garvey was always attributing the misfortunes of the Negro group to traitors and enemies. Although the identity of these "traitors" and "enemies" was often obscure, as a rule they turned out to be Negro intellectuals. The cause for such animosity against this class of Negroes is apparent when we remember that Garvey himself lacks formal education.

Garvey, who was well acquainted with the tremendous influence of religion in the life of the Negro, proved himself matchless in assimilating his own program to the religious experience of the Negro. Christmas, with its association of the lowly birth of Jesus, became symbolic of the Negro's birth among the nations of the world. Easter became the symbol of the resurrection of an oppressed and crucified race. Such naive symbolism easily kindled enthusiasm among his followers. At other times Garvey made his own situation appear similar to that of Jesus. Just as the Jews incited the Roman authorities against Jesus, other Negro leaders were making the United States authorities persecute him.

Most discussions of the Garvey movement have been concerned with the feasibility of his schemes and the legal aspects of the charge which brought him finally to the Atlanta Federal Prison. It is idle to attempt to apply to the schemes that attract crowds the test of reasonableness. Even experience fails to teach a crowd anything, for the crowd satisfies its vanity and longing in the beliefs it holds. Nor is it surprising to find Garvey's followers regarding his imprisonment at present as martyrdom for the cause he represents, although the technical charge on which he was convicted is only indirectly related to his program. But Garvey has not failed to exploit his imprisonment. He knows that the average man is impressed if anyone suffers. Upon his arrest he gave out the following statement: "There has never been a movement where the Leader has not suffered for the Cause, and not received the ingratitude of the people. I, like the rest, am prepared for the consequence." As he entered the prison in Atlanta he sent a message to his followers which appeared in his paper, the *Negro World,* for February 14, 1925. He paints himself as a sufferer for his group and blames his lot on a group of plotters. In commending his wife to the care of his followers he says: "All I have, I have given to you. I have sacrificed my home and my loving wife for you. I intrust her to your charge, to protect and defend in my absence. She is the bravest little woman I know." Such pathos he knew the mob could not resist, and the final word he sent to his supporters under the caption, "If I Die in Atlanta," with its apocalyptic message, raises him above mortals. He bade them "Look for me in the whirlwind or the storm, look for me all around you, for, with God's grace, I shall come and bring with me the countless millions of black slaves who have died in America and the West Indies and the millions in Africa to aid you in the fight for liberty, freedom, and life."

Since his imprisonment Garvey has continued to send his weekly message on the front of his paper to his followers warning them against their enemies and exhorting them to remain faithful to him in his suffering. It is uncritical to regard Garvey as a common swindler who has sought simply to enrich himself, when the evidence seems to place him among those so-called cranks who refuse to deal realistically with life. He has the distinction of initiating the first real mass movement among American Negroes.

*Kelly Miller, usually regarded as one of the moderate
black leaders of the period, offers, in the following piece,
a thoughtful and respectful view of the significance of
Marcus Garvey to black liberation.*

# After Marcus Garvey—What of the Negro?

## By Kelly Miller

MARCUS GARVEY came to the United States less than ten years ago,
unheralded, unfriended, without acquaintance, relationship, or means
of livelihood. This Jamaican immigrant was thirty years old, partially
educated, and 100 per cent black. He possessed neither comeliness
of appearance nor attractive physical personality. Judged by external appraisement, there was nothing to distinguish him from thousands of West Indian blacks who flock to our seaport cities. And yet
this ungainly youth by sheer indomitability of will projected a
propaganda and commanded a following, within the brief space of
a decade, which made the whole nation mark him and write his
speeches in their books. The Garvey Movement seemed to be absurd, grotesque, and bizarre, but the possibilities of its involvements,
as well as the ardour of advocacy and the extent and intensity of
discipleship engendered by its author and founder, filled the minds
of statesmen and thinkers with more than momentary amazement and
apprehension.

Young Garvey in his island home had tasted to the dregs the cup
of personal and racial humiliation and chagrin, and had experienced
triple ostracism on account of race, colour, and class. A personal
affront in his adolescent years sent the iron into his soul from which
it has never been withdrawn. Smarting under a keen sense of
wrong, his restless, rebellious spirit drove him from country to
country and from continent to continent, seeking rest and finding
none. His intellectual and moral faculties, though untutored,
were wildly active. His mind was swayed first by one wild notion
and then by another. The consciousness gradually grew upon him

From *Contemporary Review*, CXXXI (April 1927), 492–500.

that he was sent and commissioned to right the wrongs of his race. Suddenly the key-word flashed across his mind. Thenceforth this black John the Baptist with amazing audacity proclaimed that the kingdom of Africa was at hand. The negro race throughout the world was called upon to repent or to change its mind, preparatory to the new order of things now about to be set up, which would solve for ever the hitherto insoluble problems involved in negro blood. The federation of the black members of the human family into a world empire under self-dominion was a bold dream which no mortal had ever dared to dream before. At first Garvey possessed only a vague and visionary conception of the new kingdom. The more he preached, the clearer the vision grew, until he became firmly convinced of its immediate consummation. The fanatical propagandist is never daunted by practical impossibilities which stand between him and the realisation of his ideal. Counting the cost, as well as a cautious conscience, makes cowards of us all. A kindly fatuity saves the fanatic from the paralysis of prevision. . . .

Garvey arrived in New York at the psychological moment. The European nations were engaged in titanic conflict. America had, so far, stood aside in benevolent aloofness and apologetic neutrality. The negro caught the sound of such expressions as "the rights of the minority" and "a war for self-determination," and was thrilled by their reverberations. He seized upon the opportunity to upbraid the American conscience with the reproach of moral inconsistency. If democracy is to relieve the minorities oppressed by Germany, why not those oppressed by Georgia? Why spill American blood for oppressed peoples in the Balkan States and ignore like oppression in the Southern States? He failed to see the moral consistency in condemning atrocities in Turkey which are tolerated in Texas. Why reprove Germany for regarding an international treaty as a scrap of paper while the United States scraps the Fourteenth and Fifteenth Amendments, without self-reproof or a sense of shame? In times of revolution oppressed peoples always ask embarrassing questions. The negro, along with the rest, was conscripted to fight for the freedom of white men in Europe, himself being denied full participation in the benefits of freedom at home.

Harlem was just becoming the great negro metropolis. The necessities of the war were bringing tens of thousands of negroes to New York from all parts of the country. Thousands were also attracted from the West Indian Islands. Harlem was filled with street preachers and flamboyant orators haranguing the people from morning till night upon racial rights and wrongs. Radical magazines sprang up suddenly whose utterances were calculated to inflame the minds of the people. The West Indians were radical beyond the rest and seemed to be better adepts in mob psychology. The West Indian negro in America is a political conundrum. Conservative at home, he becomes radical abroad. About this time the negroes in New York, native and West Indian, were asserting the rights and recounting the wrongs of the race in such severe terms of denunciation as to cause the government much uneasiness. The espionage department kept the more assertive ones under surveillance, suppressed the most outspoken publications and threatened the orators, editors, and authors with serious punishment.

In those days Marcus Garvey arrived in Harlem. The West Indian contingent formed his normal point of attachment with the general situation. He immediately formed friendly affiliation with his fellow islanders to whom his appeal was more easily persuasive. He did not join in the tirade against the American people and government but shrewdly turned the energy which hitherto had vented itself in violent protestation, into new and constructive channels. He saw that the mind was ready for the sowing of new seed. He thereupon began to unfold the vision of the kingdom of Africa. First he launched the Universal Negro Improvement Association, which he had projected abortively in his native Jamaica, as a practical venture for the commercial development of the dark continent. He next established *The Negro World*, a weekly journal, as the organ and mouthpiece for the new movement. This journal reached a wide circulation among negro peoples and carried the gospel according to Garvey to all lands where the scattered children of Africa were to be found. Sections were edited in English, French, and Spanish. He built "Liberty Hut"—a crude tabernacle, with a seating capacity of six thousand, where on every Sunday evening he addressed overflowing crowds who hung breathless upon his word. The magnetic power of his charm and spell seemed never to wane.

At this stage Mr. Garvey appeared to be a crass pragmatist, relying wholly upon the instrumentality of material agencies to accomplish his remote spiritual objective. He hoped to develop race consciousness through race patronage and co-operative enterprise. Grocery stores, laundries, restaurants, hotels, and printing plants were organised under the auspices of the Universal Negro Improvement Association. These all failed as fast as they were founded. But the fanatic is never daunted by failure. How Mr. Garvey could hope that the operation of a few shops in Harlem could seriously affect the fate of the continent of Africa surpasses normal human understanding. But no whit abashed by the failure of his business ventures, the undaunted dreamer forthwith proceeded to launch the "Black Star Line" of steamships to trade with the West Indies and with the continent of Africa, a stupendous act of folly. The combined genius and wealth of America has not been able to operate competitive ocean-carrying trade. But the fanaticism and faith of Marcus Garvey performed miracles in inspiring his followers with confidence and zeal for the impossible. As fast as one steamship failed they were ready to provide for another. After all, there may be subtle method in Mr. Garvey's seeming madness. It is easier to focus attention upon a concrete project than upon an abstract ideal. A line of steamships touching African and West Indian ports, conveying not only material merchandise but also the propaganda of racial unity, was calculated to make a powerful appeal to the mind and imagination of his unsophisticated followers. Any doctrinaire reformer runs a great risk when he ventures the success or failure of his propaganda upon a single pitch-and-throw involved in a concrete enterprise. Its success may mean his triumph; its failure foreshadows his doom. . . .

It was in 1921, in the presence of six thousand of his followers and admirers in "Liberty Hut," that he proceeded to the formal inauguration of the Empire of Africa. Garvey himself was crowned President-General of the United Negro Improvement Association and Provisional President of Africa, who with one Potentate and one Supreme Deputy Potentate constituted the royalty of the Empire of Africa. Knights of the Nile, Knights of the Distinguished Service Order of Ethiopia, and Dukes of the Niger and of Uganda, constituted the nobility. The August Court was set up and actually functioned for several years, with all of the tinsel glory and barbaric splendour of oriental pomp and display. The negro's penchant for mimic display, gay regalia, and titled dignitaries was abundantly appeased. But pride goeth before a fall. The inevitable end was near. Dissension broke out within the ranks. The question of who shall sit on the right hand and on the left hand in the kingdom always precipitates unfriendly rivalry among the disciples. Internal dissensions however were easily settled by the last word of the President-General. Mr. Garvey's personal authority so far transcended that of his following that no other name than his figures conspicuously in the movement.

The Afro-American intelligentsia rose up in righteous rage and disgust at what seemed to be the absurd and ridiculous antics of this half-educated West Indian upstart. There exists fundamental opposition between the philosophy of Marcus Garvey and that of the educated American negro leaders. Their whole teaching is based upon equality of the races which they hope to enforce by appeal to the white man's conscience, reason, and aroused sense of righteousness. Mr. Garvey believes that the racial prejudice of the Anglo-Saxon is so deeply imbedded in acquired emotions, if not in natural instinct, that no amount of moral suasion or coercive force which the negro can command will have any sensible effect upon it. He believes that race consciousness is likely to become keener and more exclusive, and that the opportunities of the white men's civilisation will be reserved more and more for the sons and daughters of their own kith and kin. He looks upon the struggle for racial equality as futile and hopeless. He preaches that the negro must build on his own basis apart from the white man's foundation, if he ever hopes to be a master builder. He therefore urges the race to look to the land of their mothers across the sea for future growth and expansion. In the United States the African sojourners will never be permitted to rise above the level of hewers of wood and drawers of water. It is said that he sought conference with the rulers of the Ku-Klux-Klan, and found himself in accord with the hooded order on this basic proposition of racial relations, though each side reached the same conclusion by different processes of reason. This doctrine of inevitable subordination, naturally enough, aroused the bitterest antagonism of the Afro-American leaders who have staked all their hopes on the opposite proposition.

Again, Mr. Garvey believes, with frenzied fanaticism, in the continent of Africa as the destined end and way of all the scattered fragments of the black race who are now sojourning among the whiter nations of the earth. The educated Afro-American has little interest and no enthusiasm for his mother-land. Frederick Douglass epitomised this sentiment in the sententious saying: "I have none of the banana in me." Dr. DuBois has been trying for a number of years to promote a Pan-African Congress for the discussion of the race question on a world-wide scale. There are probably not half a dozen educated negroes in America who have evinced any genuine enthusiasm or passionate interest for Garvey's proposition. The native-born, educated negro resents as a reflection upon his American birthright any suggestion that he has a special and peculiar interest in the dark continent from which his blood was derived in whole or in part.

At the climax of antagonism, Mr. Garvey took up the apotheosis of blackness as offset to the existing deification of whiteness. He would have God painted black. This caused a violent revulsion of feeling on the part even of black men who had become habituated to bow down and worship at the shrine of a colour alien to their own. Mr. Garvey believed that not only do gods always make men in their own image, but that man, in his turn, makes God in his own likeness. Every race ascribes to its deity its own physical, mental, and moral peculiarities carried to the higher power of perfection. Mr. Garvey believes that the adoption of the colour and racial characteristics of the white man's portrayal of God paralyses the negro's racial self-respect. This was an audacious innovation in the sphere of negro thought and sensibilities which the intelligentsia had never had either the passion or the discernment to consider. They simply held up their hands in frantic disgust at such a revolting blasphemy.

With this wide difference the battle between the antagonists became war to the death. Negro newspapers and magazines were filled with criticisms and denunciations of this new and dangerous doctrine. The Garvey Movement became the Garvey menace. This interloper was denounced as a trouble-maker, dangerous to whites and blacks alike. His motive and his honesty were impugned. It was strongly urged that he should be deported as a foreigner stirring up strife among native-born Americans. His business transactions became involved in legal tangles. The "Black Star Line" had failed. Charges were filed against him by the Federal authorities for violation of postal regulations, in his quest for funds to save the sinking fortune of his ships. Upon this charge he was convicted and sentenced to five years in the Federal penitentiary. During the trial Garvey fought like a lion at bay. He and his disciples believed that he was persecuted for righteousness' sake and that the technicality of the law was invoked as a pretext to defeat his racial objective. His followers believed that in his zeal to promote a cause which he regarded as holy, he became oblivious of the technical letter of the law. No personal wrong-doing was attributed to him by way of improper personal profit. In the eyes of those who believe in him, he is as much a martyr to his cause as Gandhi of India. Both have sinned against the technicalities of the law and must suffer under the law. This is the price which the reformer must reckon to pay when his propaganda is at vital variance with established public policy.

The Garvey Movement attracted the attention of the nation and caused no little apprehension. There was general feeling that he might lash the fury of his followers to an uncontrollable extent. His name was on the tongue of every speaker dealing with racial matters. The newspapers and magazines discussed the Garvey Movement from every angle of approach and point of view. No negro, not even Booker Washington, ever received such national notoriety. He was regarded as a mountebank, a menace, a puzzle. The Garvey Movement became international in its involvements. The governments of Europe with African colonies or mandates became alarmed at the impression this Jamaican agitator was making upon the minds and imaginations of negro peoples in all parts of the earth. He admonished negroid peoples everywhere to throw off white overlordship and assert self-sovereignty. His African Empire sent representatives to the Peace Conference and sought recognition among sovereign nations. Mr. Garvey put governments with colonial control over African territory on notice that their tenancy was temporary only, until the Empire of Africa should arrive to claim rightful sovereignty over its own. He sowed the seed of self-determination in the minds of negroid peoples in all lands and found it to be a fertile soil. They had caught the suggestion from the words of Woodrow Wilson which flew round the world to its remotest bounds and darkest corners. The black heathen in his blindness heard it and was glad. It was, indeed, the gospel of great joy and glad tidings. A negro bishop to South Africa relates that whenever a white man mistreated a native, he would mark the grudge on his stick of remembrance with the suppressed murmur—"You just wait till Garvey comes." The nations were at first inclined to take the Garvey Movement as a joke, but a joke with a deep-seated undertone of seriousness. They all uttered a sigh of relief when it was learned that Garvey had been convicted and placed behind prison bars. No other negro within the period of recorded history has ever been the object of international solicitude.

Mr. Garvey is now serving a five-year term in the Atlanta penitentiary. But prison bars cannot confine the insurgence of his spirit. A weekly encyclical is issued to the faithful from a criminal's cell. His followers are still holding together the skeleton of his organisation but they miss the magic and spell of the master. His words issued from his prison house sustain their flagging courage but the glamour of the Court of the African Empire is gone. The Knights of the Nile and Dukes of the Niger have lost their brief nobility. The hour looks dark for the fate of the Empire of Africa. When the Provisional President has served out his sentence and been released from bonds he may be deported as an undesirable alien. Banished to his native Jamaica with his powers pent up by the confines of his little island, held under surveillance by the all-watchful eye of British vigilance, he will hardly be able to function effectively across the seas.

If we consider, as it now seems reasonable to do, that the Garvey Movement is a spent force, it might be profitable to consider the present and future effect of this hectic movement upon the negro race and upon the permanent relations of the black and white races. The chief achievement of Marcus Garvey consists in his quickening the sense of race consciousness and self-dignity on the part of the common people among black folks all over the world. The effect of all the movements which have been launched by the intelligentsia among negroes is that they have never been able to penetrate below a certain level of social grade. They do not reach the common people or stir their imagination. The National Association for the Advancement of Coloured People, with its capable and consecrated leadership, so far has been able to make no great impression on the heart and imagination of the proletariat. But Garvey arouses the zeal of millions of the lowliest to the frenzy of a crusade.

Mr. Garvey is by no means the only negro apostle of the return of the exiled Africans to their mother continent. The African Colonisation Society, in the early years of the nineteenth century, established Liberia as the home of Afro-Americans so soon as they could be freed. Many of the best minds of the nation, including Abraham Lincoln, believed that the American negro could build up his fortune best in his native land. Many leading negroes of that day found themselves in harmony with this scheme of repatriation. Some forty years ago, Dr. Edward W. Blyden, a West Indian negro who migrated to Africa in the wake of this Liberian movement, became an ardent advocate of the return of the race to the land of the fathers. This famous negro scholar depended in the main on the good offices of white men imbued with the missionary spirit, to support and encourage this great enterprise. Bishop H. M. Turner, of the African A.M.E. Church, sometime Bishop to Africa, became a powerful advocate of the African redemption. Various missionary societies for centuries have been operating in Africa but have made little headway in lighting up the dark continent. Now comes Marcus Garvey, if not with a new principle, at least with a new programme. He preaches race independence, race efficiency, and race sufficiency for the reclamation of Africa through political, industrial, and social conquest. He believes that philanthropy paralyses the energies of the black peoples of the world and pauperises their spirit. He has an unfathomable faith in the possibilities of his people. No greater vision has ever haunted the human mind. The accomplishment of the dream is worth a thousand years of the united endeavour of mankind. It is impossible to conceive of any task which will inure to greater advantage to the human race.

COMMUNISM

*Introducing the section on communism are three articles
by DuBois from* The Crisis. *Each one deals with specific
aspects of the radical challenge, but all share a common
viewpoint.*

# The Negro and Radical Thought

## By W. E. B. DuBois

MR. CLAUDE MCKAY, one of the editors of *The Liberator* and a Negro
poet of distinction, writes us as follows:

> I am surprised and sorry that in your editorial, "The Drive," pub-
> lished in THE CRISIS for May, you should leap out of your sphere to
> sneer at the Russian Revolution, the greatest event in the history of
> humanity; much greater than the French Revolution, which is held up
> as a wonderful achievement to Negro children and students in white
> and black schools. For American Negroes the indisputable and out-
> standing fact of the Russian Revolution is that a mere handful of
> Jews, much less in ratio to the number of Negroes in the American
> population, have attained, through the Revolution, all the political
> and social rights that were denied to them under the regime of the
> Czar.
>
> Although no thinking Negro can deny the great work that the
> N. A. A. C. P. is doing, it must yet be admitted that from its platform
> and personnel the Association cannot function as a revolutionary
> working class organization. And the overwhelming majority of Amer-
> ican Negroes belong by birth, condition and repression to the work-
> ing class. Your aim is to get for the American Negro the political and
> social rights that are his by virtue of the Constitution, the rights which
> are denied him by the Southern oligarchy with the active coopera-
> tion of the state governments and the tacit support of northern busi-
> ness interests. And your aim is a noble one, which deserves the
> support of all progressive Negroes.
>
> But the Negro in politics and social life is ostracized only tech-
> nically by the distinction of color; in reality the Negro is discriminated
> against because he is of the lowest type of worker....
>
> Obviously, this economic difference between the white and black
> workers manifests itself in various forms, in color prejudice, race
> hatred, political and social boycotting and lynching of Negroes. And

From *The Crisis*, XXII (July 1921), 102–104.

all the entrenched institutions of white America,—law courts, churches, schools, the fighting forces and the Press,—condone these iniquities perpetrated upon black men; iniquities that are dismissed indifferently as the inevitable result of the social system. Still, whenever it suits the business interests controlling these institutions to mitigate the persecutions against Negroes, they do so with impunity. When organized white workers quit their jobs, Negroes, who are discouraged by the whites to organize, are sought to take their places. And these strike-breaking Negroes work under the protection of the military and the police. But as ordinary citizens and workers, Negroes are not protected by the military and the police from the mob. The ruling classes will not grant Negroes those rights which, on a lesser scale and more plausibly, are withheld from the white proletariat. The concession of these rights would immediately cause a Revolution in the economic life of this country.

We are aware that some of our friends have been disappointed with THE CRISIS during and since the war. Some have assumed that we aimed chiefly at mounting the band wagon with our cause during the madness of war; others thought that we were playing safe so as to avoid the Department of Justice; and still a third class found us curiously stupid in our attitude toward the broader matters of human reform. Such critics, and Mr. McKay is among them, must give us credit for standing to our guns in the past at no little cost in many influential quarters, and they must also remember that we have one chief cause,—the emancipation of the Negro, and to this all else must be subordinated—not because other questions are not important but because to our mind the most important social question today is recognition of the darker races.

Turning now to that marvelous set of phenomena known as the Russian Revolution, Mr. McKay is wrong in thinking that we have ever intentionally sneered at it. On the contrary, time may prove, as he believes, that the Russian Revolution is the greatest event of the nineteenth and twentieth centuries, and its leaders the most unselfish prophets. At the same time THE CRISIS does not know this to be true. Russia is incredibly vast, and the happenings there in the last five years have been intricate to a degree that must make any student pause. We sit, therefore, with waiting hands and listening ears, seeing some splendid results from Russia, like the cartoons for public education recently exhibited in America, and hearing of other things which frighten us.

We are moved neither by the superficial omniscience of Wells nor the reports in the New York *Times*; but this alone we do know: that the immediate work for the American Negro lies in America and not in Russia, and this, too, in spite of the fact that the Third Internationale has made a pronouncement which cannot but have our entire sympathy:

> The Communist Internationale once forever breaks with the traditions of the Second Internationale which in reality only recognized the white race. The Communist Internationale makes it its task to emancipate the workers of the entire world. The ranks of the Communist Internationale fraternally unite men of all colors: white, yellow and black—the toilers of the entire world.

Despite this there come to us black men two insistent questions: What is today the right program of socialism? The editor of THE CRISIS considers himself a Socialist but he does not believe that German State Socialism or the dictatorship of the proletariat are perfect panaceas. He believes with most thinking men that the present method of creating, controlling and distributing wealth is desperately wrong; that there must come and is coming a social control of wealth; but he does not know just what form that control is going to take, and he is not prepared to dogmatize with Marx or Lenin. Further than that, and more fundamental to the duty and outlook of THE CRISIS, is this question: How far can the colored people of the world, and particularly the Negroes of the United States, trust the working classes?

Many honest thinking Negroes assume, and Mr. McKay seems to be one of these, that we have only to embrace the working class program to have the working class embrace ours; that we have only to join trade Unionism and Socialism or even Communism, as they are today expounded, to have Union Labor and Socialists and Communists believe and act on the equality of mankind and the abolition of the color line. THE CRISIS wishes that this were true, but it is forced to the conclusion that it is not.

The American Federation of Labor, as representing the trade unions in America, has been grossly unfair and discriminatory toward Negroes and still is. American Socialism has discriminated against black folk and before the war was prepared to go further with this discrimination. European Socialism has openly discriminated against Asiatics. Nor is this surprising. Why should we assume on the part of unlettered and suppressed masses of white workers a clearness of thought, a sense of human brotherhood, that is sadly lacking in the most educated classes?

Our task, therefore, as it seems to THE CRISIS, is clear: We have
to convince the working classes of the world that black men, brown
men and yellow men are human beings and suffer the same discrimination that white workers suffer. We have in addition to this
to espouse the cause of the white workers, only being careful that
we do not in this way allow them to jeopardize our cause. We must,
for instance, have bread. If our white fellow workers drive us out of
decent jobs, we are compelled to accept indecent wages even at the
price of "scabbing." It is a hard choice, but whose is the blame?
Finally despite public prejudice and clamour, we should examine
with open mind in literature, debate and in real life the great programs of social reform that are day by day being put forward.

This was the true thought and meaning back of our May editorial.
We have an immediate program for Negro emancipation laid down
and thought out by the N. A. A. C. P. It is foolish for us to give up
this practical program for mirage in Africa or by seeking to join a
revolution which we do not at present understand. On the other
hand, as Mr. McKay says, it would be just as foolish for us to sneer
or even seem to sneer at the blood-entwined writhing of hundreds
of millions of our whiter human brothers.

# The Class Struggle

## By W. E. B. DuBois

THE N. A. A. C. P. has been accused of not being a "revolutionary"
body. This is quite true. We do not believe in revolution. We expect
revolutionary changes in many parts of this life and this world, but
we expect these changes to come mainly through reason, human sympathy and the education of children, and not by murder. We know
that there have been times when organized murder seemed the
only way out of wrong, but we believe those times have been very
few, the cost of the remedy excessive, the results as terrible as bene-
ficient, and we gravely doubt if in the future there will be any real
recurrent necessity for such upheaval.

Whether this is true or not, the N. A. A. C. P. is organized to agi-
tate, to investigate, to expose, to defend, to reason, to appeal. This

From *The Crisis*, XXII (August 1921), 151–152.

is our program and this is the whole of our program. What human reform demands today is light, more light; clear thought, accurate knowledge, careful distinctions.⌐

How far, for instance, does the dogma of the "class struggle" apply to black folk in the United States today? Theoretically we are a part of the world proletariat in the sense that we are mainly an exploited class of cheap laborers; but practically we are not a part of the white proletariat and are not recognized by that proletariat to any great extent. We are the victims of their physical oppression, social ostracism, economic exclusion and personal hatred; and when in self defense we seek sheer subsistence we are howled down as "scabs."

Then consider another thing: the colored group is not yet divided into capitalists and laborers. There are only the beginnings of such a division. In one hundred years if we develop along conventional lines we would have such fully separated classes, but today to a very large extent our laborers are our capitalists and our capitalists are our laborers. Our small class of well-to-do men have come to affluence largely through manual toil and have never been physically or mentally separated from the toilers. Our professional classes are sons and daughters of porters, washerwomen and laborers.

Under these circumstances how silly it would be for us to try to apply the doctrine of the class struggle without modification or thought. Let us take a particular instance. Ten years ago the Negroes of New York City lived in hired tenement houses in Harlem, having gotten possession of them by paying higher rents than white tenants. If they had tried to escape these high rents and move into quarters where white laborers lived, the white laborers would have mobbed and murdered them. On the other hand, the white capitalists raised heaven and earth either to drive them out of Harlem or keep their rents high. Now between this devil and deep sea, what ought the Negro socialist or the Negro radical or, for that matter, the Negro conservative do?

Manifestly there was only one thing for him to do, and that was to buy Harlem; but the buying of real estate calls for capital and credit, and the institutions that deal in capital and credit are capitalistic institutions. If now, the Negro had begun to fight capital in Harlem, what capital was he fighting? If he fought capital as represented by white big real estate interests, he was wise; but he was also just as wise when he fought labor which insisted on segregating him in work and in residence.

If, on the other hand, he fought the accumulating capital in his own group, which was destined in the years 1915 to 1920 to pay down $5,000,000 for real estate in Harlem, then he was slapping himself in his own face. Because either he must furnish capital for the buying of his own home, or rest naked in the slums and swamps. It is for this reason that there is today a strong movement in Harlem for a Negro bank, and a movement which is going soon to be successful. This Negro bank eventually is going to bring into cooperation and concentration the resources of fifty or sixty other Negro banks in the United States, and this aggregation of capital is going to be used to break the power of white capital in enslaving and exploiting the darker world.

Whether this is a program of socialism or capitalism does not concern us. It is the only program that means salvation to the Negro race. The main danger and the central question of the capitalistic development through which the Negro American group is forced to go is the question of the ultimate control of the capital which they must raise and use. If this capital is going to be controlled by a few men for their own benefit, then we are destined to suffer from our own capitalists exactly what we are suffering from white capitalists today. And while this is not a pleasant prospect, it is certainly no worse than the present actuality. If, on the other hand, because of our more democratic organization and our widespread inter-class sympathy we can introduce a more democratic control, taking advantage of what the white world is itself doing to introduce industrial democracy, then we may not only escape our present economic slavery but even guide and lead a distrait economic world.

# Socialism and the Negro

## By W. E. B. DuBois

WE HAVE AN interesting letter from John H. Owens of Washington, which we would like to publish in full but can only note certain extracts. Mr. Owens says, in answer to the editorial in the July CRISIS on "The Negro and Radical Thought": "Is there not just the bare possibility that some of the issues which you consider subordinate

to your central idea (of the emancipation of the Negro) might possess the nucleus of a tangible and definite solution?"

There is more than a bare possibility, and the Negro must study
proposals and reforms with great care to see if they do not carry
with them some help in the solution of his problem. But he must not
assume that because a proposed solution settles many important
human problems, for this reason it is necessarily going to settle his.

Mr. Owens continues: "The Negro group is almost a pure proletarian group,—this fact admits of no denial. Above 90 per cent of
the Negroes are unskilled, untrained workers, and unorganized.
Thus it would seem that the race as a whole has less reason to be
suspicious of any movement of a proletarian nature than of some
scheme which offers a questionable solution for the ills of the talented minority."

The Negro has little reason to be suspicious of a proletarian movement if that movement is for the good of the proletariat; but it does
not follow that all movements proposed by the proletariat themselves
are for their own good. The workers of the world are, through no
fault of their own, ignorant, inexperienced men. It is not for a moment to be assumed that movements into which they are drawn or
which they themselves initiate are necessarily the best for them. If,
however, the Negro sees a movement for the proletariat which, after
careful thought and experience, he is convinced is for the good of the
working class, then as a worker he is bound to give every aid to such
a movement.

"Universal political enfranchisement would offer no positive relief. This the Northern Negro already enjoys; yet he suffers under
the burden of social, political, and economic injustices. His condition
is little more to be envied than that of his Southern brother."

The vote is not a panacea. It is a means to an end. The condition
of the Negro in the North because of his political power is a great
deal better than the condition of the Negro in the South. He is, of
course, hindered in the North by greater competition for work, while
in the South certain fields are open to him. The voter, white and
black, has not yet learned to control industry through his vote, but
he is learning, and only through the use of the ballot is real reform
in industry and industrial relations coming.

"Does not the editor think that State Socialism, Communism, or
even the dread dictatorship of the proletariat, offers a better solution to the problems of the proletariat than any scheme suggested by

the exploiting classes,—those who profit by the present system? And since the Negro is over 90 per cent proletarian, is it not almost logical to assume that this would also offer a better solution to this problem than anything heretofore proposed?"

I do decidedly think that many proposals made by Socialists and Communists and even by the present rulers of Russia would improve the world if they could be adopted; but I do not believe that such adoption can successfully come through war or force or murder, and I do not believe that the sudden attempt to impose a new industrial system and new ideas of industrial life can be successful without the long training of human beings. I believe that Socialism must be evolutionary, not in the sense that it must take 50,000 years, but in the sense that it does mean hard work for many generations. Beginnings can and should be made this minute or tomorrow or next year. It is precisely because of our present ignorance and our widespread assumptions as to profit and business that we cannot immediately change the world. It is true that those who today are sucking the industrial life blood of the nations get their chance to keep on by simply asserting that no better way is offered and present methods suit present human nature. We who suffer and believe in reform must not think that we can answer such persons successfully simply by saying that present industrial society is *not* in accordance with human nature. It *is* in accordance with human nature today, but human nature can and must and will be changed.

"We are both of the opinion that the present method of control and distribution of wealth is desperately wrong. We are *en rapport* on the conclusion that a form of social control is inevitable. We hold this particular truth to be self-evident,—that a change must come about. But how? I think that we both may be safe in assuming that any initiative in bringing about a better distribution of wealth must be taken by those who benefit least by the present system."

The change in industrial organization must come from those who think and believe. We cannot assume that necessarily redemption is coming from those who suffer. It may come from those who enjoy the fruit of suffering, but who come to see that such enjoyment is wrong. The point that we must hold clearly is that a proposal for reform is not necessarily good and feasible simply because it comes from a laboring man, and it is not wrong and unjustifiable simply because it comes from a millionaire. It must be judged by itself and not by its source.

"You ask the question: 'How far can the colored people of the world, and the Negroes of the United States in particular, trust the working classes?' This is a good question, and easier asked than answered. But I would like to ask further: How far can the Negroes and other dark peoples trust the exploiting Nationalists and Imperialists? Is it the English working classes that are exploiting India, sucking the very life-blood from a starving population and grinding the natives down into the desert dust in order to support English 'gentlemen' in idleness and luxury? Are the English, French and Belgian working classes raping Africa, taking ill-gotten gains from a trusting population? Are the working classes of America attempting to fasten the yoke of subjugation upon the neck of Santo Domingo, and stifle liberty and freedom of speech and press in Haiti? If we have cause to distrust the working classes, by what precept of example should we put faith in the specious promises of the masters?"

I think these questions touch the center of much modern effort and reform. I maintain that English working classes *are* exploiting India; that the English, French and Belgian laborers *are* raping Africa; that the working classes of America *are* subjugating Santo Domingo and Haiti. They may not be as conscious of all they are doing as their more educated masters, called Nationalists and Imperialists, but they are consciously submitting themselves to the leadership of these men; they are voluntarily refusing to know; they are systematically refusing to listen; they are blindly voting armies and navies and hidden diplomacy, regardless of the result, and while the individual white employee in Europe and America is less to be condemned than the individual capitalist for the way in which the darker nations have been treated, he can not escape his responsibility. He is co-worker in the miserable modern subjugation of over half the world.

*The Chicago meeting of the Communist-led American Negro Labor Congress elicited the following editorial comment from the* Independent.

# Bolshevizing the American Negro

THE RECENT attempt at Chicago of white and negro Communists to convert the American negro workingman to Bolshevism,—and incidentally to spread Communism among the colored people of the entire world,—together with the fact that young men and women of the colored race are in Russia taking a three years' course of training for the Russian "diplomatic service," reveals for the first time the aims and purposes of Red Russia where the American negro is concerned.

For several months the Department of Justice has known that more than a hundred paid Communist workers have been steadily at work in the United States and that some of them have been making a determined effort to enroll American negro workers under the Soviet banner, with the idea of eventually staging a "black revolution." No attempt was made at the American Negro Labor Congress at Chicago to hide the fact that the movement is financed and directed from Moscow. In fact, it is estimated in Washington that more than $1,000,000 is being spent yearly to organize Communism.

The ambitious program, as set forth at Chicago, would have the Negro Congress, under the leadership of Lovett Fort-Whiteman,— known as the "reddest Red" of the negro race,—take the initiative in an attempt to "rally the negro races against world imperialism." But the naming of white Communist workers on various committees is proof that the movement is not to be engineered and carried on by negroes alone. These white Communists, whose chief William Z. Foster was recently superceded by a mysterious "P. Green," have set about, with carefully laid plans and ample funds, to convince negro workers that their economic, social, and political emancipation is to be had only by affiliating with them. To quote a Chicago Communist daily:

From *Independent*, CXV (December 5, 1925), 631.

As Communists we hail this [Negro Labor] Congress as the beginning of a movement with far-reaching implications. Not merely can it be the means of starting to mobilize the negro workers for a struggle against the degrading restrictions imposed upon them as a race, but as American workers speaking the common language of the country, they can become a power in the labor movement. Furthermore, they will receive training that will enable them to play an effective part in the world's mobilization of the oppressed colonial peoples against capitalism.

There is little likelihood that the Chicago powwow, in spite of its fiery speeches and dire resolutions, will have any influence whatever upon the negroes of this country. Even if the American negro workingman were superficially deceived by Moscow's pernicious propaganda, there would be no reason for us to lose sleep over the movement to bring him into the Soviet fold. In the first place, the average negro of today is not the gullible, somewhat illiterate, and usually improvident citizen of forty years ago. In any Communist revolution —in any general attack upon private property—the American negro has proportionately as much to lose as the American white man. Moreover, he knows this.

According to Dr. Robert R. Moton, principal of Tuskegee Training School, the great negro educational institution of the South, American negroes own real estate valued at $1,800,000,000. Negro insurance companies have increased their assets in ten years from $3,000,000 to $7,500,000, and the face value of policies in force has increased from $50,000,000 to $250,000,000. Seventy-three banks in the United States, run by negroes for negroes and owned by them, have a combined capitalization of $6,250,000, and their clearings have increased from $35,000,000 to about $100,000,000. Furthermore, there are sixty negro fraternal organizations in the country today with 1,500,000 members. They own lodge buildings and other property worth $6,000,000.

The negro is naturally a "joiner," but no amount of clever talking is going to make Communists out of millions of his race who own their own homes, drive their own automobiles, manage their own stores, hotels, insurance companies, theatres, and other enterprises, conduct their own colleges, and have valuable deposits in their own banks. It will be hard for a Communistic agitator to fool them into taking part in an adventure in which they have everything to lose and nothing to gain. To assume that Chicago Communists with Moscow financial backing can move this essentially conservative race under the Red flag of Soviet Russia is to ask too much of the imagination.

This is not the first time that a "black revolution" has been forecast. During the early days of the World War, it was predicted that the negroes might be corrupted by German agents. Actually, there was less pro-Germanism among American negroes than among any other element of the population.

Nevertheless, the negro has real social and economic grievances. In various localities, the negro is disfranchised politically; he is compelled to ride in "Jim Crow" cars; he is segregated in certain large cities; he does not enjoy equal opportunities and equal pay with the white workingman. In the South there are not sufficient educational facilities for his children. These, and occasional lynchings, embitter the negro's life.

In these unfair economic and social practices lies the only real danger of the American negro's becoming Bolshevized. The way to make him a better and safer element of our population is to conduct an intelligent offensive against these real domestic menaces. If the American negro becomes a radical it will be our fault, not Russia's.

*Abram Harris was a recent college graduate in the early twenties who became a leading sociologist, administrator for the Urban League, and scholarly writer on sociological and economic matters relating to the black man.*

# Lenin Casts His Shadow upon Africa

## *By Abram L. Harris, Jr.*

Soviet Russia's avowal to organize American Negroes into a revolutionary working class movement has come to partial fruition in the American Negro Labor Congress which met in Chicago during the last week of October. This convention while not actually known to have been backed with Soviet gold was openly sponsored by the Workers' (Communist) Party of America.

Public interest focused upon the series of meetings if for no other reason than that a revolutionary meeting of Negroes violates the traditional norm of Negro group behaviour which is commonly accepted as conservative. The national press suffered paroxysms of fear. It paternalistically exhorted the Negro, on the one hand, to stand by private property institutions in which he holds such a large stake, while, like the little boy whistling in the dark, it flattered itself, on the other, into cocksureness over the Negro's unshakeable faith in American democracy.

Reflection upon the statement of grievances which emanated from the Negro Labor Congress should not lead anyone acquainted with the aspirations of various Negro advancement societies to conclude that it was a very revolutionary assemblage. It is true that the Congress, in addition to its resolves against color distinctions in American institutions, did unequivocally endorse the principal of *social equality*. Although an open advocacy of social equality by an organization may still place it beyond the pale of popular sympathy or esteem, a constant championing of the principle has robbed it of some of its ancient terror. One does not render oneself as liable in this day and time to social anathema by subscribing to a belief in social equality

From *The Crisis*, XXXI (April 1926), 272–275.

between the races as in the days when W. E. B. DuBois was blazing the trail for the then unborn militant Negro movements. So the demands of the Labor Congress, which strike at certain restraints and repressions that racial circumstance and social tradition have placed upon the Negro, should hardly be labeled as revolutionary or even as ultra-militant utterances. From another point of view, however, the Congress showed a decided radicalism. It did not attribute racial distinctions to the mental attitudes which are said to determine the quality of inter-racial associations and the extent to which they are permitted to take place in American life. The very fact that other schools of race leadership seem unable to allay the racial embroglio by correcting these mental attitudes that form the background of race prejudice led the American Negro Labor Congress to re-diagnose this affectation of the body *socius*. From its analysis it discovered that it is neither in racial intolerance nor color psychology that the problem of the races originates. Race prejudice, like all of society's multifarious ills for which communism is the only panacea, arises out of modern capitalism. Above all, the Congress uncovered an intrigue in which American capitalists have conspired for the purpose of forestalling proletarian solidarity. The capitalists are using the race question as means of carrying out its policy of *divide et impera*. Thus rang the Negro communists' indictment against capitalism: "Intent upon holding down the workers of all races as a general lower class, our masters wish to make us a general lower class within a lower class. The white worker must be made to realize that this discrimination against the Negro worker comes back against him ultimately."

This is the manner in which the Negro communist leaders of the Labor Congress diagnosed the race problem; the therapy for curing the malady logically suggests itself, viz., destroy the monster that breathes race hate.

It is not the demands of the Congress which give it a character dissimilar to that of other organizations for the Negro's political and social advancement. Nor is it by these demands that its communistic bias is revealed. It is its *modus operandi* which gives it the unbegrudged distinction of economic radicalism among the agencies for racial betterment. The question which next arises is: "Why the communistic flavor of the Convention?"

Certain writers have already suggested that communistic propaganda is being disseminated among the Negro masses by Soviet

Russia's black emissaries whose palms have been well greased with gold. The communist propagandists would perhaps enter the rejoinder that these same writers who accuse them of venality are likewise paid by the capitalists to extol the virtues of bourgeoisie and to caricature Negro communists. That Lovett Fort Whiteman—the Negro who more than any other person was responsible for the Congress convening—is in the pay of the Workers' Party which in turn is being financed by the Soviets is an incident insufficiently phenomenal to provoke comment from us whose exchange is always calculated according to the holy canons of price economy. If the servant is worthy of his hire, he expects remuneration for his labor whether performed in behalf of the Rotary Club or directed toward organizing Negroes for the class struggle. It is of little concern to me that Mr. Whiteman's radical proclivities led him to barter with the communists instead of seeking possibly more lucrative hire with the rotarians. In fact, this whole question of Soviet gold, I rule out as irrelevant to any fair appraisal of the social significance which attaches to the American Negro Labor Congress. For it is evident that no assemblage like the Labor Congress, where Negroes gathered in primary interest of their economic fortunes as wage-earners, could have come to pass merely because Soviet Russia or some of its missionaries bade it meet. Not Soviet gold but social facts furnish the explanation for the convention's radicalism and its departure from the racial assumptions and logic of the older Negro social institutions.

I have already suggested one explanation—the seeming inability of so-called bourgeois organizations among the Negro to remove race animosity by means of inter-racial education. Another explanation has to do with color prejudice in the American Labor Movement which has hampered the Negro's economic advancement.

In the late 90's the surplus Negro labor thrown off by a decadent agricultural system in the Southern States gradually moved toward the cities. Moreover the expansion of Northern industry in the first quarter of the present century and the constriction of the foreign labor supply resulted in the absorption of this plethoric supply of Southern Negro workers. But before the mass movements of 1916–17 and 1922–23 of Negroes from the South were set in motion, Negro labor had very often been imported as strike breakers. Continued migrations swelled the supply of black labor which was more and more looked upon by employers' associations and unions alike as a reservoir of potentially skilled labor whose power might be undammed as occasion should warrant, thus undermining the very foundation of organized labor. Competition between white and black workers ensued—but more directly between the unorganized unskilled white workers and the Negro than between the skilled organized white workers and the latter. Still the hostility which the increasingly great numbers of Negroes migrating to the North occasioned did not stop with the unskilled unorganized white workers. Seemingly some crafty genie had inoculated every stratum of the Northern white population with the virus of race prejudice. The most calamitous manifestation of this quickened color-psychology centered around the housing problems which faced the new and increasing black population. A sullen resentment to Negroes intruding white residential sections was and can today be easily fanned into serious race conflicts by a most trivial altercation between an individual white and black although the original cause of the fracas may have had no rational bearing upon race. No doubt these disturbances challenged any complacent faith the Negro had placed in the survival of abolitionist sentiment in the North. The Negro met this challenge with a re-vitalized race consciousness which had flowered languidly in Southern soil. Whatever the price exacted of him in social contempt or even blood shed, he seemed willing to pay it in exchange for a chance to secure higher wages, permanency of employment and an opportunity for cultural development.

In meeting this circumstance where slumbering passions had been aroused, organized labor futilely admonished Negroes not to permit themselves to be used as strike breakers. The policy of the American Federation of Labor was laissez-faire as usual. Its failure to counteract some of the competition between white and black workers by organizing the latter has been attributed to a weakness which arises out of its structure as a confederation of craft organizations. Negro labor recruited from the South was not only cheap labor but unskilled. It therefore had no place in a confederation of trade unions where possession of a craft is pre-requisite to membership. Without reviving the hoary dissension which *industrial unionism* and *amalgamation* versus *trade unionism* and *craft separatism* has occasioned, it is sufficient to say that the Federation is losing much of its conservatism in respect to organizing Negroes. Unskilled Negroes are being organized, e. g., the hod-carriers in the Building Trades Department. On the other hand, a great number of Negroes who possess a craft are kept out of the Labor movement by virtue of downright union prohibitions. The Executive Council of the American Federation of

Labor although persistently petitioned to by Negro organizations has procrastinated formulating a definitive policy toward the organization of Negroes. Therefore the exclusion of Negroes by certain unions does not seem to be merely due to the American Federation's structure which has evolved out of the experiences of the American worker. Much of the exclusion of Negro workers may be logically attributed to a color psychology which permeates the American Labor movement as it does other American institutions.

The American Negro Labor Congress appears to me to be, fundamentally, a revolt against this color psychology in the labor movement; and, incidentally, a protest against race prejudice in American life and the racial inequities arising out of it. Like most of us, the Negro communists believe that the insecurity of job and the inadequacy of income are bound up inextricably with the Negro's problems of housing, health and cultural development. But unlike some of us they believe that nothing short of a new social order can relieve the Negro of such social handicaps. Furthermore the inability of the Negro wage earners to better their economic status through collective bargaining because of the barriers set up by various unions against Negro membership; the apparent conspiracy between white employers and employees to keep Negro workers out of certain occupations; a growing disquietude among the Negro masses over the conciliatory character of present Negro organizations whose progress in race relations provokes doubtful concern; and a general dissatisfaction with the restraints placed upon the Negro by American race sentiment are factors in a racial circumstance which furnishes a field of inviting fertility for a propaganda which promises a world where economic and social equality prevails. Perhaps, most of the rank and file of the American Negro Labor Congress was wholly unacquainted with Marxian economics or the recent Leninized version of it. Nor, perhaps, was this rank and file very gravely concerned with the proposed reorganization of modern industrial society. Yet the Communist Party's appeals to it met a sympathetic response in spite of its impotence in securing any immediate economic good for the Negro or for that matter any ultimate good either for the Negro or for the white worker. But when the promise of racial equality, which although as a principle of social ethics has to await realization in a future world, is re-enforced by daily observance of equality in social practice as is done in the Workers' Party, it must have a tremendous appeal to a disadvantaged group such as is the Negro.

The Negro communist leaders, however, are more gullible than the masses whom they are proselytizing for the class struggle. They really believe that society is upon the threshold of the millennium. I have talked with many of them. Sometimes, I have left some one of these apostles with the feeling that I had come under the spell of a new evangelism. On one occasion I rushed into the street expecting to behold a great proletarian uprising which I had been told by one of my black communist visitors was just around the corner. Thoroughly drilled, and rigid "economic determinists," my communist friends argue that economic factors and the exploitation of black and white wage earners by capitalists sweep away the barriers of race. They say that the Negro and white workers are members of the same economic class; their interests are identical, *ergo*, they will unite in proletarian solidarity against capitalism. But are the interests of white and black workers identical? If white and black workers will not unite in a trade union for economic self preservation how much more unlikely is it that they will unite to promote the social revolution? These are questions which might involve interminable discussion. This much seems to me irrefutable: if their interests are identical there is little recognition of it on the part of white and black proletariat. And granting that the capitalists have entered a conspiracy to divide the untutored proletariat over the color question, the capitalists surely could not provoke race hostility between white and black workers if the workers themselves did not possess confirmed racial sentiments upon the basis of which appeals to race prejudice can be made. The conspiracy between capitalists to keep the Negro in a lower class within a low class is another illustration from which neither logic nor actual race relations in industry can deliver such doctrinaires. Not only have white workers in the organized labor movement barricaded the entrance to many types of employment against the Negro but unorganized white workers from common laborers to the white-collared aristocracy have protested against being forced by their employers to work in the same shop or plant with "niggers."

The social unrest among the Negro over which we waxed philosophical a few years back was not completely exhausted by the Garvey movement fiasco. Much of the ferment remains. Two years ago, a friend of mine wrote this about the Garvey movement: "It is just another name for psychology of the American Negro peasantry— for the surge of race consciousness felt by Negroes throughout the world, the intelligent as well as the ignorant. Tho visionary and perhaps impossible of accomplishment, it afforded a mental relaxation for the long submerged Negro peasantry. Balked desire, repressed longings, must have an outlet." My friend then queried, "After Garvey—What?" Had I known what I think I know today I would have answered, "Communism."

*Michael Gold was an articulate Communist writer and editor of the* Liberator.

# Where the Battle Is Fought

To the Editor of The Nation:

Sir: How in the name of Hank Ford can a Negro or a Jew or a Chinaman or even an Irishman escape his environment? Especially when that environment is the most insistent the world has ever known; pounding like an obsession at the ears and nerves and brain—America the gigantic?

The Negroes are not quite as isolated in America as were the Jews in Russia. And yet, even before the Revolution, the younger Jews were Russianized, were quite different from German Jews or American Jews. Even our old orthodox Jews, prisoners of ghettoes, were differentiated when they came from Salonika or from London or Prague. Environment had changed them even in the ghettoes.

If Negroes think they can build up some special racial culture in this huge America, they are either optimists or are blinded by race patriotism. It can't be done.

I have known little Chinese flappers in San Francisco, one generation removed from the joss-house, who rouge, wear silk stockings, read *Snappy Stories,* and do the Charleston. One sees hundreds of them on the streets there. If the young Chinese-Americans develop a poet, would it be proper for him to go back to Confucius and forget America? He would be as futile and reactionary if he did as some of our white poets who try to escape their age by sentimentalizing among the tombs. We Negroes, Jews, Germans, Chinese, Anglo-Saxons are all part of America, for better or worse. We are citizens of a new age, bloodier yet more hopeful than all the ages of the past.

The only real division is that of economic classes. Negro bosses will exploit and oppress Negro workers just as Jewish bosses at present exploit and beat up (with Irish police clubs) their racial brothers who happen to be poor and on strike.

From *Nation*, CXXIII (July 14, 1926), 37.

But what does this young crop of Negro intellectuals know or care about the great masses of peasants and factory workers of their race? Nothing. Almost nothing. Mr. Hughes believes with the white dilettantes that jazz and the cabaret are the ultimate flower of his people. I wish he would go out to Passaic and see a few black heroes on the picket-line, some of them captains over the white workers, the two races working as brothers in a non-racial problem—that of poverty and American culture. If the Negro intellectuals really care for their race they will forget the cabarets and colleges for a while, and go down into the life of their own people. It will make them better Negroes and better artists.

There are Negro themes, enough for a lifetime of creative activity. But white men have handled them more effectively thus far than the Negroes themselves. Eugene O'Neill has written the best play of miscegenation and Vachel Lindsay the best poetical rendering of the African primitive strain. Black men may do better some day, not because they are black, but because they are artists. Meanwhile, the field is not closed; it is open to everyone, as the Jewish life has been.

And the black race will play a great role in American history, not because it is black, but because ten million black workers will join the white workers in the unending battle for a free, civilized, and socialized America, against the black and white money-grabbers.

The Negro intellectuals can do a fine thing for their race. They can leave the cabarets of the jaded dilettantes and the colleges of the middle-class strivers, and help the mass of their brothers in the economic fight. The cultural future of the Negro soul resides in this battle, Brother Hughes, and not in Africa, Harvard, or the bootleg cabarets.

A last thought. In this battle, as I have observed him, the black worker thinks, feels, and acts very much the same as the white, yellow, or red worker the world over. Only he uses the Southern dialect.

*New York, June 27*.                                        MICHAEL GOLD

# The Faith of the American Negro

## By Mordecai Wyatt Johnson

SINCE THEIR emancipation from slavery the masses of American Negroes have lived by the strength of a simple but deeply moving faith. They have believed in the love and providence of a just and holy God; they have believed in the principles of democracy and in the righteous purpose of the Federal Government; and they have believed in the disposition of the American people as a whole and in the long run to be fair in all their dealings.

In spite of disfranchisement and peonage, mob violence and public contempt, they have kept this faith and have allowed themselves to hope with the optimism of Booker T. Washington that in proportion as they grew in intelligence, wealth, and self-respect they should win the confidence and esteem of their fellow white Americans, and should gradually acquire the responsibilities and privileges of full American citizenship.

In recent years, and especially since the Great War, this simple faith has suffered a widespread disintegration. When the United States Government set forth its war aims, called upon Negro soldiers to stand by the colors and Negro civilians, men, women, and children, to devote their labor and earnings to the cause, and when the war shortage of labor permitted a quarter million Negroes to leave the former slave States for the better conditions of the North, the entire Negro people experienced a profound sense of spiritual release. For the first time since emancipation they found themselves comparatively free to sell their labor on the open market for a living wage, found themselves launched on a great world enterprise with

From *Nation*, CXV (July 19, 1922), 64–65.

a chance to vote in a real and decisive way, and, best of all, in the heat of the struggle they found themselves bound with other Americans in the spiritual fellowship of a common cause.

When they stood on the height of this exalted experience and looked down on their pre-war poverty, impotence, and spiritual isolation, they realized as never before the depth of the harm they had suffered, and there arose in them a mighty hope that in some way the war would work a change in their situation. For a time indeed it seemed that their hope would be realized. For when the former slave States saw their labor leaving for the North, they began to reflect upon the treatment they had been accustomed to give the Negro, and they decided that it was radically wrong. Newspapers and public orators everywhere expressed this change of sentiment, set forth the wrongs in detail, and urged immediate improvement. And immediate improvement came. Better educational facilities were provided here and there, words of appreciation for the worth and spirit of the Negro as a citizen began to be uttered, and public committees arose to inquire into his grievances and to lay out programs for setting these grievances right. The colored people in these States had never experienced such collective good-will, and many of them were so grateful and happy that they actually prayed for the prolongation of the war.

At the close of the war, however, the Negro's hopes were suddenly dashed to the ground. Southern newspapers began at once to tell the Negro soldiers that the war was over and the sooner they forgot it the better. "Pull off your uniform," they said, "find the place you had before the war, and stay in it." "Act like a Negro should act," said one newspaper, "work like a Negro should work, talk like a Negro should talk, study like a Negro should study. Dismiss all ideas of independency or of being lifted up to the plane of the white man. Understand the necessity of keeping a Negro's place." In connection with such admonitions there came the great collective attacks on Negro life and property in Washington, Chicago, Omaha, Elaine, and Tulsa. There came also the increasing boldness of lynchers who advertised their purposes in advance and had their photographs taken around the burning bodies of their victims. There came vain appeals by the colored people to the President of the United States and to the houses of Congress. And finally there came the reorganization and rapid growth of the Ku Klux Klan.

The swift succession and frank brutality of all this was more than the Negro people could bear. Their simple faith and hope broke down. Multitudes took weapons in their hands and fought back violence with bloody resistance. "If we must die," they said, "it is well that we die fighting." And the Negro American world, looking on their deed with no light of hope to see by, said: "It is self-defense; it is the law of nature, of man, and of God; and it is well."

From those terrible days until this day the Negro's faith in the righteous purpose of the Federal Government has sagged. Some have laid the blame on the parties in power. Some have laid it elsewhere. But all the colored people, in every section of the United States, believe that there is something wrong, and not accidentally wrong, at the very heart of the Government.

Some of our young men are giving up the Christian religion, thinking that their fathers were fools to have believed it so long. One group among us repudiates entirely the simple faith of former days. It would put no trust in God, no trust in democracy, and would entertain no hope for betterment under the present form of government. It believes that the United States Government is through and through controlled by selfish capitalists who have no fundamental good-will for Negroes or for any sort of laborers whatever. In their publications and on the platform the members of this group urge the colored man to seek his salvation by alliance with the revolutionary labor movement of America and the world.

Another and larger group among us believes in religion and believes in the principles of democracy, but not in the white man's religion and not in the white man's democracy. It believes that the creed of the former slave States is the tacit creed of the whole nation, and that the Negro may never expect to acquire economic, political, and spiritual liberty in America. This group has held congresses with representatives from the entire Negro world, to lay the foundations of a black empire, a black religion, and a black culture; it has organized the provisional Republic of Africa, set going a multitude of economic enterprises, instituted branches of its organization wherever Negroes are to be found, and binds them together with a newspaper ably edited in two languages.

Whatever one may think of these radical movements and their destiny, one thing is certain: they are home-grown fruits, with roots deep sprung in a world of black American suffering. Their power lies in the appeal which they make to the Negro to find a way out of his trouble by new and self-reliant paths. The larger masses of the colored people do not belong to these more radical movements. They retain their belief in the Christian God, they love their country, and hope to work out their salvation within its bounds. But they are completely disillusioned. They see themselves surrounded on every hand by a sentiment of antagonism which does not intend to be fair. They see themselves partly reduced to peonage, shut out from labor unions, forced to an inferior status before the courts, made subjects of public contempt, lynched and mobbed with impunity, and deprived of the ballot, their only means of social defense. They see this antagonistic sentiment consolidated in the places of power in the former slave States and growing by leaps and bounds in the North and West. They know that it is gradually reducing them to an economic, political, and social caste. And they are now no longer able to believe with Dr. Booker T. Washington, or with any other man, that their own efforts after intelligence, wealth, and self-respect can in any wise avail to deliver them from these conditions unless they have the protection of a just and beneficent public policy in keeping with American ideals. With one voice, therefore, from pulpit and from press, and from the humblest walks of life, they are sending up a cry of pain and petition such as is heard today among the citizens of no other civilized nation in the world. They are asking for the protection of life, for the security of property, for the liberation of their peons, for the freedom to sell their labor in the open market, for a human being's chance in the courts; for a better system of public education, and for the boon of the ballot. They ask, in short, for public equality under the protection of the Federal Government.

Their request is sustained by every sentiment of humanity and by every holy ideal for which this nation stands. The time has come when the elemental justice called for in this petition should be embodied in a public policy initiated by the Federal Government and continuously supervised by a commission of that Government representing the faith and will of the whole American people.

The Negro people of America have been with us here for three hundred years. They have cut our forests, tilled our fields, built our railroads, fought our battles, and in all of their trials until now they have manifested a simple faith, a grateful heart, a cheerful spirit, and an undivided loyalty to the nation that has been a thing of beauty to behold. Now they have come to the place where their faith can no longer feed on the bread of repression and violence. They ask for the bread of liberty, of public equality, and public responsibility. It must not be denied them.

We are now sufficiently far removed from the Civil War and its animosities to see that such elemental justice may be given to the Negro with entire good-will and helpfulness toward the former slave States. We have already had one long attempt to build a wealth and culture on the backs of slaves. We found that it was a costly experiment, paid for at last with the blood of our best sons. There are some among our citizens who would turn their backs on history and repeat that experiment, and to their terrible heresy they would convert our entire great community. By every sacred bond of love for them we must not yield, and we must no longer leave them alone with their experiment. The faith of our whole nation must be brought to their support until such time as it is clear to them that their former slaves can be made both fully free and yet their faithful friends.

Across the seas the darker peoples of the earth are rising from their long sleep and are searching this Western world for light. Our Christian missionaries are among them. They are asking these missionaries: Can the Christian religion bind this multi-colored world in bonds of brotherhood? We of all nations are best prepared to answer that question, and to be their moral inspiration and their friend. For we have the world's problem of race relationships here in crucible, and by strength of our American faith we have made some encouraging progress in its solution. If the fires of this faith are kept burning around that crucible, what comes out of it is able to place these United States in the spiritual leadership of all humanity. When the Negro cries with pain from his deep hurt and lays his petition for elemental justice before the nation, he is calling upon the American people to kindle anew about the crucible of race relationships the fires of American faith.

A NOTE ON THE EDITOR

June Sochen was born in Chicago, Illinois, and studied at the University of Illinois, the University of Chicago, and Northwestern University, where she received a Ph.D. She is now Associate Professor of History at Northeastern Illinois State College in Chicago.